# THE NATION'S REPORT CARD

## EVOLUTION AND PERSPECTIVES

# THE NATION'S REPORT CARD

## EVOLUTION AND PERSPECTIVES

*Edited by*
*Lyle V. Jones and Ingram Olkin*

Published by the
Phi Delta Kappa Educational Foundation
in cooperation with the
American Educational Research Association

Cover design by
Victoria Voelker

Photograph of John Tukey by Robert Matthews, 1985
Courtesy of Princeton University

The development of this book was carried out as a project of the Education Statistics Services Institute of the
American Institutes for Research, which provided
partial funding for its publication, and with assistance
from the National Center for Education Statistics.

Phi Delta Kappa Educational Foundation
408 North Union Street
Post Office Box 789
Bloomington, IN 47402-0789
U.S.A.

Printed in the United States of America

Library of Congress Control Number 2003109696
ISBN 0-87367-848-6

*This book is dedicated to two pioneers
in the development of the
National Assessment of Educational Progress,*

*Ralph W. Tyler
and
John W. Tukey*

Ralph W. Tyler
1902-1994

John W. Tukey
1915-2000

# PREFACE

*Peggy G. Carr*

The assessment community has dedicated more than forty years to the creation of the nation's "gold standard" for monitoring the academic progress of America's children — the National Assessment of Educational Progress (NAEP). This book traces the challenges NAEP has faced since its inception. In many ways it is a documentary cataloging the unprecedented conceptual and technical advances that have led to NAEP's solid reputation for impeccable integrity and psychometric rigor.

In the 1960s many thought the notion that there would be a national assessment was wishful thinking; but after the idea gained support in 1963-64, the Exploratory Committee for the Assessment of Progress in Education (ECAPE) was established in June 1964, and the Technical Advisory Committee (TAC) was appointed in 1965. There were many periods of uncertainty about whether the project would go forward, but it survived to administer the first assessment in 1969. And NAEP has done more than survive: It has served as a source of important data and methodological innovation for 35 years.

In this book, the authors shed light on a friendly contemporary debate regarding the number and nature of NAEP's phases or milestones. Some argue that NAEP's technical history has two distinct phases, whereas others identify at least three.

Part I, *Evolution and Perspectives*, outlines the early years of NAEP, 1962 to 1982, and includes interviews with some of the best-known figures in the field of assessment. They reminisce about what was undoubtedly NAEP's beginning — the inception of NAEP as originally conceived in Francis Keppel's (the former Commissioner of Education) 1962 testimony to Congress.

In its first phase, NAEP findings emerged as national and regional summaries of item-by-item statistics for four age groups of respondents. Great efforts were taken to ensure that states and school districts included in the samples could not be identified or compared. Those were the days of unfocused block designs, taped administrations, age-based samples, and p-values, carried out by the Education Commission of the States (ECS). Reports were relatively short and straightforward. In some years, the NAEP budget was a mere $2 million and no more than three technical experts were needed to analyze and report NAEP data.

Phase two started in 1983 when Educational Testing Service (ETS) won the contract for the management of NAEP. NAEP designers entered into a new era of sophistication, and NAEP's methodology took a sharp turn toward a more complex matrix sampling design and non-classical scaling models. As described in Parts II and III, *Developing Assessment Materials* and *Sampling and Scoring,* this phase drew on the innovative work of experts who created NAEP's current distinguishing technical features: focused balanced incomplete block designs, item response theory models, plausible values, conditioning, grade samples, and advanced sampling and weighting methodologies.

This documentary also highlights the significant contributions of NAEP's external technical advisers during both its first and second phases. Many distinguished psychometricians and statisticians played critical and pivotal roles in NAEP's technical history by challenging first ECS and then ETS to examine, and eventually incorporate, many new approaches. (The innovative jackknifing procedure for variance estimation was used from the beginning and still is used today.) In phase two, the ETS staff and the TAC, later called the Design and Analysis Committee (DAC), weathered some of NAEP's most historic technical challenges.

Accounts of other significant milestones that have marked some new evolutionary paths are embedded in these pages of rich NAEP history. These paths have been shaped by NAEP's forever-changing political and methodological context and have led to significant alterations of NAEP's basic methodology and approach. Notable are the chapters that describe the emergence of the National Assessment Governing Board (NAGB), as called for in the 1987 Alexander-James report. NAGB's role was to push NAEP toward being more of a criterion-referenced system of assessments through high-profile content frameworks and achievement levels. NAGB was charged with responding to constituency demands for broad coverage of challenging content while minimizing the burden on individual students.

The political context also led to the congressional mandate to conduct NAEP state assessments — the first of which was conducted in 1990 for eighth-grade mathematics. There were many who doubted that this now very popular program component would survive, let alone flourish; but flourish it has. In fact, the demand for NAEP assessments has grown to include large school districts volunteering to participate in the 2002 Trial Urban District Assessment.

The evolution of NAEP in the 1990s introduced new issues, including the validity of the NAGB achievement levels and their relationship to state achievement levels, the effect of different state policies regarding inclusion of students with special needs, and the general effect on NAEP of the fact that state and national assessments became de facto measures of program effectiveness. In response to these issues and new technological opportunities, NAEP was able to expand access to data. In the early 1980s, when NAEP's "black box" emerged, only a handful of analysts could truly understand what was in it, and fewer still actually undertook the technically complex step of analyzing NAEP data. Today, the NAEP website provides real-time access to NAEP-released items and all NAEP reports, as well as an online data analysis tool that makes access to the findings routine and extremely user-friendly. The most nontechnical user can generate tables and graphs of the performance of individual states and groups of students within states. This new transparent NAEP might be considered its third phase and is described in the final chapter of this book.

Whether NAEP has passed through two or three phases, NAEP now is confronting what might be its most influential and challenging frontier. This newest phase began with debates that reached the level of the 2000 Presidential candidates, who took positions on NAEP's role as monitor of the educational effectiveness of individual states in reading and mathematics. Although it is true that there was no single vision of NAEP's role, all candidates gave it a leading place in their education platforms. The program was forced to prepare for several possible new roles and new relationships with its state partners.

While the dust has yet to settle on NAEP's new role, the 2001 No Child Left Behind legislation mandates that states and school districts participate biennially in State NAEP for reading and mathematics to receive federal Title I funding. Consequently, Congress tripled NAEP's budget to more than $100 million a year and altered the legislation so that the federal government pays for the cost of the administration of State NAEP. Accordingly, NAEP has nearly 3,000 test administrators and a federally funded NAEP State Coordinator in every state. The NAEP-state partnership has matured to include substantial NAEP support for increasing state capacity in areas related to assessment. The support is exemplified by the joint NCES-University of Maryland graduate certificate program in large-scale assessment and by the extensive use of web-based professional development opportunities made available to state and district staff.

The sheer increase in size and the demand for much quicker reporting has already taken NAEP around another sharp turn. Technical advances that use combined state and national samples, that pre-calibrate items from national field tests, and that employ technology in all phases of the data collection are just the forerunners of the next era of NAEP innovation, which will, of course, need to be documented in a second volume.

NAEP has evolved over a span of 40 years, during which many changes occurred, some large and some small. The presentation of the political and technical forces that fostered them makes for a fascinating story. It also is fascinating that over the 40 years, many factors remain the same.

This volume is appropriately dedicated to John W. Tukey and Ralph W. Tyler, two of the pioneering participants in the story.

We owe thanks as well to all the others who engaged in the evolution of NAEP and especially to Sylvia Johnson, professor at Howard University. Sylvia chaired DAC from 1987 until her untimely death in 2001 and enthusiastically endorsed the development of this history.

# TABLE OF CONTENTS

## PART I:
## EVOLUTION AND PERSPECTIVES

PART II:
DEVELOPING ASSESSMENT MATERIALS

PART III:
SAMPLING AND SCORING

# INTRODUCTION

In the late 1990s members of the Design and Analysis Committee (DAC) of the National Assessment of Educational Progress (NAEP) expressed an interest in fostering the publication of a history of NAEP. This suggestion was endorsed enthusiastically by the members of the attending staff of the National Center of Education Statistics (NCES), particularly Gary Phillips, Peggy Carr, and Suzanne Triplett. We, the editors of this book, then prepared a proposal to undertake that work. The proposal was submitted by the National Institute of Statistical Sciences (NISS) to the Education Statistics Services Institute (ESSI), and a contract was awarded to NISS in early 2000.

Because the origins of NAEP date back nearly 40 years, we were unsure how many individuals who played key roles in the development of NAEP would be able to contribute to the project. Fortunately, many participants in NAEP did agree to provide chapters or interviews based on their firsthand recollections.

A project as comprehensive as NAEP clearly involves many facets, ranging from the philosophy and psychology of a national assessment to budgetary arrangements, design issues, field operations, and so on. We have separated these facets into four major parts. Part I sets the foundation by recounting the evolution of NAEP. Part II details the development of assessment materials, and Part III discusses the issues of sampling, scoring, and reporting results. Part IV discusses the current status of NAEP.

NAEP was launched in 1969 following five years of intense preparation. Francis Keppel, Secretary of Education in the Johnson Administration, was instrumental in initiating the project; but its financial support until 1969 was almost wholly provided by the Carnegie Corporation of New York and the Ford Foundation and its Fund for the Support of Education. Only after the first

NAEP survey in 1969 did the project receive operational support from the Office of Education, and it has been federally funded since that time.

The essential aspects of NAEP emerged from the early leadership provided by Ralph W. Tyler, at that time director of the Center for Advanced Study in the Behavioral Sciences. His design was set forth at two conferences in December 1963 and January 1964, chaired by John W. Gardner, at that time president of the Carnegie Corporation of New York. (Appendix J is a summary report of those conferences.)

Tyler chaired the Exploratory Committee on the Assessment of Education between 1964 and 1968. The distinguished statistician, John W. Tukey of Princeton University, had joined Tyler at the 1963 and 1964 conferences in supporting the design and then chaired the initial Technical Advisory Committee (TAC) between 1965 and 1969. Tukey continued to serve as an advisor to the project until his death in 2000. In memory of these two founders of NAEP, who had such a profound influence on its future, we dedicate this history.

A chronology of noteworthy events in the history of NAEP follows this Introduction and attests to periods of uncertainty in its early years about whether the project would go forward. It also shows the shifts in emphasis during more recent years as NAEP has matured.

## Evolution and Perspectives

In Chapter One, Irvin Lehmann provides details of the planning activities from 1964 to 1969 and then of the operation of NAEP under the auspices of the Education Commission of the States (ECS) from 1969 to 1983. Lehmann served as assistant director of research for NAEP from 1968 to 1971. He bases his report on personal recollections, interviews with other NAEP staff members, and especially on the histories of NAEP during its early years that appeared as doctoral dissertations by Hazlett (1974) and Fitzharris (1993). His portrayal cites evidence of extensive pilot work and thorough review processes that were established during the early developmental years, all of which contributed to the quality of NAEP when it finally became operational in 1969.

In Chapter Two, Frederic Mosher discusses the role of the Carnegie Corporation in initiating NAEP. Mosher was a member of the Carnegie staff. In his chapter, he cites memoranda from Carnegie files that describe the earliest considerations of Carnegie to sponsor a national assessment.

Chapter Three groups together four interviews with key individuals in the development of NAEP. The late John Gardner was president of the Carnegie Corporation, and Lloyd Morrisett was a senior staff member who became the key person in the corporation's sponsorship of the project. Transcripts of recent interviews with Gardner and Morrisett provide their personal reflections on how the project was viewed in those pre-NAEP years. An interview with David Goslin serves to augment that perspective. Goslin was affiliated at the time with the Russell Sage Foundation, was a participant in the Carnegie conferences, was selected to be the conference reporter, and prepared the summary report reproduced as Appendix J. Finally, because measurement was to be an integral part of the assessment and Lee Cronbach served as a specialist in measurement, there follows a transcript of an interview with Cronbach, based on his memories of the Carnegie conferences and his service as a charter member of TAC from 1965 to 1969.

In Chapter Four the style of operation of TAC is described in journalistic fashion by Clay Allison. The chapter is an article reprinted from a 1973 issue of *Compact*, the house publication of ECS.

By the early 1970s the federal government was involved. In Chapter Five, Dorothy Gilford, the Associate Commissioner of Education at the time, presents a perspective on the federal developments affecting NAEP during its early years. Gilford reports on the skepticism within the beltway about the value of NAEP and on the budgetary consequences of that skepticism.

Archie Lapointe's perspective follows as Chapter Six. Lapointe recalls the work of Wirtz and Lapointe, a consulting firm that evaluated NAEP in 1981-82. He also discusses the proposal from the Educational Testing Service (ETS) that it become NAEP's home in 1983, as well as his service at ETS as the executive director of NAEP from 1983 to 1997.

During its first 20 years, NAEP's findings were based on national samples. Congressional legislation in 1988 established a National Assessment Governing Board (NAGB) and authorized that board to initiate state assessments, as well as to continue the national assessment of education. In Chapter Seven Ramsay Selden, associate director of the Council of Chief State School Officers (CCSSO) at the time Congress authorized state assessments, discusses the influence of the state school officers on that congressional action and on subsequent NAEP activities.

In Chapter Eight, Mary Lyn Bourque presents a history of NAGB. Bourque was chief psychometrician at NAGB from 1989 to 2001. She documents NAGB's evolution from its inception to its current status.

Except for several years in the 1970s, NAEP has been monitored within the U.S. Office or Department of Education by the National Center for Education Statistics. In Chapter Nine, Emerson Elliott, commissioner of Education Statistics from 1984 to 1995, and Gary Phillips, who has served more recently as acting commissioner of Education Statistics, provide a perspective on NAEP from the vantage point of NCES.

Chapter 10 consists of transcripts of three interviews. Chester Finn, the charter chair of NAGB, frankly presents his view concerning the need to clarify the roles of NAGB, NCES, and the NAEP contractor. Marshall Smith, undersecretary and Acting Deputy Secretary of Education in the Clinton Administration, discusses shifts in emphasis within NAEP that were responsive to budgetary constraints, as well as to political pressures from Congress, the executive branch of government, and other organizations. The interview with Jack Jennings focuses on congressional oversight of NAEP. For many years, Jennings served as director of congressional staff for the House Committee on

Education and Labor, and he shares his views about the determinants of congressional actions that affected NAEP.

Over the life of NAEP, several "outside" groups have been commissioned to critically evaluate the work of NAEP. Robert Linn chaired the initial TAC at ETS and in the 1990s participated in two congressionally mandated evaluations, one by the National Academy of Education (NAE), the other by the National Academy of Sciences (NAS). In Chapter 11 Linn describes those two evaluations, as well as earlier efforts, and discusses their effect on NAEP activities.

In Chapter 12 the late Wayne Martin provides a commentary on NAEP from his several vantage points. He was a member of the NAEP staff for more than a decade, then served as a Colorado state school officer, and most recently was the director of the State Education Assessment Center at CCSSO.

In Chapter 13 Frederic Mosher, who wrote Chapter 2 and has closely followed NAEP throughout its existence, presents his appraisal of how NAEP could become even more useful.

## Developing Assessment Materials

Psychological and educational testing emerged in the first half of the 20th century largely for the purpose of discriminating among individuals. Tests were used to aid in the classroom placement of pupils, to select college students or corporate personnel from among large numbers of applicants, to guide job placement for military personnel, or to provide certification to professional personnel. The purposes of NAEP are very different, and distinct procedures were needed to develop assessments for those purposes. In Chapter 14 Vincent Campbell and Daryl Nichols recall their creative efforts as research personnel at the American Institutes for Research (AIR) in the late 1960s, as they responded to the need for an assessment of citizenship.

In Chapter 15, Ina Mullis, a NAEP staff member first at ECS and later at ETS, illuminates the process for developing assessments in writing and mathematics.

## Sampling and Scoring

Although philosophy of assessment and issues of measurement are central to assessment planning, design and sample-survey aspects are central in assessment implementation. The design of sampling procedures and the plan for administering exercises presented major challenges as the details of NAEP were being considered in the 1960s. James Chromy, Alva Finkner, and Daniel Horvitz, all at the Research Triangle Institute (RTI), were engaged in that effort, and in Chapter 16 they explain how those planning activities were executed successfully. Further innovations in sampling and administration were required when many features of NAEP were changed in 1983 and especially in the design of state assessments in 1990 and thereafter. Westat replaced RTI as the contractor responsible for these aspects; and in Chapter 17 Keith Rust, who was in charge of NAEP sampling at Westat, presents a full description of the revised procedures.

NAEP exercises were scored initially by determining the percentage of correct responses for each exercise, and NAEP results were reported by percentages of correct response. That form of scoring and reporting was changed in 1983, when NAEP moved from ECS to ETS. Chapter 18, by Albert Beaton and Eugene Johnson, outlines the revised procedures for scoring and reporting. Both Beaton and Johnson spent many years at ETS, helping to design and implement the procedures that they discuss.

## Recent Challenges and Some Responses

In Chapter 19 Stephen Lazer at ETS, current executive director of NAEP, describes continuing improvements in NAEP to meet the changing needs of its consumers.

## The Editors' Role

As graduate students, while one of us (Olkin) worked toward a Ph.D. at the University of North Carolina (UNC), the other (Jones) earned a Ph.D. at Stanford. By happy coincidence, our academic careers have been primarily at Stanford (for Olkin) and at UNC (for Jones). Perhaps it was fated that we would work together at some time, as we did during the 1990s as participants in a series of NISS workshops sponsored by ESSI. Each of us has enjoyed prior relationships with NAEP. Jones was a charter member of TAC and later of the Analysis Advisory Committee (ANAC) until 1982. He also was a member of the Alexander-James panel, which in 1988 recommended state assessments and the formation of NAGB, and a member of the congressionally mandated panel of the National Academy of Education that evaluated trial state assessments between 1989 and 1996. Olkin was an American Statistical Association Fellow at NCES from 1988 to 1990 and, since 1987, has served on the NAEP Design Analysis Committee (DAC). Olkin currently is the chair of DAC.

For the current effort, we selected the authors and provided gentle guidance to them about the content of their contributions, and we selected individuals to be interviewed. Among the participants are some whose involvement in NAEP took place at almost every stage of NAEP's history. Each has his or her own perspective of what transpired and, because their roles overlapped in terms of chronology or positions held, the recounting of the history is at times repetitious, albeit often reflecting different perspectives. As editors we have deliberately chosen to retain some repetition in the belief that it reflects the range of vantage points of the authors and that the retelling of the evolution of NAEP is enlightened by the presentation of different views.

Inevitably, as specialists, our authors have employed technical terms that may be alien to non-specialist readers. Rather than defining such terms whenever they appear and thereby marring the continuity of the story, a glossary is provided at the end of the book as Appendix A and a list of abbreviations is Appendix B.

## Acknowledgments

The success of this effort has depended primarily on the authors and the interviewees, and we are grateful to them for sharing our enthusiasm and for responding graciously to our requests for revisions. Without their timely and constructive responses, the project would have been unmanageable.

Others also have contributed in important ways. We are grateful to Jerome Sacks, charter director of NISS, for his full support; to Alan Karr, current director of NISS; and to Martha Williamson at NISS, who has so competently handled fiscal aspects of the project.

From time to time we have received helpful comments and suggestions from members of the Design and Analysis Committee, for which we are grateful. The personnel at ESSI, ETS, and NCES were always encouraging, often providing information that otherwise was not easy to find. We acknowledge with special thanks the support of Suzanne Triplett at NCES, without which this project would not have been initiated, and the assistance so generously offered by Nada Ballator at ESSI.

Following the receipt of revised drafts from the authors, after they had responded to our initial editorial suggestions, each draft then was further reviewed by two "outside" reviewers whom we asked to provide suggestions and comments. We thank those reviewers: Sue Ahmed, Betsy Becker, Janet Johnson, Lorraine O'Donnell, and Rebecca Zwick, whose helpful and constructive suggestions resulted in further improvements.

Each of us has been fortunate to have help "at home" in the form of excellent secretarial support, from Angelica Martinez at Stanford and from Shirley Whitt at UNC. We also thank Valerie S.L. Williams at North Carolina Central University (now at Research Triangle Institute). This has been a daunting task, and she has ably managed the flow of materials that make up the present volume. She also contributed to the standardizing of formats across chapters and to the preparation of several appendices.

Our publisher, the Phi Delta Kappa Educational Foundation, played a key role in the final preparation of this book. We are especially grateful to Donovan Walling, director of Publications and Research, for managing that effort. Special thanks are directed to David Ruetschlin, managing editor at Phi Delta Kappa, whose final editorial work served to substantially improve the clarity and readability of the text.

NAEP serves the nation well. Charles X. Larabee (1991) wrote of NAEP, "It was the biggest and most innovative and very likely the most significant effort of its kind." We agree and consider ourselves privileged to have been participants in its history.

Lyle V. Jones, Chapel Hill, N.C.
Ingram Olkin, Stanford, Calif.
November 2003

# CHRONOLOGY, 1963–2003

*Lyle V. Jones**

**1963**, Spring     U.S. Commissioner of Education Francis Keppel asks Ralph Tyler, director of the Center for Advanced Study in the Behavioral Sciences, to suggest a way to evaluate U.S. education.

July     Tyler presents a responsive memorandum to Keppel.

October     Keppel turns to John Gardner, president of the Carnegie Corporation of New York, and Carnegie allocates $12,500 for two conferences.

December     First Carnegie conference is held to discuss Tyler's proposal.

**1964**, January     Second Carnegie conference is held.

April     As requested by Carnegie, John Corson (professor, Princeton University) presents a memorandum that outlines alternative structures for a national assessment of educational progress.

June     The Carnegie Board allocates $100,000 for the Exploratory Committee for the Assessment of Progress in Education (ECAPE).

August     ECAPE meets for the first time, with Tyler as chair.

*I am grateful to Nada Ballator, Eugene Johnson, Archie Lapointe, and personnel at NAGB and Westat for supplying some of the later entries.

**1965**, February  A Technical Advisory Committee (TAC) is appointed by ECAPE, with John Tukey (professor, Princeton University) as chair.

March  TAC reviews proposals from potential contractors and recommends improvements in the proposals before they are considered for approval by ECAPE. Later, contractors are chosen for first-year assessments: American Institutes for Research (AIR) for Citizenship, Science Research Associates (SRA) for Reading, and Educational Testing Service (ETS) for Science.

June  ECAPE is legally incorporated as a nonprofit corporation by the New York Board of Regents for a term of five years.

December  The Ford Foundation Fund for the Advancement of Education provides a $496,000 grant to ECAPE. The Carnegie Corporation grants an additional $2.3 million.

**1966**  The U. S. Office of Education (USOE) grants $50,000 to the University of Minnesota for a series of conferences related to national assessments.

The National Opinion Research Center (NORC) undertakes a study of interview techniques for out-of-school respondents.

The Research Triangle Institute (RTI) undertakes a study of sampling procedures and administration tools for both in- and out-of-school assessments.

The Executive Committee of the American Association of School Administrators (AASA) recommends that its members refuse to participate in NAEP tryouts or in any subsequent operational NAEP.

**1967**, February     The Executive Committee of AASA modifies its position and authorizes a 10-person joint AASA-ECAPE committee to further study participation in NAEP.

July     The National Education Association (NEA) passes a resolution to "withhold cooperation" from NAEP.

October     Preliminary discussion is initiated between ECAPE and the Education Commission of the States (ECS) concerning an appropriate home for NAEP.

**1968**, July     ECAPE is re-formed as the Committee for the Assessment of Progress of Education (CAPE).

October     CAPE meets for the first time, with George Brain (dean of education, Washington State University) as chair.

RTI is awarded a contract for NAEP sampling and field operations, and the Measurement Research Corporation (MRC) is selected to print exercise booklets and score responses.

**1969**, February     The National Science Foundation (NSF) urges all science teachers to cooperate with NAEP.

AASA revises its position, leaving to its members the decision as to whether to cooperate with NAEP.

April     NAEP assesses in-school 17-year-olds in citizenship, science, and writing.

Following a public meeting for comments, ECS agrees to govern NAEP.

TAC becomes the Analysis Advisory Committee (ANAC), and a separate Operations Advisory Committee (OPAC) is formed with John

|            | Letson (superintendent of schools, Atlanta) as chair. |
| June | After CAPE enacts a Resolution of Transfer of assets and responsibilities to ECS, ECS assumes the governance of NAEP. |
|            | NAEP assesses adults and out-of-school 17-year-olds in citizenship, science, and writing. |
|            | ECS creates the National Assessment Policy Committee: George Brain (chair of CAPE), John Tukey (chair of ANAC), John Letson (chair of Operations Advisory Committee), Ralph Tyler, California Assemblyman Leroy Greene (representing ECS), and James Hazlett, chair (newly appointed administrative director of NAEP). |
| October | CAPE is expanded, and Brain remains its chair. |
|            | USOE provides to ECS a grant of $2 million to support NAEP for one year (later renewed until 1973). |
| December | NAEP assesses 13- and 9-year-olds in citizenship, science, and writing. |
| **1970**, July | NAEP Report No. 1 is released, presenting national results from the first science assessment (authored by ANAC). |
| **1971**, April | NAEP Report No. 4 is released, presenting group results from the first science assessment (authored by ANAC). Reports No. 1 and 4 will serve as models for the NAEP reports produced by ECS in other subject areas. |
| July | NAEP headquarters are moved from the University of Michigan to ECS in Denver. |
| August | USOE transfers oversight of NAEP to the National Center for Education Statistics (NCES), with supervisors Dorothy Gilford, Assistant |

Commissioner of Education, and Iris Garfield, Monitor.

**1972**, April    The Carnegie Corporation allocates $24,000 for an evaluation of NAEP and commissions the Harvard Center for Educational Policy Research to undertake the evaluation.

**1973**    USOE support for NAEP is increased from $2 million to $3 million per year.

May    NAEP Report No. 7 is released, presenting results from the first science assessment, adjusted for selected background variables (authored by ANAC).

September    USOE announces that it will shift from supporting NAEP by grant to support by contract, "to be more tightly structured in performance specifications."

**1974**    President Nixon's budget request includes $7 million for NAEP. The House approves $6 million, the Senate approves $3 million, and $3 million is awarded.

**1977**    An evaluation of NAEP is published, *Measuring Educational Progress* by William Greenbaum with Michael S. Garet and Ellen R. Solomon, commissioned by the Carnegie Corporation in 1972.

**1978**    Within USOE, sponsorship of NAEP is transferred from NCES to the newly established National Institute of Education (NIE).

ECS is awarded a five-year continuation contract for NAEP.

**1982**                    The Wirtz-Lapointe report (funded by the Car-
                            negie Corporation and the Ford and Spencer
                            Foundations) leads NIE to entertain an open
                            competition for the new NAEP contract.

**1983**                    *A Nation at Risk* is published by the National
                            Commission on Excellence in Education.

                            *A New Design for a New Era*, by Samuel Mes-
                            sick, Albert E. Beaton, and Frederic M. Lord at
                            ETS, is published, presenting the new frame-
                            work and description of procedures for NAEP.

                            A new TAC is appointed.

         March              A new NAEP contract is awarded with ETS re-
                            sponsible for design, analysis, and reporting
                            and with Westat the subcontractor for sampling
                            and field administration.

**1984**, November   Secretary of Education Terrel Bell presents a
                            wall chart that uses SAT/ACT scores to charac-
                            terize the condition of U.S. education.

**1985**                    NAEP designs and implements the Young Adult
                            Literacy Study of 16- to 25-year-olds, adapting
                            "the NAEP technology" to do so.

                            Multivariate scaling is employed to allow the
                            reporting of mathematics and science results by
                            "content strands" as well as by composite per-
                            formance.

                            An innovative NAEP assessment is "Computer
                            Competence" at grades 3, 7, and 11.

**1986**                    The National Governors' Association issues
                            *Time for Results* by Lamar Alexander, governor
                            of Tennessee, calling for better "report cards"
                            for the nation and for states.

Secretary of Education William Bennett appoints a 22-member panel to advise about the future of NAEP (the Alexander-James study group).

**1987**    Under a grant from NSF and USOE, the Council of Chief State School Officers (CCSSO) establishes a National Assessment Planning Project to design a trial state assessment of mathematics at grade 8.

March    The report of the Alexander-James group, *The Nation's Report Card*, is published and includes a response from the National Academy of Education.

**1987-1988**    NAEP conducts an assessment of geography, with $260,000 provided by the National Geographic Society, the first NAEP endeavor to receive support from a private organization.

**1988**, April    Congress enacts P.L. 100-297, establishing the National Assessment Governing Board (NAGB) and authorizing Trial State Assessments (TSA).

December    Out-going Secretary Bennett appoints 23 NAGB members, with Chester Finn (professor, Vanderbilt University) as chair.

**1989**, February    *A World of Differences* is published by NAEP, a report of findings from the first International Assessment of Educational Progress (IAEP), an international comparative study of mathematics and science achievement of 9- and 13-year-olds in six countries.

March    The National Council of Teachers of Mathematics (NCTM) publishes suggested national standards for mathematics instruction.

September    An Education Summit of the nation's governors and President George Bush publish a set of National Education Goals.

October    As called for by congressional legislation, a panel is appointed by NAE to carry out evaluations of the TSA, with Robert Glaser (professor, University of Pittsburgh) and Robert Linn (professor, University of Colorado) as co-chairs.

December    NAGB expresses support for assessments at the school-district level.

**1990**, February    The first TSA of mathematics at grade 8 is conducted with 40 states participating; administrative procedures, administrator training, and quality-control monitoring are provided by Westat.

May    NAGB calls for reporting NAEP results by "achievement levels" and initiates a process to define them.

**1991**    The second IAEP involves 20 countries, again using NAEP technology, and findings are published as "Learning Mathematics" and "Learning Science." These studies later influence the design and implementation of the Third International Mathematics and Science Study (TIMSS).

August    NAGB consultants Daniel Stufflebeam (professor, Western Michigan University), Richard Jaeger (professor, Univeristy of North Carolina at Greensboro), and Michael Scriven (professor, Western Michigan University) produce a report that is highly critical of the process used to define "achievement levels" and that criticizes NAGB for being insufficiently qualified to make technical decisions about NAEP.

**1992**            The NAEP technology (sampling, consensus, and item development procedures, as well as an anchored scale for reporting results) is used for the National Adult Literacy Study.

NAEP first includes polytomous items into its scaling models, allowing for a more appropriate measurement of performance tasks.

NAEP initiates a Secondary Analysis Grant Program.

March        The NAE panel issues its initial report, endorsing the continuation of the TSA.

**1993**, June    The General Accounting Office issues a report highly critical of the process employed by NAGB for establishing achievement levels.

September   A report from the NAE panel judges the process for setting achievement levels to be "fatally flawed."

**1995**            NAEPEX is developed at ETS to aid secondary analysts' use of NAEP raw data.

**1996**            The NAE panel completes its work and is succeeded by a panel at the National Academy of Sciences (NAS) to evaluate NAEP.

District-level reporting is offered, with one district (Milwaukee) contracting for a report using an augmented sample.

Congress authorizes dropping the "trial" status for the NAEP state assessments.

**1998**            NAEP initiates national assessments on an annual schedule.

Web-based analysis tools are proposed, culminating in the release in August 2001 of the

NAEP Data Tool, permitting many secondary analyses that formerly required training and licensing.

Age-based samples are dropped from the main NAEP, leaving grade-only samples.

**1999**    The NAS panel evaluates NAEP, and several other committees at the National Research Council prepare reports relevant to NAEP (as called for by Congress).

NAEP data tables go on the NAEP website to provide easier public access to data.

**2000**    The NAEP Questions Tool is placed online in a public website, offering access to released questions, scoring guides, and performance data.

**2001**    President George W. Bush proposes that all states annually test all students in grades 3 to 8 in reading and mathematics and that states be required to participate in NAEP so that state results in those subjects can be confirmed by NAEP at grades 4 and 8.

A NAEP Network website is developed by Westat for states and other jurisdictions that participate in NAEP.

The NAEP public website adds State Profiles, Search, e-mail feedback, and the NAEP Data Tool.

Congress enacts the No Child Left Behind legislation that supports (in modified form) the proposal set forth earlier in the year by President Bush.

The MySchool website is developed to provide information about NAEP assessment activities to schools that are selected for the NAEP sample.

**2002**            State assessments are administered on the national model, thereby reducing the burden on schools by having NAEP staff, rather than local personnel, conduct the assessments within schools.

A federally funded NAEP State Coordinator position is established in each State Education Agency (SEA) to serve as the NAEP liaison between the SEA and NCES.

A NAEP State Service Center is established to provide ongoing support and training for NAEP State Coordinators.

In years with state assessments, the national sample now becomes an aggregate of state samples.

For the first time, all states participate in NAEP, though not all meet the requirements for reporting.

Five urban districts participate in NAEP's first federally funded Trial Urban District Assessment (TUDA).

A graduate certificate program in large-scale assessment is inaugurated, developed by NAEP in collaboration with the University of Maryland.

**2003**            Nine districts participate in the second TUDA.

Results for the 2002 reading and writing assessments become the first with a trend line to be reported with accommodations permitted for special-needs students.

Results for the 2003 assessment are the first to be reported under NCLB requirements.

# PART I

# EVOLUTION
# AND PERSPECTIVES

# CHAPTER 1

# The Genesis of NAEP

## *Irvin J. Lehmann*

For the United States, the 1950s and early 1960s witnessed what we might consider the beginning of the age of accountability. The quality of education became a contentious issue. Sputnik was launched, and Americans looked to their schools to help win the Space Race. The Supreme Court decision on the segregation of public schools in 1954 added another layer to the schools' responsibility. Educators and legislators were bombarded with criticisms of American schooling.

If the country was to meet these criticisms and improve the schools, there was a need for data to assess what our schools were doing. Prior to that time, there was no assessment program formally designed to measure the knowledge, skills, and attitudes of youth as a *group* — rather than as individuals — across the United States. Nor was any system in place to measure the *progress* of education nationally. The only recognized form of assessment at that time used standardized tests that were designed to compare individuals and not to measure individuals' learning.

In the early 1960s Francis Keppel, then U.S. Commissioner of Education, recognized the need for a national assessment that would provide technically sound and valid data regarding pupils' knowledge, skills, and abilities. As Commissioner of Education, Keppel periodically had to report to Congress on the progress of education in each of the states. But for nearly 100 years, the reports issued by previous commissioners dealt primarily with summary descriptive statistics of "input" variables in the education system, such as per pupil expenditures, attendance, number of classrooms, teacher salaries, enrollment, and so forth.

The focus of these reports dealt with the *cost* of education. Billions of dollars were spent yearly to support our education system, but the public did not know what our children were learning or the progress they were making. Only during Keppel's tenure as Commissioner of Education (1962-1965) was any attention paid to gathering data on such "output" variables as how much students are learning and what progress is being made in U.S. education. Also, before that time, standardized tests were the accepted form of student assessment.

In 1963 Keppel asked Ralph Tyler, director of the Center for Advanced Study in the Behavioral Sciences at Stanford University, to consider the feasibility of developing a plan for the periodic national assessment of student learning (Hazlett 1974, p. 26). Although both Tyler's and Keppel's interest in a national assessment was to evaluate learning, Keppel's motivation might have been heightened by his desire to use the information to provide data for his budget requests to Congress and to counter criticisms of American education.

On 1 July 1963 Tyler responded to Keppel in a five-page memorandum. What is significant, looking back, was Tyler's belief that commonly used standardized achievement tests did not provide a valid measure of what children have learned but were (and are) designed to rank students. (A more detailed discussion of Tyler's new evaluation and assessment model can be found in Fitzharris 1993, pp. 24-30, and Hazlett 1974, pp. 28-30.)

Tyler identified three problems with the standardized tests widely used in the public schools. First, the purpose of standardized tests was to identify individual differences in achievement, not to measure individuals' learning. Second, the manner in which standardized tests were scored and reported was not a meaningful way to score and report the achievements of a community. And third, the reliance of standardized tests on grade-level norms assumed some consistency within, as well as across, grade levels. Accordingly, he proposed measuring student achievement at specific ages, rather than grade levels.

Tyler's evaluation model is described in his book, *Basic Principles of Curriculum and Instruction* (1949), and eventually became the blueprint for the conduct of a national assessment. His model described evaluation as being more than the annual administration of a standardized test, a practice that was popular until the early 1960s. According to Tyler, evaluating student learning and determining changes in student behavior included two important aspects:

> (1) evaluation must appraise the behavior of students since it is changes in these behaviors which is sought in education . . . and (2) it implies that evaluation must involve more than a single appraisal at any one time since to see whether change has taken place, it is necessary to make an appraisal at an early point and other appraisals at later points. (Fitzharris 1993, pp. 26-27)

Tyler conceived of a new type of measurement instrument designed to assess identified objectives whose specifications would be determined by subject-matter and by lay people working together to reach consensus. This instrument would not focus on a single score but would use a "periodic index" to track changes over time. The index would be classified for reporting purposes in terms of regions, states, sex, socioeconomic status, and so on. The instrument would provide information on what groups of people know and can do, rather than on what score an individual receives on a test. The instrument would score and report the percentage of *groups* of pupils, not individuals, who answered the exercises correctly. And unlike standardized tests, it would not rely on grade-level norms. Rather, it would report student learning in terms of specific ages.

This bold approach differed markedly from the measurement of learning practiced at that time with standardized tests. But to activate Tyler's and Keppel's vision of a national assessment required staff and federal funding. Unfortunately, Keppel had neither; but he did provide his support and retained a high profile in the initial planning stages.

It is interesting to note that the purposes that Tyler and Keppel had for a national assessment were compatible, but they differed somewhat. Tyler envisioned a national assessment as a means of measuring learning across the United States over time. He did *not* envision the program as a means to sort students. Nor did he believe that the program should provide data to compare students, schools, school districts, or states. In fact, the sampling design prevented such comparisons (see Chapter 16). Tyler wanted the program merely to provide data that would show what students know. Keppel, on the other hand, wanted to have national data that would meet the intent of the legislation that created a Department of Education.

When Keppel proposed the idea of a national assessment in 1963, he was able to generate interest but not funding from the federal government. Accordingly, he initially approached the Carnegie Corporation of New York and later the Ford Foundation for financial support. For the first few years, private funds supported the development efforts, with Carnegie and Ford contributing more than $3 million. Not until 1971 was the U.S. Office of Education the sole source of funds for the national assessment program.

Many of the critics of a national assessment — and there were many — believed that federal funding placed the program in the political arena. In fact, this was one of the major criticisms offered by those who opposed national assessment.

## The Carnegie Corporation's Involvement

The stage was set for a national assessment and the development of a new type of assessment instrument in Tyler's 1963 memo to Keppel. However, Keppel lacked the staff and funds to develop the idea. He contacted John Gardner, president of the Carnegie Corporation, to assess Carnegie's interest in sponsoring a meeting to discuss the feasibility of a national assessment.

In July 1963 Keppel responded to Tyler and indicated that the Carnegie Corporation had a general interest in the idea and suggested a meeting of social scientists, educators, and testing experts (Hazlett 1974, pp. 29-30). Keppel asked Gardner to preside at the first meeting, and Gardner accepted. However, this action raised concern within the corporation. What was to be the direction of a government assessment program under the funding of private enterprise? Was it appropriate for a private corporation to be involved? What was the actual purpose of a national assessment? Was it to measure learning or to force changes and reform in the education enterprise across the nation?

Meetings during the first few months defined the philosophy and provided the structure for an assessment program. The first Carnegie conference was held in New York City in December 1963, with John Gardner presiding. (See Chapter 2, p. 100, for names of participants and Appendix J for David Goslin's summary report of the Carnegie conferences of December 1963 and January 1964.) Its purpose, according to Lloyd Morrisett, an executive associate at Carnegie who later was to become the corporation's point man on exploring a national assessment as a Carnegie project, was to determine the feasibility of conducting an assessment. Because the issues to be discussed centered on technical matters, eight of the 19 participants were experts in education measurement and statistics; six represented the Carnegie Corporation, the Russell Sage Foundation, and the Ford Foundation; and three were from the U.S. Office of Education (OE). One was a university president, and one represented a state department of education (Hazlett 1974, p. 35).

The issues discussed the first day of the conference, cast in the form of seven questions by Gardner, reiterated the concerns raised earlier by Tyler in his memorandum of July 1963 to Keppel:

1. How can an appropriate set of objectives be developed?
2. Can existing tests measure these objectives satisfactorily?
3. What should the specifications be for the construction of new tests?
4. How should the assessment results be reported?

5. How can the results be made meaningful?
6. To whom should the report be made?
7. Who will have access to the results and in what categories can a breakdown of the results be given? (Hazlett 1974, p. 37)

As might be expected, many concerns were expressed at this meeting. For example, the Carnegie members debated the role that would be played by the corporation. Another point of discussion centered on the purpose of a national assessment: Was it to be a barometer to measure learning or was it to be used as a lever to force changes in the education system across the nation? Without a doubt, lack of consensus about the purpose and the lack of a clear focus would haunt the assessment in the following years (Fitzharris 1993, p. 32).

There was lengthy discussion of sampling. Should the assessment be limited to in-school populations? What age groups should be assessed? How often should subjects be tested? What should be the size of the sampling unit? Should vocational education be assessed? Can existing tests be used to measure the assessment's objectives? Near the end of the conference, Tyler summarized the high points of the meeting as follows:

1. There was general approval that there should be a National Assessment of educational achievement.
2. Results should be reported by states.
3. Sampling techniques might well be used.
4. Item face validity is an important factor.
5. National Assessment instruments would differ from other tests.
6. Coverage would be fair and objective because of the formulation of objectives; there would be a danger that what is easy would be done first and that there might be a tendency to settle for less than expectations.
7. Writing is a curriculum area to be included.
8. The desirability of assessing out-of-school persons is still unclear. (Hazlett 1974, p. 40)

There also was general agreement that a national assessment was worthwhile and that the Office of Education would conduct the assessment. It was decided that the next conference should include educators and leaders with political influence, especially the chief state school officers. The expanded membership also might bring additional research and technical support.

David Goslin's formal summary of the first Carnegie conference captured the essence of the meeting:

> The general feeling among those present was that there was sufficient interest in the problem and belief in its importance to at least take whatever next steps seemed appropriate to explore further issues and objectives. All of the conferees acknowledged some feelings of anxiety about such things as possible harmful effects on school curricula and misinterpretation of the results by the general public, but there was a measure of confidence that careful planning, administration and public relations might minimize the dangers inherent in a project like the one visualized. In addition, there was firm agreement that the project would have a significant salutory [sic] effect on education by raising standards, stimulating interest in schools, and encouraging governmental support of educational institutions. (Goslin, cited in Hazlett 1974, p. 41. See also Appendix J)

Such a positive, supportive attitude no doubt piqued Morrisett's interest because he discussed setting up a tentative time schedule with Keppel and Associate Commissioner of Education Ralph Flynt. Keppel wanted 1966-67 to be the target date for the first collection of data because it was the Office of Education's centennial year.

It is evident in the early discussions that there was confusion about available and appropriate funding sources — should it be from private or federal sources? — and that there still was no clear focus for the assessment program. Possibly the most significant point coming forth from the meeting was Lee Cronbach's suggestion to design and report items that could be measured using a scale of difficulty, a scale that would permit learning to be measured over time.

The second Carnegie conference was held in New York City in January 1964. Its purpose was to explore education and public policy issues, and it was attended by 20 persons representing Carnegie and the Ford Foundation, the Office of Education, and higher education. As suggested at the first conference, there were more educators this time, with four representatives from elementary and secondary education, two school superintendents, and two representatives from the National Education Association (see Chapter 2, p. 103, and Appendix J). Whether this was a good idea is questionable inasmuch as it heightened attention to the absence of a clearly defined purpose for a national assessment. Concerns were raised about the restrictive effects of the assessment on programs and the curriculum, the possible negative effects stemming from the results when they were made public, and the effect of additional testing on the schools and on the students.

Some of the suggestions made at the meeting were as follows:

1. Assessment should begin simply and with measurable areas.
2. Funding should be from both private and public sources.
3. The Office of Education should be the administrator.
4. Valid state samples should be drawn and reporting should be done by states.
5. Results should be embedded in sociological and environmental data in the state or district tested.
6. Emphasis should be on the success levels of a task and not on an overall score. (Hazlett 1974, p. 49)

Conferees left the meeting with various interpretations of the purpose and direction of a national assessment. This might explain, in part, the opposition from professional organizations during the earliest years of the assessment's development. No doubt the lack of representation from teachers contributed to the lack of support from teachers unions.

Shortly after the second conference, John Corson, professor of economics at the Woodrow Wilson Institute at Princeton, agreed to prepare a paper developing a design for a "national testing agency" and a strategy for getting it launched. (Note the words, "national testing agency." Is it any wonder that the critics had reason to believe that the project was the forerunner of a national test foisted on the states by the federal government?) Morrisett asked Corson to prepare three papers:

> (1) a summary of issues that rose in the two conferences, (2) a timetable for test development and tryout work, and (3) "an examination of what kind of organization that might undertake this work, how it would relate the relevant interest groups, and what might be a strategy for launching it." (Hazlett 1974, p. 50)

In April 1964 Corson submitted a 24-page memorandum to Carnegie, in which he stated three reasons why a periodic assessment should be conducted. First, the 1867 statute directs the U.S. Commissioner of Education to report to the people on the "condition and progress of education in the several states." Second, the public should have an understanding of the strengths and weaknesses of education in the United States. Third, the federal authorities and Congress "need to have a more precise diagnosis of the strengths and weaknesses of state school systems" (Hazlett 1974, pp. 52-53).

Corson also referred to the two Carnegie conferences, which he felt showed a consensus among the participants that a national assessment was both feasible and desirable. He further stated in his memorandum that there are two separate and successive periods: the development period and the administrative period. In the development period, four tasks were identified as "essential and unavoidable":

> First was the formulation of objectives, "progress toward which is to be measured." This would be followed by the development of measuring instruments. The third task was to develop greater acceptance for the assessment. . . . Three groups, especially, will need to be worked with: (1) professional school administrators, (2) Catholic school administrators, and (3) "the organized Negroes." The fourth task must deal with planning how "the periodic assessment will be administered." This will require . . . "consultation with

both the executive and legislative branches of government to
get acceptance of the idea and financial support." (Hazlett
1974, p. 53)

Corson believed that the development period would take about
one and a half to two and a half years (up to October 1966) and
would require establishing a "Commission on the Progress of Education of 19 to 25 members made up of testing authorities, state
school officers, local school administrators, local school board
members, and seven or eight citizens of general esteem and distinction" (Hazlett 1974, p. 53). Various models for creating this
commission were discussed (for example, a Presidential appointment). It was decided that a small Interim Committee on the Assessment of Educational Progress of seven to nine members, aided
by staff, would carry out the necessary tasks during the period
from May to December 1964 by contracting with established
testing companies. In time, the interim committee would oversee
the assessment.

Keppel's status as commissioner of education raised some concerns among educators in general and administrators in particular.
In his book, *The Necessary Revolution in American Education*
(1966), Keppel did not wax eloquently about school administrators. He described them as myopic and preoccupied with raising
money, rather than with providing leadership. Administrators
were concerned that Keppel might be advocating a national curriculum to support a national agenda. And try as he might to nur-
ture the idea of a national assessment, the issue of trust became
one of his main obstacles.

The 1966 renewal of the Elementary and Secondary Education
Act and increased federal funds for education triggered concern
about federal control of education and whether billions of dollars
were being squandered. Because the act required that evaluation
be built into new programs, it became evident that there was no
existing source of valid data to gauge educational progress. Merwin and Womer point out: "We did not know the extent to which
various goals were being achieved; we did not know the real
nature and extent of problems which still existed. It was within

this setting that the organization of the Exploratory Committee on Assessing the Progress of Education (ECAPE) took place" (1969, p. 308).

## Exploratory Committee on Assessing the Progress of Education (ECAPE)

In August 1964, after a number of conferences and discussions, John Gardner, president of the Carnegie Corporation, appointed an interim committee to consider the development of an assessment program. This program would provide benchmarks as a basis for evaluating the changing education needs of our society over the years. The committee was composed of distinguished Americans who were broadly representative of persons vitally interested in American education. It included a city school superintendent, an assistant superintendent of public instruction, a school principal, two college presidents, two businessmen, a college professor, a representative of the Carnegie Corporation, and Tyler as chair (Hazlett 1974, pp. 75-76). Funding was provided by the Carnegie Corporation and the Ford Foundation Fund for the Advancement of Education. However, the committee lacked a technical staff director.

After considering persons who might serve in this role, Morrisett called Stephen Withey, program director at the Survey Research Center and professor of psychology at the University of Michigan in Ann Arbor, to learn whether he was interested in filling the position. Dr. Withey agreed in June 1964 to serve as staff director from 15 July 1964 to 15 January 1965, two-thirds of his time on a leave from the University of Michigan, and to tie up loose ends during January and February 1965. He further stipulated that Ann Arbor would be the location of the office of the committee and staff and that an assistant and a secretary would be hired.

In August 1964 the interim committee appointed by Gardner formally met for the first time and chose the name of the Exploratory Committee on Assessing the Progress of Education (ECAPE). The August meeting was mainly structured so that the members could get acquainted. Although many subjects were discussed, most were tabled for future meetings. The committee was well aware of the problems of formulating objectives, developing instruments, outlining procedures, and obtaining the cooperation of states, schools, and administrators. The committee decided that participation would be voluntary and anonymous, that the assessment would focus on school learning, and that the exercises would have face validity (Hazlett 1974, p. 78).

The second meeting of the exploratory committee was held in New York City in September 1964. Tyler reported on two conferences that he held with school superintendents in Dallas and in New York. The discussion centered on the matters tabled at the August meeting. According to Hazlett:

> There was also a "consensus in the need to establish a review procedure in developing goals and procedures." . . . Three kinds of people were described for the review procedure: specialists, people who know youngsters and children (e.g., guidance counselors) and lay people — "well educated laymen who can ask the question: why could this item be significant in my life when I am not a mathematician or some other specialist?" (1974, p. 80)

Recognizing the concerns of school superintendents, the committee agreed that "political units for reporting should be discouraged and suggested social-economic status, size, and kind of community and regions as appropriate data gathering and reporting categories . . . [since] sampling and reporting by states would be expensive" (Hazlett 1974, pp. 80-81). The committee also recognized the need for public relations and effective communication to the various audiences: parents, legislators, and school superintendents.

Near the end of the meeting Tyler summarized the next steps as he saw them:

> (1) holding more conferences "to enlarge geographical coverage" and to include curriculum people, (2) determine approaches to organization conferences or individual meetings with executive officers, (3) develop a blueprint of what to assess, (4) determine how to translate blueprint into tasks,

e.g., through contract, staff, seminars, etc., and (5) secure school cooperation in tryouts. (Hazlett 1974, p. 81)

When Corson translated Tyler's tasks into a timeline, it was readily evident that what Gardner initially anticipated as taking six months would take almost two years. In reality, even this was shortsighted. The assessment did not begin for another four years.

Of the four major decisions made at the meeting, one dealt with the temporary adoption of Corson's schedule and one was the preparation of a budget projection for review at the next meeting. The other two dealt with:

> (1) Formulating the objectives in Reading (and/or Language Skills), Mathematics, Science, Social Studies, Health, Vocational Education, Fine Arts, and Citizenship (Citizenship was considered a catch-all for intangibles). Health was eliminated, Fine Arts was divided into Art and Music, and Language Skills developed into Writing and Literature.
>
> (2) Developing a statement describing "what the project was and how it should be regarded, that it will continue evolving and should not be feared, and some hints on its values and uses as time goes by." (Hazlett 1974, pp. 82-83)

Tyler was constantly meeting with school personnel to "put out fires" before they could destroy the project. In September and October of 1964 Tyler met several times with school administrators and attended a meeting of instruction and curriculum specialists. The purpose of these meetings was twofold: to describe the assessment project and, more important, to obtain the participants' reactions about concerns that he and ECAPE had about the following issues:

1. What were the values, if any, in a National Assessment?
2. What hazards did the participants see in the conduct of an Assessment?
3. What problems would be encountered?
4. What curriculum areas should an Assessment cover?
5. What kind of organization should be set up to conduct an Assessment? (Hazlett 1974, pp. 84-85)

As one would expect, there were differences between what the administrators and the curriculum and instruction people emphasized as important in an assessment. Nevertheless, within each of these groups there was strong agreement about what an assessment program should be like: that the developmental stage should be vested in a private group, such as ECAPE, and not some federal commission; and that financing of the project should be with private funds. It should be noted that the group was cognizant that at some later date federal funding would be needed.

The third ECAPE meeting was held in December 1964 in New York City. At this meeting Roy Larsen, vice-chair of the board of Time Inc., an ECAPE member, and staff director Withey reported on a meeting of the Round Table of National Organizations, which they had attended the previous month. Representatives of about 30 organizations convened to discuss education testing. The meeting agenda held five topics:

1. Procedures for developing specific objectives and instruments.
2. How to make the translation to a new director and staff. [Withey would be director for only six months.]
3. The development of a commission and appropriate understructure.
4. The task and calendar aspects for ECAPE.
5. General problems of relations and support. (Hazlett 1974, p. 89)

Before considering the agenda topics, the committee declared the following positions, which were suggested at the various conferences:

1. The objectives and the curricula should be as broad as possible.
2. The emphasis of Assessment should be in terms of a national picture.
3. "Plan to measure the usual and unusual in what is to be assessed."
4. Include all areas schools devote 15-20% of their time to — therefore, all major educational goals.
5. Extend . . . instrument development until the fall of 1966.

6. Assessment procedures should be varied beyond the paper and pencil tests.
7. "Plan to report the data on less tangible areas, as well as the customary areas, in a fashion the public can grasp and understands." (Hazlett 1974, pp. 89-90)

The last point implies that the interim committee would continue its work through the stages of developing objectives, preparing exercises, selecting persons to be tested, scoring and analyzing the data, and reporting the results.

The committee also outlined the tasks and responsibilities of the contractors, noting that 1) no decision would be made until after the contractors' seminar on 5 February 1965 and 2) it would be inappropriate to have fixed-price contracts for instrument development, considering the project's developmental nature.

It should be recalled that one of the reasons proposed for conducting a national assessment was that there were many studies dealing with "input" variables but none with "output" variables, or changes that occur over time. However, when Withey undertook a study of "input" variables, he found that the picture still was murky; and no decision was made on the use of input variables.

The committee dealt with, but did not answer, questions concerning data analysis: 1) how the data gathered could be reduced to index form, 2) what would be compared as an index of progress by 1975, and 3) how schools or school systems would be compared or categorized (Hazlett 1974, p. 94). It is interesting that the committee would raise such a question when, from the beginning of the project, it was emphasized that comparisons of that nature were out of the question.

In January 1965 Tyler met with a committee of the National Association of Boards of Education. He reported that initially they had some reservations about the assessment, but a resolution was passed endorsing the project. He also reported that Carnegie granted $300,000 to extend the committee's work for another three months.

When Withey left in mid-January 1965, Jack Merwin, professor and assistant dean of the College of Education at the University of

Minnesota, was selected to direct the project, with offices now in St. Paul-Minneapolis. His staff consisted of Tom Knapp from the University of Rochester, two graduate student assistants, and a secretary. Merwin served for two and one-half years and was succeeded by Frank Womer, professor at the University of Michigan, who served from July 1967 to December 1971. After the project moved to the Education Commission of the States (ECS), Stan Ahmann, a professor at Colorado State University, succeeded Womer; and Roy Forbes succeeded Ahmann. Beverly Anderson was the last NAEP staff director before the National Assessment moved to the Educational Testing Service (ETS) in 1983. Interestingly, all of the staff directors except Forbes and Anderson were faculty members who took leave from university positions to work on the assessment project. When the project moved to Denver in July 1969, the ECS project director was James Hazlett, a former school superintendent.

In February 1965 a seminar was held with potential contractors. The seven contractors who attended were asked to submit proposals by April 1. "All proposals were required to contain assessment criteria for four age groups and for cognitive and non-cognitive items" (Fitzharris 1993, p. 44). At this meeting the contractors voiced concern about being able to meet the 1 September 1966 deadline for completion of the instruments.

At the March ECAPE meeting Tyler and Melvin Barnes, superintendant of schools in Portland, Oregon, and a member of ECAPE, reported on their February meeting with potential contractors. This took up most of the meeting. ECAPE was entering the operational phase that would focus on developing instruments, soliciting funds, obtaining cooperation and support for the assessment project, and recommending a permanent body to undertake management of the assessment. These topics would be agenda items for the next three years. As usual, the problem of federal funding was discussed.

The April 1965 ECAPE meeting was devoted to a detailed report of the potential contractors' responses and a special review panel's evaluation of the proposals from the potential contractors.

This panel, known as the Technical Advisory Committee (TAC), was chaired by John Tukey and included Robert Abelson, Lee Cronbach, and Lyle Jones. TAC is credited with giving leadership and "technical direction to all basic phases of the Assessment project — instrumentation, sampling, exercise development, data analysis, and reporting" (Hazlett 1974, p. 99).

Among the important observations by the review panel were: 1) The contractors have to work with "carefully selected teachers and committees from school"; 2) the contractors asked to submit proposals were capable of doing the work, but they "really had to learn to do the job"; 3) after the objectives have been developed, the try-out of the prototype exercises would take about four or five months; 4) writing exercises for lay validity was an almost wholly unpracticed art of unknown difficulty; and 5) time was needed to study the validity and acceptability of different approaches to developing exercises.

The review panel also made suggestions about specific proposals: 1) The health and physical education proposal could not be supported because it dealt entirely with physical fitness; 2) because the music proposal was too technical, it should be delayed in the assessment cycle for at least one year; and 3) as much money as possible should be invested in training and monitoring the contractors in order for them to be able to produce the new materials (Hazlett 1974, p. 100).

The suggestions and observations made by the review committee would, of course, require additional funds and an extension of time. However, the ECAPE members felt that, rather than reduce the project to available funds, they should think in terms of the job to be done and seek additional funding to do the job right.

Once again, how to handle the release of information came up. ECAPE recognized that they were in a difficult situation. They knew that their critics were hollering "secretiveness," but as yet they had nothing to report. Galen Saylor (then president of the Association for Supervision and Curriculum Development) prepared a five-page summary of the committee's work to date. The committee agreed that it was an excellent statement and could be distributed in response to requests for comments on the committee's work.

In July 1965 staff director Merwin and ECAPE members Katherine McBride, president of Bryn Mawr College; Mabel Smythe, principal of Lincoln High School in New York City; Corson; and Tyler met with the contractors to discuss their progress and the problems they encountered. The contractors were told that professionals *must* be included in their panels of consultants for developing the assessment's objectives. They also emphasized that the objectives should be constructed so as to be readily understood by lay people. Other subjects discussed in this meeting included:

1. Overlap of exercises between age groups were [sic] possible but this was not considered a fundamental issue.
2. Objectives should be contemporary in expressing what schools are presently doing.
3. Difficulty levels of exercises were defined as difficult (only 20% could answer), average difficulty (40% to 60% could answer), and easy (80% could answer).
4. It was decided that the assessment of non-cognitive learning would be within each subject area rather than constituting a separate assessment area.
5. There should be about six objectives per subject area as guides to the development of exercises representing behaviors relating to the area. (Hazlett 1974, p. 104)

At the October 1965 meeting of ECAPE, the discussion first centered on the public relations problems before dealing with the contractors' problems and the solicitation of funds. It was evident that there was confusion and misunderstanding not only among informed laymen but also among professionals about the distinction between the design of a national assessment and a national testing program.

To remedy the public relations problems, committee members suggested a variety of tactics, ranging from articles in *Time*, *The Nation's Schools*, and *Harper's* to increasing the membership of ECAPE to 25 persons in order to get more representation from superintendents who felt they were underrepresented in the planning stage. Some also thought that Gardner's appearance on national platforms would reduce suspicions about the project.

Because the objectives phase was completed, ECAPE outlined guidelines for selecting lay panels to review the objectives.

## Committee on Assessing the Progress of Education (CAPE)

ECAPE was formally incorporated as a nonprofit corporation for a five-year term on 25 June 1965 by the New York Board of Regents. At the December 1965 meeting, Tyler suggested deleting "exploratory" from the title because five years appeared an overly long time for "exploration." Thus the assessment project became the Committee on Assessing the Progress of Education (CAPE). The ECAPE members now became "consultants to the project" (Hazlett 1974, p. 109). Bylaws for CAPE were adopted, and Tyler was elected CAPE chair. Morrisett (who always attended the ECAPE meetings as the Carnegie officer in charge of assessment) and Paul Lawrence (assistant superintendent, California Department of Public Instruction) were elected CAPE trustees. Corson and Morrisett were elected vice chair and secretary-treasurer, respectively. An executive committee was created: Paul Johnston, Iowa Superintendent of Schools; Devereux Josephs, chair of the board of the New York Life Insurance Company; Tyler; Morrisett; and Corson.

Technical control of the project was now vested in CAPE, rather than Carnegie. For all practical purposes, except for the addition of Lawrence, the same people were involved in CAPE as were in ECAPE. Their work was still exploratory and motivated by the same charges given by Gardner. Funding from private sources increased. The total budget for FY 1967 totaled $1,280,000, all of which came from private sources (Hazlett 1974, Appendix A, reproduced in this book as Table 1 of Chapter 5, p. 178; Fitzharris 1993, p. 44).

Tyler reported that the contractors selected — Educational Testing Service (ETS), American Institutes for Research (AIR),

Science Research Associates (SRA), and the Psychological Corporation (PC) — had submitted their objectives and prototypes.

Four lay panels, each drawn from four regions and three types of communities, met to review the objectives and exercises. After the four regional meetings, the four panel chairs met in New York to consider the panels' recommendations. Barnes, who attended the meeting of the panel chairs, reported that some of those chairs felt they should have an opportunity to discuss whether the assessment should even be conducted. In fact, one of the panel chairs felt that it should not be conducted. As expected, Tyler disagreed "because the assessment will be made anyway" (Hazlett 1974, p. 110).

Merwin reported that there was wide participation in the project beyond the four lay panels. Developing the objectives involved 230 persons, and objectives were ranked by 1,300 scholars and educators.

The meeting of December 1965, like all the others, had its fill of public relations problems, speeches, reports, and questions. Reference was made to some of the opposition to national assessment, but Tyler felt that the opposition was subsiding. (Tyler did not realize the magnitude of the opposition that would confront the assessment two years later.) The meeting ended with an evaluation of the work completed and a discussion of the next steps. Work still to be done included recommending an agency to administer the assessment, developing more precise cost estimates, and developing a sampling plan.

The contractors met in January 1966 to review the lay panels' recommendations and to work on the next steps in item development. They agreed to develop cost estimates, and the CAPE executive committee was authorized to enter into contractual arrangements.

In February a meeting was held with social studies specialists from schools, contractors, and testing companies to clarify problems identified by the Technical Advisory Committee at their meeting in December. At the March 1966 meeting of CAPE, most of the time was spent discussing public information activities and problems and the shortage of funds to complete instrument development. Tyler and Merwin still were attending meetings of professional organizations, such as the American Association for the Advancement of Science, the American Educational Research Association, and the Department of Elementary School Principals, to do "damage control." Between 24 January and 20 March 1966, Tyler attended 10 meetings, while Merwin spoke at five meetings in five states to convey the message of national assessment — its purpose, methodology, scoring, and reporting.

CAPE was cognizant of the inordinate amount of time assessment personnel, particularly Tyler, spent on public relations. However, they rejected the idea of using a public relations firm. Instead, they suggested hiring a communications specialist. Morrisett's proposal to develop a public relations approach was not successful. As Hazlett (1974) said, "The future history [of national assessment] may have been different had they accepted his idea" (p.118).

Once again, funding was a problem and an "all-consuming subject." Some alternative solutions proposed by Tyler included: 1) having the contractors reduce their activities or providing some pro bono service; 2) eliminating some of the subject areas, which would be unfortunate since there was such a nice balance between the "three Rs" and the other areas; 3) having Tyler and Merwin develop exercises in-house, but this was silly because neither had the time nor the staff; 4) spreading the work over two years and using money obtained the next year; and 5) approaching Ford and Carnegie for additional money (Hazlett 1974, pp. 118-19).

A three-part decision was reached. First, the staff should "squeeze out all the fat" possible without damaging the project. Second, the contractors should be encouraged to consider part of their work as a contribution that will result in dividends later. Third, additional money should be sought from Carnegie, which incidentally had a positive attitude to the need for additional funds.

At the September 1966 CAPE meeting, Tyler reported that instruments should be ready for tryout early in 1967. He said that instruments would be reviewed by staff and by lay panels, with the latter paying particular attention to offensiveness. Tyler reported that, though money was a problem, it was possible to stretch things; staff would have responsibility for tryouts, and contractors would be expected to give some service pro bono.

Regarding ownership of the exercises, the contractors initially were told that they were the property of the Carnegie Corporation. Later, however, they were told they could keep those exercises that were not selected for the assessment. Possibly this would help in reducing the contractors' costs.

Merwin reported that lay panels and subject-matter specialists would review all exercises. He said that one lay panel met in May, another was to meet in September, and panels probably would meet once a month throughout the fall of 1966.

Once again, the group discussed using private funding for development and federal funding for review. The latter was a concern from the early days of the project and was continually mentioned by its critics.

Some issues other than the perennial public relations problems were discussed, including: 1) the most beneficial way to reduce opposition to the project might be through the education committees in state legislatures and through state board members; 2) they needed to develop a sampling plan that would protect the privacy of the respondents and their schools; 3) since the exercises were not yet developed, it was difficult to plan for their administration; 4) the cost of assessing individuals in and out of school was estimated as $5 and $50, respectively; and 5) meeting the costs of the try-outs and the problems of packaging, administering, and developing exercises for the three difficulty levels. Tukey suggested that an additional $1.1 million to $1.2 million would be required to complete the committee's work. Once again, John Tukey prevailed and a motion was made to request that the executive committee forward a proposal for $1.2 million.

The group discussed the organization, agency, or commission to undertake the assessment project but made no decision. However, Morrisett was to write to the committee members asking them to give some thought to this prior to further discussion at the December meeting.

At the December 1966 CAPE meeting, the first order of business was designating an agency to conduct the assessment. Corson stated that he had discussed options with various persons, the consensus of opinion being that a consortium of states would be that agency. This was in contrast to the prestigious presidential commission that Corson proposed in the early days of ECAPE.

Corson, in his inimitable fashion, summarized the discussion by saying that: 1) there was no doubt the assessment should take place, 2) the number of students or regions should not be reduced as a method to save money, and 3) the committee should be enlarged by adding membership from schools, especially parochial schools. When Corson suggested that the Office of Education be encouraged to submit a budget item for congressional review, it can be assumed that no decision was made on the selection of an agency to conduct the assessment. Corson suggested a meeting in March 1967 "to look at the cost of try-outs, the try-out plan, and the progress being made with the Office of Education and the Congress in securing federal funding" (Hazlett 1974, p. 130).

Tyler reported that the tryouts should be concluded by fall 1967. Merwin reported that the TAC made some suggestions about undertaking a few studies. One would be to see if the contractors met the specifications established for the exercises. If they didn't, CAPE would have the data to challenge them. Another idea dealt with the tryout of some mathematics exercises so that the TAC would have data that might give them ideas for reports and analyses. Still another thought was to begin feasibility studies to test the various approaches considered for administration, for example, the use of audiotapes for administering the exercises.

At the March 1967 CAPE meeting, Tyler reported that, since the previous committee meeting in December 1966, he had met with lay committees (50% of whom were school board members) and with nine other groups to promote understanding of the assessment. For a change, instead of reporting on the opposition to the national assessment, the meeting opened with a list of individuals and groups who *opposed* the American Association of School Administrators (AASA) position that previously asked its members not to participate in an assessment. The National Association of Secondary School Principals and the National Congress of Parents and Teachers adopted a resolution supporting the assessment, and the elementary school principals were expected to do the same. Insofar as the Association for Supervision and Curriculum Development (ASCD) was concerned, Tyler said he didn't know their stand on the AASA resolution. The *Wall Street Journal, Houston Post,* and *Washington Post* also had taken stands *against* the AASA position.

Tyler reported that AASA unexpectedly requested that a 15-member committee be established to review the assessment and to answer questions about which the AASA felt it had not yet received satisfactory answers. This committee would include five CAPE members, five AASA members, and five others to be selected by the other 10 members. Tyler suggested that CAPE would be happy to have its members meet with AASA, but he was opposed to forming a new group.

Tyler estimated the cost of the assessment at $2 million per year or $6 million for a complete three-year cycle. Josephs felt that private funds should not be used unless the federal government would not do it. Tyler suggested that another avenue to obtaining funds would be to sell the exclusive publication rights to some publisher or newspaper. He felt that federal funds should not be used if it meant losing the support of school people.

Once again, discussion centered on the agency to conduct the assessment. Should it be a continuation of CAPE, a consortium of universities, a consortium of states, or the creation of a presidential commission?

Merwin reported that, though the rejection rate for exercises was less than 1%, the revisions might take more time than anticipated. He also reported on the two studies that TAC requested. One was a tryout of mathematics exercises to provide TAC with data that they could use to look at possible analysis and reporting methods. The other was the administration of a sample of "easy" exercises to see if, in fact, they were "easy."

Feasibility studies were to be conducted by the American Institutes for Research (AIR) and the Educational Testing Service

(ETS), using various approaches for administering the exercises, such as filmstrips, audiotapes, and so on.

At the June 1967 meeting, Tyler told the committee that the meeting's purpose was twofold: to discuss, first, the review committee suggested by the AASA and, second, the progress in developing instruments for the actual assessment. ("Exploratory" was restored to the name of the committee, possibly in recognition that exploration still was a part of the formal corporate name.)

At this meeting, it was reported that exercises labeled as "easy" were, in fact, not so. The exercises often were incomprehensible, especially in social studies. TAC recommended that special efforts be made to secure more 90% items, particularly for the nine-year-old group. Doing so would delay the start of the assessment until fall 1968. Also, the revision of many of the exercises would further contribute to the scaling down of the tryouts

Merwin reported that the lay reviews had been completed and the cooperation of schools in the tryouts was very good. He also said that a variety of studies were conducted, including looking at the format of the exercise booklets, scoring procedures, sampling procedures, and interview techniques for the out-of-school sample.

At the October 1967 ECAPE meeting, five ECAPE members who had been meeting with the AASA reported that, though there still was some negative feeling, many AASA members accepted the assessment and were pleased that it was in good hands. Another meeting of the groups was planned. TAC also had met with the contractors on 16-18 August 1967 to discuss measurement problems. Although it had been implied for some time, now there was no doubt that "the real directing force in setting the quality of the instruments and the pace of their development was this advisory group of four people which Tyler had put together" (Hazlett 1974, p. 139).

TAC recommended (and the committee concurred) using a three-year cyclic approach, such as four subjects the first year and three subjects each of the following two years. Conferences with contractors revealed new problems, necessitating another round of exercise reviews. Tryouts might begin in December 1967 and run through the spring. Depending on the sampling design, a pilot study was to be conducted to test the feasibility of the assessment procedures. Tyler estimated that the first cycle would begin in fall 1968.

Staff Director Womer reported that two studies had revealed some problems in the wording of some exercises and in the directions for administration. Ten conferences had been held to study the validity and comprehensibility of the exercises. Womer reviewed each subject area and pointed out reviewers' comments, such as "Music was not sufficiently comprehensive in coverage . . . the exercises in mathematics . . . were too text-bookish, very technical, and too difficult . . . the language was too difficult . . . there weren't enough easy items . . . further work . . . was needed" (Hazlett 1974, pp. 140-41).

It was evident that there was a communication gap between reviewers and exercise writers, especially insofar as writing imaginative exercises was concerned. Accordingly, the group suggested that conferences be held between the item writers and reviewers to try to remedy this problem. They also discussed audiotaping the directions for administering the exercises, alternate administration sites if schools weren't available, the sampling design, and other matters. Again, the need to select an agency to manage the assessment was brought up. The compact known as the Education Commission of the States (ECS) was mentioned again, a compact of 43 states and territories initiated by the Carnegie Corporation to discuss education problems and coordinate activities. The ECS Steering Committee had been approached, and they were not in favor for a variety of reasons. Tyler was to talk with Wendell Pierce, the ECS executive director, while Corson and Eli Evans, an aide to North Carolina Governor Terry Sanford, then the ECS Chairman, would follow up with needed action.

At the meeting of ECAPE in January 1968, the agency to carry out the assessment again was considered. Corson indicated four possibilities: 1) the Education Commission of the States, 2) the

National Committee on Accrediting, 3) a reconstituted CAPE that would include representatives from the Big Six (six major national associations of educators) plus a Catholic organization, and 4) a presidential commission. Corson urged an early decision "so that the OE could be asked for . . . [a] million dollars . . . in their current budget before the fiscal year is up on June 30th" (Hazlett 1974, p. 145).

After much discussion of the pros and cons of each possibility, a reconstituted CAPE committee was chosen as an appropriate vehicle to manage the project. The ECAPE members agreed to submit a report to the presidents of the Carnegie Corporation and the Ford Foundation stating that their work was complete. They also suggested that the foundation presidents invite some of the ECAPE members to serve on a reconstituted committee, along with representatives from the Big Six, ECS, and other persons to serve as trustees.

Womer reported that exercise reviews in literature, citizenship, writing, and social studies were already completed and that science would soon be ready. From these five areas, science, writing, and citizenship were selected for the first year's assessment. He said that tryouts would be conducted in schools and homes from February through April 1968 to detect problems not identified earlier. Womer also said that a conference was being planned to look at the objectives — both specific and general — in vocational education, the relationship between vocational and technical education, and problems associated with assessing the disadvantaged. TAC still was working on the sampling design with the Research Triangle Institute (RTI). Some consideration also was given to the feasibility of using a mobile van for administering the exercises. Womer reported on the work of TAC on the various feasibility and special studies under way, the size of the sample to be used, the types of reports and their release schedule, and the decision that each booklet would contain exercises from all areas being assessed in that cycle.

At the April 1968 meeting, two major items were discussed: the reconstitution of the committee and the preparation of a public report of ECAPE's work. There was agreement that the following points should be emphasized in the statement to be issued:

1. The statement should note that, after two years, the Committee feels that an Assessment can now be made.
2. The statement should emphasize the broad involvement of all kinds of people.
3. It should be widely distributed through mailings and released to educational journals.
4. There should be two reviews . . . one by the Office of Education to check the content and "one from the standpoint of public understanding.". . .
5. The report should be addressed to the educational community "to report . . . on a pioneering educational venture."
6. The statement was to be sent to all who had participated on panels and conferences . . . to all fifteen organizations who had cooperated . . . to "relevant committees of Congress." (Hazlett 1974, p.148)

Because many people felt that the assessment was secretive and sinister, it was deemed advisable to issue a public report. Also, such a report could be used by Commissioner of Education Harold Howe in requesting funding. Howe also said that funding for fiscal year 1969 should be limited to $2 million, which might result in ECAPE setting priorities.

The committee also agreed with Corson and Morrisett about features of the restructured committee, including:

1. The membership should consist of twenty-five members selected by the present members.
2. Members should be associated with educational organizations but they would be serving as individuals and not as spokesmen of their organization. Geography, race, politics, and urban or non-urban residency would be considered in the selection.
3. A few critics should be included so that some would think "assessment was under relatively safe leadership."
4. James Allen . . . would be an appropriate chairman because he was a chief state school officer, a[n ECS] Compact official, and an innovator.

5. The legal name of the Committee for Assessing the Progress of Education would be used and the by-laws would be changed to permit a three-year rotation scheme subject to reelection.

6. Corson, Morrisett, and Smythe were appointed to contact a number of people suggested from [different] organizations and/or position types . . . [to include] unions. (Hazlett 1974, pp. 149-50)

The committee agreed that the next meeting with the AASA should take place *after* the announcement of the reconstituted committee so as to demonstrate the assessment's independence.

It was reported that TAC made two recommendations: formation of an Operations Advisory Committee (OPAC) to advise in the actual conduct of the assessment, and delay of data gathering until January 1969 to allow for staffing, training, and developing the sample.

In July 1968 the Exploratory Committee issued its final report and turned over the assessment instruments and the plan that was developed for the conduct of the assessment to the Committee on Assessing the Progress of Education (CAPE), which then assumed responsibility for the national assessment that began collecting data in February 1969.

## Reconstituted Committee on Assessing the Progress of Education

The meeting of CAPE in October 1968 was the first meeting of the reconstituted committee, made up of the core group plus nine new members representing professional organizations, politicians, and educators (see names in Hazlett 1974, p.151). Tyler briefly reviewed the assessment's history and pointed out the duties of the committee. He also said that CAPE would have a rotating membership to provide "new vitality" from time to time. Once again, there was discussion on how to reach local professional leaders. It was hoped that the descriptive brochure prepared by the Carnegie Corporation would help not only to inform people about the project but also to remove the concerns and misconceptions of the critics.

As might be expected, there was lengthy discussion on identifying the opposition to the assessment. George Brain, dean of the School of Education at Washington State University and a past president of AASA, as well as chair of the special AASA Committee on Assessment, felt that the AASA would support the project if they knew *how* the results were to be used. AASA still feared that administrators would be blamed for the educational status of students. How would the press and Congress treat the results? Brain and John Letson, the superintendant of schools in Atlanta, both felt that the superintendents — especially those from large cities — believed the assessment to be a waste of money because the data already existed in the schools. This again demonstrated the lack of understanding about the nature of the assessment that permeated the education establishment.

Brain was elected chair of CAPE to replace Tyler. It is ironic that the new chair of the body appointed to manage the assessment was the past president of an organization that was so opposed to a national assessment that it urged its members not to cooperate. As Hazlett (1974, p. 160) wrote, "Who converted whom?"

Womer presented two budget estimates, one for 1968-69 and the other for 1969-70. The first was for $2.5 million to cover assessing out-of-school 17-year-olds and young adults. The second was for $4.12 million to assess nine- and 13-year-olds and in-school 17-year-olds. Womer reported that bids for administering, scoring, printing, and initial reporting were sent to 12 organizations; but only six responded. He said that TAC would evaluate the bids. Corson, however, reminded the group that this was really a function for the proposed Operations Advisory Committee.

As usual, there was discussion of the agency that would assume governance of the assessment. With Robert McNair (governor of South Carolina) and New York Commissioner of Education James Allen, ECS chairman and vice-chairman respectively, present at the meeting, the discussion centered on ECS assuming the task.

McNair said that, though this would improve the image of ECS, he felt their staff was too small to take on the task. However, both he and Corson thought that if ECS was able to contract out most of the work, they *might* be interested.

Corson estimated the annual cost of the assessment from $3 million to $5 million, but only $2 million would come from the OE. The remainder would have to come from other sources. Because of uncertainty of funding, Tyler said that data would be gathered first in April, rather than January 1969. Morrisett said that delays or cuts in the age groups or target subjects also were possible ways to save on costs.

Morrisett reported that the restructured CAPE was still short three members to bring the list to 25 and that he, Corson, and Roy Larsen (ECAPE member and vice-chair of the board of Time Inc.) would prepare a list of recommended names. (When CAPE met for the last time in May 1969, full membership was established. However, the resignation of Paul Lawrence because of a possible conflict of interest — he was elected director of the Western District of the United States Office of Education — meant that an additional member would have to be added.)

At the meeting of CAPE in April 1969, it was noted that ECS management of the assessment had been discussed by CAPE in October 1968. It was reported (though not in the minutes of the October meeting) that ECS Executive Director Wendell Pierce was personally supportive but believed the compact was not ready to assume the task. Pierce attended the CAPE meeting in April 1969, where Brain introduced him and indicated that there were discussions between the two groups. Brain reminded CAPE that he was authorized to seek out ECS' interest in assuming management of the assessment. McNair recommended that someone from CAPE attend the December 1969 ECS Steering Committee meeting.

Brain indicated that he and Womer had attended an ECS Steering Committee meeting in Wilmington, Delaware, in December 1968. They proposed that because the OE and many professional organizations wanted ECS to assume the assessment program as one of its projects, they should do so. They felt this would place the assessment in an "on-going body which is legally responsible and responsive to the electorate of the states" (Committee on Assessing the Progress of Education 1969*a*). No doubt this action played a significant role in ameliorating the critics' opposition. In fact, AASA — one of the most critical bodies — rescinded opposition to the program at its annual meeting in February 1969. Pierce indicated that CAPE's role would be *advisory*. And as far as making any adjustments to the budget was concerned, that would be ECS' responsibility. The group passed a resolution authorizing Pierce to enter into negotiations with the affected parties "for the governance, management, and administration of the project" (Hazlett 1974, p. 161). The first of July 1969 was chosen as the effective date because it was the beginning of the fiscal year for both ECS and the OE.

Brain noted three administrative concerns: 1) What would CAPE's future role be? 2) Who was the ECS person the NAEP staff director would relate to? and 3) What relationship would there be between CAPE staff and ECS? It was evident that the relationship between the two staffs was not very smooth. Although there was no outward hostility, the CAPE staff felt that ECS wasn't really interested in the project except for the overhead that would provide support for their own projects. Two additional questions raised at the meeting were: 1) What did the ECS person know about assessment? and 2) Would the ECS person's role be directive or liaison? Although Brain was not concerned about the administrative details, he felt that the larger question was how Pierce viewed "the role of CAPE and its continuing relationship with the National Assessment project" (Hazlett 1974, p. 162).

Brain's questions were more significant than they may appear. CAPE members eagerly looked forward to having some other agency take over the management of the project, but they were now concerned about the conditions of its continuation. It seemed that ECS was the boss and that CAPE should be considered advisory.

Womer reported on the status of the assessment of the 17-year-olds to date, at that time in its fourth week of field operations. He reported 90% cooperation from the schools contacted, which was amazing considering the early criticism. He also said that few problems had been encountered.

The big questions facing staff dealt with whether three or four areas should be assessed in the second year and if new areas should be developed. Because it took three years to develop an area, it was necessary that work begin immediately for a new area to be ready by 1972. These questions were forwarded to the Operations Advisory Committee for advice.

Near the end of the meeting, Tyler — who had designed the assessment project, secured funding from private sources, guided it for six years, and had been pilloried by many professional organizations, especially the AASA, for being secretive and developing a project that would eventually result in a national test and place the curriculum under federal control — thanked "the chairman of the AASA Special Committee [Brain] for negotiating a governance plan that depended on federal money and state direction" (Hazlett 1974, p. 166).

The May 1969 meeting was the last meeting of the original CAPE (also known as the "Exploratory Committee" or just the "Committee") that had been meeting three or four times a year for nearly five years. Little had the original members realized that they would spend this much time; they had thought that they would be involved for only about six months. All but two of the original members of ECAPE (Father Reinert and Devereux Josephs) stayed even after the committee was reconstituted. Three new members had been added: Martin Essex, Ohio Chief State School Officer and former AASA president; James Stratten, past president of the San Francisco Board of Education; and Donald Wilson, president-elect of the Association of Classroom Teachers. With the exception of having to replace Lawrence, full membership on CAPE was realized.

## The Birth of NAEP

In June 1969 a "Memorandum of Understanding" was signed by Allen and McNair that set the stage for the transfer of responsibility from CAPE to the Education Commission of the States. With OE now responsible for funding, ECS assumed responsibility for the direction, management, and operation of the assessment. "This structure appeared to be a perfect blend of state and federal efforts" (Fitzharris 1993, p. 50). The transfer became official on 1 July 1969, when CAPE was reduced to an advisory committee and the project became known as the National Assessment of Educational Progress.

The essential points of the Memorandum of Understanding concerning administration were: 1) The role of the present chairman of CAPE would be assumed by the chairman of a newly created Policy Committee, who would be an ECS employee. 2) The director and staff would continue in their present working relationships. 3) The staff director would report to the chairman of the Policy Committee. 4) CAPE would become an advisory committee to ECS (Hazlett 1974, p. 168).

Not only did the organizational memorandum place supervision and control of the project and staff with the Policy Committee, but it stated that its membership would include the chairs of the Advisory Committee, Technical Advisory Committee, Operations Advisory Committee (these were Brain, Tukey, and Letson, respectively), and the ECS vice-chair. The Policy Committee chairman's duties were spelled out: responsibility for seeking funds; relationships with Congress, chief state school officers, and professional organizations; and developing guidelines for officially announcing the project's results. Membership on the Policy Committee was controlled by the ECS Steering Committee.

When Womer said that he hoped he would be able to go to the Advisory Committee, Pierce outlined the procedure that he would have to follow. It would appear that Womer would not be able to go to the Advisory Committee directly but would have to go through the Policy Committee Chairman, who would be the channel to the Advisory Committee. Pierce was quite insistent when he said, "But we have no intention of skipping any of these steps . . . you see" (Hazlett 1974, p. 170). Without doubt, it appears that CAPE was emasculated and had no power. It was only *advisory* to ECS. It should be mentioned here that, though concerns were raised about some sections of the memorandum, the Resolution of Transfer and Responsibility was passed by CAPE.

Womer talked about plans for the coming year that would include getting ready for Year 04, which would involve re-administering the areas assessed in Year 01. He recommended that after discussions with the Operations Advisory Committee, specifications be sent out to develop exercises in consumer education, health and physical education, and speaking and listening and that one of them would be chosen for a new area of assessment. Morrisett was very supportive of the idea of having the NAEP assume a broader role. He also recommended assessment of mathematics, music, and literature in Year 02 and social studies, reading, art, and career and occupational development in Year 03.

Womer brought up four problems discussed at the last meeting: 1) invasion-of-privacy problems in California, 2) objections to the content of some exercises, 3) some local superintendents asking for endorsements from state education agencies, and 4) apparent underrepresentation in the sample of students from large cities. Of the four, the California problem was the most serious because having some items deleted could skew the results for those items. After considerable discussion, it was decided that, when reporting about problems, California should not be identified.

Womer said another problem was related to the type of information to be reported. Should it be simply factual data? Should they give any explanation and, if so, to what extent? Initially, TAC and the Operations Advisory Committee said the reports should concentrate on the facts. It was evident from the discussion that a statistical report complete with jargon would not suffice. Pierce echoed a point often made by the ECS constituency:

> I am particularly conscious of the fact that the lay person — and I would put politically-oriented people in that category— just don't dig our jargon, and we've got to find a way of overcoming that because if we just put it out in our jargon, we are going to miss the whole boat in this thing in my opinion. (Hazlett 1974, p. 173)

Brain interpreted the sense of the committee when he said Womer should assign the highest priority to reporting, "sparing no effort and using language understood by the common citizen" (Hazlett 1974, p. 173).

This meeting, the last of CAPE as a corporation directing the assessment's affairs, ended with Brain paying tribute to Tyler for his devotion and direction for the past six years despite the many criticisms leveled at the project, as well as at him personally.

In July 1969, CAPE ceased to exist. All its assets were transferred to ECS, which became responsible for the management and administration of the national assessment program.

## The Assessment Plan

Developing a plan for a national assessment had been the goal of ECAPE. The committee's plan was designed to answer two fundamental questions: 1) What are the current education attainments of our population? and 2) What change is there in the level of attainments of our population? Although these goals aren't unusual in other testing programs, the methods and design used by NAEP had a number of unique aspects.

It was readily evident to the ECAPE members that the tools and techniques available at the time were inadequate for meaningfully reporting education progress at the national level. Accordingly, a new assessment plan was needed. This involved specifying the objectives to be assessed, seeing to it that exercises were developed to implement the plan, selecting the individuals to be tested, specifying the manner in which the data were to be analyzed and reported, carrying out any research that was needed, and recommending a new group to handle the actual assessment.

The overall design for the assessment was to select a national sample of census tracts, randomly select school buildings and households that fall in each census tract, and randomly select a small number of students of a given age within a school building. This sampling plan then permitted the following reporting units:

1. Four geographical areas: Northeast, Southeast, Central, West.
2. Four types of communities: large cities with an urban fringe, middle-size cities, small cities, and rural areas.
3. Four ages: 9, 13, 17, and young adults 26-35.
4. Two SES levels: below poverty level and above.
5. Sex.

Although race/ethnicity was not considered as a stratification variable in the initial sampling plan, it was considered as a reporting category on the recommendation of various groups concerned about the education of minority groups.

Ten subject matter areas were to be developed: citizenship, science, writing, literature, reading, music, mathematics, social studies, and career and occupational development (initially called vocational education).

It is readily evident that more than the "three Rs" were to be assessed. Although five areas were ready for administration during the first year of the assessment, only three subject matter areas (citizenship, science, writing) were to be assessed; another three (or four) the second year; and the final three (or four) the third year. This would complete the first cycle.

From the outset, the national assessment staff was essentially a planning and monitoring staff, though there was some in-house development of exercises and small research studies. The sampling, administration, printing of exercise booklets, scoring, reporting, and most exercise development activities were contracted out.

*Developing Objectives.* The identification of goals and objectives provided the framework for developing assessment measures. The Exploratory Committee had decided that the objectives had to satisfy three criteria: "They should be objectives that (1) the school currently is seeking to attain, (2) scholars in the field consider authentic to their discipline, and (3) thoughtful laymen would consider important for American youth to attain" (Merwin and Womer 1969, pp. 314-15). For the national assessment, goals had to be expressed in behavioral terms and be a clear guide for developing assessment exercises.

The objectives had to be important to three groups of people. First, they had to be considered important by scholars of a given subject area. Mathematicians, for example, should generally agree that the mathematics objectives were worthwhile. Second, the objectives had to be acceptable to most educators and be considered desirable teaching goals in most schools. Finally, in contrast to most other achievement tests of the time, the national assessment's objectives had to be considered desirable by thoughtful lay persons, that is, there should be agreement among parents and persons interested in education that an objective is important for our country's youth to know and that it is of value in modern life.

ECAPE recognized very early that it did not have — nor would it be able to build — an in-house staff with the skills and capabilities needed to produce the exercises. Therefore it executed item-writing contracts with existing organizations that had professional staffs and access to subject-matter specialists. This, of course, required additional funding; and Carnegie provided an additional $300,000. Also, the original timeline of six months was revised to two years.

The seven contractors who submitted proposals by the 1 April 1965 deadline were ETS, SRA, PC, AIR, Measurement Research Center (MRC), National Opinion Research Center (NORC), and the University of Michigan Survey Research Center (UMSRC). All proposals were reviewed by TAC, which later became the Analysis Advisory Committee (ANAC). Tukey served as Chairman of TAC and was the initial chairman of ANAC.

The review panel (TAC) recommended that proposals be accepted from four companies in the following areas:

ETS: Language arts, mathematics, science, social studies, foreign language, citizenship, and study skills, interests, and attitudes.

SRA: Mathematics, reading, and vocational education.

AIR: Citizenship, social studies, vocational education, and health and physical education.

PC: Science and mathematics (Hazlett 1974, p. 99).

Because of the unusual nature of the national assessment and the importance of objectives in developing exercises, ECAPE felt it would be valuable to obtain different points of view, and so they used two different contractors to work independently on developing the objectives for four areas — citizenship, science, social studies, and vocational education — and the mathematics objectives were looked at by three contractors: ETS, SRA, and PC. TAC recommended excluding health and physical education and delaying the development of music for at least one year.

The contractors were given complete freedom to bring together consultants whom they felt were competent in developing the sets of objectives.

*Lay Reviews.* TAC's chief concern was to develop procedures to ensure the consistency and quality of the objectives and related exercises. To help achieve this goal, a series of reviews and conferences was held to review the objectives and exercises.

> The uniqueness of the new types of items and the early criticism of the National Assessment project made the review of the test items crucial. Test items were reviewed from November 1966 to March 1969 under the direction and control of the Technical Advisory Committee (TAC) . . . the types of reviews included an analysis of the difficulty level of the items, the correlation between multiple choice items, open-ended items, and the feasibility of testing adults no longer in school. . . . A final step included administration of approximately one-third of the items in classrooms to determine if they were valid and reliable items. (Fitzharris 1993, p. 58)

One of the unique aspects of the national assessment project — and there were many — was involving lay persons in developing and reviewing the objectives and exercises in the early stages of development. Approximately 1,300 educators and content specialists evaluated the objectives. To get nominations of lay persons, ECAPE approached the officers of various state and national organizations, such as the U.S. Chamber of Commerce, the NAACP, and the National Catholic Education Association, and asked for their assistance. From the nominations, ECAPE selected 99 lay persons from each area of the country; from different races, religions, sexes, and economic levels; and from different organizations interested in education. These individuals were invited to attend one of four conferences held in 1966 and 1967 to review the objectives. The first regional conference was held in Chicago. Similar conferences were held in Philadelphia, Atlanta, and Dallas.

Eleven lay panels were organized, each chaired by one of the lay panelists. One ECAPE staff member was present on each panel to serve as a resource person. Each panel had a complete report from the contractor responsible for developing the objectives and spent two days reviewing and discussing all the objectives that had been developed, thus providing 11 independent reviews. The panel chairpersons were then brought together to pool their recommendations to ECAPE.

Suggestions were made for minor revisions; but in general, there was good agreement not only among the lay panels but also between the lay and professional judgments regarding the objectives. The lay panelists accepted the contractors' objectives as important goals for American youth in all subject matter areas except for social studies (Merwin and Womer 1969, p. 315). The panelists felt that the objectives for social studies had problems and recommended more work before producing exercises.

Following the lay-review meetings, a special conference of social studies teachers, professors of social studies education, and experts in those disciplines contributing to social studies was convened to consider the social studies objectives and to form guidelines for further work. Following this conference, a revised set of social studies objectives was developed and approved.

It is interesting to note that when a study was made of the relationship between the objectives of the 10 national assessment subject areas and other objectives in these areas that previously appeared in the professional literature, "it was clear that National Assessment had not produced a set of new objectives . . . [but] its objectives represented a reorganization, restatement, and something of a summarization of objectives which frequently had appeared in print in the last quarter century" (Merwin and Womer 1969, p. 316). Because one criterion for the objectives was that they be ones that were in schools' curricula, this similarity was desired and expected.

*Development of Exercises.* The Exploratory Committee turned to the same four contractors that had been involved in the development of the objectives and asked them to develop the exercises that would meet three specific criteria:

> (a) each exercise must sample the behavior of one of the objectives; (b) each exercise must have enough face validity to communicate achievement information meaningfully to laymen; (c) one-third of the exercises should be ones that practically all individuals of a given age level could do, one-third that approximately half could do, and one-third that only the most advanced could do. (Merwin and Womer 1969, p. 317)

Within this framework the contractors were encouraged to "ignore practical limitations and to produce the best plan they could for developing exercises that met the criteria" (Merwin and Womer 1969, p. 317). They were encouraged to be bold and creative, such as requiring students to perform for a music exercise or conduct an experiment in science. They were told to not limit themselves to the traditional pencil-and-paper exercises.

Regretfully, the opportunity to be creative and different resulted in failure. Some new approaches were developed, such as using tape recorders for presenting the stimulus and recording the response; using a national TV-type male voice for administering the group exercises; and having an "I Don't Know" alternative for almost all of the multiple-choice exercises. In the main, however, the first set of exercises received from the contractors was disappointing. It seems that the professional item writers couldn't extricate themselves from the form and content of the types of items found in conventional achievement tests.

*Initial Exercise Reviews.* The original plan for developing exercises called for two reviews, one by lay people and one by subject matter specialists, followed by a tryout of the exercises. The purpose of the lay review was 1) to identify exercises that might be construed as being biased or offensive and should be eliminated, and 2) to rate the exercises for social importance. The reviews by subject matter specialists were to ensure that each exercise 1) was valid and assessed the objective for which it was written, 2) accurately represented the discipline and had no identifiable flaws, and 3) was appropriate. Conferences of six to eight consultants worked with NAEP staff over a three-day period. Differences of opinion were resolved through discussion. The revised exercises were tried out again and reviewed at a later conference. There also were technical reviews by the NAEP staff to eliminate or minimize possible problems in administration, scoring, analysis, and reporting.

Approximately 10,000 items were developed by the contractors. The test items were reviewed from November 1966 to March 1969 under the direction of TAC. The review was conducted among three groups: NAEP staff, a panel from the ECS, and the OE, which was primarily concerned with invasion of privacy. A final step in the review process involved administering about one-third of the exercises in classrooms to ascertain their validity and reliability.

*Lay Review of Exercises for Offensiveness.* At the same time that the subject matter specialists' review was going on, a series of conferences was initiated to learn whether the exercises were an invasion of privacy or were offensive in any way. Lay persons who previously reviewed the objectives reviewed the exercises using the following criteria: 1) Would I want my child to be given this exercise? 2) Would anybody in my community be offended by having this type of item in a national assessment? The national assessment staff also reviewed some of the items, such as those in mathematics, to identify those items that might be deemed to be offensive.

The exercises were assembled in booklets and given to the reviewers for discussion at five lay conferences. Every exercise was reviewed by two to four panels of reviewers. Of the 1,215 exercises reviewed (6% of the exercises submitted by the contractors), 25% were judged to be offensive and recommended for elimination from the pool, 15% were considered being somewhat offensive and were revised, and 60% were judged to be acceptable as written (Finley and Berdie 1970, p. 41). As expected, some subjects — citizenship, social studies, and literature — were more sensitive than others, such as mathematics, science, and writing, which had very few offensive exercises. As a result of this review, some exercises were deleted and some were revised to correct the problem while ensuring that the item still measured the objective for which it was written.

For citizenship, especially, it became evident that to measure citizenship, some sensitive areas would have to be covered. As one panelist said, "If we remove everything about politics, sex, religion, race, minority groups, and the police, there isn't much meaningful material left in the area of Citizenship" (Merwin and Womer 1969, p. 319). There was no problem with exercises that dealt with knowledge or generally accepted behavior. However, for those items that dealt with actual practice, there was much uneasiness expressed. Because of disagreement about what actually constitutes good citizenship, much rewording and revision was necessary to obtain consensus.

*Mail Review of Exercises by Subject Matter Specialists.* Although professional subject matter specialists were involved in developing the exercises, ECAPE considered it desirable to obtain an independent review of each exercise by specialists who had *not* been involved in its construction. It was hoped that such a review would provide another view "in regard to the content validity and appropriate sampling of the behavior" (Finley and Berdie 1970, p. 47). Thus, as soon as exercises were judged to be nonoffensive by either staff or a lay conference, they were mailed to a subject matter specialist for further review. To locate these reviewers, the committee consulted 12 national organizations, such as the National Council on Social Studies, the National Science Teachers Association, and the American Vocational Teachers Association, to nominate reviewers from their organizations. Three to five reviewers, each a nationally recognized expert in the field who had experience in writing exercises, were selected for each subject. The reviewers were asked to consider a number of questions, such as:

> (1) Does this exercise sample the objective indicated? (2) Is the answer indicated the correct answer to this exercise? (3) Does it contain any flaws that would make it ambiguous . . . or a poor exercise? and (4) What proportion of __-year-olds in this country do you estimate would answer the exercise correctly?" (Finley and Berdie 1970, p. 48)

The percentage of negative comments received from the mail reviewers varied from 13% of items in music to 52% in reading. Overall, about 30% of the 15,000 items reviewed had some type of negative comment, but outright rejection of exercises was less than 1%. About 25% of the exercises required some reworking as a result of the comments, and they were returned to the contractor for revision (Finley and Berdie 1970, p. 49).

The reviewers' comments were helpful for revising existing exercises and writing new ones, eliminating those with obvious flaws, and pointing out the need for more easy exercises. Many of the exercises contractors said were "easy" (those which should be answered by 90% of the students) did not receive such a rating from the reviewers.

The mail review by subject matter specialists did not accomplish all that was anticipated. Regretfully, the reviewers' comments often were unclear to the exercise writers, which made it difficult for them to correct the exercise. It also became clear that there had to be more interaction between the exercise writers and reviewers; the reviewers obtained only the objectives for the exercises they were reviewing and therefore didn't have a complete picture. As one reviewer commented, "Apparently you sent me a portion of the total test . . . at least two objectives I didn't have — II-A and III-AA . . . If my comments on objectives don't make sense, its obviously because I'm not seeing the whole picture" (Finley and Berdie 1970, p. 51).

The results garnered from the mail review of exercises resulted in a decision to convene a number of item-review conferences during the summer of 1967. The participants were subject matter specialists and others working in, or closely related to, each area. The reviewers' tasks were twofold: 1) to evaluate each exercise in relation to the objective it was designed to measure, and 2) to suggest editorial and other changes which they felt would improve the item. In addition, the reviewers could see all the exercises and objectives written for a given age level, thereby getting a complete picture for that age. Also, there could be inter-action between the reviewers and exercise writers, and ECAPE staff members were present to ensure that criteria considered important to exercise development were followed.

*First Subject Matter Review Conferences.* The first set of sub-ject matter review conferences took place in the summer of 1967. The number of reviewers per conference ranged from three to 16. A different panel was assembled to review the exercises for each age group. Staff members were present, as well as one or more of the contractor's exercise writers, to answer questions about scor-ing, purpose of the exercise, etc.

There was some flexibility in the organization of the confer-ences. At some, smaller groups reviewed all the exercises of a set, while at others, the reviewers dealt with only a portion of the set and then convened to discuss the total set. Time permitting, the reviewers tried to edit those exercises that required just minor revision.

Many problems were identified at these conferences. The nature of the specific comments varied from conference to conference, age to age, and subject to subject. For some subjects, the exer-cises were considered "too text-bookish" (particularly those writ-ten to assess knowledge), required only rote memory, or were too simplistic. In other subjects, the language was pedantic, imprecise, or wrong. Most reviewers considered the vocabulary to be excessively difficult, particularly for nine-year-olds, and too middle-class. In many areas, reviewers found gaps in the coverage. At all the conferences it was obvious that more work was needed on the exercises to meet the reviewers' criticisms. The suggestions were sufficiently specific in five of the subject areas that they could be implemented within a few months. In the other five areas, the defects were so serious that a major overhaul of the items or approach was judged to be necessary, and many completely new exercises were required. At this point, ECAPE asked item writers *other than* the original ones for help to fill some of the gaps that the reviewers identified (Merwin and Womer 1969, p. 321).

In all subjects, the contractors were asked to revise exercises and to produce more exercises for certain objectives. These new or reworked exercises also would have to be reviewed, so plans were made for a second series of subject matter conferences.

*Second Subject Matter Review Conferences.* The second set of conferences was held in winter 1968. Based on some of the comments made at the first conferences, it was decided that this review should include people who were working with low-achieving students because they would be more familiar with the language and "should be able to offer suggestions for non-middle-class-oriented materials" (Finley and Berdie 1970, p. 71). In general, the conferences were organized by subject matter into four panels, one for each age. Each panel:

> had to include at least one person with experience in working with low socio-educational children, one person with a measurement background in the subject, and two or more who were subject experts at either the appropriate teaching level or at colleges of education with specialization in the specific subject area. (Finley and Berdie 1970, p. 71)

Each panel had a staff member acting as recorder, and contractors were available to consult with the panels. Again, the emphasis was on the validity of each exercise, the appropriateness of the content for the age, the overall coverage of each objective, the appropriateness of the difficulty estimate, and the comprehensibility of the vocabulary. Two weaknesses pointed out in many of the reviews, the clarity of the vocabulary and the directions, were stressed.

It should be obvious from the many review conferences that ECAPE's goals were not easily achieved. Being creative in developing imaginative exercises that measure important education objectives while still being worded so simply that the exercise is easily understood is not easy to accomplish.

Two additional matters considered at the second review conference pertained to "clustering" and "directionality." Some exercises were grouped together, "clustered," because they contained related information; and the reviewers were asked to consider which ones could be de-clustered and still be meaningful. The directionality issue was more difficult.

*Directionality.* One of the major considerations in developing exercises for NAEP, which the TAC considered an "absolute," was the need for directionality. This means that every cognitive exercise must have a correct answer; and for every noncognitive or attitude exercise, there must be a defensible positive direction for the attitude assessed. Without directionality, progress could not be measured between results obtained at different cycles. Thus, if directionality could not be met, the exercise would have to be reworded or deleted.

There was not too much difficulty in meeting the "directionality" requirement for the cognitive areas. However, this was not so for the noncognitive or attitudinal assessment. For example, assessments of citizenship would be almost impossible if there isn't always a clear "right or wrong" answer. It was not impossible to meet the directionality requirement for attitudinal exercises, but it was much more difficult to define and reach agreement on the desired direction of change.

As would be expected, different problems arose depending on the age level and subject matter. For example, the reviewers for science items felt that insufficient attention was paid to the understanding of scientific principles, while the mathematics reviewers felt that the language used was too formal. In the end, these reviews were extremely valuable because the quality of the selected exercises was excellent.

## NAEP: A Large Research Project

Not only was the national assessment a data-gathering endeavor, it was also a large-scale research project because there were so many questions that had to be answered. Although content validity is stressed in standardized achievement tests, item quality is often supported by predictive or construct validity. This was not so for the items to be used in the national assessment. The purpose of the national assessment exercises was to describe the knowledges, skills, and attitudes of American youth as a group. It was not to predict or identify "traits or clusters of anything" (Womer 1968*a*, p. 34).

In fact, TAC was so concerned with content validity that it emphasized that everything possible should be done to maximize an examinee's understanding of what he is being asked to do in each exercise. Accordingly, a number of feasibility studies were undertaken in the spring and summer of 1967 to test the general content validity of the exercises. Questions such as the following were investigated: "Are there any problems in administering difficult or complex items to low-ability examinees?" "Was having a great variety of item formats an asset or a hindrance?" "Was mixing different subject areas in the same booklet an asset or hindrance?" "Was it feasible to administer ECAPE exercises by personal interview in the respondent's home?" "Should classroom teachers be used to administer the exercises?" "Should the directions and even the exercises themselves be read aloud to the examinees, excluding the reading test?" Answers to such questions were necessary because different item formats would be used in the assessment, there would be exercises from different subject areas in each package, and there would be both in-school and out-of-school assessments. The answers to such questions would not be found in the measurement literature.

To answer the skeptics (of which there were many) and critics regarding their opposition to the many research studies conducted, Tyler gave the following persuasive rationale for undertaking these studies:

> The need for these try-outs was clear from the initial planning of the project. Tests currently in use concentrate their exercises on the performance of "average" students. Very few if any exercises in tests now on the market are directed towards the performance of slow learners or of the more advanced. We have no way of ascertaining from comparable tests the progress made in education by the lowest third and the highest third of school children. Hence, one of the specifications for the assessment exercises was that approximately one-third of them represent the educational performance of the lowest third of the age group, one-third represent the educational performance of the middle third and one-third of the exercises represent the educational performance of the top third. Since test constructors have not heretofore had to meet this specification it is very necessary to find out by try-outs whether the exercises do, in fact, represent this distribution.
>
> Another new feature of this project was that the plan called for assessing the educational performance of a representative sample of 9-year-olds, 13-year-olds, 17-year-olds both in and out of school and adults between the ages of 26 and 35. These ages were chosen as the approximate ages at which the majority are completing primary education, elementary education, and secondary education. Furthermore, age 17 is the oldest age at which a majority of youth is still in school. Age 26 is a time when the great majority of adults have completed all formal schooling including professional education.
>
> However, nearly half of the seventeen-year-olds were not in school and most adults are out of school. Hence, to assess representative samples at these two ages requires the persons to take the assessment exercises in the home or at other

non-school situations. Heretofore, civilian tests have not often been given in out-of-school situations. Therefore, it is essential to try out procedures for assessing educational performance in out-of-school situations to see how feasible this is and how similar are the results obtained when compared with assessments conducted in the school situation. (Tyler 1967, reported in Finley and Berdie 1970, pp. 53-54)

Contractors for the in-school studies were ETS and AIR; the out-of-school studies were conducted by NORC.

## Feasibility Studies

Because the method used to develop the NAEP exercises was a radical departure from that traditionally followed in developing standardized tests, it is not unreasonable to expect that such questions as the following would arise:

1. How should the exercises be "packaged," that is, should different subjects be interspersed in one package or should all exercises in a package be of a single subject area? Could students handle a great variety of different formats in one assessment period?
2. Since the exercise writers were encouraged to be creative, "think big," and use new and unique formats, which would be unfamiliar to students, would students be able to understand what they were expected to do?
3. Is the vocabulary at a level that can be understood by low-achieving students?
4. Could enough "easy" exercises (ones that could be correctly answered by 90% of a particular age group) be written?
5. Are there any problems that might arise in administering the exercises?
6. Are the exercises equally distributed for different levels of achievement, including exercises for the lowest third, middle third, and upper third of each age group?
7. Are there appropriate exercises for each of the four age groups (9, 13, 17, and young adults)?
8. Is it feasible to assess individuals in an out-of-school situation?

9. Are there any problems administering difficult or complex exercises to low-ability students?

To try to answer such questions, the Ninety-Percent Study and two feasibility studies — Children in School and Adult and Out-of-School Youths — were completed during spring and summer 1967. Their findings had a profound influence on exercise development.

*The Ninety-Percent Study.* Many of the items that were supposed to be so "easy" that nearly everybody of a particular age group could answer the item correctly were so difficult that they couldn't meet this criterion. In fact, the item writers' estimate of item difficulty was often considerably different from the estimate of the ECAPE staff. Accordingly, a study known as the Ninety-Percent Study was designed by ECAPE staff and conducted in April and May 1967.

The purpose of the study was to see whether the contractors were able to write enough "easy" exercises, that is, items that practically everyone of a particular age group could answer correctly. This was done for each of the 10 subject areas assessed. The study was conducted by the Southeastern Education Laboratory (SEL) in Atlanta and the Eastern Regional Institute for Education (ERIE) in Syracuse, New York. Although a "true" representative sample was not drawn, ECAPE staff felt that rough estimates of the difficulty of the items for a national group could be obtained.

Correct responses to the exercises that the item writers labeled as "easy" were given by as few as 4% and by as many as 100% of the group tested. Only a small number of the items in any subject area met the goal, and in one area the highest percentage of correct responses for any item was between 50% and 60%.

It was readily evident from this and other studies that exercise writers in general, and commercial item writers in particular, were unable to reliably judge the difficulty level of exercises intended to be easy. Because of this, the difficulty of the items — particularly the "easy" items — had been grossly underestimated, particularly at the nine-year-old level.

*Early Tryouts.* The first large-scale tryouts of national assessment exercises consisted of a series of studies in the spring and summer of 1967 to test the content validity of the exercises, to learn whether there were any general problems with the exercises as a group, and to determine whether the exercises were appropriate for the age levels for which they were designed.

Fairly large samples of unedited exercises were tried out in classrooms or with adults and out-of-school youths to see if any problems existed with "stimulus presentation and/or response procedures and/or scoring schemes of the exercises" (Merwin and Womer 1969, p. 320). The results of these feasibility studies were based primarily on comments from teachers, students, and interviewers. For the in-school sample, an important purpose of the study was to detect any problems related to vocabulary, clarity, understanding, and administration when difficult or complex exercises were administered to students of low ability. The assumption was that if low-ability students had no problems understanding the tasks, the same would hold for students of average or high ability. For convenience, samples were selected from grades 3, 7, and 11, rather than by age, and were chosen to include large numbers of students of low ability. The exercises administered were purposely chosen to include the most difficult ones available. Classroom teachers presented the packages of exercises in classrooms, with one or two contractor representatives as observers. A small number of students, judged to be least able, then were interviewed to learn whether they had problems with the exercises.

> The major problems with the exercises were directions that were too complex or . . . use of vocabulary that was so difficult that low achieving examinees had trouble understanding the task or the question. The post-test interviews were particularly productive in identifying specific words, phrases and directions that were incomprehensible to many students. (Finley and Berdie 1970, pp. 61-62)

The feasibility of using classroom teachers to administer the tests also was considered. Regretably, the two contractors disagreed. Both agreed that there were problems getting directions to the teachers, having them read the directions beforehand, following the directions explicitly, and familiarizing themselves in using such special equipment as tape recorders. They disagreed, however, on whether the problems could be overcome in the actual assessment.

Results of the various feasibility studies, based primarily upon interviewer, teacher, and student comments, were both positive and negative. Although the major conclusion was that the exercises as they existed in spring 1967 were basically usable, they still needed considerable revision. The major deficiencies with the exercises were that 1) the directions were too complex or involved, and 2) the vocabulary was so difficult that low-achieving students had difficulty understanding the task or question.

In applying the general principle of "maximizing student understanding," it was decided to:

1. Hold a series of conferences during the summer of 1967, in which subject matter specialists would review each exercise for content validity and for simplicity of wording.
2. Attempt to reduce the number of unique exercise formats by adopting a standard multiple-choice format, a standard short answer format and other standard formats.
3. Move ahead with the decision to include two or three subject areas in each package for the actual assessment.
4. Investigate methods of test administrations in which both the directions and the exercises would be read aloud to examinees.
5. Investigate individual administration of National Assessment exercises. (Finley and Berdie 1970, p. 64)

The study of adults and out-of-school youth was conducted using individual interviews to determine whether questions of a cognitive nature could be successfully asked in the home or other non-school situation. Much to everyone's surprise, it was found that it was no more difficult to get adults and 17-year-olds in the home to respond to achievement exercises than it was to respond to opinion items. In fact, many of the respondents enjoyed the tasks.

The major conclusion of this study was that "it is feasible to administer exercises by a personal interview . . . in a respondent's home. None of the exercises was impossible to administer and there was little reluctance to begin the task or carry it through" (Finley and Berdie 1970, p. 65).

Additional conclusions were:

1. Much editing is necessary in tone, clarity of instructions, and vocabulary.
2. Respondents are not troubled by varying content areas. Grouping exercises by item format was suggested.
3. Having respondents mark multiple-choice questions themselves was suggested.
4. Open-ended exercises should be asked orally. When answers are cursory, interviewers should probe for a more complete response.
5. Packages of an hour's length or more are feasible. (Finley and Berdie 1970, pp. 65-66).

*Formal Tryouts.* In the spring of 1968, formal tryouts were conduced of the citizenship, literature, science, social studies, and writing exercises by three contractors. These tryouts dealt with both the individually administered and group-administered exercises. The information obtained from the tryouts was used to identify special problems in the exercises that were not eliminated in the earlier reviews and tryouts.

In addition, information was obtained about the time required for each exercise. The tryouts also provided logistical information, that is, experience dealing with securing the cooperation of school systems and with the actual administration of the packages of exercises. These formal tryouts led to the revision of exercises to be used in the actual national assessment.

## Special Studies

As mentioned earlier, the national assessment project was a research study that had many questions that were unanswered in the professional literature. Hence a number of special studies had to be conducted. These studies were designed to answer specific questions about the exercises and how best to administer them.

*In-School Versus Out-of-School Administration.* This study, conducted by Gertrude Cox of RTI, investigated whether the physical setting of testing, in school or in the home, would have any effect on the results. This information was vital because the design for testing 17-year-olds differed depending on whether they were enrolled in school or had withdrawn. When used in the school, the group exercises were given individually to one sample and in groups to another sample. When used in the home, they were given only individually. The major conclusion was that there were no statistically significant differences between in-school and in-home results on either the individually administered or group-administered exercises.

*Regional Voice.* A study designed by the ECAPE staff but conducted by AIR, RTI, and the Southern Regional Laboratory investigated possible differences in results depending on whether the directions were read by a person with a national TV or a radio-quality voice or one whose voice reflected a definite regional accent. The first part of the study used a "national" male voice, a regional male voice, and a regional female voice. Examinees hearing either male voice did significantly better than those hearing the female voice. Between the two male voices, girls did significantly better when hearing the regional male voice, but boys did not.

In two replications of this study, using only the two male voices, there were no significant differences between the two taped voices for either boys or girls (Merwin and Womer 1969, pp. 328-29). It was decided to administer the group exercises using a TV-type male voice.

*Mathematics Study.* ECAPE's reviewers were very concerned about the formal wording of the mathematics exercises. Whereas mathematicians insist on precise and accurate wording, mathematics educators prefer to use less precise language because it is more easily understood. ECAPE staff designed and carried out a study to learn whether there was any difference in results for exercises worded formally and those worded with simpler language. In addition, the same exercises were presented in both multiple-choice and open-ended formats, and all multiple-choice items were administered with and without an "I Don't Know" response. It was found that:

1. The wording used in most exercises made little difference with respect to the difficulty of the exercise. Regardless of the wording, "easy" exercises were easy and "difficult" ones were difficult.
2. The "I Don't Know" option made a significant difference in item difficulty. Also, guessing appeared to be reduced when examinees were given an "I Don't Know" option (Merwin and Womer 1969, p. 329).
3. In about 40% of the comparisons, the open-ended exercises were more difficult than the multiple-choice versions.

The second finding was an important reason for adding the "I Don't Know" alternative to almost all the multiple-choice exercises proposed for the national assessment.

*Choices Study.* In this study, the staff investigated whether there are differences between examinee responses that are related to specific alternatives in a multiple-choice exercise. Three knowledge-type social studies exercises were used to compare results obtained from giving three versions of the same multiple-choice question along with the same question in an open-ended format. The four item types were: 1) contractors' original exercise, 2) ECAPE revision with alternatives designed to make the exercise more difficult, 3) ECAPE revision with other "logical" choices, and 4) open-ended version. The general results were:

1. Some exercises were so easy that there were no differences in the difficulty between the four versions.

2. For about two-thirds of the exercises, there were large differences in the difficulty between the four versions. In nearly all cases, the open-ended version was more difficult. Occasionally, the three multiple-choice versions showed large differences.
3. The "I Don't Know" response was often selected for the multiple-choice questions; but the examinees tended to omit an answer for the open-ended exercises, rather than write, "I Don't Know" (Merwin and Womer 1969, p. 330).

*Modes of Administration.* This study investigated various methods of administering the questions in order to maximize understanding and to minimize the students' problems with reading, formats, and item directions. The study was conducted by AIR with nine-year-olds who were poor readers. "Easy" exercises were purposely used, the assumption being that, if these students encountered problems with the "easy" exercises, they surely would have problems with the more difficult ones.

The major recommendations were:

1. At least for the nine-year-olds, all directions, exercises, and alternatives should be read aloud by paced audiotape, with the exception of the reading exercises.
2. Consideration should be given to having all open-ended exercises administered individually, with the interviewer recording responses, or to taping the examinee's verbal responses.
3. Some consideration had been given to using a "trailer or van" to administer the exercises. As a result of this investigation, this idea was put on hold.

## The Involvement of the Education Commission of the States, 1969-1974

Political considerations in the late 1960s figured prominently in selecting the ECS to manage the assessment, which needed a home with a national but not a federal basis in order to placate the critics screaming, "federal control."

Several organizations, such as the American Association of School Administrators and the Association for Supervision and Curriculum Development, were hostile to the project. Professional educators feared that NAEP would foster invidious comparisons of student achievement between states, districts, and even schools. The fact that funding shifted from private funds to federal funds raised many questions and fears about the *true* purpose of the project. Was this an attempt to establish national performance standards or a national curriculum? Was this the first step toward the eventual establishment of federal control over education?

After more than two years of debate, the governance and administration of the national assessment were transferred to ECS in July 1969, just as it became fully operational. It was, by far, the largest and most controversial project run by ECS. It was ECS' most expensive project, operating on a multimillion-dollar annual budget. NAEP constituted more than 50% of the ECS annual budget, and more than 40% of the ECS staff was employed by NAEP.

It is not surprising that CAPE selected ECS to manage the program. First, it had the blessing of the education establishment, particularly the AASA. Wendell Pierce, the ECS executive director, once was on the AASA Executive Committee. Second, ECS, though a state-oriented organization, was national in scope and was free from federal control. Third, both ECS and ECAPE had their beginning with funding from Carnegie. Fourth, when CAPE expanded its membership, three of the most prominent ECS Steering Committee members — Allen and McNair, who were ECS chairman and vice-chairman, respectively, and Senator Richard Webster of Missouri — were asked to serve on CAPE. Allen and Webster were not only ECS Steering Committee members, but they also represented state governments.

The first mention of assessment at an ECS Steering Committee meeting was in 1967, where Pierce mentioned he had received informal inquiries about the commission's interest in governing the assessment (Layton 1972, pp. 132-33). This was slightly less than two years before ECS actually assumed management and nine months after the letter AASA sent to its membership urging them to boycott the project. The ECS Steering Committee rejected the project in 1967, but in 1969 Pierce was authorized "to investigate . . . and report back to the Executive Committee" (Hazlett 1974, p. 233).

At the March 1969 meeting, a public hearing was held to consider again whether ECS would govern the assessment. At this meeting, Wayne Shaffer, the future president of the Association of State Boards of Education, said his organization had three concerns:

1. Who would set policy, CAPE or ECS?
2. Who would receive the grant, CAPE or ECS?
3. It was imperative that there be more representation from elementary and secondary education on the commission (Hazlett 1974, pp. 235-36).

Although the AASA and NEA were adamant in their opposition earlier, now they said they would assist in procuring federal funds. As Hazlett (1974, p. 162) wrote, "How quickly the taint of federal funds became neutralized with ECS as the grantee!"

After considerable debate, the steering committee authorized Pierce to "enter into active negotiations with CAPE, the U.S. Office of Education, and others . . . to arrange for contractual arrangements to transfer the governance, management, and administration of National Assessment to the Education Commission" (Layton 1972, p. 132). This action was not the end of the matter. In fact, at the 1969 ECS Annual Meeting, there still was opposition to ECS assuming management of the project.

The steering committee met in June 1969 to approve the three documents Pierce had negotiated. These documents clearly showed that ECS would be in complete control of the national assessment. CAPE was reduced to an advisory committee (Hazlett 1974, pp. 245-50). Only Wyoming State Superintendent Harry Roberts and Minnesota Governor Harold Levander (both of whom had voted the previous March against giving Pierce authority to negotiate) were against the project (Hazlett 1974, p. 244).

As a result of assuming management of NAEP, there was a change in the leadership and a restructuring of ECS. The key elements in the new structure were the creation of a Project Policy Board and designating as its chairman the ECS "chief executive officer for the project who would be responsible to the ECS Executive Director for effective conduct of the project." The policy board would have five other members: the chairmen of the general advisory committee, the technical advisory committee, and the operations advisory committee; the ECS vice-chairman; and the ECS executive director. The steering committee could add "representatives of . . . governmental, foundation, educational, or other organizations" to the membership of the Board (Hazlett 1974, p. 249).

The policy board would be "responsible for the overall administration and direction of the project, the establishment of general project policy, the making of major operational decisions, and the supervision of basic administrative practices" (Hazlett 1974, p. 249). Perhaps of greatest importance was that the policy board maintained the project's "quasi-independence" from the federal government. The board had full power to run NAEP and did so for the first four years of ECS management.

When the policy board was established, the old CAPE became an advisory committee to the policy board. The executive committee also authorized adding five more positions to the advisory board. Both the advisory committee and the policy board included members from both ECS and CAPE. Interestingly, the advisory committee urged the staff not to have these groups dominated by educators.

Both the developers of national assessment and the ECS Steering Committee felt that decisions at the policy level should involve the participation of lay citizens, legislators, and government officials. Accordingly, when ECS assumed responsibility for the project in 1969, the steering committee created an 11-member National Assessment Policy Committee consisting of the chairman of the policy board, three persons from state government, three school superintendents, a statistician, a business executive, a measurement and evaluation specialist, and a representative from higher education. Changes in both the number of members and their duties were made in 1973 and again in 1978.

At the 1969 ECS Annual Meeting general business session, the matter of whether ECS should have undertaken governance of the NAEP was once again questioned. It should be noted that those contesting the decision were not always in agreement about reasons for their opposition. Their reasons varied from the view that it was just an inappropriate activity for ECS to questioning the constitutionality of the action.

Once the ECS took over the NAEP, it was a topic of discussion at all subsequent meetings of the steering and executive committee meetings. These discussions centered on four topics: 1) funding problems, 2) assistance to states, 3) reporting policies and practices, and 4) management practices.

## Funding

Initially, all funds to support the national assessment came from the Carnegie Corporation and the Ford Foundation, together contributing $4,128,900 from 1963 to 1969. When the management of the project was taken over by ECS, all financial support came from the U.S. Office of Education. The uncertainty of funding and other budget problems had a large effect on the assessment.

In October 1969 the policy committee made three significant changes in the cycle for administering the assessments. While originally there was to be a three-year cycle for all 10 subjects, this was changed to a three-year cycle for reading, mathematics, and science and a six-year cycle for the other seven subjects. This change reduced the budget needed for FY 1970 from $4 million to $3.5 million. Commissioner Allen was told that funding below that figure would seriously harm the project and that anything less than $3 million would injure the design (Hazlett 1974, p. 255). The policy committee also delayed the second year of data gathering from February 1970 to September 1970 and moved the reading assessment from the third year to the second year

(Hazlett 1974, pp. 254-55). No doubt the uncertainty of funding was an important reason for these changes.

Funding concerns plagued ECS from the time it assumed governance until it lost the contract to ETS. Funding for NAEP could be compared to a roller coaster; at no time was there assurance of how much it would receive or when it would receive funding. The FY 1970 budget presents a good example of these problems. By the fifth month of that fiscal year, ECS still did not know how much funding the project would receive. One problem was the multiple layers of decision making in the U.S. Office of Education; the Department of Health, Education and Welfare; the Office of Management and Budget; appropriation subcommittees and committees in both houses of Congress; presidential signatures and vetoes; the release of funds once appropriated; and the threat of impoundment (Hazlett 1974, p. 256).

Even if piecing together funds from various sources would allow NAEP to run for the year, the uncertainty of funding concerned Utah Governor Calvin Rampton, who said in 1970:

> I am a little bit disturbed about the role which the Commission has been forced to play in this Assessment. . . . I . . . was very much in favor of taking it on, but only on the assurance . . . the financing of it would not be difficult. . . . Now we are cast in the role of a seeker of funds. We have to . . . entreat individuals to bring funds in to us . . . I think we should have some kind of understanding with the Office of Education that they are going to take care of this *or this is our last year.*" (Hazlett 1974, p. 263, emphasis added)

Pierce said he came to the same conclusion three weeks earlier and said that if assurance was not forthcoming, he would recommend that the project be discontinued.

## Assistance to States

At the November 1969 meeting of the steering committee, Hazlett reported that 16 states were interested in state assessments in order to learn how their students compared with the national results. Hazlett stated that there were three options: 1) do nothing because of lack of money, staff, and time; 2) offer information and assistance; or 3) have ECS contract to do state assessments. Oregon Governor Tom McCall suggested convening an informational meeting of state department representatives to discuss state assessments. Nearly half of the nation's state departments of education then were asked how ECS could help the states. The consensus was that ECS could deal with the exchange of information and coordination, but that NAEP should limit itself to its original purpose.

At the last session of the 1970 Annual Meeting, Hazlett proposed a revised policy on the relationship of ECS and NAEP to the states. The following recommendations were made:

1. The national assessment program should continue in its present design, and the staff resources should be restricted to the conduct of the program. However, there was a consensus that states could "piggyback" on the national assessment by paying for the administration of NAEP exercises to a valid state sample concurrently with the collection of NAEP data in that state.
2. ECS should provide a forum for the exchange of information and offer consultant services at cost.
3. ECS should provide chief state school officers with specimen sets of packaged items, instructions, and scoring cards and provide advice on their use (Hazlett 1974, pp. 267-68).

For the first time, the NAEP budget included "provisions to assist in the application of National Assessment methodology and materials, such as consultant services to states and school systems who request them, informational workshops and systematic dissemination and conference with professional and lay organizations" (Hazlett 1974, p. 273). There was considerable discussion as to the implications of this move and of the support for it provided by the U.S. Office of Education, which included an allocation of $6 million for FY 1972 and $7.25 million for FY 1973. Hazlett reported that, since the adoption of the new policy on working with states, there were six requests for specimen sets and that NAEP was making its materials available to the Education Research Information Center (ERIC). Even so, he felt that "more aggressive follow-up is needed to show the consequences and implications of the policy" (Hazlett 1974, p. 270).

In addition, in 1973 NAEP negotiated with the Right-to-Read Office about conducting a mini-assessment in reading for 17-year-olds during 1973-74. Although an "index" had been proposed by Cronbach earlier, this was "the first time an expectancy level was established for a group of exercises and a standard made against which results could be compared" (Hazlett 1974, p. 278).

## Reporting

Of prime concern to the policy committee was the reporting of data. Governor Levander felt that the reports were going to be so complex that a new research project would be needed to explain the findings.

The committee set a policy that required data to be presented in a manner that the average reader could understand. The committee also was adamant that conclusions and interpretations be avoided. However, the staff was bombarded constantly by the press about what the results meant; and they felt that they could not hold off until change data were available. In addition, the staff felt that the reports did not encourage others to draw inferences about the data. Thus they believed that some interpretations had to be included in the reports.

Because of the demand for information, the policy committee created the Department of Utilization-Applications to assist states in using the "NAEP model and materials for their own state assessments and generating efforts by professional organizations and others to draw inferences from the data" (Hazlett 1974, p. 284).

## Management Practices

When ECS assumed control of NAEP, it inherited all the NAEP subcontracts that had been awarded by CAPE. The ECS staff developed a bid policy to handle new contracts. Essentially all activities, with the exception of research-and-development tasks that could be done in-house, were to be awarded on the basis of competitive bidding.

One point of contention was who would approve the contracts. Hazlett proposed that the staff award contracts on all low bids and refer their recommendations to the executive committee. An amendment was offered that would have all contracts awarded by the executive committee, but one member said that this would reduce the executive committee to an administrative agency, which was not their role. The amendment was defeated, 10 to 9.

In August 1971 Commissioner Sidney Marland transferred the monitoring of NAEP from the National Center for Educational Research and Development to Assistant Commissioner of Education Dorothy Gilford and the National Center for Education Statistics (NCES). Although Gilford was personally interested in the national assessment, this was not a positive omen. "This transfer, subtle as it may have appeared, moved NAEP from a research branch to one designed to gather data" (Fitzharris 1993, p. 52). Also, for the first time, NAEP experienced extensive line-item budgeting as its funding was changed from grant support to a contract (see Chapter 5).

It became evident that NAEP had to be known and understood by federal government officials who had budget and policy roles. Thus, with the full approval of Marland and the encouragement of Gilford, NAEP sponsored a full day of orientation for the staff of the U.S. Office of Education; the Office of Management and Budget; the Department of Health, Education and Welfare; and the National Science Foundation.

In late fall 1972, the NAEP staff was asked to prepare a five-year plan outlining the program's goals, methods to achieve them, and the costs estimated for each year. The five-year plan specified the tasks called for in the basic NAEP design, as well as some internal research studies to increase the meaningfulness of the results. The annual basic costs were estimated to be about $7.5 million, only $500,000 above the President's budget for national assessment for 1973-74.

The euphoria came to a grinding halt in spring 1973 when NAEP was advised to use $6 million as a planning figure for the next five years, though the President recommended $7 million for FY 1974. A real uneasiness developed in fall 1973 when the Senate Appropriations Committee recommended $3 million. By December 1973, the budget was increased to $4.5 million; but this still amounted was a reduction of $1.5 million from the already reduced planning figure.

This reduction was devastating to NAEP. The assessment of two subjects per year had to be delayed, which resulted in a change in the original testing cycle. The second young adult writing assessment was postponed. Special studies aimed at operational improvements were cancelled (Fitzharris 1993, p. 79). There were constant "discussions about and decisions made on a variety of matters deemed necessary to adjust or refine the operations of the design as experience and the availability of funds suggested" (Hazlett 1974, p. 282).

Pierce and NAEP staff pleaded for more involvement from top-level members of the Office of Education. In July 1973 Gilford arranged for a full-day meeting of all deputy commissioners, the director of the National Institute of Education (NIE), and others to discuss the national assessment. It came as a shock to Gilford, Pierce, and the NAEP staff when the only top official in attendance was John Evans, assistant commissioner for planning and evaluation. Unknown to NAEP at the time was that those in attendance (none of whom were deputy commissioners) were charged by Marland to be a review committee to evaluate NAEP's future.

The national assessment was again broadsided when, at a meeting in Marland's office in September 1973, Marland announced that the assessment would be shifted to a contract arrangement and "had no priority among grants and contracts which OE administered and must fit into all the considerations of tight budgets and OE priorities" (Hazlett 1974, pp. 287-94).

In October 1973, John Evans was asked to explain the rationale for changing from a grant to a contract and why the Office of Education felt it should have more control than before. As might be expected, eight of the nine policy committee members who were present felt strongly about Gilford's response to Hazlett, which pointed out the reasons why the the Office of Education wanted to make some significant changes. In fact, "their position against the OE control beyond the annual approval function was unanimous . . . and some staff felt that the Policy Committee might recommend abandoning Assessment" (Hazlett 1974, p. 295).

Commissioner Marland's transfer of monitoring responsibility to Gilford and the NCES resulted in hard feelings within the ECS/NAEP staff. The period from fall 1971 to fall 1973 was one of increased questioning by the Office of Education about the value of the national assessment, "particularly with reference to how it could serve the interests of the Office of Education itself, and a period of requiring more precise management and budgeting" (Hazlett 1974, p. 285).

Although initially there was little objection to ECS administering NAEP, that changed in the mid- to late-1970s. Later, when the 1983-88 NAEP contract was up for renewal, other organizations entered the fray. An external evaluation of ECS suggested that the National Assessment of Educational Progress be reviewed to consider the possibility of its operating better under other management.

In February 1983, the National Institute of Education awarded the NAEP contract to ETS, having judged its proposal to be superior. ETS promised to make the "assessment data more useful to the states, to increase the role of the policy-making committee, and to provide a wider range of statistical analysis of the data collected" (Layton 1985, p. 275). Also, ETS was willing to subsidize some of the costs.

Some ECS staff members felt that this was not the whole story. They argued that for several years relations had not been good between NIE officials and those at ECS who directed the project. In addition, some had "different interpretations of an external evaluation of the NAEP conducted by a Washington consulting firm" (Layton 1985, p. 275). The co-investigator of the consulting firm of Wirtz and Lapointe subsequently became the director of NAEP at ETS. Other ECS staffers felt that they deserved much of the blame for the loss of NAEP. From the beginning of the ECS involvement with NAEP in 1969, some ECS officers and staff were ambivalent about ECS sponsorship, feeling that ECS was biting off more than it could chew and that other ECS programs were suffering.

# CHAPTER 2

# The Age of Innocence

*Frederic A. Mosher*

In 1963 Education Commissioner Francis Keppel decided that he ought to have some way to discover and report on how U.S. students were doing. He probably also had in mind that if he could show that U.S. students were not doing well in some respects, or that there were substantial inequalities in the performance of significant groups of students or regions of the country, it would strengthen the case for some form of federal assistance for the schools, an issue that was then being hotly debated. Keppel invited Ralph Tyler, then the director of the Center for Advanced Study in the Behavioral Sciences, to give him some ideas about what might be possible.

Sometime in mid-1963 Keppel had an informal discussion about his ideas with my new boss, John Gardner, then the president of the Carnegie Corporation of New York, a grant-making foundation concerned with education. At that time, I had been working for the corporation for less than a year and, because I worked in the areas of international affairs and development, I had no direct involvement with the corporation's role in the origins of NAEP beyond joining general discussions in staff meetings.

I became more involved in education issues in the later 1960s and handled Carnegie's grants for two evaluations of NAEP, the first by William Greenbaum and his colleagues at Harvard (Greenbaum, Garet, and Solomon 1977) and the second by Wirtz and Lapointe (1982). The Greenbaum book includes a thorough description and analysis of the early planning of, and the early expectations for, the assessment. It also contains a thoughtful consideration of the implications of trying to develop a "social-indicator" measure for education and discusses the conflicts in the expectations of the assessment's founders. Much of the following discussion has its roots in Bill Greenbaum's study and in conversations with him. In addition, I used materials in the archive of Carnegie Corporation papers held in the collection of Columbia University's Rare Book and Manuscript Library. Those papers were winnowed to some extent before being turned over to Columbia, so some relevant material, including the original Tyler planning memo or memos, is missing. Where I can fill in from memory or from extrapolation from knowledge of how things worked at the corporation, I have done so, I hope with appropriate cautions.

On 5 September 1963 Keppel wrote to Gardner, saying that he would like to "follow through on the discussions we had about Admiral Hyman Rickover, Ralph Tyler, and the development of some kind of national examining and reporting system." He wanted to know whether Carnegie would be willing to take responsibility for exploring the question and providing some of the needed support. The reference to Rickover referred to the admiral's advocacy of a national test that could be used to select talented students who could benefit from enhanced school programs, particularly in science and mathematics. Neither Keppel nor Gardner seemed to favor Rickover's idea.

On September 11, Gardner sent a memo to Alan Pifer, Carnegie's vice-president, sharing Keppel's letter and asking what he thought about the idea of the corporation supporting two informal one-day conferences to consider Keppel's idea. The first conference would be on the "technical problems of getting the job done." The second conference would focus on "the organizational and practical questions of how to mount such a project," including whether it should have government or private funding or both, how to build support and avoid opposition, and so on.

Gardner's note indicated his concern that this idea should "not be discussed outside the office at the present time" and that it would be best if it were done "without any official responsibility whatever." (I think he meant without federal government responsibility, but I am not sure.) He wrote that he was "frank to say, I hope we can see our way clear to do it."

Pifer responded on September 13, saying that he and Lloyd Morrisett, at that time a senior Carnegie program officer and special assistant to Carnegie's president, agreed that it was an idea worth pursuing and that Carnegie "should retain a large measure of control in the initial stages, and to do so may require some delicacy." He suggested that Morrisett should be the officer in charge of pursuing the matter, though he would need logistical help. Pifer also wrote that the conferences could be held at the Carnegie Corporation, or they might consider asking Tyler to host them at the Center for Advanced Study in the Behavioral Sciences at Stanford University.

Pifer said that the Tyler memo (which is no longer in the Carnegie Corporation archives) "provides a useful start but doesn't take us very far." He reported that Morrisett thought that "it doesn't cover all the potential purposes which might be served by national examinations, and, LM believes, is questionable in its comments on the shortcomings of presently available standardized tests." Nevertheless, he said: "We believe a move should be made on the project quickly, to forestall some other initiatives, particularly a governmental one. This would mean action at the October ExCom" (the periodic meeting of the Executive Committee of Carnegie's board). Pifer went on to discuss possible parallels — the "11 Plus" and O and A Level exams in the United Kingdom and the New York State Regents exams — and he called attention to Harvard University President James Conant's work that was being supported by the Carnegie Corporation. Conant (1964) made the point that Congress was limited in its authority over public education and in its ability to sanction performance with reference to standards, in contrast to what the states could do given their constitutional responsibilities. There was a question,

Pifer said, whether "even making the appropriation of Federal funds for education purposes conditional would be constitutional."

Gardner responded on September 19, accepting all of Pifer's recommendations. He agreed that the Carnegie Corporation should retain initial control; and concerning the need for "delicacy," he wrote, "I'm sure that we can work it out quite candidly with Frank." He reported that Keppel would like him to chair the first conference and that New York would be more convenient than Stanford. Concerning the questionable constitutionality of using federal funds, Gardner wrote that they "would present the test not as a way of 'forcing' standards, not as a way of measuring individuals, but as a device to enable them to report on the state of American education." If the states and localities chose to use them as a basis for standard setting "that would be their privilege." He ended, "Will you schedule an early staff discussion on this? Then perhaps we should have a more definitive talk with FK."

Morrisett immediately accepted responsibility for handling Carnegie's involvement in the project. In his September 23 memo he said, "Carnegie Corporation's interest in this project is that it offers a lever with which to get at the heart of the problem of national standards in education." The initial discretionary grant for support of the meetings must have been approved in subsequent staff discussion, but the archives show no record of it until an indication in January 1964 of an allocation of $12,500 from the corporation's discretionary grant fund "for exploration of the feasibility of a national assessment of educational achievement." (This was after the first conference had already taken place; things were more relaxed in those days.) Following approval, Morrisett quickly organized the meetings.

Morrisett reported an October 3 conversation with Keppel and David Seeley, then a Keppel aide, indicating that Keppel "also believes that budgetary requests would be more soundly based if viewed from a measurable perspective." Keppel thought that the tests "in some measure should represent what a well educated person should know in the given areas. This view is in distinction to having them represent an expert's idea of what should be known." Keppel, Morrisett wrote, argued for including in the conferences a few people with broad concern for education; "Conant is a prototype." In addition, Keppel believed that "putting it on a sampling basis would remove, or at least help reduce, objections to the project." Keppel thought that the invitation should say that the conferences were sponsored by Carnegie Corporation "with the cooperation of the Office of Education," and that is the way the invitations went out.

In an October 14 memo to Gardner and Pifer, Morrisett proposed that the first conference should be to determine the "means of ascertaining the educational level attained through American public education." The focus would be on assessing feasibility — whether currently available tests could be used or, if they could not, what should be the specifications for constructing new tests. Other topics would be the ways of reporting test results, the categories that should be used, the sample sizes required, and so on.

In an October meeting with Orville (Bert) Brim, president of the Russell Sage Foundation, and his colleagues David Glass and David Goslin, Brim suggested that general policy questions ought not to be ignored, echoing a point made in the Carnegie staff discussion, probably by Peter Caws, then a program officer and now a philosophy professor at George Washington University. The proposed invitation seemed to assume that a national assessment would be a good thing, but that assumption would be worth some consideration in the conference. Greenbaum and his colleagues (1977, p. 8) report this comment, which probably was found in the "pink sheets" of staff comments attached to a circulating proposal docket. Unfortunately, those pink sheets were destroyed by the corporation's former secretary, Florence Anderson. I remember the issue being raised, and I think it was Caws who made the point, though in a recent exchange he indicated that he could not remember that, nor claim otherwise.

It was decided to add a dinner discussion the evening before the main meeting to consider the value of gathering such information. The November 20 invitation indicated that the purpose of the conference was "to explore whether developments in testing and in methods of sampling now enable a fair assessment of the level of national educational attainment." It went on to say, "Some of the issues which we hope to cover are: the desirability of periodic national assessments of educational attainment; possible objectives of an assessment and methods of developing an appropriate set of objectives; presently available tests and their capacity to measure these objectives; specifications for the construction of new tests; ways of reporting the results of an assessment — How can these results be made meaningful? To whom should the report be made? Who will have access to the results? In what categories will the breakdown be given? — and sampling problems — size and methods."

In the time before the convening of the first meeting, Alan Pifer pursued his set of questions about the A and O Level exams and the 11 Plus tests with acquaintances in the United Kingdom. He asked H. Lionel Elvin, Director of the Institute of Education, University of London, whether he could get samples of any of them, and whether the 11 Plus results had ever been used to assess the relative achievement of different schools, cities, counties, or other units, or were they "as I understand, used mainly as selection devices?" His inquiry seems to have been referred to W.D. Wall of the U.K. Foundation for Education Research, who said that copies of the A and O Level papers were available and would be sent, but that one could not get copies of the 11 Plus unless, perhaps, one promised to keep them "under lock and key." Wall said that data on the results were available on schools. Wall also referred Pifer to the International Assessment of Educational Achievement, which included comparative studies of national achievement levels in selected subjects among 13-year-olds in 12 countries. Wall mentioned Benjamin Bloom, professor at the University of Chicago, and Robert Thorndike, professor at Teachers College Columbia University, as key participants in the U.S. participation in these studies. In a subsequent memo, Pifer asked Morrisett if he knew about the IEA.

The files don't contain a response. However, they do contain a copy of a memo to James Allen, the New York State Commissioner of Education, written by his colleague, Lorne Wollatt, commenting on the invitation to the conference and suggesting some parallels in Project Talent and in the efforts New York had undertaken in its "Quality Measurement Project," which had reviewed the commercially available standardized tests as a possible way to get data for New York's schools on some common scale. That project also had looked into using other measures of schools' quality, such as their "holding power" (that is, ability to minimize dropouts), and other measures, such as students' socioeconomic backgrounds and the status of the schools' communities. Wollatt wrote that reporting on national achievement levels might contribute to the improvement of quality, but it also might "supply ammunition for the arguments of the extreme proponents and opponents of public education (Could and should private education be included?)." Woolott suggested that trying to get national results for local schools or districts would likely prove to be too hard and that they probably would have to be satisfied with regional results, or perhaps state-by-state results and comparisons, which the states might be comfortable to have reported publicly if they first were given a "heads-up." Such reports might confirm that some states are well behind others, "which now can only be assumed based on such input differences as the length of the school day or year, levels of teacher training, and per-pupil expenditures."

The files also contain a lengthy paper by William D. Firman of the Bureau of Education Finance Research of the State University of New York. The paper was written for the Committee on Education Finance of the National Education Association and concerns the relationship of cost to quality in education, detailing some of the considerations involved and the difficulties of establishing such relationships.

These documents, Pifer's inquiries, and a later background paper by Robert Thorndike are the only indication that the Carnegie Corporation paid much attention to the technical and policy issues involved.

Thorndike's paper pointed out that, if the purpose of an assessment was to characterize the performance of groups, then

"normative" scores would not be meaningful. It is hard to interpret the meaning of a group percentile or its equivalent, and it is
more relevant to report in terms of a task, or the kinds of tasks,
that members of a group can accomplish. He also suggested that
it would be important to consider whether and what background
information should be collected on students and schools in order
to provide a basis for interpreting the achievement results. It is not
clear whether this paper was shared with the second conference.

The first conference was held at the Carnegie Corporation on
18 and 19 December 1963. The participants included Keppel,
Gardner, who chaired the meeting, Pifer, Morrisett, Frank Bowles
of the Ford Foundation, Brim and Goslin from the Russell Sage
Foundation, Ralph Tyler, Lee Cronbach from Stanford, John
Fischer from Teachers College, John Tukey from Princeton, John
Flanagan from the American Institutes for Research, Henry Dyer
from the Educational Testing Service, John Holland from the
National Merit Scholarship Corporation, Peter Rossi from the
National Opinion Research Center, Ralph Flynt and David Seeley
from the Office of Education, and William Firman, who then was
at the New York State Department of Education and sat in for Jim
Allen.

Early in the discussion, Tyler reported on the preliminary work
that he and Tukey had done at Keppel's request, and he laid out a
proposed structure for the assessment. As Greenbaum, Garet, and
Solomon  summarize it, he suggested that:

> (1) the assessment would test general levels of knowl-
> edge, "what people have learned, not necessarily all within
> the school system," (2) the tests would not be aimed at dis-
> criminating among individuals, unlike most educational tests,
> (3) there would be an attempt to assess more accurately the
> levels of learning of the least educated, average, and most
> educated groups in the society, (4) some sort of matrix sam-
> pling system would test individuals only on a small number
> of questions but results could be aggregated to reflect the
> knowledge of particular subgroups in the population,
> (5) adults might be included in the sample, (6) stages, such

as the end of elementary school, the end of intermediate school, and the end of high school, should be used in connection with specific testing ages rather than at specific grade levels, and (7) the effects of the tests themselves would have to be carefully considered because they might become standards for educational curricula and might also reflect on the status of particular communities. (1977, p. 10)

The subsequent discussion concentrated on what ought to be measured: Should the focus be on general learning or knowledge, regardless of whether it was learned in school, as Tyler's opening position suggested? Should it try to distinguish between what the schools accomplish and what is learned elsewhere, for example, from families or television? Should the objectives include values and social skills, as well as academic subjects? And if the focus is on school subjects, should the assessment focus on what the schools were trying to do at that time or on what they ought to be trying to do? Greenbaum, Garet, and Solomon (1977) report that these issues continued to play a central role through these planning meetings and the extensive consensus-seeking process that characterized the development of NAEP in the following years. In the end, the process led to a focus on what the Greenbaum report calls the "cardinal rule," attributed to Tyler, that is, that the assessment should focus on what the schools are trying to do in academic areas. The category of "citizenship" was used for the "intangibles," such as social values and behavior; but when certain reform ideas had strong constituencies, that rule was often loosely applied to include those reforms.

There seems to have been agreement that a national survey of achievement would produce information that would be useful to policy makers and the public, but there was remarkably little attention to exactly how the information could be used or interpreted, beyond the idea that areas of concern could be identified. For example, the results might show that particular demographic groups or areas of the country were doing poorly or that particular subjects or skills were showing weakness. Parallels were drawn with the uses of unemployment or epidemiological statistics.

There was an impression that the data might also inform the search for solutions to weaknesses. There also was remarkably little attention to the implications of Tyler's emphasis on trying to measure performance directly in terms of what students knew, rather than in terms of their performance relative to each other. That was probably because the psychometric assumptions of norm-referenced testing were so deeply ingrained in this group that they were held almost unconsciously, and thus the group could not recognize the radical implications of Tyler's proposal. Tyler himself, given his experience with the "Eight Year Study" (Smith, Tyler, and the Evaluation Staff 1942), had a much clearer basis for his distaste for conventional tests; but even he did not seem to understand or anticipate the implications of a thoroughly different approach. At its conclusion, the first conference reached a clear consensus in favor of a national assessment of achievement and of the general approach suggested by Tyler.

In a 30 December 1963 memo following the first meeting, Morrisett laid out for Pifer and Gardner the steps he thought would have to be taken if a national assessment were to be developed in time to make its first report in the 1966-67 centennial year of the U.S. Office of Education. These steps included developing support in the education community, finding or developing an organization to spearhead the activity, and gaining financial support. He suggested the purpose of the second conference, to take place in January, should be "primarily to begin developing widespread support for the national testing project." Keppel had said that the Office of Education was not in a good position to develop or fund the necessary organization. "He would like CC [Carnegie Corporation] to take the responsibility at first, i.e., the responsibility of choosing the right organization and person to spearhead the project." He said he had begun to think about what organization might be asked to manage the work, and said one possibility was the Russell Sage Foundation, with someone like Harold Howe (then superintendent of schools in Scarsdale) to run it. Morrisett said that Keppel indicated that the Office of Education probably could contribute only about $50,000 at that point, enough to fund some summer work, but that there might be up to $2 million in future budgets. Morrisett said that might mean that they would not need large amounts of private money, but "this may be a case where broad and diversified support would be desirable." He asked to what extent the Ford Foundation or similar organizations might be interested. He had asked Robert Thorndike to do a substantive prospectus for the project.

The second conference was held on 27 and 28 January 1964. A number of key education leaders were added to the original group, and a number of the testing experts and researchers who were at the first conference (Brim, Cronbach, Dyer, Firman, Flanagan, Holland, Rossi, and Tukey) were not invited. The new participants were: James Allen from New York; Leon Minear, Superintendent of Public Instruction in Oregon; William Carr, executive, and Robert Wyatt, president, of the National Education Association; Logan Wilson, president of the American Council on Education; Edward Mead of the Ford Foundation; William Golden, a businessman and member of various boards who was knowledgeable about science policy; John Corson, of Princeton and McKinsey and Co. (who was asked by the corporation to develop an implementation plan for the project); George Stoddard of New York University; and Robert Thorndike of Teachers College Columbia University.

Morrisett made an opening presentation to the gathering, summarizing the idea, its origins, and the results of the first conference. His outline, in the archives, contained these items:

1.  Concern with quality
    A. Because of effects on individual - occupation, personal satisfaction
    B. and Nationally - status as a nation
2.  How to know quality and develop standards of judgment
    A. Reporting Function - comparative information
    B. Research Function - leading to improvements
        - education related to employment, costs, background factors
3.  Interest of the Office of Education - information for public policy

4. Interest of CC - helping to raise national standards and aspirations. Create model to forestall less effective efforts.
5. What kind of survey?
   A. objective, unbiased
   B. aimed at group achievement, not individual sampling
   C. Broad enough to fairly reflect aims of education
      Deal with modern as well as traditional curriculum
   D. Optimally, several age levels, including adults (perhaps start on a smaller scale)
6. First Conference - purpose and results
   A. Feasible in terms of testing and sampling
   B. Need to develop techniques
   C. Worth further exploration, hence present meeting focusing on issues of public and educational policy
7. Potential uses of survey
   A. Local planning, stimulate improvement
   B. National policy

The conference itself seems to have gone much the same way as the first, including spending a lot of its time on the question of what should be measured and in the end giving assent to the general plan. There was some advice offered about potential sources of resistance and ways to overcome them, but most of the operative thinking about those issues seems to have been left to John Corson.

Morrisett had asked David Goslin to take notes on the two meetings and to summarize the results. At the time, Goslin headed a Carnegie-supported study of achievement testing at the Russell Sage Foundation and seems to have been a candidate to manage the development of the national assessment project if the Russell Sage Foundation took responsibility for it, which they declined to do the following June.

Based heavily on Goslin's summary (see Appendix J), Greenbaum and his colleagues derived a list of five types of objectives for the assessment. The earliest objectives for the national assessment were:

A. Major Short-Term Objectives
   1. To obtain *meaningful* national data on the strengths and weaknesses of American education (by locating

deficiencies and inequalities in particular subject areas and particular subgroups of the population).

2. To provide this [sic] data to Congress, the lay public, and educational decision makers so that they could make more informed decisions on new programs, bond issues, new curricula, steps to reduce inequalities, and so on.

3. To provide this data to researchers working on various teaching and learning problems, either to answer research questions or to identify specific problems which would generate research hypotheses.

B. Major Long-Term Objectives

4. To continue collecting the national data at regular intervals so that comparisons could be made over time concerning national levels of achievement, performance in various subject areas, and performance in various subgroups, vis-à-vis themselves and other subgroups. This would provide a census of educational progress in America.

5. To forestall the development of "less effective or misdirected" attempts at assessment. Some backers of the Assessment disapproved of plans for a California assessment and the national proposals of Admiral Hyman Rickover, both of which were less interested in reducing inequality than in separating elites from the average population so "excellence" could be pursued efficiently.

6. To make international comparisons possible once sampling and testing problems could be resolved.

C. Subordinate Objectives

7. To promote concern about more meaningfully defining the nation's educational objectives.

8. To provide comparative data to stimulate competition among the states and local communities (without encouraging invidious comparisons).

D. Major Low-Profile Objectives

9. To lead a movement away from relying solely on norm-referenced testing, which discriminates among

individuals, and toward some form of objective- or criterion-referenced tests that assess how much an individual or group actually knows about a particular area of knowledge.

10. To lead a movement away from current testing which relies largely on measuring knowledge in ways that overemphasize memorization and that underestimate actual skills, understandings, and attitudes.

11. To encourage new modes of testing that are better fitted to the kinds of information being gathered and the particular characteristics of the respondents.

E. Operational Objectives

12. To create an independent committee to manage the development of the Assessment.

13. To develop widespread acceptance among the educational establishment so that the Assessment could gain access to school systems.

14. To develop widespread political support so that the federal government would take over funding of the Assessment, while at the same time assuring [sic] that representatives of state and local governments would not be too uneasy about the project being federally funded.

15. To develop lists of educational objectives that would "fairly reflect the aims of American education" and serve as guides for the exercise writers. (Greenbaum, Garet, and Solomon 1977)

Following the January meeting, Morrisett moved ahead on the operational objectives.

Corson's report on possible alternative approaches to developing the assessment was completed in early April 1964. He pointed out that the process so far had not involved the education community very widely and that opposition, particularly from representatives of school administrators and governing boards, was quite likely. There would have to be a campaign to convince opinion leaders that this was a good, and feasible, idea. There also were a great many issues to be worked out both about what objectives should be measured and how the technical problems of sampling, assessment, and reporting could be solved. Corson anticipated that the Office of Education could be expected to fund the work eventually but that they would probably choose to contract with a private organization to carry it out and that the design work, the public relations issues, and the choice of the organization or organizations to do the work would probably have to be undertaken by an interim working group supported privately, presumably by Carnegie and perhaps other foundations. He thought it would be at least a year, if the groundwork were completed by then, before the Office of Education could become substantially engaged (Greenbaum, Garet, and Solomon 1977, pp. 15-16).

Following Corson's advice, Morrisett wrote a 28 April 1964 memo to Gardner and Pifer outlining a plan for an interim committee. Morrisett suggested that the developments be reported to Carnegie's full board at their May meeting for general discussion and then that the executive committee be asked to grant funding for planning and development at their June meeting, when more details would be available. Gardner responded on April 29 with general approval but suggested that Morrisett consider "separating out the technical side and starting now — and run them in parallel."

Morrisett drafted a background memo for the board's discussion of granting support for "organizational expenses for a national educational assessment." The draft memo said, in part:

> Local control of education has very well known merits. However, at the same time it leads to schools of varied excellence and makes it extremely difficult to discover the standard of quality being met in any given school. This same situation also leads to failures of educational planning at the national level, since it is almost impossible to provide either the Office of Education or Congress with information on educational quality which would lead to sound decisions.

The memo that actually went to the board did so under the agenda heading, "For discussion of a national educational assessment" (these agendas were often substantially edited by Florence Anderson). It argued that the Office of Education gathers vast amounts of information every year; but with minor exceptions, this information has nothing to do with educational achievement. It deals with enrollment but tells nothing about the educational performance of those enrolled. "Such an assessment will provide national agencies with information for their own planning, and at the same time would allow individual states, school districts, or schools to rate their own accomplishments."

The memo argued that 1) the experts said the project was feasible and 2) it was worth a try. Both of these arguments continued the tendency seen in the two conferences to assert the proposition that information about achievement could usefully inform policy decisions. And, as in those conferences, the memo did not specify just what kind of decision actually could be warranted by the sorts of information that a sample-survey type of assessment would provide. In addition, the samples were hardly likely to provide information about districts or schools, or even, as it turned out until recently, about states. However, that was not a detail that troubled the corporation's board.

The board discussion seems to have gone well. In June, the executive committee approved a grant of $100,000 to support the work of an initial planning committee and the initial technical work through the summer and into the fall. Morrisett pursued the possibility that the Russell Sage Foundation might take responsibility for both aspects, but they opted out in early June. He tried one or two individuals who were known to the Carnegie Corporation staff; and then, probably on the advice of other social scientists, he turned to a young professor at the University of Michigan's Survey Research Center, Stephen Withey, as a candidate to staff an interim committee. Withey had the background to oversee the beginning of the technical work. After a meeting at Michigan at the end of June, Withey agreed.

On July 6, Morrisett asked Ralph Tyler if he would serve as chair of the interim committee. Tyler accepted. Working with Tyler, Morrisett identified the other members of the interim committee. They were: Melvin W. Barnes, superintendent of schools in Portland, Oregon; John Corson; Paul F. Johnston, superintendent of public instruction in Iowa; Devereaux C. Josephs, New York Life Insurance (and a Carnegie board member and former president of the corporation); Roy E. Larsen, Time Inc.; Katherine E. McBride, president of Bryn Mawr; the Reverend Paul C. Reinert, president, St. Louis University; Mabel Smythe, New Lincoln School, New York City; and Morrisett himself, representing Carnegie.

The committee's first meeting was in August 1964, and they chose to call themselves the Exploratory Committee on Assessing the Progress of Education (ECAPE). Their assignment was to "Develop a greater consensus among influential educational groups that a periodic national assessment of education is feasible and desirable; develop the instruments for assessing the status of education; and plan how the assessment could be administered and monitored in the public interest" (Greenbaum, Garet, and Solomon 1977, pp. 16-17). They were supposed to take five months.

ECAPE continued for four years, and in 1968 it became the Committee on Assessing the Progress of Education (CAPE). ECAPE received about $2 million in grants from Carnegie and Ford (initially from its Fund for the Advancement of Education). CAPE received another $3 million from the two foundations and from the federal government. Carnegie's total contribution to the development of the assessment project was $2,432,900.

In June 1969, CAPE found its first "permanent" organizational home at the Education Commission of the States (ECS) in Denver and became NAEP, the National Assessment of Educational Progress. ECS was itself just four years old, having grown from a suggestion in James Conant's Carnegie-supported book, *Shaping Educational Policy* (1964). Conant argued that several states should form an organization that could represent their interests and take responsibility for developing a consensus about a "national" education policy, as opposed to a federal one developed in Washington.

ECS seemed to be a good answer to the question of how to make NAEP acceptable to the states. However, as Greenbaum points out, the negotiations with the states and the extensive consultations with the wider education establishment meant that the design of NAEP had to be made as unobjectionable as possible. In particular, it meant that results would be reported by regions and demographic groups, rather than by identifiable states or districts. These were not concessions that particularly offended Ralph Tyler's sense of what the design could or should be, but they have been a source of continuing disappointment to those who thought that the assessment could somehow directly affect policy.

Greenbaum, Garet, and Solomon (1977) claimed that there was always a crucial contradiction between what Tyler and Tukey thought were the possible uses of the assessment and the expectations of many others, including the staff at the Carnegie Corporation. In their discussions, the Carnegie staff implied that the assessment would provide information that would both inform policy and answer research questions. These expectations assumed that the assessment data could be used to establish what is working or failing or to test hypotheses about what might work.

The truth is that the kind of sampling involved in NAEP does not allow researchers to establish any causal or evaluative relationships. At best, the data might provide hints about associations that would suggest hypotheses that would have to be tested with more robust designs. In addition, the validity of the measures has been challenged; but even if the researcher accepts them, there is a very limited number of valid conclusions that can be drawn. The researcher can, indeed, talk about where (within the terms of the samples) and in what groups there is success or failure, and the trend data will allow conclusions about whether these things are changing over time. But the data cannot be used to explain why anything happens.

Tyler knew this, and he was careful never to claim otherwise. But he did not go out of his way to force others to recognize this limitation, perhaps because it would have undercut the support for NAEP. But because of these limitations, NAEP has always proved disappointing to those who hoped for answers and puzzling to those who don't understand the intrinsic problem.

There have been many suggestions for improving NAEP. For example, the recent National Research Council report, *Grading the Nation's Report Card* (Pellegrino, Jones, and Mitchell 1999), proposed that NAEP's results should be placed in the context of a much larger set of indicators so that a more comprehensive, and conclusive, picture of American students' achievement can be constructed.

However, perhaps it would be best to focus on and improve what NAEP has been trying to do all along, and that is to measure achievement with reference to our best understanding of the knowledge and skills that the schools are trying to teach and to our standards for what we would consider satisfactory, or better, in the core knowledge and skills. If NAEP could do that job better than it does, then it might provide the lever on national standards that Morrisett originally hoped for.

When my colleagues and I discussed NAEP in the early days, we were innocents. We had yet to see the changes brought about by the Elementary and Secondary Education Act and the Coleman report (1966) and the many shocks that followed. True, it does not compare to Adam's fall; but for many of us, it was a pretty big deal.

Seen from today, it really is remarkable that, when this story began, how small and tidy the world looked to Keppel and Gardner and the rest of us. But time and experience have taught us a different lesson. It is a credit to Tyler and Morrisett that they were able to stay the course, learn the lessons, and bring NAEP to reality. That, too, was a pretty big deal.

# CHAPTER 3

# Interviews

*An Interview with John Gardner*

This interview with John Gardner was held 24 April 2001 in his office at Stanford University, conducted by Ingram Olkin and Marshall Smith.

**Olkin:** John, as you know, we are trying to obtain perspectives from various key persons who were involved with NAEP in its early days. You were unequivocally one of the leading architects of NAEP. So we would like to get your recollections and views.

**Gardner:** Do you want me to ramble?

**Olkin:** By all means, let's start that way, and then go on to more specific topics.

**Gardner:** Frank Keppel and I and Ralph Tyler were in very close communication, just trading ideas, keeping one another up to date; but it was Frank who first called me about this idea of a national assessment. We talked about it at some length, and very early concluded that we needed to tap the best thinking around — getting Ralph in, getting John Tukey in, getting the usual suspects. I think that that preceded the memorandum from Ralph. But Ralph was surely thinking about this from the beginning because he was, like myself, a very close talking partner with Keppel.

The Carnegie Corporation of New York, not the Carnegie Foundation, was the one that was involved from the beginning. This was a time when the Carnegie Foundation had no money.

We convened the conference that included all the individuals we thought would be interested in this idea. I think that Roger Heyns [chancellor, University of California at Berkeley] attended one of the conferences; I would have thought that Henry Chauncey [president of ETS] would be in that group, but maybe not. John Corson worked at McKinsey, and he was a consultant kind of person we would call upon to prepare a memo. I do not think of him as one of the key architects of the plan.

We allocated $100,000, that is, the Carnegie Corporation of New York. I guess I was president of both the corporation and foundation at the time. Ralph then took the ball and did a very good job, as you would expect.

**Smith:** Were there other people from Carnegie involved in this? Fritz Mosher? Lloyd Morrisett?

**Gardner:** Not Fritz; possibly Lloyd Morrisett because his field was education, as you know, and it was possible that I handed it over to Lloyd; but not Fritz — he was not trained in this.

**Smith:** As you talked to Frank — he was U.S. Commissioner of Education at that point — do you recall how he thought about this? You were soon to become secretary of HEW (Health, Education and Welfare), but you did not know it at that time.

**Gardner:** It was a long conversation running through the preliminaries of the Elementary and Secondary Education Act [ESEA], and Frank was very taken, as was I, with the idea of testing the school — that is, not testing every child — but by sampling the school you could test the school. This was the very thing that almost shot us down when the school administrators heard about this idea. They zeroed in on that with fierce concern that they would be measured. But that was Frank's original idea. He wanted evaluation beyond what we could get. Basically we had all been focused on individual evaluation. The thinking was toward individual assessment. He was thinking like a commissioner of education, and a very imaginative one, and that's what reached him finally.

**Smith:** So he wanted at that point to create a mechanism to evaluate the quality of the school, rather than to focus the assessment on the individual student.

**Gardner:** His first concern was to find a tool for his own evaluation of how the nation was doing, how states were doing, how school districts were doing. Somewhat naively we thought the schools would welcome this. They didn't at all. We were thinking about the school boards really.

I remember I was on the education committee of the Scarsdale Schools, and it would have been a great device for us because we thought we were awfully good.

Frank had a very keen grasp of his national responsibility, and the absence of metrics and tools to do some of that evaluation — where are we headed, how are we doing? Both Ralph and I had been brought up on testing. So that was really what pulled us into it. I got brought into it fairly early. The Ford Fund for the Advancement of Education was in it also, and I suspect that it was because of Clarence H. Faust [then president of the Ford Fund].

By that time I was at HEW. I went there in August 1965.

**Smith:** Was Frank gone by then?

**Gardner:** No; Frank was very much still there.

**Smith:** He was there how long?

**Gardner:** He was there well into 1966.

**Olkin:** By the way, in 1965 the Carnegie grant of $100,000 was a lot of money. If money doubles every eight or ten years, that was a very considerable amount in terms of current dollars.

**Gardner:** It was a very big grant, and I thought that we were very successful in tapping the best thinking. You can't beat people like Ralph and John Tukey. I do think that Fred Mosteller was in there at some time, and I am not sure whether Roger Heyns was in there, but he was very wise.

**Smith:** He was not a testing person.

**Gardner:** No, he certainly wasn't a testing person. What else should I tell you?

**Smith:** As this began to take some shape, both you and Frank were in key government positions; and in the summer of 1966, along came the Coleman report, which in some ways was an attempt to evaluate the country. And federal Title I passed in 1965. Did you see NAEP as part of this larger picture of increased federal participation?

**Gardner:** Oh, yes, absolutely. Both Frank and I were very out-and-out believers in federal involvement in this, but not in a meddlesome way. NAEP is a perfect example of just giving the educational world a tool that they could do what they wanted with. But what the school administrators were saying was a part of my education in how extremely tough the professional lobby could be. I came to Washington with a picture of a lobbyist being a fat guy with a cigar representing the tobacco industry. But I discovered that some of the toughest ones were my own professional colleagues, and some of the administrators were just that. They were just absolutely cold, tough, self-interested.

**Smith:** This is the AASA, the American Association of School Administrators.

**Gardner:** That's right. They didn't want anybody to measure them, and they fought hard. I had a terrible time getting it on the tracks because of them.

**Smith:** They are like the firemen, they have people in every community, so every congressman has to be aware of them. How did the unions react to this? Of course, they weren't calling themselves unions at that point.

**Gardner:** The NEA [National Education Association] decided to back the school administrators. That was again a cool lobbyist game, not thinking about American education, but thinking about the profession.

**Smith:** The Council of Chief State School Officers probably did too.

**Gardner:** That's right.

**Smith:** So, the education establishment lined up against you.

**Gardner:** Yes, that's right. We had to make compromises. We had to say that NAEP would not be used for any direct comparison of schools, that it would be used for assessing year-to-year progress, not district versus district. It is amazing that it survived considering all the things that they tried to put onto it. But it was so necessary and valuable.

**Smith:** It is an interesting mixture of private philanthrophy and federal governance. It is quite possible that Frank couldn't have pulled it off by himself just at the federal level because of these various pressures.

**Gardner:** They could have blocked him and killed it in its cradle. But we assembled a pretty good weight of professional opinion from ETS, SRA, AIR, Psychological Corporation. They were forces, too. They weren't powerful. I look back and they were utter innocents in not understanding the lobbying in its cold-blooded form. But nevertheless, they had a fair amount of weight and we had lined them up.

**Olkin:** Were there any congressional hearings? Did Congress get involved in discussing this?

**Gardner:** Later on, when we went after federal money. Yes, absolutely. That was a tough battle.

**Smith:** That was the time when you were still at HEW.

**Olkin:** What year are we talking about now?

**Gardner:** That must have been around 1967.

**Smith:** In 1967 NEA passed a resolution to withhold cooperation from NAEP. So at that point it had reached the highest levels at NEA. They were not just lobbying. They were passing internal resolutions.

On another note, you mentioned earlier today that Oregon Senator Wayne Morse had influence over Frank as they worked on the ESEA. Did Morse get involved in NAEP at all?

**Gardner:** This was the whole thing about federal funding to the schools. It had always been blocked by the religious issue, and some on the civil rights issue, and also just the bare fact that the rich schools didn't want to find their money ending up in poor states, which is practically the heart of why you get the federal government involved. And we brought this up. It was time to deal with the fact that when Mississippi put into education a vastly large percentage of its state resources, it still isn't going to make it.

I think the most vivid expression of that was by Ribicoff [Connecticut Senator Abraham Ribicoff]. Frank and I were on the John F. Kennedy task force on education. Ribicoff was chairman of the commission, and he flat out said, "If you think that I am going to watch these guys from the South come up and steal my people, and then send money to them to steal some more, no way."

Frank had gotten from Wayne Morse — bless his heart — this idea that we won't talk about rich states and poor states, but we would talk about rich and poor school districts. That broke the thing. It meant you weren't constantly pointing to Mississippi. Every state had poor districts. It just cut through the thing, and we built that into the ESEA.

At that time I was chair of Lyndon Johnson's task force on education, and I got Frank to sit in, not as a member, but just to be there. It was very amusing because he shared with his top people all the ideas that were floating around. Sometimes they would act on it or did away with it, which was devastating for the scholars who came along later, trying to find out where this idea came from — did it come from the task force? But it is a very profitable way to function. The idea of getting at the committee report, carrying it over to this Office of Education, and having them read through it saying, do I agree? It cuts through a lot of work.

**Olkin:** Did schools of education react in any way? Was this a topic at meetings of the American Educational Research Association?

**Gardner:** It was a topic with professional educators. The testing wing was very active and saw this as a real opportunity. They were on board.

**Smith:** How do you see it now? That is, that the federal government would put a tool out there. How do you evaluate it over time?

**Gardner:** I think NAEP was always extremely valuable. I made the point at the time, and two or three others did as well, that the testing field had to be prepared to mount a rival measure if the federal measure didn't work. There had to be an alternative. It would be a terrible mistake to assume that our government is always right about these things. But as long as the field has enough guts and leadership to say, "OK, we're going to do our homework in the way that Jim [James] Kelly [then program officer for the Ford Foundation] did with teacher certification," then we are perfectly capable of it.

But the fact that the federal government puts forth enabling measures is one of the valuable things they can do. They are not saying that you have to do it. They are not saying that it has to be done in any particular way. They are just saying: "Here is an instrument we set up. Take a look at it and see if you want to use it," which is what Jim Kelly did with teacher certification.

I spent a lot of time on the cities, and we are all spending time trying to figure out not only how the federal government could be in, but how could it be in without throttling the creativity of the local people. It is so easy in the legislation, in regulations, to limit, as you know, the choices of the local people. It doesn't need to be. There is a lot of room for choices.

I put together the first move away from categorical grants; and we had, I think, 15 grants. Each one had its own little package: maternal health, venereal disease, and so on. Each went down its silo to the local official, the state official. They did not have to talk to one another at all. We put this together and put a little planning money in and said to the governors, "We will give you the money, and you figure out the little packages." That's the kind of liberating thing that you can do.

If you look at the governmental transportation agency, it's a marvel of saying to the local people: "OK. You figure it out. We will give you the money; but you have to figure out how much for light rail, how much for highways, for configuration." NAEP is very much in that mode. It doesn't cramp the local districts, and it vastly enables schools — and even school districts that fought against this — to decide. We needed some comparison pill.

**Smith:** It sounds as if you and Frank and others shared a common set of perspectives and a direction that you wanted to go in. And NAEP did go in that direction. Any reaction to that?

**Gardner:** No question that there was emerging — and I may be prejudiced in thinking that Frank played a major role in that — a really impressive change in education thinking nationally, thinking in terms of a possible federal role. . . . They were thinking nationally. If they had done it ten years before, they couldn't have succeeded with NAEP. The Office of Education had to emerge. The times were right.

**Smith:** Did Conant [James Bryant Conant, former president of Harvard University, U.S. High Commissioner to Germany, and ambassador to Germany] play a role in any of this?

**Gardner:** No. Conant was in Germany [as an education advisor on a Ford Foundation grant] when this was going on; and when he came back, he was deeply interested in the schools as schools. He set out to visit schools. When I first put the thing to him, I said, "We understand that you are coming back, and we would love to see you tackle some issues in the field of education." He said, "Well, I would like to study the high schools."

**Smith:** Did President Johnson have any perspective on this.

**Gardner:** No, he didn't. He was passionately interested in education, that and welfare. But he never talked about it.

We needed a site for the study of high schools, and we picked Chicago, the one site that could have knocked us out of the picture. Richard Daley was, on one side of his personality, absolutely in tune with Lyndon Johnson. They were old pals.

The insurmountable problem seems to me to be the different inputs in terms of kinds of students who come to a high school. There was a person around the western part of Chicago, and he was just passionate about keeping the kids in school. And if you measured his school's dropout level, he was a hero. But if you measured the test performance at the school, he didn't look good; and he was totally aware of it. He just said, "I resign myself. I'm not going to be a high-ranking school." That's hard.

**Smith:** Well, probably the school was ranking low because he kept in so many students.

**Gardner:** Exactly. For a lot of years I've worried that Americans really don't want to look at the lowest part of the intelligence distribution. They don't want to look at it. They don't want to think about it. And in all these discussions of standards, that is a kind of lurking thing. If you really get tough, you'll make that 80-IQ kid come up to snuff; and it's heartbreaking because it always ends up hurting the 80-IQ kid. But don't you think the whole thing of standards is somewhat crass?

# An Interview with Lloyd Morrisett

This interview with Lloyd Morrisett was held 12 July 2001 at One Lincoln Plaza at Sesame Works, conducted by Ingram Olkin.

**Olkin:** In the interview with John Gardner, he mentioned that early on, when the whole idea of a national assessment came into being with the Carnegie Corporation, he turned a lot of it over to you because you were more knowledgeable in that area. I wonder if you could tell us of your recollections.

**Morrisett:** As is indicated by your list of key events, this was all started in the summer and fall of 1963. I don't remember exactly when John Gardner first talked to me about this. It was certainly some time in the fall of 1963 because I did attend both the first two Carnegie conferences, the first in December 1963 and the next one in January 1964. I don't remember all of the people who were at the conferences, but it was a fairly diverse group, as would have been typical of what Carnegie did in those days. For example, my memory is that William Golden was at one of them, perhaps both. Bill was a very wise man, a financial investor not particularly associated with education, although he had been a good friend of John Gardner and later became a good friend of mine. I'm just mentioning him as one kind of person who was there. Bill had been with the Atomic Energy Commission before that, so he had some political background.

**Olkin:** So the conference was quite diverse in the kinds of background represented.

**Morrisett:** It was a diverse group in both cases, and the agenda for those conferences was to examine whether this initiative made sense — educationally, politically, and scientifically. And second, to perhaps begin developing some notions of how to proceed in an organized way if it were determined that the idea was a good one.

**Olkin:** Was there some kind of white paper, or was it just a verbal presentation?

**Morrisett:** I believe that there was some documentation given to people that had attended the conference beforehand, but it was not extensive.

**Olkin:** So there was no plan in effect.

**Morrisett:** No.

**Olkin:** It was primarily ideas of what might be.

**Morrisett:** That's correct. The background was presented; there was a discussion of the current state of education; there was a discussion of the educational and political atmosphere in Washington and in the states. There was a discussion of possible scientific approaches to doing something like this, but there was no plan. Ralph Tyler had presented in advance a memorandum to Keppel, but it was more of a schema than what you would call a plan.

The general reaction of the people at those conferences was that it was a good idea and that it was worth pursuing. And at that point, again as you have indicated here on the chronology, John Gardner approached John Corson. John Corson was still then, I think, a partner in McKinsey. He had not retired. He had had an education specialty at McKinsey. He had been more or less McKinsey's partner dealing with the education practice, and he was also a good friend of John Gardner at Carnegie. So John Gardner asked John Corson to present some alternative structures for a proposed national assessment of education. And it was somewhere in this time period in the Spring of 1964 when I believe that John began to involve me more formally as the liaison between Carnegie and what was about to happen. I think that, rather than trying to follow the chronology of events, what I ought to do now is to talk about some of the specific issues that came up and some of the problems that ECAPE faced, as far as I remember them.

It was very clear from the beginning that to undertake something like a national assessment meant overcoming very substantial political resistance in the educational community. The idea of local control was strongly held in most of the states and in most school districts. There may have been some notions of what would then have been called standardized testing floated before this, but all such efforts had failed. I'm not clear in my memory about that, but I believe that was part of the background. I'm sure about the political resistance because that was discussed extensively.

**Olkin:** John Gardner referred to that and said that it came as a surprise that people he thought he could count on were actually to some degree hostile.

**Morrisett:** One of the main tasks of the committee, and particularly the Technical Advisory Committee [TAC] when it was constituted, was to devise a plan that would afford a snapshot of the state of education and, over time, its progress. It was important that it be in a form that would not seem to be dangerous to the people that resisted the idea of comparative testing. Certainly the feedback that we got at that time was that states did not want to be compared with each other, and districts did not want to be compared with each other. So, as you well know, the original sampling plan that was finally devised was in a form where students were randomly selected and the samples were done in such a way so that you could not compare districts, schools, or states.

**Olkin:** That was a critical part of the plan.

**Morrisett:** A very critical part of the plan; and in my view, it was the part of the plan that eventually led to enough acceptance so that the assessment could take place. We had, as I am sure you are aware, a brilliant technical advisory committee. John Tukey was superb in the initial role of chair; and the other members of the committee, Bob Abelson, Lee Cronbach, and Lyle Jones, provided wonderful support, although as I said, Bob did not participate as extensively as Lee and Lyle did.

**Olkin:** And also Ralph Tyler.

**Morrisett:** That's right, Ralph Tyler. So the next thing that I remember is that we were extremely fortunate in being able to obtain Steve Withey at the University of Michigan as our initial staff director. Steve was an excellent choice. He had the right combination of talents for the job. He understood the technical necessities of such an assessment. He was a good organizer, and he had enough sensitivity about educational values. He was just the right person for the job, and he was excellent. Once we had a plan, there needed to be testing items devised that were appropriate for the plan. And, of course, then the notion was that we were not trying to test directly what the schools did, but we were trying to test the behavioral outcomes that we hoped the schools would produce. Ralph and Lee Cronbach both, but Ralph particularly, were important in defining that distinction in a way so that it could be made operational by people who devised testing items. Steve Withey and Ralph were involved in a series of meetings with subject matter experts to talk about what it meant to have an appropriate, let's say, junior high school reading level or an appropriate understanding of mathematics at the sixth grade. What should a child be able to do if he or she was at such a grade level.

**Olkin:** Were there meetings with, say, the mathematical community, for example?

**Morrisett:** Yes, there were. I think I participated in at least a few of those meetings, although I did not participate in many. My memory is that the meetings included mathematics — I'm taking mathematics as an example — mathematics teachers from schools, mathematicians, and may well have included — because I really believe that my memory is accurate on this — lay people who could provide a citizen's judgment as to whether or not the things that were being talked about were relevant in the real world. This wasn't simply an academic exercise.

**Olkin:** And this would be true in reading or in any of the other areas?

**Morrisett:** Yes, those committees were pulled together in the same way, but the subject matter area varied.

**Olkin:** Were they pulled together by Tyler?

**Morrisett:** Ralph and Steve, but I think that in each case they probably contacted key people in relevant communities and got names and ideas from them. Because in no way did the people on our committee have the range of contacts in localities and throughout the country that would have allowed them to do that in all the subject matter areas.

That process of trying to define testing items that were age and grade appropriate, and represented behavioral outcomes that were desirable and relevant in the real world, that was a key part of it. So two things were going on — the devising of testing items, and the devising of a sampling plan. To make it work, we had to have people who would put that together and put it into an operational framework. And one of the key initial problems, and here I'm not sure in the chronology where it fits, was who or what institution was going to do this. By all odds, ETS was thought to be a very strong possibility; and as far as the people at ETS were concerned at the time, they thought that they were probably the only logical possibility. However, when it came down to it, we requested proposals from a variety of institutions; and we felt that ETS had not given it their best efforts. So we chose others to do that job, those initial jobs.

That provoked a strong reaction from Henry Chauncey, who was president of ETS at the time. He had quite an indignant reaction as to how this could have happened, because they were the best in the business and why didn't we choose them?

Now later, of course, all of that turned around and it became vitally important to ETS, and it has indeed over the years been a central part of ETS activities in the last 20 years.

**Olkin:** Were some of the specialists in tests and measurement at ETS involved, for example, Sam Messick, Fred Lord, Norman Frederickson, William Angoff?

**Morrisett:** They might have well been involved at some point. My memory is not going to be sufficient to answer that question, specifically. However, the indignant reaction really came from Henry Chauncey.

**Olkin:** What was the liaison between Carnegie and other groups? Was it monitoring, was there reporting, or was Carnegie just a helpful friend of the community?

**Morrisett:** During that initial time, I think that I would have to say two things went on. The direct monitoring was done through the staff director, initially Steve Withey. I was involved to a minor degree. That is, I wasn't independent of the committee or Steve Withey, but I did participate with them in those discussions that led to those kinds of decisions. And I was the liaison between the staff director and Carnegie. Carnegie did also receive reports from time to time from Ralph Tyler about what was going on. But the sort of day-to-day kinds of information were channeled through me. Carnegie, I would say, was a helpful advisor and ready to do what seemed to be necessary to move things along.

**Olkin:** How long was Carnegie involved before others took over?

**Morrisett:** We were certainly involved through the decision about those initial contractors. I was personally involved through the time that Jack Merwin was staff director in 1967.

John Gardner left Carnegie in 1965 to become the Secretary of Health, Education and Welfare. At that point, Alan Pifer became president of Carnegie and I became vice president. So I would think that sometime around 1965 or 1966 my own role in this phased out; and I suspect that's when Fritz Mosher took more of the responsibility because, as vice president, I had quite a different set of responsibilities than I had had when John was there.

**Olkin:** There was a lot of discussion about how this would be different from other kinds of testing programs. Perhaps you can think back about some of the conversations along those lines.

**Morrisett:** I am thinking about Ralph Tyler in particular because it was his philosophy, if you will, that I think led to much of what you are asking about. Ralph had been very active and supportive of the cooperative education movement. I'm not as familiar with it as I should be; but as I recall it, in the cooperative education movement, students were, in effect, apprenticed, as well as going to school at the same time, so they obtained real-world skills while they were obtaining academic formal learning. And Ralph believed in that. You know Ralph's personal history, and so I won't go into that. But I think that probably informed his outlook about what sorts of outcomes of education were important to measure. That it was not simply what went on in school, not simply what went on in teaching to standardized tests, but the important thing was that schools, and education generally, produced citizens who could be effective in using the skills that they had gained in doing real-world tasks. Therefore, what was desired was that a student who had supposedly learned to read could actually read the newspaper. And, indeed, reading the newspaper was one of the early testing items. It may still be, as far as I know. But it certainly was one of the original ones. And be able to read the things that a citizen would need in order to be an informed person. Similarly, in mathematics at whatever age level, it wasn't simply that you know the multiplication tables or conduct simple division in your mind depending upon the age level, but that if you went into a store to buy some candy and you had a certain amount of money, could you figure out how much candy you should get for that money.

And that was formed by Ralph Tyler's philosophy, and I believe one could probably trace some of Ralph's philosophy back to John Dewey. It happened that, because John Tukey was the chair of the TAC at that point, it reinforced this view. John's orientation toward statistics was that statistics needed to deal with the data that you found in a way that made them meaningful.

**Olkin:** So everything pointed to Ralph's philosophy, in effect. That is, the committee was very positive toward that point of view in its own thinking.

**Morrisett:** No question. So it all fit together beautifully in that regard. And, of course, that also fit very well with the eventual removal of the fear of people in education about this approach to testing. Because if you are testing the outcome of whether somebody can read the newspaper, that doesn't necessarily map back directly to what went on in a particular class. Because, presumably, that results not only from your instruction in reading in school but your work in English, your work in social studies, and other things, too, that would contribute toward your ability to understand what you read when you read the newspaper. So that philosophy was, I think, important in the long run in helping remove the fear of some people in education about comparative testing.

**Olkin:** Who were the people who were involved in the actual selling? I mean, clearly this committee was a very academic type, and they would not be involved in the political aspects. Was John Gardner the lead person in trying to get Francis Keppel to pursue this?

**Morrisett:** I can't say. Both of them certainly exerted what influence in appropriate ways they could. But John went to HEW in 1965; and what he may or may not have done in that position with respect to this, I don't know. My guess is that he had very little time or thought to give to this because HEW was a huge job.

Frank Keppel was very sensitive to political issues in education, and I am sure that he lent what weight he could to it. But I think Ralph Tyler was the main sales person. It was because Ralph could participate in educational meetings because of his background, because he didn't represent Washington, D.C., and his reputation allowed him access to meetings where he could easily talk to people about it. I also believe that to some extent Steve Withey was a salesperson for ECAPE.

I'll say one other thing. Part of the sales work for the committee was really done through those meetings that were called together to devise testing items, where you had teachers, where you had lay people talking together. So you had teachers who had participated in discussions and had come to feel that this might be a good thing, who could go back to their localities; and they were then local salespeople. At least they weren't oppositional. And it would be known in their local communities and in their organizations that they had participated in this. And I am sure they were asked about it.

**Olkin:** Did the media report on this? Nowadays, the *New York Times*, for example, would have articles on education and articles on science and medicine. I'm not sure in the late 1960s whether this was true.

**Morrisett:** I don't remember any media reporting. However, when the results came out, that was different of course. Along the way, I don't remember anything like that. Now, and even during the time I was still at Carnegie, once the initial results came out, there were a few people beginning to talk about the desirability of having more specific results. That is, some state school officers began to think it would be useful to know how their state stacked up, at least against the national average, if not compared to other particular states. So once the assessment began, you could see that people began to think how this might be used to further their own agendas.

Ralph saw this happening. But he was so concerned to protect the integrity of the assessment process, especially when it was young and fragile, to shield it from any organized opposition, that he resisted that for a long time.

**Olkin:** Moving to a totally different area, do you have any thoughts on what's happened since your departure from involvement with NAEP in its early days?

**Morrisett:** Well, of course, I have been extremely pleased to see it become institutionalized and regularized and an important part of our knowledge about education. Currently, with the discussion of mandatory testing throughout the country, I suspect that in the next few years we will see NAEP have renewed importance in various ways, which I cannot now define. But the recent controversy in Texas about high-stakes testing and the discrepancy with what Texas found using its own tests and the NAEP results, those are matters that will have to have explanation over time with appropriate studies. I am sure they will be carried out. NAEP will provide a benchmark. With NAEP having now 35 years or so of history, I think that it gives an anchor to which almost all educational testing will be referred.

**Olkin:** Lloyd, are there any other recollections about the members of the committee?

**Morrisett:** Well, let's start with Ralph Tyler. Ralph had an encyclopedic background in education, and one of Ralph's characteristics is that he had eidetic memory. He really did have it. That is, he could go on a plane and he could take a set of papers and a book and he could leaf through them, and then he could see those pages in his mind later in the meeting. So this ability that he had, this memory store, was of enormous use and a great amazement to anybody who encountered Ralph. All this stuff that he knew, it was available to him, very effective.

**Olkin:** This was without having to go to the Web.

**Morrisett:** Oh, he was the Web. He was a live Web. Was there a study done? Oh, that was done by so-and-so in such a year. He knew it. He was also a wonderful storyteller. He had a fabulous store of jokes — scurrilous, scatological, funny — he had an endless supply of jokes. So at a dinner meeting, for example, he could regale the group for half an hour or an hour and never repeat himself. And that went along with the memory, obviously, because this was part of his memory store. He had a wonderful ability as a raconteur and as a teller of jokes.

It provided a sort of lubrication for a lot of meetings that was very useful. Ralph was also, as we have said, thoughtful and very concerned about the integrity of what we were about and protecting it. And he was an excellent leader. He also had a lot of energy, even when he was well up in his 80s. He still had quite a bit of energy. He was a very energetic man.

John Tukey was clearly a genius. He would regularly sit in the back of meetings, and he would have a set of computer printouts that, let's say, he was doing multivariate analysis with. And he would be working on that and he could listen to the meeting at the same time; and when a point came up that he wanted to talk about, he would just look up and say something and he would continue working. He had that kind of ability, and it was all so amazing.

Lee Cronbach was a wonderful psychologist. He was an extremely sophisticated experimentalist in education. Much of educational research has not been as well designed or as well controlled as it might be, and Lee was always a person who did those things extremely well and paid a lot of attention to it. So Lee was a very precise man, I would say, and fit in very well with TAC.

**Olkin:** Was Bob Abelson involved in the committee?

**Morrisett:** Bob was not involved. Bob was one of my very good friends at Yale. He was a young instructor when I was a graduate student at Yale in the Psychology Department, and so I knew Bob very well. But as we have said, he really was not very involved in this process.

**Olkin:** Did John Gardner attend these meetings?

**Morrisett:** No, I don't believe he attended any meetings after the first two conferences. John was a kind of person who had many ideas. His method of operation at Carnegie was essentially to seed a number of them and hope that some flowers would bloom. And so, in effect, these first two conferences were his way of seeding this idea. And after that, it began to bloom and he didn't give it his attention in the same way as at that initial time.

# An Interview with David A. Goslin

This interview with David Goslin was held 23 March 2001 in his office at the American Institutes for Research (AIR) office in Washington, D.C., conducted by Ingram Olkin.

**Olkin:** My recollection is that you wrote a report now referred to as the Carnegie Report; perhaps you could review your involvement with the Carnegie Corporation and how this report came to be.

**Goslin:** The answer to that question begins when I was a young graduate student in sociology finishing work at Yale. At a meeting of the Eastern Sociological Society — it must have been 1960 — I met Bert Brim, who at that time was a staff person at the Russell Sage Foundation in New York [he later became president of the foundation]. The upshot of that meeting was that subsequently Bert asked if I would be interested in joining the staff of Russell Sage Foundation in New York when I finished my doctoral work. When I asked what I would do at the foundation, he described an idea he had been thinking about for several years, namely, a study of the social effects of standardized testing. He noted that standardized testing in American society is a very important sociological phenomenon and expressed the view that someone should do a series of studies on the social effects of standardized testing in America. That was the kind of grand vision — grand idea — that Bert Brim became known for in the years to come; and he persuaded me to spend my first year after graduate school at the foundation.

I went directly from graduate school in September 1961 to Russell Sage and spent that year learning about standardized testing in American society. I visited the Educational Testing Service, I visited other test publishers, I visited schools, and I interviewed most of the major figures of the day in the testing field. Then in May 1962, I sat down and wrote a book called *The Search for Ability: Standardized Testing in Social Perspective,* which Russell Sage published the following year. In addition to a broad overview of the use of standardized tests in society, the book included a theoretical analysis of the possible social consequences of testing in society, as well as an outline for some possible research to take place over the next decade. This turned into a long-range program of research that ultimately was funded by Russell Sage Foundation, by the Carnegie Corporation of New York, by other foundations, and, indeed, by the federal government at one point. I ended up staying at Russell Sage for 13 years, during which time I participated actively in the program of research on the social effects of testing, as well as a variety of other activities.

In any case, two years before the Carnegie Corporation organized its first planning conferences on NAEP, I had become involved in studying the social effects of testing, and I was working with Bert Brim. When Bert was invited to participate in the first planning conference on December 18 and 19, 1963, convened by John Gardner, John asked Bert if he had any ideas on who might attend the conference and who might serve as a reporter for the conference. Bert suggested me for the latter role. Thus, while I did not have anything like the stature of the individuals who gathered at Carnegie in December 1963, I was able to attend and participate as a member of a truly extraordinary group of experts who began to explore for the first time the idea of a national report card on American education.

That was the first planning conference that Carnegie organized, and the report that you are now holding is the report I wrote in my role as conference reporter right after that conference in 1963. There was a second conference a month later in January 1964. Instead of writing a separate report of the second conference, I summarized the deliberations of both conferences in a summary report on two conferences, which is the second document that you have. [See Appendix J.]

**Olkin:** Do you remember any of the interactions, any of the personal aspects that occurred at these conferences?

**Goslin:** It's a difficult question to answer because in the subsequent years I've had the opportunity to work with and get to know well almost everybody who was there. For example, John Flanagan was a participant, who of course was one of my predecessors here at AIR, and Bert Brim and Ralph Tyler. I have a hard time recollecting any individual anecdote out of that meeting, except that it was quite an extraordinary collection of people. They took the task very seriously. There was, as I recall thinking to myself at the time and thereafter, a predisposition to think this was a good idea. Obviously, they wouldn't have been there in the first place if there had not been some momentum behind the idea. But they were very concerned about the political problems that might occur if you compared states with one another as a result of this test.

It does not come through in my report quite as clearly as I remember it subsequently, but it was a major consideration at the second conference, where the participants began to zero in on the notion that no student would take the entire exam. This idea developed between the first and second conferences, as I recall, the notion that individual students would take only a sample of items from the test. This idea solved the problems of generating individual test scores, as well as reducing the burden on test takers. There was still some talk of comparisons of schools with one another or cities or states. Everyone recognized that those were potentially difficult political problems. In addition, the notion clearly came through — though the term "criterion-referenced tests" never appeared in my report, and I don't remember whether it was ever used during the conference — that the scoring should be linked to what students actually are able to accomplish, rather than some normative frame of reference. This was a theme that ran through the conference from beginning to end. And, indeed, from the very beginning there was agreement on the notion that items should be divided into those that 10%, 50%, and 90% of the population could pass.

**Olkin:** Did they have any names for those cutoff points?

**Goslin:** They did not use the words, "proficiency levels," as I recall.

**Olkin:** But there was a notion of defining levels for the general public, translating levels into something that the lay person could understand.

**Goslin:** That was clearly understood as a major imperative for the program, namely, that it had to be meaningful to the population as a whole.

**Olkin:** What about the notion of teaching to the test?

**Goslin:** That certainly was another theme. I had just written my book on the social consequence of testing. The tendency of schools to teach to the test was one of the major effects of testing that I had talked about in my book. The New York State Regents exam was a focus of attention at that time, due to accusations that the Regents exam had a stultifying effect on the school curriculum in New York State. It is interesting that we are now in a period where we are reinventing the New York Regents exam.

**Olkin:** Tell me a bit about your book. What were the basic themes about testing?

**Goslin:** The purpose of the book was to provide a conceptual framework for planning a series of research projects that would look at different aspects of the social effects of tests. The conceptual framework included effects on kids who took the tests (on everything from the experience of taking it to their life chances), the effects on parents, the effects on schools, and on all other institutions in society. As a sociologist, I saw standardized tests as an important institution that could and did have an effect on a wide range of individuals and other institutions.

**Olkin:** Did any of these ideas influence the thinking at the conferences?

**Goslin:** I don't recall myself as having been silent at these meetings, and I am sure that these thoughts entered the discussions about NAEP over the next half-dozen years. For example, I was subsequently engaged at Russell Sage on a study of the use of tests by teachers.

**Olkin:** Were you or the group at Russell Sage involved with NAEP, or were the origins of NAEP moving from other directions?

**Goslin:** The development of NAEP proceeded independently from the program of research that we were working on at Russell Sage, though many of us at Russell Sage had connections with NAEP at various times.

**Olkin:** What are your thoughts about where NAEP has been or about the future?

**Goslin:** I find it interesting that it is only eight or nine years ago that the trial state NAEP comparisons began. Until that time NAEP did not enable comparisons among states. Now we are talking about trial city comparisons. I think I made the comment in one of those original conferences that someday comparisons would be made because it would be irresistible that NAEP would be used to compare organizational units. Now we are talking about an individual NAEP.

I pointed out in my report that NAEP eventually would have an impact on curriculum, that it would drive curriculum, and the phrase that would be used was that it was going to constitute a national curriculum. Today NAEP is the closest thing that we have to national standards for education. There is no other framework that could be regarded as a national curriculum framework.

I think the group was prophetic in some respects in terms of predicting where this was going to go, although there were those in the group who thought that it would never happen. Moreover, if the conference participants had predicted these outcomes at that time, NAEP might not have come into existence. I think that as a political position, nobody could acknowledge then that you might one day have comparisons of states, localities, and schools on the NAEP test. Second, the idea that this would be the basis for a national curriculum would have been an anathema; it would not have gone anywhere.

**Olkin:** In the new presidential proposal on education, one of the tasks that has been asked of NAEP is that it will confirm what the states do in terms of growth; NAEP will be used as the barometer for how well the schools are doing.

**Goslin:** The problem is that as soon as stakes are attached to NAEP, people will want to make sure that they do well on the test. If you attach stakes to NAEP, for example, that poorly performing states will lose funding from the federal government, then you are likely to fundamentally change the character of NAEP and the response of schools to it.

# *An Interview with Lee J. Cronbach*

This interview with Lee Cronbach was held 19 February 2001 at Channing House in Palo Alto, conducted by Ingram Olkin and Marshall Smith.

**Cronbach:** My first contact in this was by being included in the meeting that was held in John Gardner's office to get a reading on whether the project should go ahead with or without Carnegie support, and it was a mixed group. You can get a transcript of that meeting. Carnegie kept one. I saw a write-up based on it, so I won't even try to say anything about that.

The next contact I had was in 1965, to join what was called the Technical Advisory Committee at the time, and I said I was going to Japan. They said that sounded all right because they were going to move slowly and I would be needed on this committee by the time I would get back. The committee consisted of John Tukey as chair, Bob Abelson, Lyle Jones, and me. Ralph Tyler was in most of the meetings; but in some, when he was absent, the staff director or another staff person sat in.

The composition of that committee is itself instructive. Tyler, of course, was identified with educational measurement. None of the others, except possibly myself, was identified with educational measurement. I had mapped myself into psychological measurement. In part, that was because everywhere that I taught, for instance at Chicago, there was someone already in place who was specializing in educational measurement. It's funny for me to do psychological measurement. It meant that I was strongly in psychometrics, even though I had never dealt with one construction of an achievement test, for example.

In general, the philosophy here was to get away from tradition, and that dominated almost everything that the committee did. The committee met probably every six weeks, on average, and took a great level of responsibility, in the sense that we not only judged

proposals from outside, where test development firms were prepared to do a section of the test, but when the instruments came
in, we reviewed them item by item. We re-wrote items, sent the
whole thing back, or rejected large chunks, saying this didn't
meet the requirements.

The point I would like to stress is that everything that I can recall
from the efforts of that committee were diametrically opposed to
what has gone on since NAGB took over. I'm not saying that
NAGB was solely responsible. I don't have that history clear, but
NAEP in recent years has been very much different in philosophy
and style, not to mention, of course, all the technical embellish-
ment that ETS put in.

The initial point of view came from Tyler. I was a Tyler student;
the others were not. And there had been concern from the beginning, as is evident from the meeting at Carnegie, that we wanted to
avoid evaluation driving the curriculum. We did not want teaching
to the test, and there was a concern that a "national curriculum"
driven by the assessment was to be avoided as being inappropriate
under the structure. You may recall that a prime mover in all of this
was Frank Keppel, the Commissioner of Education, and he was
highly sensitive to questions of the federal role.

TAC was asked to agree about subject areas for which there
would be surveys and, therefore, instruments; and each one was
developed pretty much independently, except as we imposed a
common style or, in the end, staff combined some of them in trial
assessments.

The point of view was to try to identify aspects of educational
development of what kids could learn and be assessed on, almost
regardless of the particular lessons they had studied. So we would
avoid technical vocabulary because we wanted to detect whether a
person had reasoned mathematically given a mathematical problem,
regardless of jargon they had been taught. We not only avoided
technical vocabulary as much as possible, but we would try to get
generalized items on whatever the topic was within a field that
persons could come to understand regardless of what particular
topics their course had covered.

This was very different from what achievement test construction was normally like in the Sixties. By then, all the firms that built the tests that were in use would lay out a table of topics, and within the subtopics would lay out the other directions, the type of item to be used, when there was a problem to be solved or recalled, etc. The test constructor set up what was seen as a canonical curriculum outline — which of course was reviewed by people from a lot of schools — and then had his staff or contractors write a lot of items, cell by cell, and then there would be an assembly process to put together the whole test.

We didn't work that way. We worked with comparatively large ideas, and we encouraged the development of items that set up situations and required a prediction or analysis or explanation.

By that time, standardized testing was committed to scores, to norms, and to multiple-choice items almost exclusively. We took the position — or Tyler took the position, and we accepted it — that what we were trying to do was to influence teaching by getting teachers to think in terms of these larger principles, points of view, and so on. The principle would aid almost any course of learning from any particular chapter out of a textbook.

First, then, there was interest in making the results comprehensible to teachers in terms that they could put to use in their teaching. Second, the reports to the public were to be as free as possible from measurement technology, of anything that would come between the citizen and the information about the quality of education. The idea of scores was dismissed pretty much outright. I don't think that we spent more then an hour on this aspect of the problem. The decision — which wasn't entirely practical, we ultimately found out — was to report the items as they stood. No one could misunderstand that; and prose could be added to explain why this was considered something more than a sentence to be drilled on, that this represented a way of thinking about a test as an application to a new situation, that sort of thing. In the end, we thought we could establish something a bit like opinion polling — which at that time was not being done hour by hour, but was being done in a fairly regular way — and that the Gallup Institute or others would prepare newspaper columns and prepare newspaper releases and have columns in which they laid out the questions and the data that came back. We thought that NAEP could be fed into educational thinking by getting newspaper days. At one point I remember that there was a thought of a NAEP exercise being released and being made the subject of a small item that could be presented as a box in a newspaper, and we thought that this could be done every day.

But the idea was to directly report the exercises together with the percentages correct. It might have been presented first for all students, and then for whatever subgroups were to be identified.

**Olkin:** Were all grades considered early on, or were fourth, eighth, and 12th grades chosen from the beginning?

**Cronbach:** I am sure it was not 12th. The original plan was to sample students from a particular age so as to get away from school promotion policies, and these tests would be administered to a fraction of the students. The sample would be determined from outside, that is, by the sampling formulas. The school knew the ages of the pupils, so a pupil would go in regardless of whether he was still in the third grade or had been moved to the fourth. I don't remember the ages selected, but I would have said perhaps fourth grade is right — about age 10 — and eighth grade would be age 14. That is a bit high.

**Smith:** Nine, 13 and 17?

**Cronbach:** Yes, nine, 13, and 17 would seem pretty good as ages. I am pretty sure that we were not thinking in terms of a final high school evaluation. The emphasis was on what could be done with children of this age in their subsequent education.

I am reasonably certain that we came down toward the sophomore year, but this is a memory from the very distant past. I am right, I am sure, about the use of age rather than grade because we were trying hard to get away from making the data a reflection of school policies as such.

**Smith:** One of the points you made earlier was that that you were hoping to use the test to provide to teachers information about larger ideas. Was there a theory driving that? Was there a conceptualization of those larger ideas that someone had put together?

**Cronbach:** Well, I don't recall anything being used that represented a laying out of principles like this. Of course, Tyler in his work with the progressive schools had worked with teachers to get these principles in a great many secondary subjects. So, in the background, there was thinking of this kind. But I am pretty sure there was never anything comparable to a curriculum outline in what we were doing.

I don't think anything that went on deserves the name of a theory, but there was a pretty common understanding that the educated person can analyze a situation and see elements in it. Something of that vague character certainly influenced our view of what constituted a good assessment exercise.

**Smith:** ETS used to use language about the SATs as being measures of a more general ability not related to the curriculum. I wonder if you could comment on the similarities or the differences between the two approaches.

**Cronbach:** Well, the developed abilities notion that ETS used was highly general and would be good to use in subsequent instruction of, let's say, mathematical thinking; and that does happen to go together with one of the curriculum areas. But on the whole, the ETS thinking was as far from the curriculum as they could get. They were dealing with reasoning interpretation in general; reading would be included as an ability that was a valuable tool.

Now in our situation, we really thought that the curriculum included courses, for instance, in different areas of science. Within biology you would have the possibility in one part of the country of emphasizing things in its environment that wouldn't appear in another part of the country. We were interested in framing questions so that a student who had not studied the desert at all could still think about an ecological question and put the pieces together. So there was an attempt to free the questions from dependence on the lesson system, free it from the lessons the student had studied. But the understanding was that it was going to influence the teacher to think about whatever this teacher had been doing to promote ecological thinking, and that was fairly specific to the biology course. That is quite different from anything that ETS was thinking about.

We were not dealing with a general ability, whereas ETS was promoting a theme very close to that. We are dealing with reporting here. It was not at the level of aggregates. We didn't talk about scientific thinking. The ideal that we started out with was that we were going to get attention on a given Saturday to an ecological exercise; and, in principle, if there had been two or three ecological exercises, they supposedly might have gotten into the same article. But we never got to that point. The idea of release through newspapers collapsed; we never did find a way to make the exercise-level reports used. I cannot remember what was ultimately released in those days. But, of course, we were an agency of the exploratory committee for a national assessment, and our job was to identify issues and difficulties and possibilities. No samples were being drawn with the thought that we were going to be reporting to the public. We were at a much earlier stage. So I guess there probably was never any piloting of such reports. But I say that now without a definite memory.

There was, of course, a large concern at the outset with the idea that these fairly small samples would be used to compare states. The states were highly resistant; and during this period of seeing whether the boat would float, Tyler negotiated a deal whereby the headquarters of the project would be at the offices of the Council of Chief State School Officers or whatever it was called in Denver [the organization was the Education Commission of the States]. And while they, as far as I know, didn't exert much control, they felt comfortable with that and were promised that there would be no reporting by state. So we started the sampling plan with the understanding that sampling would be by region and that reporting would be by region and not by state.

**Olkin:** I'd like to focus a bit on the big picture. One is the set of policy decisions. Also any operational difficulties that you people were thinking about. The issue of evaluations, either internal or external, and any technical innovations that people were thinking about. You had a high-powered statistical group, for example, so were there any other policy decisions of a large nature?

**Cronbach:** Well, the policy decisions in general were incidental. You start working within a subject area, and you find some things that you can do and some things that you can't do. But the one dominant policy that our committee operated by was: Don't think about past practice as a model. Try to figure out what will serve this particular field; and if you have to go away from multiple-choice questions, that is perfectly all right. This is a policy of latitude, if you will; and I can't remember anybody announcing it. I think it was understood from day one that creativity was to be encouraged on the part of the various contractors.

I think I might deviate somewhat from your list of questions. The best example of this was that AIR [American Institute for Research] wanted to work on the social studies area, in particular on the skills of citizenship; the word *citizenship* floated around somewhere in the initial discussions, and citizenship was included as an area to be covered in the very first assessment.

Vincent Campbell, a social psychologist, had been studying student discussions and had a fairly elaborate idea of what information you could get. I don't recall his mechanism exactly. I do recall that he would introduce a policy question in the form of a problem situation and have students think about it and discuss it, and I believe he would record the discussion of the group of students as a unit. He had a scoring scheme so that he could summarize what one group did, what another group did; and we were highly enthusiastic about this. He was strongly encouraged to run pilot studies. It shows that we were getting away from the student as a unit of measurement. In this case, the school was the unit of measurement, because we had groups in several schools that would be compared, and you would not be comparing people within groups.

The use of qualitative scoring of performance in a group to be converted to numbers that could be compared over groups was perhaps without precedent in achievement measurement and was an ancestor of much that has been done to score performance tasks. The use of matrix sampling of test content allowed different pupils to respond to different questions. Yet the score on the different items could be compared. That was a first application of some ideas of Fred Lord.

**Smith:** Was John Flanagan involved in this?

**Cronbach:** Not directly. He obviously had been supportive of Campbell, but we had no interaction with John's level in AIR. There were some places like AIR where we understood the thinking of the individual investigator. In other cases, like the Psychological Corporation and ETS, we were dealing with an organization; and somebody at the top of that organization fielded the request and decided how it would be managed, and we had no direct influence. Our influence came afterward when we looked at the product.

Psych Corp, in particular, seemed to have been inclined to take each request, break it down into whatever table of specifications it had been using to file its stock of items, and then to lift items from its stock and send them back to us as a test. The probabilities that these were items that had been written with any of the principles we had in mind were fairly low. I think the same problem arose with ETS, but I'm not as definite in my memory there. We were a lot happier when we were in communication with people who could understand what we were looking for.

There were large operational questions on sampling, which we handled by delegation. I don't remember whether Westat was the primary consultant in the earliest days.

**Smith:** I think maybe RTI at Research Triangle Park, maybe with Dan Horvitz.

**Cronbach:** Yes, it was a matter of asking them to study the requirements and to make some suggestions. What we got back was a highly technical proposal; and our review of it was limited, as I recall, to saying yes, they were on the right wavelength. That is, we didn't see anything there that was in conflict with the other aspects of the plan. But there was a case where somebody who really needed to know sampling, like Abelson or maybe Lyle [Jones], could point to technical innovations. I don't know whether they did things that were new or just packaged things that they always had ready for use. It was an elaborate plan. On the psychometric side, the decision not to aggregate items, which was not abandoned during my years on the committee, that decision made psychometrics almost irrelevant, because all psychometrics is based on an aggregate of items.

**Olkin:** Did that have many implications?

**Cronbach:** Yes. The only statistic that was of great interest to us was the standard error and the percentage correct on each item in turn. Well, the whole point, you see, was to get away from reports about "people are proficient," "people are meeting the national objectives," or whatever. The plan for reporting was not to abstract at the level of "here is some evidence on the objective of application of science to everyday life." The objectives were not units for reporting. If the exercises did not strike the public as being educationally useful, OK, that was a reasonable matter for public discussion, for a school board to consider. But we were just giving the facts on things that somebody had thought was a reasonable part of educational growth.

You asked about evaluation. At that time, nothing that our committee did made any provision for evaluation. The assumption was that the public would be interested in the facts and would debate them where they saw issues. So there was never a mechanism for going beyond the score reports to anybody's judgment about the worth of the project. I think that is an accurate statement.

I don't remember how long I was on the committee. I would have said that four years is likely. It was understood to have been preliminary to a decision to go from pilot work on a small scale to operational trials.

**Olkin:** There was a question also about technical innovations, but you may not have been in on that part.

**Cronbach:** Our position from the beginning was that we were going to offer minimally processed reports on what was observed in student performance. We did not expect any user to need technical understanding to deal with the reports. Obviously, we had this terrible tri-bandwidth reporting scheme that collapsed of its own weight. Nobody took it seriously. But this was still the basis for deciding that an assessment exercise was satisfactory. I recall criticizing and rewriting some exercises on the grounds that when this exercise is in the newspaper, there will be criticism for its lack of good public understanding. The exercise had to be transparent to an educated person. But that is a logical editorial judgment, not at all in technical areas. I don't think that in spite of the qualifications of Abelson, Jones, and to some extent myself, that we drew much on that. I do think that Lyle had a large interest in the sampling questions, but I can't remember that we did anything really more definite than to say get a good contractor.

**Olkin:** What was John Tukey's role in this?

**Cronbach:** He was first among equals, or something like that. John played an active role. He was just as likely to be critical of the wording of an item as the rest of us. We thought nothing of rewriting the stem of a question to put it in language that was more directly comprehensible. We were far more than a passive review committee, and John was an active part of that review.

I am sure that if we were able to look back on a transcript of a meeting we would find that he did some chairman-like things, such as making sure that we covered the agenda in the course of the meeting. My largest impression is that he acted like a very bright member of the committee.

**Olkin:** We are talking now about the early 1960s to somewhere around 1968.

**Cronbach:** The only thing that I have mentioned prior to 1965 was the Carnegie meeting. And so what we have been talking about is the period 1965-69.

**Smith:** The first trend NAEP came into being in about 1973. The versions of NAEP for the last 27 years or so are very much of multiple-choice items measuring curriculum areas. Did that come into the discussions? This was not the same as the early NAEP that you describe.

**Cronbach:** Well, I think that what must have happened was that I left the committee before 1971. It was always understood that it was a short-term appointment.

**Smith:** I think ETS came in the early 1980s. That sounds like it was a really major shift in the orientation of NAEP, when the contract was awarded to ETS.

**Cronbach:** ETS was given a very large role in redesigning the reporting because people wanted something that fitted more with the idea of accountability. We went to great lengths to avoid anything that smacked of accountability or reporting to higher authorities. From our point of view, the teacher was in charge of the classroom rather generally, and so we were trying to upgrade the wisdom of the teachers' individual decisions and were solicitous to design not making any provision for drawing conclusions about the merits of individual teachers or schools. So that went into the sampling plan.

**Smith:** Frank Keppel changed his views over the years and really supported a national curriculum toward the end of his life. In 1989, 1990, 1991 he was very supportive of it.

**Cronbach:** I don't know what he thought in his heart back in the Sixties. I know he was playing the role of commissioner, which is extremely limited, and he wanted everyone to understand that he wasn't overreaching. The point that Frank kept as a basis for his original approach to Tyler and then to Gardner was that, in Washington, he discovered how much clout public health statistics gave the people seeking funds for medical research, and he thought that appropriate educational assessment would do the same thing for educational funding. In some sense, that is what we are seeing now, given the slogans about accountability. We also have all those clauses about funding for places where performance is poor. I haven't heard anything quite as strong about translating NAEP into money for educational research. But Frank just might have favored in his heart a national curriculum even back in the 1960s.

**Olkin:** Do you have any thoughts about what has happened to NAEP from the 1980s to now? I think you commented a little about that.

**Cronbach:** Well, yes, but almost everything that I mentioned compares the way we are now with the way we were thinking then about the assessment problems. The reverse dominates the scene today. You start with this idea that scores should be traceable. I don't think NAEP is thinking about reporting for students, but state assessments sure are. And NAEP may not have plans at the moment for reporting at levels lower than demographic subgroups within the state. But the idea of pointing the finger at institutional structures that are doing badly is precisely the opposite of where we were. We weren't dealing in our thinking with institutional structures. We were thinking about a public interested in education, speaking to the school boards and through them to the teachers. From our point of view, the only thing that we had agreed upon was that we were not going to make comparisons across states. That did not distress us any, whereas it is now standard in all the thinking.

The aggregation to study proficiency is a major technical difficulty that ETS may or may not have solved, but is just the opposite of what we were doing. I'm not sure what NAEP is doing now in the various subject areas; but there were nine areas, as I recall, which we were trying to assess equally seriously and with comparable principles. In the record I see now, it is reading and mathematics, and I am not sure how advanced mathematics is; and I am not sure that things like the international studies include real secondary school mathematics. I don't know what NAEP is doing, but the other curriculum areas have largely disappeared. From where I sit, I never see reference to them, and I don't know whether assessment in subject matter fields other than these basic skills is being attempted or not.

**Smith:** It is, but it's just infrequently.

**Cronbach:** With reporting of what sort?

**Smith:** Of the same sort, proficiency in science.

**Cronbach:** Because, of course, the label of proficient is a non-unified development that throws together an enormous diversity of achievements.

**Smith:** Do you think it makes sense in a unified field?

**Cronbach:** Well, you can read a student's short composition and allow for a lot of variation and still read the paper for comprehensibility, structure, and interest. That is to say, you can apply some general questions where the goal is general and the way the task is performed is diverse. So what happens is that something like written expression, which is really idiosyncratic and not uniform, is still subject to assessment. But I don't see science as lending itself to this at all, or social studies. Actually I don't think we were ever given social studies as a target. I think that from the beginning, we had citizenship as an area, even though that doesn't correspond to any curriculum subdivision. It would be interesting to check back and find out what the nine areas were. But I remember we were concerned with reading, mathematics, science, and citizenship, and I just don't remember what else we fumbled with. I don't think there were any triumphs in these other areas, or I would have remembered that.

In general, what went on in our meetings was reported by whatever representative of the staff, from Tyler on down, was present. That information was taken back to the Exploratory Committee on the Assessment of Education. Sometimes it was the idea of sending out a new request for proposals, if we were dissatisfied with what we received, and sometimes it was just a point of view that the staff could develop in its own ways. So our feedback was highly informal. I think it really depended on the messenger. That is to say, I am pretty sure that Tukey was not asked to go after our meetings and give them a summary.

**Smith:** So there was no staff person from the Exploratory Committee or the chiefs there?

**Cronbach:** Tyler was present. I don't think anyone else was. And ECS, of course, came in late during the time I am describing, so they weren't in at the start. When Tyler didn't come to meetings, sometimes [Jack] Merwin, the staff director, came; and after that [Frank] Womer, Merwin's successor. I think that Tyler usually did attend those meetings.

**Smith:** While you were there, were no assessments run?

**Cronbach:** That is correct. Everything was done at the pilot level.

**Smith:** Do you recall reports on the pilots?

**Cronbach:** No, I don't. The pilots were more like collecting item data and sending the thing back to the test developer.

One summary impression is worth saying. I look back on that and felt that issues of feasibility loomed very large. We started with a plan that was driven by some ideals of what you might do with an assessment, and some of the more imaginative things proved to be infeasible on the national assessment scale. But I don't remember now where the breakdowns came.

**Smith:** The power of technology is particularly great now to organize information and apply it. Is there any way of thinking about having the original vision of the assessment be computer administered?

**Cronbach:** Well, except for Campbell's work with groups, I don't see anything that couldn't be handled by computer; and, indeed, with modern technology you would be a lot freer with graphics. The question becomes aggregation. The bandwidth of information about pupil's educational development is simply enormous; and to be used by any audience, it has to be packed down. ETS chose something that was fairly consistent with its aggregations and was fairly congenial to NAGB. That's one way of packing down, but I don't believe that we thought of a qualitative compilation being attempted.

In principle, you can do qualitative things and aggregate them, most obviously you can ask did the student or didn't the student use metaphor in writing. This is a straightforward yes-no question, and it aggregates. You can ask more subtle questions about the metaphor, but I think that we haven't begun to deal with qualitative information that any teacher reading a composition wouldn't do automatically. It is just a very different process from adding up errors or storing overall judgments.

**Smith:** Suppose that the assessments, by using technology, adhered entirely to your original ideas of having no aggregation.

**Cronbach:** The issue with reporting at the item level is that you don't have any teachers or other readers in your report to want to sit in front of the screen and go through 100 items at a clip. You can collect information on a tremendous number of items. But when you try to aggregate items and say these items all require understanding of measurement principles, that is so remote from the subtle item itself that most of the information is getting lost because the different questions will have different meanings. You may want to check on a particular issue, such as, is a continuous scale appropriate or should categories be used. You could have lots of items of that character. But you can't run an assessment at that fine grain.

The issue of the width of the audience attention span is how much information the audience wants. It's a great difficulty. You can always, in doing any kind of evaluation, collect ten times as much information that is intrinsically interesting, and even potentially useful. Then you can try to get your clients to pay attention. Their mechanisms aren't designed to receive a highly variegated input. So we have problems in communication here as distinct from just getting the information right.

# CHAPTER 4

# Technical Giants of National Assessment*

*Clay Allison*

## The Analysis Advisory Committee

Fine Hall, a modern, 14-story tower of brick and stone, stands between Washington Road and Palmer Stadium in the southeast corner of Princeton University's 225-year-old campus. On a Saturday afternoon during the fall, when the varsity is at home, one can go to the top floor of Fine and see as much as a quarter of the gridiron and, if lucky, catch glimpses of the Tigers locked in one of their traditionally deathless struggles.

Most of the faculty and students, whose workday lives center in the department of mathematics and the department of statistics, which crowd into every corner of Fine, are more interested in such things as multivariable calculus and "analysis on manifolds and differential geometry" or perhaps combinatorics, stochastic process or homological algebra.

On the fourth floor is Room 408, the office of John Wilder Tukey, professor of statistics and associate executive director at the Bell Telephone Laboratories at nearby Murray Hill, New Jersey. The office is plain and simple, offers no amenity other than

---

*This article was first published by the Education Commission of the States in *Compact* 6 (February 1972), and is reproduced here with permission.

one overstuffed chair that has seen better days. There is a rack containing miscellaneous books and pamphlets, a table piled high with papers, and Professor Tukey's desk stuffed into one corner and in a state of what might be described as disarray. The room is more of a workshop than an office.

Across the corridor from 408 is a long, rather narrow classroom with blackboards on three sides. On the fourth side the windows look out on a green sward between Fine Hall and Ivy Lane. This classroom often serves as a meeting room for a small group of topflight statisticians and quantitative psychologists banded together in ANAC, national assessment's Analysis Advisory Committee, which "puts the frosting on the national assessment cake."

First organized in 1965 as the Technical Advisory Committee for the budding national assessment program with Dr. Tukey as chairman, the original committee consisted of Dr. Tukey; Dr. Ralph W. Tyler, a "founding father" of national assessment and the first director of the Center for Advanced Study in the Behavioral Sciences at Palo Alto; Dr. Lee J. Cronbach, professor of psychology and education at Stanford; Dr. Robert Abelson, professor of psychology and chairman of the department of psychology at Yale; and Dr. Lyle V. Jones, professor of psychology, vice chancellor, and dean of the graduate school at the University of North Carolina.

It became the Analysis Advisory Committee in 1969 with Dr. Tukey continuing to serve as chairman and Drs. Abelson and Jones continuing to serve as active members. In September 1970, Dr. Frederick Mosteller, professor of mathematics and statistics at Harvard and vice chairman of the President's Commission on Federal Statistics; Dr. William E. Coffman, professor of education and director of Iowa Testing Programs at the University of Iowa; and Dr. John P. Gilbert, staff statistician at the Harvard Computer Center, became members of ANAC.

## Preparing the Package

In its early operations, the advisory committee did such things as give advice on agency contractors who conduct the actual sampling of young Americans in the 9, 13, 17, and young adult (26 to 35) age brackets to determine what they actually know in specific subjects: for example, science, citizenship, mathematics, writing, etc.

Said Dr. Jones at a recent ANAC meeting: "We not only gave advice on agency contractors, but we even designed exercises. There was no one else and no other agency to do the work. We continued in this way until the exploratory work was over, and it was assured there would actually be a national assessment program.

"Then the sampling schemes had to be worked out, the exercises had to be selected, and we had to decide on the form and organization of the reports. We had to settle on the definitions of size and type of community, educational level of parents, etc. Finally we had a package to sell. Ralph Tyler and others then spelled it out, funding followed and national assessment became operational, complete with procedures and staff."

Dr. Tyler, a bouncy and vigorous near-septuagenarian, thinks national assessment is forging ahead "despite the fact that we were delayed at least a year by the job of getting proper exercises. The exercises at the outset did not really sample, nor did they give us enough information. The need to develop exercises that more faithfully reflect the objectives of the school is still with us. The second critical problem is how to report these data in ways that will be most meaningful and proper."

Although Tyler sits in on ANAC meetings only occasionally these days, the committee's objectives are in line with his thinking. Chairman Tukey and his associates see their principal jobs as analyzing data and deciding on how it should be reported.

## The Heart and Guts of NAEP

The committee wrote Science Reports 1, 4, and 7, which reported the raw data of science sampling in 1969-70 on the basis of sex, region, race, parental education, and size and type of community. While ANAC did not prepare the reports issued thus far on citizenship and writing, it reviewed them before they were published by NAEP.

"The general strategy today is that the committee's contribution in its present form will be complete when we finish the science reports," said Dr. Lyle Jones. "We feel that as consultants, we are doing too much operational type work in analysis and reporting. We have had the major responsibility in science, but when we have finished with it, it should serve as a model for the other categories. In the future ANAC will be much more advisory and will leave the analyzing and writing of reports to the national assessment staff.

"Essentially what we have done is take the responsibility to clear up the methodological situation and try to find out how to analyze things so they make good sense. Our experience has been that if they make good sense in science, then they make good sense in other areas as well."

Said Dr. Abelson: "There are many problems in an assessment program, but among the basic ones are these: preparation of adequate and proper exercises to be administered to selected groups (in the case of national assessment: to 9-, 13-, and 17-year-olds and to young adults, age 26 to 35) on a nationwide basis. The first question is, will the exercises do the job? Once the sampling has been done and the exercises scored, a check must be made for errors of omission and commission. Then they must be analyzed and reports written. This is where ANAC comes in and is why it might be referred to as 'the heart and guts of National Assessment.'"

Figures, results and scores, standing by themselves, don't mean very much or may be actually misleading. Professor Tukey has a favorite story to illustrate the point: "In this community there were two hospitals doing the same kind of anesthesia and surgery. The statistical results at one hospital were much better than at the other. Judging from the figures alone one had a good record in administering anesthetics and performing surgery, the other fell short. But study showed that the one with the good record did most of the 'easy' jobs while the other handled the tough emergencies brought in off the street and the aged poor. When these factors were taken into consideration in analyzing and balancing the statistics, the records of the two hospitals were much closer."

## Overcoming Biases

Judgment, then, must be used in handling and interpreting statistics, along with the mathematical tools always used by such master statisticians as the members of ANAC. The process of "balancing the data" was created by ANAC to assist in judging the results properly.

"Sometimes you have to make special fixes for various kinds of troubles that show up in statistics; and when done correctly, they may very well be the best thing to do. In handling data we must always determine if a number used one way is going to be more informative than if used in another way. So you make a judgment. You always have to wind up using judgment in analyzing data, and we hope that whatever biases the members of ANAC may have are sufficiently diverse so that we get good answers and good judgment. Nobody is without biases . . . and under the right circumstances the world seems to do pretty well in canceling biases out. That is clearly what we want to do in analyzing national assessment data. It is secondary, it seems to me, to the exercise of good statistical inside knowledge and all the sort of thing that goes into doing a good analysis, but one has to include judgment."

All of the members of ANAC have professional careers in full swing at their respective universities and some of them hold down several posts, but they are very busy consultants for NAEP. They meet an average of eight to ten times per year and each time spend a couple of days and nights pouring over the assessment data, arguing about what it says and what it means, and writing reports.

Since they all have demanding schedules, it is no mean feat to get them together from five scattered states. About half of the meetings are held in Tukey's Princeton aerie, the remainder in Palo Alto or Washington or Chicago or someplace else.

## John's Team

When they do get together they organize quickly, lay out the ground rules for the meeting, and get right to work. There is no formality, no pulling punches, no hanging back. Each man is an expert in his field (statistics, psychology, psychometrics, educational measurement), each is aware of his command of his subject and of the outstanding professional capabilities of his fellow committee members. Most of them have been associated at one time or another with the Center for Advanced Study in the Behavioral Sciences at Stanford University in Palo Alto. They have worked together for a long time, pull together easily as a team.

The committee uses a jargon of its own coupled with terminology from their respective disciplines and the bright new world of data processing. In addition to the all-committee terminology, Chairman Tukey has some favorites of his own, some of which can be as difficult for a visitor or a new member of the committee as the committee's acronyms. When Dr. Tukey wants his committee to think about some debated point, he is apt to say, "Well, let's marinate on that for a time." And when he says, "Illuminate me," he wants a more detailed explanation. Another Tukey favorite: "I hear your words, but I'm not sure what you mean."

A strong, stockily built man with sparse, collar-length graying hair, Dr. Tukey's conduct of a committee meeting can be quite a show for the uninitiated. He favors black, short-sleeved knit pullovers, suntans and Keds, uses his horn-rimmed glasses to do paperwork, stare over, and as a sword for conversational thrusts, slashes, and parries.

He has a round, suntanned, expressive face. He peers, stares, grins, and when making an important point, often screws up his right eye until it is tightly shut.

Another Tukey habit which can startle, amuse, or annoy strangers and visitors is his custom of doing paperwork while conducting a committee meeting or carrying on a person-to-person conversation. He typically runs an ANAC meeting for two nights, a day, and part of a second day, and says, "I am of the opinion, and I think it's right, that the proper duration of a committee meeting in terms of its effect is not the number of days, but the number of nights. When we have two night meetings instead of one, I think we get more done. Our meetings have a nasty habit of being on weekends . . . [long interlude] . . . which doesn't fit well into anybody's schedule . . . [long interlude] . . . though we have a certain amount of doing together."

The meetings usually start Friday night, continue Saturday and Saturday night, and then go for a while on Sunday.

A Tukey-chaired meeting is apt to be a long meeting. He thinks in terms of a half hour break for dinner, may arrive for a meeting that starts at 5 p.m. equipped with a jar of peanut butter and a box of crackers, keeps the committee going on and on into the night. The members gradually sink lower and lower in their chairs, may wind up sprawled on two or three chairs. Tukey sometimes stretches out on his back on two or three chairs, locks his hands behind his head, and conducts the meeting while staring at the ceiling or with closed eyes.

He is also a prune man. At some point or other during ANAC gatherings, cellophane bags of ready-to-eat prunes appear. Tukey eats them thoughtfully and puts the pits on the table in front of him, in a mathematically straight line. So do his colleagues.

While this sort of thing might lead an outsider to believe that ANAC meetings are fun and games, they are no such thing. Chairman Tukey and his committee members are highly professional, dedicated men doing a serious and important job for NAEP. They believe the program is important to education and to the nation.

## Fifty Pounds of Data

At a given meeting each member, including Chairman Tukey, will have a specific assignment. For example, at a meeting in Princeton to work on the results of sampling young people on their knowledge of science, each member was asked his preference, then assigned to interpret the data in a specific category and write a report: Dr. Coffman to regions, Dr. Abelson to race, Dr. Jones to education of the young people's parents, Dr. Gilbert to communities. Dr. Tukey took the one remaining: sex.

They worked at a long table with a cardboard box containing fifty pounds of data set out for each man. The material, after it had been gathered from the field, had been scored and put on tape by the Measurement Research Center in Iowa City, Iowa, then forwarded to the Princeton Computer Center. The computer run, which required the services of 10 technicians, had cost $14,000.

The discussion went on for the entire weekend and will be a continuing one for ANAC meetings in the months ahead.

The general procedure is that once they have a meeting of the minds on a specific batch of data, each man writes his assigned report, then circulates to the others. The next step is a conference call in which the entire committee participates. During the call, which is usually at night and continues without interruption for five or six hours, the members edit each report, word by word, line by line, paragraph by paragraph.

After each chapter is approved by the committee, Tukey writes a summary, which gets the same treatment. The chapters and summary then become the technical report, which is published by National Assessment of Educational Progress and is made available to educators and others who have an interest in the assessment results.

Dr. Coffman, who, with Dr. Gilbert, is one of the newer members of the committee, has a slightly different view of ANAC meetings and procedures as a result of his long identification with traditional testing programs at the University of Iowa. The traditional test compares students with fellow students, whereas the national assessment makes no such comparisons, and instead seeks to learn what students actually know about specific subjects.

Said Dr. Coffman: "I've been interested in looking at data from a new point of view, though I must say I'm amused by some of the criticisms made of traditional testing. Today I hear people blaming reading specialists because children can't read, but that simply isn't true.

"But the effort to look at testing data from a new perspective and summarizing the material item by item will result in new ways.

"Actually the individual teacher (already) has more information than she can cope with, just as our analysis committee has more information than we can really handle.

"However," Dr. Coffman continued, "the important thing about the way we are doing national assessment is that no individual gets more of a test (sample or exercise) than he can handle, so we can administer more complex items in an hour's time. We can set up laboratory experiments. All this gives us more flexibility in what we measure; it gives us the kind of information we need to make general judgments.

"A teacher does this in his or her mind for his or her pupils, but you can't very well summarize what is in the heads of thousands of teachers.

"The NAEP ability to generalize because of careful sampling and widespread cooperation is a great asset. National assessment didn't ask for much time and as a result got better cooperation from the schools and a better sample than anyone ever got before. Not the biggest, but the best," he concluded.

Some members of ANAC are beginning to wonder, after their tough years as an operating body, if they will be able to find the same challenge in a purely advisory role, but all are anxious to give it a try.

The members of ANAC are not only former members of the Center for Advanced Study in the Behavioral Sciences at Palo Alto "club," but most of them have worked together on other projects. For example, Tukey, Abelson, Jones, and Gilbert have worked together for NBC Election Returns.

But, happily for NAEP and ANAC, there is still another bond. Said Mrs. Tukey: "They are all John's friends."

They are important friends of the national assessment project, also.

# CHAPTER 5

# NAEP and the U.S. Office of Education, 1971 to 1974

*Dorothy M. Gilford*

This chapter provides a history of the National Assessment of Educational Progress (NAEP) from my viewpoint as Assistant Commissioner for Education Statistics of the U.S. Office of Education (USOE) and director of the National Center for Education Statistics (NCES) from 1968 to 1974. From 1971 to 1974 NCES was responsible for monitoring the USOE grants for the NAEP project.[1]

Funding for NAEP was provided by the Carnegie Corporation in 1968, 1969, and 1970, and by the Ford Foundation in 1969. USOE funding started in 1968 and continued beyond the period covered by this chapter (Hazlett 1974).

In July of 1969, the Education Commission of the States (ECS) assumed administrative responsibility for the NAEP program.[2] Prior to that time, a nonprofit organization in New York state, known as the Exploratory Committee on Assessing the Progress of Education (ECAPE), with Ralph Tyler as chairman, had been responsible for NAEP.

During the period from 1968 to 1971, Herbert Conrad, special assistant to J. Louis Bright, Associate Commissioner for Research and Development, monitored the USOE grants for NAEP project activities. After Conrad's death in 1971, Thomas Moorefield,

Chief of the Basic Research Branch of the National Center for Educational Research, became the monitor.

On 25 August 1971 the Commissioner of Education, Sidney Marland, wrote to Wendall H. Pierce, executive director of ECS, informing him that oversight of NAEP had been transferred to NCES. Marland noted that Pierce, in a letter that reached then-Commissioner Terrel Bell, had raised the question a year before about the proper placement of NAEP in the USOE. Marland's letter explained, "Now that much of the exploratory work has been accomplished, it seems to make sense to transfer the project from the National Center for Educational Research to the National Center for Educational Statistics."

The NAEP project was a welcome addition to the National Center for Educational Statistics' program because it would provide data on student attainment, data that were essential to the center's mission of measuring the character and progress of American education. National assessment was "designed 1) to obtain, at regular, periodic intervals, census-like data on the knowledge, skills, understandings, and attitudes possessed by various subpopulations in the United States, and 2) to measure the growth or decline in educational attainment that takes place over time in learning areas of educational concern" (Ahmann 1976). For the first time for education in the United States, NAEP's systematic data collection provided such information on the country's youth and reported it to people involved in the on-going process of improving education.

Until 1971 the data collected by NCES were primarily inputs to education: data from state and local education agencies on such topics as enrollment by grade, full-time equivalent staff by major employment category, and finance data including revenues by source (local, state, federal) and expenditures by function (instruction, support services, and non-instruction).

My predecessor as Assistant Commissioner of Educational Statistics, Alex Mood, recognized that NCES needed to measure other aspects of education. To fill this need he established a small group of analysts to develop models of the education process. He planned to use the models to identify important data elements for inclusion in the NCES data collections, but this program was not completed. Mood also was a proponent of the national assessment. Hazlett summarized a memorandum written by Mood and dated 2 May 1966:

> if Carnegie or some other agency did not undertake a nationwide sample to secure achievement data then the Office might do that in 1967 for two purposes; namely, the general purpose of determining the "educational composition of the population" and the specific purpose of "coordinating the evaluation of Title I of the Elementary and Secondary Education Act which will be done by the various state departments of education." (Hazlett 1974, p. 317)

In 1967 he wrote a thoughtful article enumerating many of the potential values of NAEP (Mood 1967).

I shared Mood's concern about the character of the NCES program and in 1971 was taking steps to change it. At the time NAEP was transferred to the center, two large studies that would complement the center's input data were in the design phase: the Survey of Public Secondary School Offerings, Enrollment, and Curriculum Practices, 1972-73, a curriculum study that would provide information about what was being taught in the schools, and the National Longitudinal Study of the High School Class of 1972, which would provide information about the outcomes of education and transition into the world of work. The data from these two programs, combined with the input data already collected by NCES and the rich output data from NAEP, would indeed improve measurement of the character and progress of American education.

The balance of this chapter addresses four categories of NCES activities related to the NAEP project. The first, NCES oversight of the NAEP project, involved an all-day meeting of top staff members from ECS/NAEP and USOE, site visits to ECS, and actions related to quality concerns about the NAEP program. The second category describes the NCES activities in 1972 to avert the termination of USOE funding for NAEP. This budget crisis highlighted the importance of a third activity, a dissemination program spearheaded by NCES to provide NAEP information focused on each of the following groups: USOE policy makers, other Federal policy makers, state policy makers, and national education organizations. The fourth describes NCES project management related to the financial history of NAEP. This includes the funding history of NAEP.

## NCES Oversight of the NAEP Project

At the time NAEP oversight was transferred to NCES, the staff members responsible for NAEP at ECS were James A. Hazlett, administrative director; J. Stanley Ahmann, staff director; and George H. Johnson, associate staff director.

I appointed Iris Garfield as NCES monitor of the project. In this capacity she regularly reviewed the project with the ECS staff and represented the Office of Education at ECS meetings and meetings of NAEP's national advisory committees. She also worked closely with the NAEP Analysis Advisory Committee (ANAC) on methodology, as well as with departmental managers in order to evaluate project status, solve data problems, and provide guidance and recommend changes in resource allocation to the NAEP departments.

In response to frequent requests from ECS and its NAEP staff for involvement with top-level Office of Education staff, I talked to Commissioner Marland, who agreed to setting up a day's meeting away from the office to which top officials of both OE and ECS would be invited. NAEP staff worked with NCES staff to plan the agenda. The meeting was held on 1 October 1971, less than two months after NCES assumed monitorship for NAEP. According to Hazlett (1974, p. 346), Commissioner Marland and ECS Executive Director Pierce were among the 34 people from USOE and 12 ECS/NAEP staff members who attended. Also present were six people from the U.S. Office of Management and Budget and 15 NAEP resource people, including members of the NAEP Policy Committee and ANAC.

The summary report of the working groups at the meeting stressed that NAEP staff must become more involved in the interpretation of results. The NAEP Executive Committee was responsive to this finding and authorized inclusion of funds in the NAEP budget to promote the use and application of NAEP results (Hazlett 1974, p. 347). Presumably this authorization was for the FY 1972-73 budget, as the 1971-72 fiscal year had already begun on October 1.

During 1971-72, Iris Garfield, the NCES monitor of the NAEP project, and I made several visits to ECS to attend meetings of the Analysis Advisory Committee (successor to the Technical Advisory Committee) and to meet with NAEP staff to obtain a better understanding of NAEP program operations. The NAEP staff was consistently very cooperative in providing background information about the program and in responding positively to suggestions we made, though this was not always true for the ECS Policy Committee and ANAC.

At the first ANAC meeting I attended, I was surprised to find the committee responsible for analysis engaged in reviewing the content validity and clarity of the exercises for the next assessment. I later learned that this was the second of three reviews before an exercise was included in an assessment. The first review was by lay people to determine that each exercise was asking meaningful information. The third review was by the USOE to determine whether any of the questions might be interpreted as an invasion of privacy (Finley and Berdie 1970).

In characteristic style, John Tukey called this review process "icking the questions." He would give each committee member around the table the opportunity to state whether the question should be "icked" (dropped) and, if so, why. The committee would then decide whether to retain the question. Committee work was done rapidly and with a sense of humor. The congenial atmosphere was further improved by Fred Mosteller finding a superb pastry shop nearby and coming to meetings with several delicious pies for all to sample.

My purpose in attending the Analysis Advisory Committee meeting was to discuss steps that might be taken by NCES and

NAEP to facilitate the work of researchers interested in studying associations between NCES input data and NAEP outcome data. The committee chair was not willing to put this item on the committee's agenda but gave no reason for his position. Later I learned that both he and Ralph Tyler took a very conservative stance on including background factors in the analysis of output data, feeling that the magnitude of the study of background factors was such that it could cloud the issues related to collecting data for output measurement (NAEP Staff 1973).

Nonetheless, the FY1974 budget for NAEP included $142,170 for a literature search to identify studies that had been concerned with background factors, to assess the results of these studies, to convene two conferences to determine factors that should be identified for further study, and to study the questions related to developing measuring instruments to assess those factors (Hazlett, Ahmann, and Johnson 1973, p. 32). An early product from this activity was the report, *Associations Between Educational Outcomes and Background Variables: A Review of the Literature* (Bryant et al. 1974).

## Quality Concerns

As NCES staff became more familiar with the NAEP project, several concerns were raised. For example, questions were asked about the number of children in the sample who had been excused from the test (for example, learning-disabled students or students for whom English is a second language). Iris Garfield, the NCES monitor of the NAEP project, posed this question on her next visit to ECS and was frustrated that she could not get an answer. On a second visit she learned that NAEP did not collect this information.

Although it would be difficult to name a more outstanding group of specialists than those on the Analysis Advisory Committee, NCES staff thought it would be desirable to obtain the views of a group of individuals who had not been closely involved in the project. Therefore, NCES initiated a series of annual project site reviews at ECS using national experts in testing, education research and evaluation, statistical methodology, dissemination, and policy analysis. Recommendations made at these reviews provided the basis for pushing the project to include data relevant to national policy concerns, including information on student background characteristics, and to provide adaptations of NAEP for state and local assessments.

## The First Budget Crisis

In 1972, a year following the transfer of NAEP oversight to NCES, John Evans, the assistant commissioner for Planning, Budgeting, and Evaluation, told me that he planned to delete the NAEP project from the next year's budget because the data lacked policy relevance. I met with him to protest and to try to convince him that NAEP should be retained in the budget.

At this time the only published data for NAEP were data for the 1969-70 assessments of science, citizenship, and writing. It was too early in the sequence of assessments to have trend data or even to have data on the same subject for two points in time. Because one stated purpose of NAEP was to measure the growth or decline of student achievement over time, graphs of some hypothetical trend projections for NAEP were in order — in particular, some trends that would be sufficiently provocative to stimulate policy action if they were real. Therefore we prepared hypothetical graphs showing trend lines moving in opposite directions over time for various subpopulations of students.

I met with John Evans and argued the importance of having information on what students are learning, how this is changing over time, and the relative changes for subpopulations. The argument, plus the shocking trends in the graphs, won the day; and the NAEP project stayed in the budget. This budget episode highlighted the importance of demonstrating the potential policy relevance of NAEP data and of disseminating information about NAEP to as many categories of potential users as possible. Many of the future NCES efforts concerning NAEP were focused on this activity.

## Focused Dissemination Program

The center undertook, or urged NAEP staff to undertake, or supported NAEP in undertaking, several projects to disseminate information concerning NAEP to potential users of the NAEP data. These projects were focused on policy makers at the federal and state levels and on national professional organizations concerned with education.

*NAEP Information for Office of Education Policy Makers.* One outcome of the 1 October 1971 meeting between ECS/NAEP staff and top federal education policy makers was a request that NAEP conduct two special reading assessments for the federal Right to Read Program. These mini-assessments of 17-year-old students were eventually conducted in 1974 and 1975. The summary and highlights of the findings of the two assessments are included in the report, *Functional Literacy: Basic Reading Performance* (Gadway and Wilson 1976).

Another request stemming from this meeting came from staff of the federal Adult Education Program. They requested and received assistance from the NAEP staff in the development of their Advanced Placement Level testing instruments and methodology.

*NAEP Information for Other Federal Education Policy Makers.* Another information activity concerned social indicators. Federal agencies were devoting considerable effort to developing social indicators in the late 1960s and early 1970s. One of several major publications on this topic during this period was *Toward a Social Report* (U.S. Department of Health, Education and Welfare 1969).

NAEP data were a potential source for social indicators. To explore that data, NCES contracted for a study reported in *National Assessment and Social Indicators* (Mushkin 1973). The report illustrated ways in which data from NAEP questions could be used in connection with indicators of the health status of the population, measurements of equality of opportunity, and views on freedom and participation. The report also set forth the possible use of national assessment data for an Educational Product Index (EPI) that would be applied in much the same way as the Consumer Price Index, an index of change over time.

Finally, at the request of the National Advisory Council on Equal Educational Opportunity, the NAEP staff provided special analyses comparing NAEP data for racial and ethnic minorities (Sauls 1975).

*NAEP Information for State Policy Makers.* While housed in the ECS, NAEP staff members were well aware of the importance of demonstrating the utility of NAEP to state policy makers. In fact, in 1971 and 1972 they convened state assessment workshops. My awareness of this issue was perhaps even more acute than that of the NAEP staff because of the many difficulties I had encountered with states in fielding NCES national surveys of education.

State policy makers must understand the potential value of a survey or an assessment if they are to continue to support it. Therefore I urged the NAEP staff to place even more emphasis on their program to explain the policy relevance of NAEP-type assessments to states. The NAEP staff established a Department of Application and Utilization (probably in 1972 or 1973) to produce interpretative reports, targeted materials, and technical assistance to assist states in using NAEP.

The NAEP newsletter for February 1973 featured an article titled, "States Incorporating NAEP Methods in Their Assessment Programs." The article describes the assessment activities in 14 states that were using NAEP materials as groundwork for assessment and revising them to fit state needs. The article noted that:

> state education officials find NAEP-type data useful in two ways:
>
> 1. State assessments with nationwide or regional comparability give educational decision makers new insights into areas of strength and weakness in school programs, and
>
> 2. NAEP-type assessment results, because they describe student achievement in terms of concrete items of knowl-

edge, can give the public a clear idea of what students are learning. (NAEP 1973)

The 1974 NAEP Yearbook describes a Model Utilization/ Adaptation (MU/A) program that NAEP developed to encourage and facilitate the adaptation of the assessment by state and local education systems. The program provided services to state and local educational systems in three ways:

(1) consultation between MU/A staff and state or local officials to determine the feasibility of adapting the NAEP model to meet local needs,

(2) technical assistance to state and local officials in the use of the Assessment model or certain aspects of it, and

(3) workshops and seminars that provide an exchange of ideas between NAEP and state and local assessments. (NAEP 1974, p. 35)

The program is clearly a valuable service to states. It provides an opportunity for consultation with NAEP staff to discuss questions about adapting the NAEP model, technology, or materials for a state assessment. The NAEP staff also provides continuing technical assistance to states that adopt some aspects of the NAEP program. Finally the program provides annual workshops for state personnel to discuss their experiences with assessment and to benefit from the assessment experiences of other states.

*NAEP Information for National Education Organizations.* The center urged NAEP to include a program of small contracts to enable national organizations to explore the usefulness of NAEP findings for their program areas. Contracts were let with the National Science Teachers Association (NSTA) and the National Council for the Social Studies to review the NAEP findings in Science and Citizenship, respectively. The NSTA was the first professional organization to examine the NAEP findings for implications for teachers and teaching. The NSTA study team provided a list of recommendations to NAEP (NSTA 1973a) and published a report *National Assessment Findings in Science 1969-70: What*

*Do They Mean?* (NSTA 1973*b*). The National Council of Teachers of Mathematics also planned an interpretive study of the results of the first Mathematics Assessment in 1974-75.

## Financial History and Project Management

During the first years that ECS administered the NAEP program, it was conducted as a research program funded by grants from the Carnegie Corporation, the Ford Foundation, the Fund for the Advancement of Education, and the U. S. Office of Education. Hazlett (1974, Appendix A) provides a chronology of NAEP funding and its distribution by source, shown here in Table 1. As seen in this chronology, funding grew gradually from 1964 until 1969-70, when the first assessment was conducted. Three subjects were assessed that year: Citizenship, Science, and Writing, and two subjects were assessed each year for the next four years. The budget continued to increase through the year 1973-74 not only because each new assessment brought new data and reports, but because NAEP continued to issue additional reports on the prior assessments, to publish announcements of their availability, and to fill orders for reports.

As the funding grew to $6 million in FY1972 and FY1973, closer oversight became appropriate for a federal program of that magnitude. In late fall 1972, NCES asked the NAEP staff to prepare a five-year plan for the period 1975-79. This allowed ample time for NAEP to prepare the plan and for NCES to review it and interact with NAEP before the proposal for FY1975 would be prepared.

The opening paragraph of the plan notes that:

> effort has been devoted to a comprehensive examination of the goals of the project; possible needs for extensions, refinements, or validations; current status and problems; future directions and necessary action to move toward them and the necessity for planfulness [sic] and anticipation of needs and problems rather than "crisis management" and its attendant pressures and unpredictable outcomes. (Hazlett, Ahmann, and Johnson 1973, p. 1)

The plan was based on the following goals that were established jointly by the National Assessment Policy Committee, Analysis Advisory Committee, and staff:

> *Overarching Goal*: To provide information useful to educational decision-makers and practitioners in identifying problems, setting priorities, and determining progress.
>
> *Goal I*: To measure change in selected aspects of the educational attainments of young Americans.
>
> *Goal II*: To make available on a continuing basis comprehensive data on the educational attainments of young Americans.
>
> *Goal III*: To utilize the capabilities of the National Assessment organization to conduct special interest "probes" into selected areas of educational attainment.
>
> *Goal IV*: To provide data, analyses and reports understandable to, interpretable by, and responsive to the needs of a variety of audiences.
>
> *Goal V*: To encourage and facilitate interpretive studies of National Assessment data, thereby generating implications useful to educational practitioners and decision-makers.
>
> *Goal VI*: To facilitate the use of National Assessment technology at state and local levels as appropriate.
>
> *Goal VII*: To continue to develop, test and refine the technologies necessary for gathering and analyzing National Assessment achievement data.
>
> *Goal VIII*: To conduct an ongoing program of research and operational studies necessary for the resolution of problems and refinement of the National Assessment model. (Hazlett, Ahmann, and Johnson 1973, pp. 3-6)

The plan submitted to the NCES provided for the basic NAEP design and added internal research and operational studies needed to improve its operations and refine the assessment model. Also added for possible inclusion in NAEP was the investigation of background factors related to achievement. This would increase the usefulness of NAEP for understanding factors related to school success. The plan provided annual cost estimates for its various components. The proposed annual budgets for the plan increased from $7,997,500 for FY1975 to $11,283,300 for FY1979.

Starting with the NAEP proposal for FY1973, NCES began using external reviewers to take advantage of expertise not available in NCES and to get a broader perspective on the merit of the activities proposed by NAEP. Though using such reviewers is common in federal agencies that fund research, top-level ECS and NAEP staff were quite irate about this procedure. However, the reviewers' suggestions for improvements in the NAEP project were relayed to the NAEP staff, who not only gave them careful consideration but adopted some of the suggested improvements.

The NAEP proposal for FY1974 was $7 million, an increase I supported successfully within the Office of Education and at the Office of Management and Budget; so the President's budget for NAEP was at the $7 million level. The budget provided costs for research and analysis, exercise development, utilization/applications, operations, data processing, and administration.

However, the House of Representatives approved only $6 million. Hazlett (1974, p. 297) cites the fiscal note of the Subcommittee on Appropriations (Report 93-305, 1 June 1973) that accompanied the markup (House modifications to the President's proposed budget) as saying, "The committee fails to see the need to expand statistical surveys and studies by the Office of Education particularly while the budget elsewhere is proposing reductions in programs and educational services to local schools."

According to Hazlett (1974, pp. 297-98), the NAEP Policy Committee developed a strategy to see if the Senate would restore the $1 million deleted by the House. They made contacts with key senators and with HEW Secretary Casper Weinberger, who sent a letter to Washington Senator Warren Magnuson, Chairman of the Senate Appropriations Committee, supporting the restoration to $7 million. In spite of these efforts, the Senate reduced NAEP funding to $3 million; and only $3 million was awarded.

Early in the summer of 1973, internal budget discussions in the Office of Education concerning the FY1975 budget led to the decision that the annual planning figure for NAEP for the next five years should be $6 million. This amount was drastically different from the expectations of NAEP staff when they prepared

Table 1. NAEP funding and funding sources.

| Fiscal Year* | Source | Amount | Annual Total |
|---|---|---|---|
| 1964 | Carnegie | $ 112,500 | $ 112,500 |
| 1965 | Carnegie | $ 260,000 | $ 260,000 |
| 1966 | Carnegie | $ 70,400 | $ 566,400 |
| | Fund for the Advancement of Education | $ 496,000 | |
| 1967 | Carnegie | $ 640,000 | $ 1,280,000 |
| | Fund for the Advancement of Education | $ 640,000 | |
| 1968 | Carnegie | $1,000,000 | $ 1,372,358 |
| | USOE | $ 372,358 | |
| 1969 | Carnegie | $ 350,000 | $ 1,910,000 |
| | Ford Foundation | $ 560,000 | |
| | USOE | $1,000,000 | |
| 1970 | Carnegie | $ 350,000 | $ 2,750,000 |
| | USOE | $2,400,000 | |
| 1971 | USOE | $4,500,000 | $ 4,500,000 |
| 1972 | USOE | $6,000,000 | $ 6,000,000 |
| 1973 | USOE | $6,000,000 | $ 6,000,000 |
| | | | $24,751,258 |
| | | | $ 100,000 ** |
| Total | | | $24,851,258 |
| Distribution by source: | Carnegie | | $ 2,432,900 |
| | Ford Foundation | | $ 560,000 |
| | Fund for the Advancement of Education | | $ 1,136,000 |
| | US Office of Education | | $20,372,258 |

*The NAEP fiscal year starts October 1.
**This $100,000 represents two USOE grants to the University of Minnesota of approximately $50,000 each for fiscal years 1966 and 1967. Hazlett (1974, p. 317) quotes Mood as saying, "The purpose of the grant was to establish liaison between Carnegie and the Office in the development of Assessment, to keep the Office informed, and to encourage educators and intelligent lay citizens to participate in conferences and on lay panels."

the five-year plan that started in FY1975. When I informed the NAEP staff of this USOE decision, Pierce, the ECS executive director, and Hazlett, the NAEP administrative director, requested a meeting with top-level USOE staff. The meeting was held on July 11, but the only top-level USOE staff member who attended was John Evans. Hazlett (1974, p. 288) relates that the five-year planning level of $6 million, combined with this unsatisfactory meeting, led Pierce, Hazlett, and the NAEP staff to determine to seek reaffirmation of the partnership described in the 1969 Memorandum of Understanding between USOE and ECS. Hazlett drafted a statement titled, "Reaffirmation of USOE-ECS Agreement on National Assessment," which was approved by the ECS Policy Committee. When Assistant Secretary of Education Sydney Marland was in Denver on July 23, Pierce and Hazlett met with him briefly. Marland said that discussion was obviously needed and that he would arrange a meeting of top ECS/NAEP officials and Acting Commissioner of Education John Ottina and others.

The meeting was held on September 18 in Marland's office and was attended by top-level staff of ECS and USOE. According to Hazlett (1974, pp. 290-91), his preliminary remarks reviewing the spirit of the 1969 Memorandum were cut short by Marland's handing out a prepared statement titled, "Meeting, September 18, 1973, ECS— Education Division HEW." Marland stated that NAEP had no priority among grants and contracts that USOE administered and must fit into all the considerations of tight budgets and USOE priorities. Then the statement said that NAEP funding henceforth would be a contract, not a grant, "broadly structured upon agreed terms" for FY1974. "In the succeeding year, as USOE and OCS [sic] have time to work out the specifications, the contract will be more tightly structured in performance specifications, while giving ECS latitude in meeting the agreed upon specifications."

The ECS representatives were stunned by the outcome of the meeting, which they had expected to be only a discussion. The brusqueness of Marland's presentation of the change from a grant to a contract was probably due to the fact that he was clearing his slate of important issues before he announced his departure from government service later that day.

Prior to this meeting I had not heard of the 1969 Memorandum of Understanding; perhaps none of the USOE personnel in the room had heard of it. The memorandum, dated 2 June 1969, was signed by James E. Allen Jr., commissioner, for the Office of Education, and Robert E. McNair, ECS chairman and then governor of South Carolina. Hazlett (1974, pp. 245-47) lists the highlights of the six-page memorandum. Three of them pertain to USOE (OE in the memorandum):

> 3. OE is committed to the implementation of the Assessment on a continuing basis and will give it all possible support and assistance.
>
> 4. OE recognizes that ECS must have considerable flexibility in developing its grant budget, both because of the nature of the Assessment and because of the uncertainties inherent in the initial assumption of responsibility for the Assessment.
>
> 8. OE grant terms and conditions are intended simply to meet its obligations to keep informed on the status and progress of federally supported projects, to assure that grant funds are expended properly to carry out the grant, and to see that adequate records are maintained to account for public funds expenditures. OE has no desire to impose its will or to substitute its judgment for that of ECS. Its role will be to assist, advise, and support ECS, as it has CAPE, in this important undertaking.

Considering this memorandum, it is not surprising that NAEP staff chafed at the increase in controls imposed by USOE. However, the agreement was four years old; the annual USOE funding had grown from $1 million in 1969 to $6 million; and, as Evans stated in a letter to Hazlett, "the nearly total independence which has characterized the NAEP grant thus far is not a satisfactory type of relationship for us to insure that the work of the NAEP is maximally policy relevant" (Hazlett 1974, p. 294).

The day following the meeting with Marland, I met with Hazlett and Johnson of ECS and with some NCES staff members to discuss details of the impending contract. Hazlett noted that "Most of the material [in the contract] had been lifted from the NAEP prepared proposal and the progress reports were not unlike those under the grants of previous years." However, he objected to a new requirement that subcontracts must be approved before initiating further work. Hazlett said that negotiations must cease unless this requirement was deleted. He asked to meet with Evans, who affirmed that USOE's accountability to Congress required closer supervision and approval of the designated steps. Hazlett said that the matter was contrary to the Memorandum of Understanding and would have to be reviewed by the Policy Committee on October 19-20 and possibly by the ECS Steering Committee at the end of the month. Evans authorized a two-month contract through November 29 by telegram because the NAEP fiscal year was to begin October 1.

As Hazlett (1974, pp. 293-96) describes in great detail, the position of the ECS Policy Committee against USOE control was unanimous. Ultimately, both sides of the argument compromised a little; and the contract for FY1974 was signed without the explicit controls urged by Evans.

The contract required several management procedures, many of which had been included in previous grants. It included a system of program budgeting and accounting, deliverable products, quarterly financial reports, and tracking of major milestones to assess cost effectiveness of survey design, data collection, data analysis, reporting, and dissemination.

In 1974 the Department of Health, Education and Welfare audited the Education Commission of the State's financial reporting for the NAEP contract. In view of the magnitude of the contract, it is not surprising that it was singled out for an audit. Although NCES staff members were present at one meeting related to the audit, they were not involved in the decision to audit the USOE contract.

The audit resulted in reduction of the overhead rate and the institution of new accounting procedures by ECS for the NAEP program. The change in accounting procedures obviously required some extra work, but that was temporary. However, the reduction in overhead rate would be permanent and a serious change for ECS because the NAEP project was the major source of overhead funding for ECS.

## A Last Word

I was a strong proponent of NAEP because of its potential for measuring the character and progress of U.S. education and for providing data to a variety of education policy makers. Consequently, NAEP received a great deal of my attention. The actions taken by NCES between the fall of 1971 and December of 1974 were always motivated by a desire to strengthen the NAEP program and to ensure its viability. The actions were designed to have the following effects:

- To stimulate dissemination to potential users.
- To provide technical assistance to users of NAEP data.
- To ensure the financial support needed by NAEP as the amount of data and reporting increased.
- To improve program management.

I would be remiss not to acknowledge that the NAEP administration was quite effective prior to the USOE interventions. Between fall 1971 and the end of 1974, NAEP successfully conducted the first round of assessments for five subjects: music and social studies in 1971-72, mathematics in 1972-73, and career and occupational development and writing in 1973-74. They also conducted the second assessment of science in 1972-73. They had designed and were in the field with first assessments of art and the index of basic skills and the second assessment of reading.

In addition, NAEP had published a large number of reports. They had published NAEP report cards[3] for four subjects: science in 1972, reading and mathematics in 1973, and writing in 1974, as well as other national reports listed in the *Directory of NAEP Publications* (NCES 1999). This directory provides lists of many other types of reports published during this period and thereafter: state reports, abbreviated documents, technical reports, focused reports and special studies, conference proceedings and commissioned papers, and subject area objectives, frameworks, and achievement levels. The NAEP program was indeed meeting its overarching goal "to provide information useful to educational decision-makers and practitioners in identifying problems, setting priorities, and determining progress."

# Notes

1. Special appreciation is due to Iris Garfield (NCES monitor for the NAEP project from 1971 to 1975) for her help in preparing this document. It is very difficult to recall details of actions taken a quarter of a century ago without files or records. A one-page entry in Iris' job description was the only record we had of NCES monitorship of the NAEP project; it provided the skeleton for this chapter. The absence of records is responsible for vagueness about dates or the sequence of some activities. I also want to acknowledge my appreciation to staff at the National Center for Education Statistics. Unfortunately a great deal of material that might have been useful was destroyed in the last move made by center staff, but Suzanne Triplett was helpful in retrieving budget information and Steven Gorman sorted through the center's files and found several publications that provided useful information. Among these was James A. Hazlett's doctoral dissertation, *"A History of the National Assessment of Educational Progress, 1963-73,"* which stimulated my memory and provided a number of duly-cited details about NAEP-related actions of the Education Commission of the States that were new to me.

2. At that time ECS was a compact of 45 states, Puerto Rico, and the Virgin Islands, whose purpose was to promote cooperative action in improving education at all levels. Each state could name seven members of the commission, usually the governor, two representatives of the state legislature, and four others appointed by the governor (Hazlett 1974, pp. 224-25).

3. NAEP report cards report main assessment data, address the needs of national and state policy makers, and present the results for selected demographic subgroups defined by such variables as gender, race or ethnicity, and parents' highest level of education. Report cards present primary findings and are typically the first reports to be released after data analysis (NCES 1999).

# CHAPTER 6

# A New Design for a New Era

*Archie Lapointe*

In 1978, when the National Institute of Education requested proposals for the National Assessment of Educational Progress, they received a single submission. The Education Commission of the States (ECS) had been managing NAEP for almost ten years and submitted the sole proposal.

The NIE engaged a panel of reviewers to evaluate the ECS proposal. After an initial review process, the four members who were present agreed that the proposal was inadequate and that NIE reject it. When the fifth reviewer, Gregory Anrig, commissioner of education for the State of Massachusetts, arrived, he pleaded with his four colleagues to alter their recommendation.

The reviewers finally suggested that NIE forward the panel's criticisms to ECS with a request that ECS resubmit the proposal after making appropriate changes. The staff of the Education Commission of the States reacted positively to the criticisms, changed the proposal, resubmitted it, and it was accepted. Another five-year contract with ECS was launched.

Anrig felt strongly that NAEP was an important asset, and he was unwilling to risk its sudden demise. He had been an official in the U.S. Office of Education responsible for the desegregation efforts in the 1960s and early 1970s, and he was well aware of the importance of the kind of information that NAEP was beginning to provide. He was also a colleague and great friend of Frank Keppel, who is widely considered to be the "Father of NAEP."

NAEP was a very important project to the Education Commission of the States. It was its largest single project, representing about two-thirds of its revenue; and the staff working on NAEP represented about 60% of the total staff of ECS. One suspected reason for the lack of any competitive proposals was the general feeling that the NAEP contract was the "property" of ECS. Since ECS membership included governors, important legislators, and chief state school officers from 48 states, it was generally believed that their political clout would be impossible to overcome. Therefore, none of the other organizations that could possibly implement NAEP, such as Educational Testing Service (ETS), American College Testing (ACT), or the major publishers, considered it reasonable to expend the effort to submit a proposal.

Early in 1980 Frederic A. Mosher, a program officer with the Carnegie Corporation, became concerned about the future of NAEP. Mosher had been involved with NAEP as a young professional at the Carnegie Corporation when the project was launched. He had attended, commented on, and later funded many of the initial meetings in the 1960s that imagined, designed, and created the National Assessment of Educational Progress. After following NAEP's progress rather closely over the decade of the 1970s, he was disappointed in the prospects for its future. Its funding from Congress was in decline, its data were not being widely used, and the project management seemed to be growing weary of addressing the constant technical and operational problems.

Mosher convinced the Carnegie Corporation, as well as his counterparts in both the Spencer and Ford Foundations, to fund an evaluation of the National Assessment of Educational Progress. He referred to the project as "an assessment of the assessment." He then approached a small Washington consulting firm called Wirtz and Lapointe. The questions Mosher asked Wirtz and Lapointe to examine were: Is there still a need for the national assessment? Should the project be continued? Should its objectives be altered or changed in any way to make the reports more useful and more effective?

Willard Wirtz had been Secretary of Labor during the Kennedy and Johnson administrations. He was deeply concerned about and committed to issues involving youth unemployment and, specifically, the transition from school to work. He knew about the existence of NAEP but had no feelings one way or the other about its effectiveness.

My career had included assignments at Educational Testing Service, general manager of the California Test Bureau-McGraw-Hill, senior vice president for Science Research Associates (SRA), and president of the National Institute for Work and Learning. While at SRA, I worked closely with Ralph Tyler, one of the creators of NAEP, who at the time was urging that all of the test publishers play some role in helping develop and implement the national assessment. However, most of the publishers viewed NAEP as a possible competitor and therefore a threat to their business.

Wirtz and I prepared a proposal, submitted a budget, and initiated what ended up being a two-year project attempting to address three major questions:

- Should there be a NAEP?
- If the answer is yes, should it be changed in any significant ways?
- How can it become more effective?

The project was launched in late 1980, and Wirtz and I relied heavily on Paul Barton, a policy specialist and at that time vice president of the National Institute for Work and Learning. In addition, Stephen Koffler, who at the time was director of testing and research for the state of New Jersey, took a leave of absence to join the team.

Recognizing the multidimensionality of the questions involved, it was decided that a council of several wise individuals would be invited to join the staff to consider the questions and to ponder ways in which NAEP could be made more effective.

Seven creative individuals representing significantly different backgrounds were invited to form an Assessment Policy Committee, later referred to as the "Council of Seven," to act as a sounding board, prod, and conscience and to guide the work of the team. These individuals were:

- Gregory Anrig, Commissioner of Education, Commonwealth of Massachusetts
- Stephen Bailey, professor, Graduate School of Education, Harvard University
- Charles Bowen, program director for education development, IBM Corporation
- Clare Burstall, deputy director of the National Foundation for Educational Research, England and Wales
- Elton Jolly, executive director of Opportunities Industrialization Centers, an organization dedicated to minority youth employment
- Lauren Resnick, co-director of the Learning Research Development Center, University of Pittsburgh
- Dorothy Shields, director of education, AFL-CIO

Each of the participants took a personal interest and responsibility for what was deemed to be a very important issue. During the course of the project, their discussions were candid, stimulating, and frustrating; and their opinions were both conflicting and complementary. Each viewed the potential of the national assessment to serve the needs of his or her own constituencies: the children in the schools of Massachusetts, minority dropouts looking for work, the need for skilled employees in a high-tech corporation. Steve Bailey's historical and policy perspectives continually broadened the debate, and Lauren Resnick's concern with learning and rigorous curricula enriched the discussions significantly.

The presence of Clare Burstall, from a different culture, lengthened the horizons even further. The independence, variety, and creativity of the British schools at that time represented a significant contrast to the focus in the United States on what was then referred to as "the back to basics movement."

In addition to these principal players, it was agreed that many other individuals and organizations would be asked to provide input concerning how to improve the National Assessment of Educational Progress. The project's final report lists more than 150 individuals who were invited to submit written comments and opinions or to agree to an in-depth interview probing various questions related to their potential interest in NAEP, its findings, or its continued existence. Many of these were educators in the schools across the country who had participated in the national assessment in the past. Others were associations of parents, teachers, and school administrators. Also invited to participate were policy makers, state legislators, school board associations, both state and local organized labor, and representatives of large industries. Finally, measurement experts from both the United States and abroad were asked their opinions about the NAEP experiment. As the project progressed, responses were collated, tabulated, and discussed at meetings of the Council of Seven.

During the initial year of the project, the Wirtz and Lapointe staff attended all of the meetings of the Assessment Policy Committee as it progressed. ECS graciously opened its archives and its operations and invited the participation of Wirtz and Lapointe personnel at ECS staff retreats, planning sessions, and press conferences. Reciprocally, Wirtz and Lapointe shared the information it was collecting with the ECS staff and management and elicited their reactions.

The work of this project was described in the forward to its final report, *Measuring the Quality of Education: A Report on Assessing Educational Progress* (Wirtz and Lapointe 1982).

> Although this report will inevitably be taken as passing judgment on the National Assessment of Educational Progress (NAEP), this will miss both its purpose and any real value it may have. What is set out here will be worthwhile only as it informs the political process that is shaping the Assessment's future course. Realizing this has prompted particular effort to make the report more than an expression of merely personal points of view.

These meetings with the Council were extraordinary personal and intellectual experiences. The inquiry and discussion started from examination of the broad concepts of educational assessment, and this became the context for considering the National Assessment itself. It was the Council's suggestion and eventually its decision to shape the entire report in terms of the Assessment's potential role in developing higher and more effective educational standards. Where we [Wirtz and Lapointe] had been timid about this, the Council moved boldly. They were right.

In 1982, the Wirtz and Lapointe study concluded that "educational standards are here to stay, and that the Assessment's future depends on its capacity to improve their effectiveness." The report then identified 13 separate recommendations to guide future efforts toward a more effective national assessment.

1. The national assessment should be continued because, if it did not exist, a similar program would have to be initiated.
2. Two curriculum subjects should be assessed each year for cost efficiency.
3. Testing time for each assessment should be increased from one hour to two.
4. NAEP should "be expanded to provide state-by-state and locally useful results."
5. Age levels, 9, 13, and 17 should be replaced by grade levels, 4, 8, and 12.
6. The standard-setting process should be broadened to include wider participation from various sectors of society.
7. The assessments should include a broader range of question types.
8. Reports of individual item-level data should be replaced by more useful aggregated "scores" of curriculum "domains" and sub-domains.
9. NAEP should develop and maintain a fuller research and development program.

10. NAEP should be re-designed to maximize its service function to state and local education assessment and standard-setting agencies.
11. Assessment results should be reported in forms that can be used more easily by researchers, particularly those interested in possible causal relations between certain factors and student achievement.
12. Specific periodic assessments should be developed to illuminate particular policy issues.
13. There should be a National Educational Advisory Council that would synthesize data from multiple sources and take actions to improve the communication of the meaning and significance of education statistics.

## The 1983 Request for Proposals

The National Institute for Education (NIE) was determined to encourage a broad participation in the NAEP competition of 1983. Several publishers and nonprofit testing agencies were contacted to call their attention to the upcoming competition. A further step was taken to heighten interest by offering "planning grants" to organizations in order to prepare ideas and designs for possible proposals. Six organizations received the planning grants, and five ultimately submitted proposals for the five-year grant to administer the national assessment.

By that time, Gregory Anrig, a member of the Council of Seven, had become president of ETS. Because of the ongoing controversies surrounding ETS, largely related to its "dominance" in the measurement field and the major programs it administered for the College Board, Greg felt that it would be almost impossible for the NIE to award the grant to ETS. However, he did feel strongly that ETS should participate in the competition because it might generate some useful ideas for the improvement of NAEP.

Anrig asked Garley Forehand, a distinguished ETS researcher, to prepare a paper on the issues involved and a possible course of action for ETS. A large internal committee of ETS researchers and test developers was then convened under the chairmanship of

Sam Messick. Some outside consultants were included in the conversations. An agreement was reached with Westat to assume responsibility for the field administration should the team win, and a decision was taken to apply for a planning grant and to submit a proposal. Financially, it was the most expensive proposal ever written by ETS, largely because of the involvement of its most senior scientists, including Fred Lord, Sam Messick, and Al Beaton, and because the effort was identified as an "ETS Presidential Initiative." Indeed, Anrig personally read several iterations of the document as it was being developed.

The ETS proposal, titled "A New Design for a New Era," proposed 12 of the 13 recommendations included in the Wirtz and Lapointe study. The psychometric design was completely changed, freeing the student data from the "booklet-bound" situation that limited data-analysis options. By creating a Balanced Incomplete Block (BIB) design and using imputation techniques, background-question information could be compared across a large number of one-hour-long test booklets covering a broad range of curriculum content. The proposed, and later established, Technical Advisory Committee included some of the best minds in the country.

While there was a great deal of intellectual excitement created during the proposal-writing exercise, there was real concern within the senior management at ETS over the financial viability of the project. First, it was a grant, which meant that ETS had to make a modest annual financial commitment to the program. Second, NAEP was to be level-funded for the five-year period at 3.88 million dollars per year with no adjustments for inflation. Finally, ETS was proposing some dramatic and creative changes in design, and the risk of unforeseen problems was significant. Anrig cast the deciding vote, and the proposal was submitted by the deadline.

The first series of clarifying questions submitted to ETS asked the company to discuss the possible ramifications of awarding this national project to the largest and most influential test company in the country. ETS proposed establishing a separate center within ETS that would report directly to the president in order to "insulate" the project from the other programs administered by the company. I was to act as the executive director of the project.

Immediately after the grant was awarded, Anrig and I appeared before many education and policy groups in Washington and at numerous conventions across the country, describing what was planned for the national assessment and inviting opinions and recommendations. The dialog was sometimes fruitful, but more often it was disappointing because of the meager awareness of NAEP by most of these leaders.

It was decided by the new Assessment Policy Committee, then chaired by William Cody (Kentucky Education Commissioner), that a concerted effort would be made to implement an aggressive and consistent campaign to publicize the findings of NAEP. An outside book designer was engaged to design each new NAEP report, page by page, so that lay readers would be attracted to the publications and be able to easily understand the prose and the data. Instead of the previous 3,000 copies, 25,000 copies of each report were distributed nationally.

Over the subsequent five years, press conferences were held at the National Press Club in Washington, D.C., with appearances and comments by the presidents of the two major teachers unions and a variety of educational and policy personalities. Cornell University professor Carl Sagan and an MIT physicist presented their reactions to the science data, as did the president of the National Geographic Society after the geography results were disclosed. Officials from the National Council of Teachers of Mathematics and selected social scientists defined the significance of NAEP data, and reading and literacy experts debated phonics, whole language, and basic literacy from NAEP's podium. CBS produced two one-hour TV specials on education that featured NAEP data. The "Today" show regularly discussed the latest NAEP results.

When President Reagan declared war on adult illiteracy, Secretary of Education Terrel H. Bell asked NAEP to use its assessment design to develop and administer the Young Adult Literacy

Study. Working with Westat, ETS collected and reported literacy data on young Americans aged 16 to 25 in 1987. The National Adult Literacy Survey (NALS) expanded that study in 1990 to include all American adults from age 16 to 100. That project also used NAEP technology, though it measured different content and skills: prose, document, and quantitative literacy.

The recommended and proposed state-by-state change to NAEP was finally adopted in 1990, after Congress had approved a "trial" state assessment. Thirty-seven states, the District of Columbia, and two territories volunteered to participate in the first such assessment, involving eighth-grade mathematics.

Finally, another use was made of the NAEP design when two international studies were conducted by ETS: International Assessments of Educational Progress (IAEP) I and II. Six countries participated in the first, and 20 countries were involved in IAEP II. The design of these assessments had a significant effect on the Third International Mathematics and Science Study (TIMSS), which incorporated many NAEP features.

# CHAPTER 7

# Making NAEP
# State-by-State

*Ramsay Selden*

When it began in the 1960s, NAEP specifically was designed *not* to provide comparisons among states. This was done for political reasons, so that the assessment program would be palatable to the education community and to the states. It is not insignificant that NAEP was conducted initially by the Education Commission of the States, an organization representing governors, chief state school officers, state legislators, and state board members. This gave the states control of the program, ensuring that it would not be used to compare them.

By the early 1980s, the political climate had changed. *A Nation at Risk* and other reports called the condition of the education system into question, and the country was looking for ways to reform the system and to hold it accountable. The Education Department's Office of Planning and Evaluation issued what were referred to as wall charts: state-by-state compendia of the best available data on the condition of the education system in each state. Data on spending, enrollments, and dropouts were included, as were average SAT and ACT scores, the best available achievement measures. While there were shortcomings in many of the data that were provided, it was widely recognized that state comparisons were healthy and appropriate.

In the climate of concern about the health of the U.S. education system, the states no longer could resist being monitored and compared. States were the main players, responsible for the majority of funding, for the curriculum, for standards governing teaching, and for other key factors. At the same time, it was recognized that the states had to provide open and comparative data to the public, to policy makers, and to educators.

The Council of Chief State School Officers (CCSSO) played a key role in developing state-by-state achievement data. In a critical series of policy actions and organizational developments, CCSSO endorsed the concept of state-by-state comparisons and set up a structure for developing good data for comparing the states. In policy positions at its annual meetings in 1983, 1984, and 1985, CCSSO endorsed complete and valid comparisons of the states' education systems and set up a State Education Assessment Center to design methods to collect and disseminate the information.

The key issue the CCSSO center had to address was comparative achievement assessment. This was the *sine qua non* of state-by-state comparisons. In 1985 no satisfactory program existed to provide valid achievement measures across states. Average SAT and ACT scores were available for each state, but the students taking those tests were not a representative sample of students in the states. In addition, college-entrance exams are questionable measures of the overall achievement of students or of the output of the education system.

Providing comparative data for the states faced two problems. One was that a means was needed for acquiring this data; the other concerned what to test.

There were two main options for collecting the data. Either the NAEP program could be changed to collect it, or a new testing program could be created especially for this purpose. Congress commissioned a panel, co-chaired by Lamar Alexander and Thomas James, to determine whether NAEP should be adapted to a state-by-state program and, if so, how. The panel concluded that NAEP could be used in this way if it were done carefully and appropriately. The panel also addressed the policy structure that should be put in place if NAEP were taken in this direction.

Among other decisions, the panel argued that NAEP would need to be organized in three parts: the NAEP project or contractor to conduct the program, the National Assessment Governing Board (NAGB) to set NAEP's content and other significant policy parameters, and the National Center for Education Statistics (NCES) to provide technical direction and oversight. The panel stressed that this structure was essential in order to keep the policy and technical aspects of NAEP independent of each other.

It was not a foregone conclusion that NAEP would be used for state comparisons. During 1985 to 1987, this was debated regularly at the National Conference on Large-Scale Assessment. Archie Lapointe, the director of the NAEP program, argued for its use; I and others raised questions about using NAEP and emphasized that other options had to be explored. Concerns included whether this would overburden NAEP, what the costs would be, whether NAEP was the best mechanism from a technical standpoint, and so on. One major concern was that, while NAEP was a good overall assessment and was a leader in some areas, such as writing, it was not state of the art in all areas.

In the end, CCSSO agreed to adapt NAEP into a state-by-state program. This avoided creating a redundant new program at the national level, and it saved CCSSO's members the additional cost that would have been involved in creating a new program.

The other problem was what to test. Because states set their own priorities for education, it was conceivable that large differences in what was taught might exist among the states. In that case, consensus would be difficult, if not impossible.

Working in conjunction with NAGB and NCES, CCSSO and others in the field developed consensus frameworks for the state-by-state assessments. In 1987, the first framework, for the 1990 mathematics assessment, was agreed on; and this was followed by consensus frameworks for reading, science, U.S. history, geography, the arts, and civics. This process resulted in a statement of the subject matter and related cognitive skills to be assessed in each subject.

The consensus-setting process used a carefully developed structure. Participants from all levels in the education system were involved, as were parents, business people, and policy makers. The process was open and involved a great deal of advise and consent, including comments from a wide array of communities.

CCSSO structured its part of the process in two committees. A planning committee consisted of curriculum specialists, teachers, researchers, and other specialists in the particular subject area. The policy committee included representatives from the policy-making community, businesses, parents, and the public. The planning committees would develop initial proposals of the assessment frameworks and testing recommendations, and the policy committees would review and respond. States also were given several opportunities to review and respond to the directions being developed for the assessments.

In this process, attempts were made to identify current directions of instruction in the country, major approaches in the field, and the extent of diversity among state curricula, local curricula, and teacher practice. This was seen as an essential base on which to make decisions concerning subject matter. In mathematics, the key question was how much of the emerging national voluntary professional standards should be incorporated. In reading, the issue of phonics versus other approaches had to be addressed. In science, U.S. history, geography, and civics, instructional consensus and directions had to be determined. A gratifying quality of this effort was that, in every subject, the opportunity was taken to set an ambitious standard. The participants could have lobbied for a least-common-denominator approach or for expectations that would not really stretch the system, but in no case did they elect to do that. It is also a credit to NCES and NAGB that they never directed or rejected the recommendations for what should be assessed. They always honored the consensus process.

An interesting part of this process was a give and take that existed between the consensus-panel recommendations and the state of the art of assessment in NAEP. Typically, the planning groups wanted NAEP to move to a more technically sophisticated approach in some areas. For example, many participants wanted the assessments to include open-ended items or other activities beyond multiple-choice items. Also, the planners typically wanted the assessment to measure more sophisticated aspects of learning in the subject, something that was consistent with the drive to establish the NAEP achievement levels, including the advanced one. The push for these innovations and changes often resulted in enhancing NAEP's methods.

Shifting NAEP to a state-by-state program was a very interesting period in its history. The excitement surrounding the process and the profundity of the issues involved reflected the unique events that were occurring in education at that time: assessing the quality of our system, striving for reform, and putting a focus on the states.

CHAPTER 8

# A History of the National Assessment Governing Board

*Mary Lyn Bourque*

The National Assessment Governing Board (NAGB) was created by federal legislation and signed into law in April 1988 (Public Law 100-297, 1988). The bill, sometimes called the Stafford-Hawkins Act after the legislators who introduced it in Congress, covered the reauthorization of the National Assessment of Educational Progress (NAEP) that had been in existence since 1969.

Like many federal programs, NAEP was created in response to a perceived need to report to the American people on the academic progress of students. Just as NAEP was a congressional response to a perceived need, the creation of NAGB was a congressional response to a report by Alexander and James (1987) that included among its recommendations the creation of an independent policy board for NAEP. This policy board would have a broadly representative and bipartisan composition. Members would serve for short terms (for example, three to four years) and would be responsible for setting policy for the NAEP program in every area from assessment content to assessment design, standards, and reporting. The Alexander-James report, along with the Commentary by the National Academy of Education, formed the basis for the Stafford-Hawkins Act (Public Law 100-297, 1988).

This chapter is not a scholarly, in-depth study of NAGB, but a history of how NAGB carried out the major congressional tasks with which it was charged. I was a staff member and was intimately involved in all but the first two official NAGB meetings, and I was on two board committees for 12 years, the Achievement Levels and the Design and Methodology committees.

## The Composition of NAGB

The 1994 reauthorization of the legislation specified that NAGB would have 25 members, including two governors or former governors and two state legislators from different political parties, two chief state school officers, one local superintendent, one representative each from a state and local board of education, three classroom teachers (one each from grades 4, 8, and 12), one representative of business and industry, two curriculum specialists, three testing and measurement experts, one nonpublic school administrator or policy maker, an elementary and a secondary school principal, and four members of the general public, including parents. The original legislation specified one less general public member and one less testing and measurement expert, for a total membership of 23. And, at the time this chapter was written, the most recent legislation (Public Law 107-334, 2002) placed restrictions on the selection of the four general public representatives: none may be employed by a local, state, or federal education agency; and at least two must be parents. In addition, the assistant secretary for the Office of Educational Research and Improvement (OERI) is an ex-officio (non-voting) member.

Since 1988, there have been more than 80 members serving on the National Assessment Governing Board. (Appendix E provides a complete list of NAGB members as of 2003.) The original membership of NAGB included those persons who were members of the Advisory Policy Council, an advisory panel to Educational Testing Service, on 28 April 1988, the date of enactment of the Stafford-Hawkins legislation. Thereafter, members were appointed by the secretary of education.

The NAGB Nominations Committee proposes to the secretary of education at least six candidates for each open category (NAGB 2000c). Individual nominees must match the category for which they are nominated at the time of appointment; they must have no apparent conflict of interest with NAEP or its contractors; and they must be willing to serve and be able to attend board meetings. The nominee pool must be diverse from a racial, ethnic, gender, and geographic perspective.

Board members' four-year terms begin on October 1. In 1994, the terms were changed to three years (Public Law 103-382, 1994); but the FY 2001 appropriations bill extended all current Board members terms by one year, that is, from three- to four-year terms.

There has always been a term limit in the legislation, allowing no more than two consecutive terms for members (see Public Law 100-297, 1988, and Public Law 103-382, 1994). However, this limit has been implemented independently for each NAEP reauthorization. That is, the Office of General Counsel for the Department of Education has interpreted the legislation as meaning that the term limit applies only for the duration of that specific legislation (for example, Public Law 100-297 applied from 1988 to 1994, while Public Law 103-382 applied from 1994 to 2000). Because the two pieces of legislation are independent of each other, members could serve for two terms under the earlier legislation and another two terms under the later legislation, for a total of four terms. Consequently, some members' service on the board has exceeded the usual six to eight years.

## NAGB's Structure and Role in NAEP

Public Law 100-297 (1988) was very clear in providing a list of NAGB responsibilities. This was not some maverick group of individuals that could go off on its own. It was a duly constituted body given a congressional mandate. Board members needed to take their charge very seriously. The legislation states that the board shall be responsible for:

- Selecting subject areas to be assessed.
- Identifying appropriate achievement goals for each age and grade in each subject area.
- Developing assessment objectives.
- Developing test specifications.
- Designing the methodology of the assessment.
- Developing guidelines and standards for analysis plans and for reporting and disseminating results.
- Developing standards and procedures for interstate, regional, and national comparisons.
- Taking appropriate actions needed to improve the form and use of the national assessment (Sec. 3403, (6)(A) ).

To meet these mandates, the board organized itself in a way that maximized its ability to handle many different topics while, at the same time, providing for full board involvement in the decision-making process. It adopted a standing committee structure, with *ad hoc* committees on an as-needed basis. Each member of the board serves on at least one committee, and each committee chair is also a member of the NAGB Executive Committee.

Recently, due to a realignment of the committee structure, there is now a chair and vice chair for each committee, both of whom are members of the Executive Committee. The Secretary of Education appoints the board chair each year, while the vice chair is nominated each year by the Executive Committee and elected by the full board.

One problem faced by NAGB from the start was just who was in charge of what. The legislation created a tri-partite, shared administration in which NAGB's role was not fully articulated, the relationship between policy and administration was blurred, and policy and technical issues had considerable overlap. Furthermore, when NAGB was instituted in 1988, there were some valid differences of opinion between a lay board of policy makers and the government staff who had been administering the NAEP program for nearly 20 years. These differences have been resolved over the years on an *ad hoc* basis, with some solutions being more satisfactory than others.

The National Assessment Governing Board had its first meeting in Chicago in late 1988. There is little or no written documentation for that meeting. The board's first officially documented meeting was in late January 1989, during which the members adopted its bylaws, formalized its committee structure, and tackled a number of other goals. One of the most important issues considered at the January 1989 meeting was developing a "consensus process" for determining the content of the 1992 reading assessment (NAGB 1989).

NAGB has never adopted a formal policy on the consensus process, even though it is one of the main policy charges in the legislation. However, I have observed the consensus processes in reading, writing, U.S. history, world geography, science, and civics. The principles described below in large measure are what govern the work of the groups. These principles, developed by the NCES under contract to the Council of Chief State School Officers (CCSSO), appeared in the NAGB January 1989 *Briefing Book*.

1. The process should be participatory, visionary, iterative, structured, explicit, stable, of sufficient length, and supported by adequate resource.
2. The discussion of consensus committees should be managed in a value-free way, so as to be free-flowing, to encourage opinions, spontaneity and creativity, and to avoid curtailing or intimidating the participants.
3. The consensus planning process is an activity that should be mutually educational for those involved.
4. Values and constraints governing the process should be stated up front.
5. Changes in the basic structure or rules of the consensus process while it is going on must be avoided.
6. Solicitation of comment by formal committees representing the field, either on content or procedures, is needed only in response to draft recommendations.
7. Board members must decide carefully with which people from state departments of education and other constituencies they will work.

8. Work on the subject-matter objectives and on procedural and analytic plans should be a staff function of the governance process, and review by the field should be part of the planning process.
9. The consensus process should be "self-evaluating."
10. The planning process should have a built-in buffer to ensure that recommendations that are made are thoughtful and appropriate. (NAGB 1989, Tab 2, pp. 10-14)

I have written about this process as employing the *participatory* and *balance* principles (Bourque 1999). The participatory principle reflects the opportunity for all points of view to be represented at the consensus table. The law requires this, and the board embraces this principle. The balance principle reflects the delicate weighting of what is with what should be, so that the NAEP assessment reflects what is being currently taught in America's classrooms as well as what should be taught. The hallmark of each NAEP assessment framework is its ability to achieve both principles in the development process and to be widely accepted as state-of-the-art in large-scale assessment programs.

The CCSSO report cited in the NAGB *Briefing Book* (1989) lists a series of recommendations for developing the objectives of the assessment. The first recommendation is:

> an explicit policy is needed by NAGB to direct those developing objectives on the balance of assessing what students do know and can do and objectives that are primarily based on the belief of what should be taught students. While "cutting edge" curriculum development should, to some degree, be included in the assessment, if it gets too far outside what schools are currently teaching the willingness to participate will diminish. This must [be] guided from a high-level governing body. (NAGB 1989, Tab 2, p. 14)

Achieving this principle has been accomplished by a stated goal in the Request for Proposal to contractors, by verbal guidance by NAGB staff, and by ongoing monitoring by the appropriate board committees.

There are several recommendations in the CCSSO report that deal with achieving a balance between state frameworks and earlier NAEP objectives with those objectives being developed in a current consensus process. However, the most striking recommendation states that the "NAEP planning process should become an event which *drives consideration and development of national goals for education in a subject,* through the process of helping determine what to test" (NAGB 1989, Tab 2, p. 17, emphasis added).

This recommendation directly supported the National Council of Teachers of Mathematics curriculum standards. The report suggested that, as other standards become available in science, history and civics, they also needed to be factored into the NAEP assessment development process. However, NAGB has tried to avoid adopting a strong position (favorable or otherwise) on any of the curriculum standards offered by the professional associations because even a back-door approach to a national curriculum is not consistent with its goals. This does not mean that the various curriculum standards are not considered in the assessment development process; they are. But curriculum standards are one of many sources that inform the board's work. Other sources include best practice, current research in the field, curricular issues in the field, policy papers having major national implications, feasibility for large-scale assessment practices, and cost, to mention a few.

One final CCSSO recommendation that warrants mention states:

> Over time, what each successive assessment measures in a subject should be dynamic, reflecting changes in what practitioners, scholars, and interested citizens believe should be taught. Otherwise, the assessment will discourage curriculum development and be unresponsive to innovation in the discipline or to circumstances in the world that justify change in our view of what is important for students to know and be able to do. (NAGB 1989, Tab 2, p. 19)

This has been a more difficult recommendation to deal with than one would at first suspect. It gets at the very heart of NAEP, that is, to report progress over time.

At its meeting in January 1989, the board was briefed on the NAEP reading anomaly. They were sensitized almost immediately to the importance of stability over time. As Beaton (1988*b*) said, "If you want to measure change, don't change the measure." Little did NAGB know back in 1989 that the issue of how to balance change and stability in the NAEP assessments would plague them for years to come.

The issue of both long-term and short-term trends has been considered on more than one occasion. During the 1996 NAEP redesign effort (Forsyth et al. 1996), NAGB decided to maintain the long-term trend assessments (some of these date back to 1969) on a less frequent basis (every four years instead of every other year), but failed to decide what it would do to handle short-trend assessments as new assessment frameworks come on-line in 2004 (mathematics) and 2006 (reading). NAGB also decided as part of its redesign policy to maintain assessment frameworks for no less than a period of 10 years.

Forsyth and his colleagues (1996) recommended a principle called *managed change*. Basically, this means *rolling* long-term trends that would remain stable for about 10 years, after which a new long-term trend assessment would move into place. For now, the original 1969 long-term trend would be maintained. However, when a new short-term trend assessment in a particular subject comes on-line, both the new and current short-term trend would be administered for at least one or two NAEP cycles, at which point the current short-term trend would become the new long-term trend and the 1969 long-term trend assessment would be retired. Such planned obsolescence is one way (perhaps the only way) to restrict the proliferation of "many NAEPs," each one administered to a separate sample of students, as is currently the case. This same notion of rolling trends was also recommended by the capstone report of the National Academy of Education's evaluation of the national assessment (Glaser, Linn, and Bohrnstedt, 1997).

The board has not adopted the principle of managed change, but perhaps in the future there will be no choice. The ultimate effect of not adopting a managed change approach to NAEP may be to lose the short-term trends that have been so influential in guiding state policies and moving the education reform movement forward during the last decade.

## NAEP Test Specifications

Another major responsibility of the board found in the legislation is to "ensure that all items selected for use in the National Assessment are free from racial, cultural, gender or regional bias" (Public Law 103-382, 1994, Sec.412 (e)(4)). The legislation also gives NAGB final authority on the appropriateness of cognitive items. The board committee responsible for the framework development in the subject areas implements both of these requirements. Usually this is done on an annual basis, with board reviews preceding the use of any items in field or operational testing. The committees are staffed by both NAGB and NCES staff members. NAGB policy also allows for retaining outside content experts if needed.

Since NAGB's inception in 1988, the board has developed assessment frameworks in eight content areas: reading, mathematics, U.S. history, world geography, science, writing, civics, and the arts (NAGB 1999*b*, 1999*a*, 2000*d*, 2000*b*, 1999*d*, 1997*a*, 1997*b*, and 1994*a*, respectively). For each framework there are concomitant test specifications that articulate the technical requirements for the particular assessment. Originally, these documents were not widely available because they identify specific content on the assessment, provide sample test items, and give the reader a fairly exact picture of what the assessment will look like when fully constructed. However, over the last decade the merits of making these publicly available became obvious; and they are now a regular part of the assessment distribution information.

During the consensus process on the 1990 mathematics framework, no test specifications were developed. Instead, the decisions about the details of the assessment were left to the operations contractor to develop. The lack of test specifications created serious gaps in the item pool and made the selection of items largely dependent on the contractor staff. This may have resulted in uneven content coverage and, perhaps, item development and selection decisions that were prejudiced by personal interests, rather than by NAGB policy. Consequently, developing test specifications has been part of every consensus effort since the 1990 mathematics development effort. In the more recent framework development projects, NAGB has encouraged and supported a Technical Advisory Committee to the consensus contractor for the sole purpose of ensuring that assessment development in general and the test specifications in particular are driven by attention to policy adopted by the board.

The test specifications lay out the item formats to be used, the ratio of multiple choice to constructed response items, the percentage of items to be devoted to each content area in the domain (for example, currently NAEP assesses algebra as about 25% of the mathematics assessment), and other critical technical factors that help construct the item pool. These decisions are no longer left to happenstance but are captured in the NAGB test specifications document.

## Background Variables

The third part of the assessment development involves the background variables included on the questionnaires for the students, teachers, and schools. The background variables include instructional practices, homework, preservice and inservice teacher preparation, and home-related variables.

NAGB currently has explicit policy authority over the selection and approval of background variables (see the No Child Left Behind Act, Public Law 107-334, 2002). Before this law, NAGB had only an advisory role in decisions about this part of the assessment. The final decision rested with NCES in consultation with the operations contractors. However, even under this advisory relationship, NAGB always developed recommendations on the set of variables that should be included and which accompany the frameworks as part of the consensus work. These were forwarded to NCES in an effort to provide input from the perspective of the consensus panels.

In the mid-1990s there was an effort to develop a parent questionnaire in order to improve some of the proxy variables for socioeconomic status. A parent questionnaire was proposed for field-testing with about 3,500 parents in 1995. Although the field test never went forward, some of the questions to which the board objected as being too intrusive were included in the student questionnaire for the 1995 NAEP field test. The board reviewed the questions on the survey only after that field test was administered, and they expressed concern and displeasure at being left out of the review loop. Following this incident, the board adopted a comprehensive policy on collecting and reporting of background data (NAGB 1995*a*). This policy required a board review of all background questions to be used in either field testing or operational NAEP and limited the nature of the questions to those that were directly related to reporting academic achievement on NAEP, as the 1994 legislation directed. In June 2002, Lawrence Feinberg, assistant director for reporting and dissemination at NAGB, told me that the board was working on a new policy for the background questions because the board is responsible for their selection and development on all subsequent NAEP assessments. The new policy, approved in 2003, entails establishing a framework for background questions.

In 2000 a contract was let by NCES to develop a framework for background variables that might cut across subjects. When this article was written, only a draft of that document was available; but the work represents a major advance in thinking about background variables for NAEP (Greenberg et al. 2001).

## Developing Achievement Levels

Undoubtedly the board's most controversial responsibility has been developing student performance standards for NAEP. This responsibility has concerned the board since its first meeting in 1989.

While Public Law 100-297 included more than one reference to setting goals, the legislative intent was not so clear.

At the first NAGB meeting one topic that received the board's attention was the interpretation of Public Law 100-297. There was more than one reference in that legislation to setting goals. One part of the statute directed the board to "identify appropriate achievement goals for each age and grade in each subject area to be tested" (Sec.3403, (6)(A)). In yet another section it stated that "Each learning area assessment shall have goal statements devised through a national consensus approach" (Sec. 3403, (6)(E)). The legislative intent was not so clear. However, in order to interpret the intent of Congress, the board leaned heavily on the advice of the National Academy of Education, which had been asked to review and comment on the Alexander-James report (1987). In that document, the panel members argued that "for each content area NAEP should articulate clear descriptions of performance levels, descriptions that might be analogous to such craft rankings as novice, journeyman, highly competent, and expert. Descriptions of this kind would be extremely useful to educators, parents, legislators, and an informed public" (Glaser 1987, p. 58).

The first policy statement on the NAEP achievement levels was adopted in May 1990 (NAGB 1990*b*). This was developed during the first 18 months after the board was formed and was completed in consultation with many technical and policy experts (Angoff 1989; Beaton 1989; Hambleton 1990; Johnson 1990). There would be three student performance standards: Basic, Proficient, and Advanced. (The term, "Below Basic," is not a standard set by NAGB, though it has been reported in all tables of achievement levels.)

The levels became the primary means of reporting NAEP results for the nation and the states. They were used for the first time to report the 1992 NAEP mathematics assessment. In developing the levels, a modified Angoff method would be used with a panel of judges who would develop descriptions of the levels and the cut scores on the NAEP score scale. While the policy was simple and straightforward, its implementation was complex and very contentious.

*The 1990 Mathematics Initial Effort.* The first standard setting was a learning experience for both the board and the consultants it engaged. NAGB did not realize the resources it would take to carry out a project of this magnitude, nor had NAGB members thought through many of the specific details of the process. Such questions as who should be impaneled as judges, how long would setting standards take, what kind of training should the judges have, how much information about NAEP do the judges need in order to complete their task, and many other questions went unanswered until it became clear that decisions were required. Consequently, the inaugural effort was carried out on an ad hoc basis.

The judges' panel met for three days in Vermont. A consultant conducted the meetings, with the NAGB staff assisting as needed. As this meeting unfolded, it became clear to all involved that the panel of judges was not appropriate for the task, time was too short, and a myriad of other unanticipated problems emerged. Some corrective measures were implemented later, for example, a follow-up meeting to complete the work and a series of replications in four states. However, the board decided that these initial levels would be a trial for 1990 and that the levels would be developed afresh in 1992. The full details of this initial effort are well documented (Bourque and Garrison 1991a, 1991b; Hambleton and Bourque 1991).

The board hired its own evaluation team to monitor and advise on the quality of the 1990 project and its outcomes. Stufflebeam, Jaeger, and Scriven (1991a) prepared a fairly negative evaluation report on the project. The report was submitted in draft form to the board in early August 1991. Simultaneously, the authors also distributed the draft (without NAGB's permission) to some 39 other "reviewers," many of whom were well connected with congressional leaders, their staffs, and other influential policy leaders in Washington, D.C. The board saw this as a direct strike against their work and as an effort to "kill" the achievement levels. The board quickly ended the contract (the correct language was "termination for the convenience of the government"), paid their bill, and asked the evaluators to do no more work.

This event often has been described in somewhat pejorative language, for example, "NAGB fired the evaluators." In fact, it was NAGB's prerogative as the contracting agency to terminate the work at any time. Because the content of the evaluation failed to provide NAGB with any insights on how to improve the process in the future, NAGB did not find it useful and chose to terminate.

This event still was being discussed at an American Educational Research Association symposium in 2000. Ronald Hambleton, the principal investigator for the 1990 NAGB standard-setting effort, was invited to make a presentation on program evaluation efforts from the stakeholders' perspective. In his remarks, Hambleton made two points: 1) he "respectfully disagree[d] with [his] three colleagues [Stufflebeam, Jaeger, and Scriven] who felt they prepared an 'accurate, clear, and fair' summative evaluation report," and 2) "achievement level setting on NAEP and in the country on state assessments and credentialing exams is better for the debate that took place in 1990 and 1991" (Hambleton 2000, p. 2). However, Hambleton's detailed rebuttal of the Stufflebeam evaluation was published in 1993 and was, in part, responsible for NAGB's moving to contract with ACT and taking on an ambitious research agenda over the next decade.

*The ACT Contracts, 1992-2000.* Following the 1990 standard-setting trial, NAGB decided to put more resources toward the effort and awarded a three-year contract to ACT for setting standards on the 1992 NAEP mathematics, reading, and writing assessments. ACT recommended several improvements over the 1990 effort, including using sampling to select a more representative panel of judges, intensive and improved training for panelists, and use of feedback during the process (American College Testing Program 1992). Levels were developed in reading, writing, and mathematics but were not recommended in writing (American College Testing Program 1993). The 1992 writing assessment had too few prompts to allow setting three achievement levels on the score scale. Standards for writing would wait until the 1998 assessment.

The board awarded two additional contracts to ACT, the first to develop standards on the 1994 U.S. history and world geography assessments and the 1996 science assessment, the second to develop standards for the 1998 civics and writing assessments. To date, NAGB has adopted achievement levels in seven NAEP subjects. All NAEP subjects tested during the last decade, except for art education, have student performance standards.

During the decade of development, ACT completed a number of research studies that are important for understanding the board's contribution to the field of setting standards. Reckase (2000) describes these in some detail in a report prepared during the last months of the most recent ACT contract. In addition, Loomis and Bourque (2001) also review a number of methodologies piloted, field tested, or used during the ACT standard-setting work.

During the entire last decade, a continuous barrage of evaluation reports provided extensive qualitative and quantitative analyses of the NAEP achievement levels. One researcher has said that NAEP has the most evaluated student performance standards in the world (Ronald K. Hambleton, personal communication, 1996). The Stufflebeam report (Stufflebeam, Jaeger, and Scriven 1991*b*) spawned a whole series of subsequent evaluations of the achievement levels. The first to follow was an investigation by the U.S. General Accounting Office (1993). This was followed by a series of reports that emanated from a five-year contract, authorized under the NAEP legislation, between the NCES and the NAE (Glaser, Linn, and Bohrnstedt 1992, 1993*a*, 1993*b*, 1996, 1997). Most of these reports made recommendations regarding the board's initiative to set levels. For example, in the second-year report that focused exclusively on the achievement levels, the NAE panel made the following recommendations:

1. Discontinue use of the Angoff method.
2. Discontinue reporting by achievement levels.
3. Invite experts to comment on the meaning of NAEP results and the desired performance standards.
4. Publish achievement levels separately from the official NAEP reports and report these as drafts or developmental.

5. Use percentile scores to monitor achievement in future assessments (Glaser, Linn, and Bohrnstedt 1993*a,* pp. xxiv-xxvii).

It was in this series of reports that the term, "fundamentally flawed," was used to describe the methods for setting the levels. In a second 1993 report that focused on the trial state assessment, the NAE panel recommended that:

> NAGB discontinue the use of the Angoff method to set achievement levels, discontinue reporting using the flawed 1992 levels [in reading], and not reinstate achievement levels as the primary reporting mechanism until the following conditions are met: (1) a new, more defensible way of reporting the achievement levels can be developed, (2) the achievement levels have been empirically evaluated prior to using them as the primary NAEP reporting mechanism, and (3) assessment content is better articulated with emerging national content and performance standards. (Glaser, Linn, and Bohrnstedt 1993*b,* p. xxviii)

A three-year contract between the U.S. Department of Education's Program Evaluation Services office and NAS followed the NAE long-term evaluation. The NAS evaluation concluded that "NAEP's current achievement-level-setting procedures remain fundamentally flawed" (Pellegrino, Jones, and Mitchell 1999, p. 182). The NAS panel also made the following recommendations in their final report:

> 5A. The current process for setting achievement levels should be replaced;
>
> 5B. NAEP's current achievement levels should continue to be used on a developmental basis only; and
>
> 5C. NAGB should explicitly communicate that achievement levels result from an inherently judgmental process. (Pellegrino, Jones, and Mitchell 1999, p. 183)

The NAS panel based its evaluation in large measure on the earlier work of the NAE and, therefore, reached similar conclusions.

Each of the evaluation reports cited above has been refuted by a long list of scholars (Cizek 1993; Hambleton 1993; Kane 1993*a,*

1993*b*; Bourque 1995; Hambleton et al. 2000). One of these rejoinders to the NAS evaluation was particularly explicit in its concerns regarding the conclusions reached by the NAS. It states: "Our review of the evidence suggests that Chapter 5 on 'Setting Reasonable and Useful Performance Standards' for NAEP constitutes a one-sided, incomplete and inaccurate accounting of the NAGB/ACT standard settings conducted during this decade. As such, Chapter 5 of the NAS Report is a disservice to NAGB, educational policymakers, educators, and the public" (Hambleton et al. 2000, p. 13).

Many of these rejoinders have laid out in clear terms the technical improvements that were made in the process over the years. There is evidence to suggest that the Angoff method is not "fundamentally flawed" as some have claimed (Reckase 2000). Yet even today there are those who remain convinced that this has been an inappropriate initiative by NAGB. Some still believe that 1) NAGB should not be setting levels in the first place; 2) the Angoff method is fundamentally flawed; 3) the levels adopted by the board are set too high; and 4) the levels are not reasonable and valid as specified in the current legislation.

In late 1998 Congress again asked the board to examine the levels yet one more time in conjunction with the development of the Voluntary National Test. The authors of that self-study provide evidence for the validity and reasonableness of the levels (Bourque and Byrd 2000).

The evaluations have served a very important catalytic role in the whole field of standard-setting research. If all had been judged well, NAGB and its contractors, as well as others in the field, might not have pursued the research program so aggressively. Each evaluation during the last decade spawned yet more research. For example, the search for improved methods and the criticisms of the Angoff method have led to the development of many newer methods, including the Bookmark method (Lewis et al. 1998), the Generalized Examinee-Centered method (Cohen, Kane, and Crooks 1999), the Body-of-Work method (Massachusetts Department of Education 1998), and others. The work of such researchers as Hambleton and Plake (1995), Impara and Plake (1997), and others has been mounted because of the criticisms leveled against the Angoff method by evaluators of the NAEP achievement levels. The field is far better off today than it was 10 years ago, at least in part because of NAGB's tenacity, conducting its business as Congress intended.

NAGB's role needs to be put into the larger context. During the last decade, Title I legislation required student performance levels similar to the NAEP achievement levels. Similarly, 49 out of the 50 states now require students to reach goals similar, often nearly identical, to the NAEP achievement levels (Nellhaus 2000). It is not surprising that such reform activity precipitated the flood of research in the field.

## Resolving Technical-Policy Issues

A second sensitive area of NAGB activity is the confluence of technical matters and policy issues. This area became so contentious in the early 1990s that there was a change in the board's legislative mandate. The original 1988 legislation stated that the board was responsible for "developing guidelines and standards for *analysis plans* and for reporting and disseminating results" (Public Law 100-297, Sec.3403, (6)(A), emphasis added). In the 1994 legislation the above statement was abridged to include only reporting and dissemination plans, and four new conditions were inserted. The first stated that the board "shall design the methodology of the assessment, *in consultation with appropriate technical experts,* including the Advisory Council established under Section 407" (Public Law 103-382, Sec.412, (e)(1)(D), emphasis added). The second condition expanded the Advisory Council on Education Statistics (ACES) from its original nine members to 18 members. The third condition is found in the law under a new subheading, titled "*TECHNICAL*." It states, "In carrying out the duties required by paragraph (1) [references the board's duties], the Board may seek technical advice, as appropriate, from the Commissioner and the Advisory Council on Education Statistics and other experts" (Sec. 412 (e)(5)). The fourth and final condition changes the membership of the board from two testing and measurement experts to *"three testing and measurement experts, who shall have training and experience in the field of testing and measurement"* (Sec.412 (b)(J), emphasis added).

Targeted changes in legislation such as those described above do not happen without a concerted effort. Congress did not divine such changes by themselves. They were encouraged to make such changes. There were those who thought that a lay board such as NAGB had no business having policy authority over technical matters. There are those who still remain convinced that this area should be one where the board treads lightly. The Castle bill described later in this chapter would refocus this approach and give the board full responsibility for both policy and the administration of NAEP.

*Statistical Analysis of NAEP Data.* One of the more important technical issues that the board has dealt with over the years is the analysis of NAEP data. Initially, the board was in no position to change any of the analytical techniques already in use by the operations contractor, ETS. However, the board made every effort to learn about the policy ramifications of each technical issue. For example, as early as the August 1990 meeting, the board was discussing the merits of cross-grade scaling versus within-grade scaling. At the same meeting, board members discussed the possibility of adding Asians as one additional subpopulation in the 1992 assessment (NAGB 1990*a*).

*District and School Assessments.* Another technical area remaining largely unresolved today is the issue of assessing districts and schools. The 1984 legislation, Public Law 98-511, was silent on state and below-state assessments. The federal government did not report any NAEP results below the regional level; but jurisdictions, for example, states and local districts, could oversample and report their own data at their own expense. The Southern Regional Education Board (SREB) did collect data at their own expense on state performances long before the trial state assessments were authorized by statute.

The 1988 legislation (Public Law 100-297) specifically prohibited anyone from collecting below-state data, no matter who was paying for it. The law did authorize the trial state assessment.

The prohibition on district and school assessments was lifted in the 1994 reauthorization. At that time the board expressed an interest in pursuing this as a policy option for interested districts residing in states participating in NAEP.

There are approximately five districts in NAEP that are "naturally occurring" districts in which no oversampling of schools is required in order to reach a sample large enough to report the results. There are several other districts, mostly in large urban areas, that would require modest oversampling in order to meet the requirements for school sample size.

In 1996 NAGB encouraged eligible districts to participate in this initiative. Although more than 20 districts expressed initial interest, only one, Milwaukee, actually received a district report.

In 2000, however, a Great City Schools proposal was submitted to the board and forwarded to Congress for consideration in the reauthorization in 2001 (Council of Great City Schools 2000). This proposal outlined a trial *city* assessment, starting with the 2002 NAEP, modeled after the trial *state* assessments begun in 1990. NAGB gave full support to this at their November 2000 meeting and considered sample designs and cost proposals at the March 2001 meeting. Five of the largest NAEP districts (New York City, Chicago, Atlanta, Houston, and Los Angeles) participated in the 2002 trial district assessment program in reading, and results were released in July 2003. Reactions to the trial urban assessment will be watched very closely in this new age of accountability.

*The 1996 Redesign Policy.* The 1996 NAEP redesign policy was an effort by NAGB to change some of the fundamental assumptions of the NAEP design (NAGB 1996*a*). Some of the major features of the redesign called for:

1. Measuring all subjects identified in the Goals 2000 legislation.

2. Refocusing NAEP reports for the American public.
3. Reducing time lag between data collection and reporting.
4. Simplifying NAEP trends.
5. Moving NAEP into the technology age through innovative assessments.
6. Achieving balanced measurement by stability of frameworks and an appropriate mix of item formats.

The policy plan was far-reaching and forward-thinking. In review, it received support by a broad number of technical experts (see, for example, Forsyth et al. 1996). The redesign has been implemented in at least two stages by NCES since its adoption in 1996. Since much of the redesign work is contingent on contractual agreements between NCES and the operations contractors, it has been necessary to phase in various parts of the plan over a period of years. Not all the policy goals have been achieved, but it is hoped that future changes in NAEP will support states' use of the data to inform policy decisions and state reforms.

*Accommodations and Exclusions in NAEP.* The issue of accommodating children with special needs is clearly an area in which the political and technical aspects of NAEP are joined. Since passage of the Americans with Disabilities Act in 1990 and the Individuals with Disabilities Education Act in 1997, providing special accommodations for children who are not proficient in English or who have special needs is a requirement in most states.

NAEP also offers some limited accommodations on all assessments. These first were provided in the 1996 NAEP mathematics and science assessments. However, these nonstandard administrations have not been included in the NAEP reporting samples. There are several issues that still need to be resolved before an aggregated NAEP reporting sample will include both standard and nonstandard administrations.

First, there is the issue of including or excluding particular students in the sample. This decision usually is made at the local level using students' individual education plans (IEPs). However, the IEPs often require a *modification* in the assessment, rather than an accommodation. Because modifications are likely to result in a change in the construct being measured, they are not allowed in NAEP. For example, one common modification for reading tests is to read the test aloud to the student, which would change the nature of what is being assessed in NAEP. During the 1998 cycle, several states' exclusion rates soared over rates in previous years. An investigation found that these states required modifications that NAEP does not allow.

Second, states do not have consistent policies for developing and implementing student IEPs. Since the IEP drives the assessment conditions for students, NAEP needs to develop guidelines and standards for the use of these in making NAEP assessment decisions.

So far, the NAEP long-term trend assessment has resisted change in this area, and no accommodations are allowed. However, the short-term trends in reading, mathematics, U.S. history, world geography, and science have at least two data-trend points. The changing inclusion/exclusion rules and nonstandard administrations undoubtedly have created unknown changes in the student samples and, consequently, have had an unknown influence on trends in these subjects.

NAGB has supported an aggressive research agenda in this area, and NCES engaged the National Institute of Statistical Sciences (NISS) to provide advice on inclusion policies for large-scale assessments (Jones and Olkin 2000). For reporting 2002 NAEP performance at the national and state levels, results were aggregated over both standard and accommodated samples.

## Reporting and Dissemination Policy

NAGB's first policy statement on reporting and disseminating NAEP data was adopted in November 1990 (NAGB 1990c). The guiding principles governing reporting of NAEP data included accurate and timely results; uneditorialized text free from partisan political considerations; comprehensive information on sampling, methodology, scoring, and scaling; and achievement data informed by contextual information. With respect to disseminating NAEP data, the board's guiding principles supported a wide distribution network; identified NAEP's key audiences as teachers, principals, and parents; and encouraged the notion of customized materials for different audiences.

This policy was not embraced by Christopher T. Cross, the Assistant Secretary for OERI, who believed that the policy went beyond the authority given to the board in the authorizing statute. However, the board stood its ground, and the policy did not change (NAGB 1991).

The 1990 policies that would govern NAEP reporting were partitioned into three broad areas: 1) report preparation and content; 2) public release of NAEP results; and 3) dissemination.

*Policies on Report Preparation and Content.* The policy authorized the preparation of NAEP reports by the commissioner of education statistics in accordance with the standard NCES clearance and review procedures (sometimes referred to as "adjudication"). This initial policy disallowed causality statements in NAEP reports unless strongly supported by the NAEP data.

The board also went on record for the first time to state that the achievement levels shall be the primary means for reporting NAEP results. This was the first of four different occasions when the board adopted such a resolution (see NAGB 1992, 1995*b*, 1996*c*). Because this was the first time that state results would be reported, NAGB authorized the inclusion of contextual variables, both those collected by NAEP questionnaires and co-statistics available from other reliable sources, (for example, per capita income, pupil/teacher ratios, average teacher salaries, etc.).

*Public Release of NAEP Results.* The public-release policy is quite clear in its intention, stating that:

> Public reporting and release procedures for NAEP shall be apolitical, similar to those of other Congressionally-mandated data-gathering programs. By insulating NAEP from partisan political considerations, the release procedures should serve to uphold the credibility of NAEP data and to encourage the continued voluntary participation of schools,

> school districts, and states in NAEP surveys. (NAGB 1990c, p. 3)

The policy also required the commissioner to prepare a release plan to be approved by the board in advance of the public release. Similarly, the board required review copies of the report 10 days in advance. The commissioner was designated as the federal official to release the results. Both NAGB and NCES could invite speakers to provide commentary on the results. Supplementary reports could be available at the release if their authors and sponsorship was clearly identified. All nonofficial reports and materials required prior approval by the board for inclusion in the press materials. Embargoed materials could be made available in advance, and the board normally would issue press statements at the time of a release.

*Dissemination.* NAGB pledged to consult with education, business, and civic organizations in order to improve the "form and use of NAEP," as stipulated in the legislation (Public Law 100-297, 1988). The policy also pledges NAGB and NCES to making concerted efforts to disseminate NAEP to and through organizations of parents, teachers, school board members, principals, and other educators. Similarly, the policy encourages NAEP presentations and briefings by NAGB, NCES, and their staffs, warning that inappropriate interpretations and conclusions of causality are disallowed.

In the mid-1990s the board engaged the services of a public relations firm to examine NAGB's dissemination strategies and to conduct focus groups with various NAEP publics. The Widmeyer Group report (Widmeyer and Blaunstein 1993) was thorough and forward-looking, recommending 35 dissemination approaches to ensure that the NAEP message would receive wide circulation. The price tag was estimated between $700,000 and $800,000.

Unfortunately, the recommendations and suggestions came at a time when NAEP was not awash with federal dollars, and many of the good ideas never materialized. NCES reviewed the report but found that it could not implement many of the suggestions for cost reasons. However, NCES did agree to include some new dissemination initiatives in the next round of requests for proposals with the operations contractors (NAGB 1994*b*).

*Ten Years of NAEP Reporting*. In late 1998 the Reporting and Dissemination Committee undertook a 10-year review of its policies and procedures for reporting NAEP. By and large, the policies adopted in November 1990 have withstood the test of time. There have been some modest amendments, including accommodation to the NAEP redesign and several smaller policy statements covering such topics as the formats for state-by-state comparisons or prohibitions on the use of adjusted scores in reporting NAEP data.

The board adopted a streamlined and consolidated policy the following year, reaffirming the principles that had been governing NAEP reports for a decade. However, there are several significant differences between the 1990 and 1999 policy statements.

First, as a result of the 1996 redesign, NAEP's primary audience was redefined as the general public, not simply parents, teachers, and school administrators, as in the 1990 policy. Second, the board reaffirmed the importance of reporting NAEP results using the achievement levels. Third, the new policy reaffirmed the importance of insulating NAEP from political influences.

This latter point has been a difficult one for the board from time to time. For example, in mid-1992 when George Bush was campaigning for president, he prematurely released embargoed reading results at a campaign rally (Rothman 1992). The board responded in writing to all parties involved, including then-Commissioner of Education Statistics Emerson Elliott.

Another incident occurred during the early stage of Al Gore's presidential campaign. The Vice President, without the knowledge or authorization of the board, invited himself to release the results of the 1998 reading assessment at the NAEP press conference. However, instead of releasing the short-term trend data (covering 1992, 1994, and 1998), Gore chose to focus solely on the 1994–98 gains and not to acknowledge the 1992–94 losses. Again, all parties were put on notice regarding the inappropriateness of the misinterpretation.

These events precipitated a change in NAGB's reporting policy. The 1999 *Policy Statement on Reporting and Dissemination of National Assessment Results* states that the "reporting and dissemination of National Assessment results shall be insulated from partisan political considerations and processes. The initial release of NAEP data shall be independent and apolitical, separated clearly from other programs and policies of the Department of Education" (p. 2). It continues:

> At press conferences for the release of NAEP results, the Commissioner of Education Statistics and/or his designees (NCES staff or representatives of the NAEP contractor or grantee) shall present major data findings. The National Assessment Governing Board shall select members to participate in each press conference to provide commentary about the meaning of test results. In addition, either the Commissioner or the Board may invite other officials or experts to comment on the significance of the results in accordance with the specific plan approved by the Board or one of its duly constituted committees. (p. 6)

For 10 years, the "official" press release generally came from the office of the Secretary of Education, even though the commissioner released the official results. This current policy changes the picture entirely, with the "official" press release now coming from NCES. This is not unlike the policy of other government agencies. For example, the bureau chief of the Bureau of Labor Statistics releases the monthly unemployment figures following a briefing for the Secretary of Commerce about 30 minutes in advance of the release.

The board hopes that this new approach to releasing NAEP data will protect the integrity of NAEP and maintain its credibility with the American public. A recent review of 10 years of press packets used at NAEP releases and the resulting news media stories has demonstrated that there have been marked improvements in reporting NAEP data over that period (Hambleton 2000). Hambleton reports that "Our findings revealed a complex pattern of NAEP score reporting by the press since 1990 but, in general, score reporting appears to have improved considerably over the time period" (p. 149).

## The VNT Era: From Napkin to Item Pool

The idea for an individual version of NAEP was born when the Clinton Administration asked staff at NCES what such a test would look like if it could exist. In February 1997 President Clinton announced the Voluntary National Test (VNT) in his State of the Union address.

Gary Phillips, deputy commissioner of NCES, recounted that the design of the VNT was first conceptualized on a napkin during lunch at a local restaurant. It would be modeled on NAEP and would use the NAEP frameworks in mathematics (at grade 8 only) and reading (at grade 4 only). The design would need to be adjusted to accommodate individual scores.

*Department of Education Contracts.* Initially, the U.S. Department of Education administered the project with funding from the Fund for the Improvement of Education (FIE) in the Secretary of Education's budget. The department contracted with the Council of Chief State School Officers and MPR Associates to develop test and item specifications for reading and mathematics. These test and item specifications would be based on the NAEP assessment frameworks but would accommodate individual student scores. This work was completed on 15 September 1997. The department also awarded a contract to the American Institutes for Research (AIR) Consortium to develop the item pool, construct student booklets, conduct linking studies, and conduct other research associated with the VNT development.

*Authorizing Legislation.* The initial implementation did not have supporting legislation. Congress caught up with the VNT about nine months later and, in an historic move, gave NAGB "exclusive authority over all policies, direction, and guidelines for developing voluntary national tests" (Public Law 105-78, 1997). This legislation moved the AIR contract from the Department of Education to NAGB and required the board to review the contract and make a decision to modify or terminate it within the first 90 days after enactment. This was intended to align the contract with the requirements of the legislation.

The conference report for Public Law 105-78 provides the intent of the Congress and specific recommendations not stated in the legislation. Of primary importance was the notion that the VNT be built on NAEP frameworks and that the VNT test specifications be consistent with NAEP's content and achievement levels. The conference report stipulated that the VNT be linked to NAEP "to the maximum extent possible."

*NAGB's Initial Review and Planning.* The AIR contract was, in fact, a contract with a consortium of major testing firms. The American Institutes for Research was the prime contractor, with seven sub-contractors, including the Council for Basic Education (CBE), CTB/McGraw-Hill, ETS, Harcourt Brace Educational Measurement, National Computer Systems (NCS), Riverside Publishing, and Westat. After the board's review, the work being conducted by CBE was deemed unnecessary to fulfilling the legislative intent; and that subcontract was terminated.

The original contract with the Department of Education was for a period of five years and in excess of $60 million dollars. The board's review of such a massive contract was not simple, especially because the completion date specified by Congress was 90 days from enactment of the law on 11 February 1998. The board appointed an ad hoc committee to conduct the review and to make recommendations to the full board at an extraordinary meeting held in January 1998.

The committee conducted an initial review of the department's original request for proposals (which articulated the scope of work) for conformance with the authorizing legislation and relevant NAGB policies. They also reviewed the contract proposals and all cost proposals. The committee recommended modifications to, rather than termination of, the contract, and the contract was renegotiated with the prime contractor (NAGB 1998). The contract was converted to a series of one-year contracts, renewable each year for a period of five years. The total five-year costs were projected at more than $40 million if Congress authorized all five years.

Funding for the VNT always remained separate from the NAEP/NAGB budget. Congressional appropriations continued to fund the program out of the Fund for the Improvement of Education, part of the discretionary funding in the Secretary of Education's budget.

*AIR Contract Work and NAS Evaluations.* The initial work on the VNT under NAGB's guidance got under way in early 1998. However, the legislation limited the use of fiscal year 1998 funding to test development and planning activities. Pilot testing and field testing, though being planned, were expressly not allowed.

The legislation also called for three National Academy of Science studies. The NAS studies looked at the issue of fairness, linking the VNT to commercial assessments, and the accuracy of the information that might result from the VNT (Feuer et al. 1999; Heubert and Hauser 1999; Koretz, Bertenthal, and Green 1999).

During this first year, NAGB proceeded carefully and cautiously. The original plans called for the VNT to be fully operational by the spring of 2000. Pilot testing would have been scheduled in the fall of 1998, field testing in the spring of 1999. NAGB's first move was to delay that schedule, postponing full operational testing until at least spring 2001.

*Policy and Administration.* Initially, the board committees had more questions than answers. However, the contractors and staff focused the agenda of each board committee so that policy decisions were made in a timely manner and with the benefit of board and committee discussions.

The Assessment Development Committees handled all aspects of test development, conducted all item reviews, monitored construction of test specifications in both subjects, and provided oversight guidance to the contractor's research. The Design and Methodology Committee was largely responsible for all the technical aspects of the testing, including pilot test and field test designs, test forms construction, linking the VNT to NAEP and to the grade 8 mathematics performance of American students on the Third International Mathematics and Science Study, and the use of accommodations on the VNT. The Achievement Levels Committee was responsible for ensuring that the VNT design would support reporting the NAEP achievement levels on the VNT score scale, while the Reporting Committee monitored development of reporting strategies.

From November 1997 through March 2001 the board worked to ensure that the VNT would be developed as Congress intended. By April 2001 there were more than 2,000 grade 8 mathematics items and nearly 2,000 grade 4 reading items linked to more than 100 reading passages. However, Congress called a moratorium on the VNT in 1999, limiting the allocation of funds solely to test development and prohibiting pilot testing of items and field testing of student forms.

At that time, the board stated that if Congress did not specifically authorize and fund pilot testing and field testing in the next appropriation, then the board would terminate the contract. In the FY 2001 appropriation, Congress did not authorize funding to continue the development work, and the prohibition on pilot testing and field-testing was not lifted. Therefore the board terminated the contract as of 22 December 2000. The contractor prepared well-documented electronic files of the item pools for NAGB in case the items might be used in the future (NAGB 2000*a*).

The board sponsored hundreds of hours of work with focus groups all over the country in an effort to meet their legislated responsibilities, namely, to articulate purposes for the VNT and the nature of "voluntary" and to deal with such thorny issues as data aggregation and reporting mechanisms. The contractors devoted hundreds of hours to research on important topics relevant to the success of such a testing program. Technical experts and the contractor's staff committed their professional resources to developing a high-quality item pool for the VNT. Millions of tax dollars were spent on this project, the outcome of which is doubtful. It would be unfortunate if such an investment of human capital and scarce fiscal resources could not be put to some good use in the future.

## NAGB's Future Role in NAEP

The No Child Left Behind Act (NCLB) was signed by President Bush in January 2002. It is making some very significant changes in NAEP. For one thing, NAEP has always been a low-stakes assessment. However, NCLB changes that and makes it a high-stakes test.

NCLB makes it mandatory for states and local districts to participate in NAEP assessments in both reading and math at grades 4 and 8. If states and districts do not participate in these assessments, they will not be eligible to receive funds under the Elementary and Secondary Education Act. Furthermore, the math and reading assessments will be conducted every other year.

While states' participation is mandated, individual students are not required to participate, nor are they required to "answer questions they are uncomfortable answering" (House Education and Workforce Committee 2001). In addition, parents may exclude their children from participation if they wish. Finally, state samples exempt home schools, home school students, private schools, and private school students from all testing requirements.

As a policy board for NAEP, NAGB has functioned quite effectively with its committee structure and four meetings each year. However, there now will be daily, even hourly, decisions that must be made in implementing NAEP. In the past, the board has resisted delegating authority to staff or to contractors. Yet, as the new legislation changes the nature of NAEP, the board will have a difficult time keeping up. If the board does not delegate some of its authority and functions to qualified staff members, the plan will fail.

# CHAPTER 9

# A View from the NCES

*Emerson Elliott and Gary Phillips*

By any measure, the most momentous change in the national assessment between 1980 and 2000 was to begin trials of state-by-state assessments, authorized by Congress in 1988 (Public Law 100-297, 1988). Of course, there were many other important elements in the 1988 amendments, including establishing the National Assessment Governing Board and authorizing achievement levels to interpret and report NAEP results. Other features of the law mandated maintenance of "valid and reliable trend reporting" in NAEP and required "appropriate actions needed to improve the form and use" of assessment. Each of these features created technical challenges for assessment designers and conductors.

Events surrounding government actions offer temptingly easy explanations for why NAEP was changed so significantly in 1988. Some obvious "causes" of those changes, the Study Group on "The Nation's Report Card" (Alexander and James 1987) and the 1983 report of the National Commission on Excellence in Education, *A Nation at Risk*, are certainly part of the story. Another part is the 1989 meeting of President Bush and the nation's governors in Charlottesville. Only the third meeting in history of the nation's leaders from both the national and state levels, its sole subject was education. Its chief outcome was agreement to establish national goals in education, which followed a few months later in 1990, and to monitor progress toward achieving them on an annual basis. These goals made state reporting of achievement data more urgent and visible as the principal means for reporting on progress toward the student learning goals, as well as more likely because of interest from the President and the governors. But the subsequent changes in the National Assessment of Educational Progress, and the debate about them, have roots extending back to the earliest concept for a national assessment of student performance.

The beginning of this chapter describes these roots and the later pages address the technical challenges. The portrayal makes no pretense of recounting the whole story of the national assessment. Rather, it selects from three time periods: the years of concept and early development, the decade or so following NAEP's first national testing, and the fast-moving changes in NAEP's context in the middle 1980s.

## The Founders' NAEP

In a 1962 testimony before Congress, U.S. Commissioner of Education Francis Keppel noted that there was "no present mechanism remotely comparable to the guidelines of the Bureau of Labor Statistics or the Bureau of Standards which would enable us merely to suggest levels of proficiency for our autonomous school districts" (Hazlett 1974, p. 353). Hazlett concludes that the commissioner was advocating academic standards. But Mr. Keppel's public commitment, set out in that testimony, was "to seek scholarly and expert advice in the desirability of developing voluntary national academic standards."

As he began his search for scholarly and expert advice, Commissioner Keppel stated his goal as testing "what a well educated person should know," rather than "an expert's idea of what should be known" (Hazlett 1974, p. 32).

At the first discussions of an assessment of student achievement, states were conceived as the logical level of reporting. Commissioner Keppel sought the counsel of one of the nation's most eminent contributors to twentieth century assessment, Ralph Tyler. Tyler became a key figure in these discussions; and he — along with others soon to be associated with the exploratory assessment efforts — viewed cross-state comparisons as highly useful additions for consideration of education policy.

Decisions about what should be included in the NAEP tests would be reached through consensus discussions among subject-matter specialists and nonspecialists. "The purpose is to obtain exercises to assess educational attainments, each of which either appears on its face to be valid or its significance can be explained to and understood by the interested laymen" (Hazlett 1974, p. 28, attributed to Ralph Tyler).

The NAEP design would draw on state-of-the-art testing technology. Tyler's plan was to conduct assessments on samples of students, since the intent was to assess achievement in schools or districts or in states, rather than on individuals. Matrix sampling also made it possible to use more items on NAEP than could be found in most standardized tests. For example, in an hour of testing, most standardized tests can administer only 50 to 60 items in a given subject because each student has to take all items. However, on NAEP, several hundred items could be administered because different students were taking different sets of items. The assessment would test general levels of knowledge, not be aimed at discriminating among individuals, as most standardized tests do. Test instruments would differ from those used in other tests. Items would have face validity so the public could believe they were good questions. Reporting would be by individual items (Hazlett 1974, p. 38).

But as elements of the plans for assessment became more public, strong opposition emerged. The American Association of School Administrators (AASA), the most vocal opponents, pronounced the proposal seriously flawed. In January of 1967, AASA sent a letter to its members recommending that they refuse to participate in the tryouts of these tests. Among the reasons advanced for this opposition were that common questions asked of students across the country would not allow for population and financial diversity, and also that a national testing program would be coercive, leading to teaching to the test and federal control over curricula (Hazlett 1974, pp. 186-87).

Tyler and his associates responded to this opposition with some modifications of the initial NAEP structure, especially geographic reporting. The NAEP design that was in place when the first assessments were conducted in 1969:

- Provided coverage of subject matter for population groups, rather than by smaller subgroups, localities, or individuals.
- Sampled students by age, rather than by grade.
- Reported results at the exercise level in addition to reporting by curriculum unit or topical areas.
- Administered different items to different students and provided greater coverage of the curriculum, while limiting analyses of trends and correlates with achievement.
- Concentrated almost exclusively on the assessment of cognitive skills, rather than including background and attitude questions that would suggest curricular and policy changes (National Institute of Education 1986, Appendix, p. 1).

Another activity begun by the founders of the national assessment was the annual "large-scale testing conference." In 1969 the assessment's staff director, Frank Womer, proposed that the commission meet periodically with state testing directors. State testing was beginning to develop rapidly in the early 1970s; and the NAEP technology, such as item development and sampling, could be adapted for use in state assessments.

Originally staffed entirely by ECS and attracting participants from just a few states, the conference now is sponsored by the Council of Chief State School Officers. The conference continues to draw large and growing numbers of participants because it serves as a forum for exchanging test items, testing technology, and analyzing the policy environment for testing. By the late 1980s, the conference had created a community of large-scale testers who had sophisticated knowledge about the purposes and conduct of the national assessment.

## NAEP Faces Its Critics

The features adopted for NAEP, moderating original concepts with practical political realities, provided a new basis for critical review. In 1976, NAEP was seen by the General Accounting Office

(GAO) as flawed for its lack of usefulness to education decision makers. Among the GAO recommendations was one to improve the interpretation of NAEP data. The report said:

> A factor contributing to the lack of interpretation of National Assessment data is the lack of standards against which test data can be compared to judge performance. An example of a performance standard might be: "80 percent of the 9-year-olds should meet this objective 90 percent of the time." . . . To increase the use and improve the usefulness of National Assessment data, we recommend that the Secretary require project management to . . . provide for comparison of its test results with performance standards by giving greater emphasis to developing the procedures needed to compare those results to generally acceptable non-Federal standards. (Comptroller General of the United States 1976, pp. 28, 35)

In their responses to the GAO report, both the Department of Health, Education and Welfare and the Education Commission of the States provided apparently positive reactions to the recommendation. But they pointed to the problem of finding or creating standards that would be appropriate for such comparisons.

Little followed from the GAO report; and in the early 1980s a survey of public opinion, reported by the director of the National Institute of Education — then the overseeing federal office — concluded that "NAEP was justly viewed as essentially a census of education progress, not as a tool to explain problems, to support particular solutions, or to predict future trends" (National Institute of Education 1982, p. 5).

There was a powerful reluctance to conduct the assessment with state representative samples and to provide comparisons based on performance standards. A 1982 study by Willard Wirtz and Archie Lapointe determined that "the Assessment [should] not be expanded to permit reporting of results on a state-by-state basis; but . . . arrangements [should] be made to facilitate use of the Assessment by state or local school agencies for comparisons with nationwide student achievement levels" (Wirtz and Lapointe 1982, p. 21).

The study went on to express concern about "translating statistical gibberish into terms people can understand" (p. 33), yet concluded that one possible alternative for reporting — based on setting standards for performance, as the GAO recommended — must not be undertaken by NAEP. Wirtz and Lapointe said:

> Setting levels of failure, mediocrity, or excellence in terms of NAEP percentages would be a serious mistake. Whatever educational standards are developed in this country will properly be made operative only at the local or possibly the state level. Even the making of judgments about what is "good" or "bad" is reasonable and responsible only in terms of particular educational environments. (p. 33)

Instead, the report called for an "independent council . . . with responsibility, among others, to improve public understanding of this type of data" (p. 33). Wirtz and Lapointe also called for a new research and development emphasis, drawing on and extending the state of the art in large-scale testing, as NAEP had set out to do at the beginning.

By the early 1980s, funding had eroded; and NAEP was barely maintaining its original technology. A large investment was needed to renew and update all aspects of NAEP, from subject objectives to final analysis and reporting (Wirtz and Lapointe 1982, p. 34).

As the Educational Testing Service (ETS) took over the assessment management responsibilities in 1983, there was renewed investment in these areas, as reflected in an NIE review, including:

- Emphasis on collection of grade data.
- Retention of age data, but standardized to the calendar year.
- Expansion in the number of background items and collection of much more background information.
- New data collection methods, including Balanced Incomplete Block (BIB) spiraled sampling.
- Reporting through behaviorally anchored scale scores (National Institute of Education 1986, pp. 13-14).

Many elements of the NAEP design have been consistent over a long period of time. Descriptions of the NAEP design in 1980, for example, could seem quite similar to descriptions from the first wave of testing in 1969, and in some ways not too distant from current ones. At the beginning of the 1980s, NAEP would use an objective-referenced approach to report on what students knew and could do.

> NAEP develops both general and age-specific objectives for each learning area assessed, and then, with extensive involvement of scholars, teachers, subject matter and curriculum specialists, and lay people, develops exercises (questions or items) designed to measure what youngsters know in these subject areas. (National Institute of Education 1982, p. 11)

There was matrix sampling to minimize burdens placed on schools and respondents. There were both multiple-choice and open-ended exercises. When the assessment was administered to students, a paced tape or exercise administrator in an interview situation read the items (except for the reading assessment), though after the early 1980s this was retained only for trend reporting.

Further advances during the 1980s were introduced to, or adapted by, NAEP. BIB spiraling, a variant of matrix sampling, made it possible to calculate correlations and cross-tabulations among exercises in different test booklets (National Institute of Education 1986, Appendix, pp. 4-5). Item Response Theory (IRT) was applied to NAEP to simplify the measurement and interpretation of group differences and trends over time (National Institute of Education 1986, Appendix, p. 9). Behavioral Anchoring shifted the NAEP reporting of percentages of correct responses on single exercises or sets of exercises to scale scores with descriptions of student competence and achievement corresponding to the scales.

In a set of "guiding principles" for NAEP issued in 1985, Secretary of Education William Bennett supported the gathering of background information about students, teachers, households, and schools, asserting that "if we want to improve, we also need deeper understanding of the sources of, and impediments to, educational achievement." He urged the use of examples that measure "excellence," as well as minimum competence, and also called for better means of interpreting and understanding education performance. Yet he permitted only ambiguous advocacy of state-by-state testing:

> States should be encouraged to participate more fully in the National Assessment program to enable them readily to gauge the performance of their students against the performance of the nation as a whole and of other states. . . . The Department of Education should work with state and local policy makers and educators to develop satisfactory means whereby they can — if they wish to — satisfy more of their needs for comparative education performance data with the assistance of NAEP (National Institute of Education 1986, pp. 21-22).

## The Alexander-James Study Group

Through roughly one year of meetings, and with the advice of 46 commissioned papers, a study group formed by Secretary Bennett reached this straightforward conclusion: "The single most important change recommended by the Study Group is that the assessment collect representative data on achievement in each of the fifty states and the District of Columbia" (Alexander and James 1987, pp. 11-12).

The Alexander-James report called for NAEP to take full advantage of state-of-the-art advances in testing, sampling, computer-adaptive procedures, and analysis:

> The national assessment should also use new measurement technologies to develop assessment methods that go beyond the limitations of the standard multiple-choice format. . . . We urge NAEP to build upon the recent developments in cognitive research and measurement technology, as well as its own special strength as an assessment program, to explore more effective strategies for identifying and measuring higher-order thinking. . . . Replacing paper-and-

pencil with computerized testing, which is now feasible, would offer a number of benefits. . . . Advances in computer technology and in our understanding of problem-solving behavior now make it possible to identify where students "go right" or "go wrong" with a task, and can thus provide valuable clues for improving instruction. New technologies also allow for more efficient use of time. . . . Finally computerized testing could shorten the time between the collection of data and the dissemination of results. (Alexander and James 1987, pp. 17, 28)

The study group also recommended an increase in testing time. In addition, it included some crucial words about NAEP reporting and interpretation of test results — barely noticed during congressional consideration in 1987 and 1988 — that became the basis for setting achievement levels by the National Assessment Governing Board.

The chief responsibility of the new council would be to shape each assessment, selecting the content areas to be tested, defining conceptually the ground to be covered in each area, setting test specifications, and identifying feasible achievement goals for each of the age and grade levels to be tested. (Alexander and James 1987, p. 32)

One of the papers commissioned for the Alexander-James Study Group addressed "Roles, Governance, and Multiple Use for a New NAEP." That paper, prepared by Michael W. Kirst, called for a new "charge" for an assessment policy committee to encompass "advice on the feasible and important achievement targets and performance standards at all three levels of education governance" (Kirst 1986).

The idea had been discussed in a regional meeting convened in San Francisco for the study group. One participant was the California State Superintendent of Public Instruction, Bill Honig, who had created a "target" goal for each school as a way to encourage advances in California achievement test scores. The school target was based on the previous performance of students in the school and the school's characteristics. Others attending the meeting thought this might be applied in some form to the national assessment. The idea provided a platform for new ways to report and interpret NAEP results.

By spring 1988, Congress enacted legislation authorizing state assessments and achievement goals. The act stated, "In carrying out its functions under this subsection, the Board shall be responsible for . . . identifying appropriate achievement goals for each age and grade in each subject area to be tested under the National Assessment" (Public Law 100-297, 1988, Sec. 3401 (6)(A)(ii)).

There is no record to clarify the congressional intent about this language. Certainly the achievement levels created by the National Assessment Governing Board, and the reporting of student performance within those levels, bear little resemblance to Superintendent Honig's targets for California schools. What was actually created evolved from the National Assessment Governing Board's own interpretation of the law, tempered by their sense of the direction the national assessment should take in the 1990s.

## NAEP in the 1980s

The study group's recommendations seemed to move NAEP to an entirely new plane, one that could not be so boldly stated even two years earlier. So what else transpired during the 1980s that could have so changed the policy environment between 1985 and 1988?

The report from President Reagan's National Commission on Excellence in Education, *A Nation at Risk*, is probably overcited as a leading cause of education reform. The commission's recommendations called for student achievement assessments in language that emphasized student accomplishment and the diagnosis of learning problems, rather than accountability or evaluation of schools or education systems. The recommendation read:

> Standardized tests of achievement (not to be confused with aptitude tests) should be administered at major transition points from one level of schooling to another and particularly from high school to college or work. The purposes of these tests would be to (a) certify the student's credentials;

(b) identify the need for remedial intervention; and (c) identify the opportunity for advanced or accelerated work. The tests should be administered as part of a nationwide (but not Federal) system of State and local standardized tests. This system should include other diagnostic procedures that assist teachers and students to evaluate student progress. (National Commission on Excellence in Education 1983, p. 28)

*A Nation at Risk* created a strong incentive for policy makers, especially governors, to pay attention to education. Leaders in such organizations as the Southern Regional Education Board (SREB), the National Governors' Association, and the Education Commission of the States undertook projects to develop organizational consensus and to make recommendations for actions to improve education achievement. Most of these recommendations involved state assessments in some form. SREB pioneered the concept of stating goals for education and then gathering state data periodically to evaluate progress.

These discussions, recommendations, and state-testing mandates, in turn, influenced chief state education officials. Their governors and legislators were asking new questions and demanding more evidence about education in their state compared to other states. So one outcome of *A Nation at Risk* was an expectation for more comparative education data, especially assessment data.

In 1984 the Council of Chief State School Officers voted, by a one-vote margin, to take a "national leadership role in the formulation and coordination of policies regarding the assessment of the K-12 education system." The CCSSO also formed a Center for Assessment and Evaluation. Previously the council had not favored cross-state comparisons; but at the council's 1985 annual meeting, a unanimous vote committed the council to support state education indicators and an annual report that would make it possible to compare states, including comparisons of student achievement.

Another outcome was growth in states' use of national assessment technology, not only for designing their own tests, but also in their contracts for NAEP-based services (National Institute of Education 1986, pp. 18-19). The annual large-scale testing conference — and collegial contacts evolving from it — were by this time a significant influence in these discussions.

By the mid-1980s, 38 states and numerous local education agencies had established testing programs. Many of these assessments drew on the pools of NAEP items, and by 1984 more than 500 sets of NAEP items were distributed for public use. Thirty-two states in that year reported that they used NAEP materials and methods, though in different ways from state to state. New Jersey reported that its assessment used NAEP methods. Connecticut and Michigan reported incorporating NAEP items into their assessments and using the results to place their state findings into perspective. New York administered the NAEP writing materials to its students. Massachusetts was planning to test every student in grades 3, 7, and 11 using NAEP items. Several states in the Southern Regional Education Board were administering an identical set of NAEP reading items to a sample of 17-year-olds in 1985 and again in 1986.

At the federal level, governors asked then Secretary of Education Bell for information on the performance of their state in education. The secretary's response was to create the Department of Education "State Education Statistics Chart," published for a half-dozen years beginning in 1984. The chart listed each state down the side and provided comparative data for many aspects of education — school-lunch population, dropouts, enrollment, finances, and teachers. It also included SAT and ACT scores as indicators of student performance. State education agency staff frequently complained about the accuracy of data on the chart; and while these data were made more consistent and reliable, one criticism did not end until the charts ceased publication: The measures of student performance were for a self-selected population (students who expected to attend college), bore no relation to the taught curriculum, and failed to represent the better test forms that NAEP and states were using more frequently in their own testing programs.

Thus when Secretary Bennett created the Alexander-James Study Group in 1986, and when Congress finished action on the subsequent legislation in 1988, there was a far more receptive climate for comparable information on student achievement at the state level.

The new NAEP of the 1990s came with significant assessment-design challenges. From the state authorization, the issues included sampling, participation of private schools, state administration, and maintenance of trends. Because of fast-moving events in assessment technology, IRT, BIB spiraling, behavioral anchoring, new forms of assessment items (such as performance items), and richer background information all created new technical demands.

## Methodological Developments in the 1990s

There are a number of methodological characteristics of NAEP that NCES either directly introduced or financially supported in order to further research and development. Each of these practices is now an integral part of the statistical machinery of NAEP.

*Separate National and State Samples.* The NAEP legislation required that state assessments (at the time called the Trial State Assessments) be administered by the states. This was included in the legislation because Congress wanted the state to pay part of the cost of the assessment. In order to comply with this requirement, NCES decided to have the national contractor collect data in the national NAEP sample and the local staff collect data in the state samples. The government then could count the services provided by school and state staff as in-kind contributions that fulfilled the cost-sharing requirement of the law.

A technical problem with this decision was how to control for the effects of different modes of administration. For example, if the local staff and national contractor administered the items differently, the average student achievement on one could be higher than on the other. Over time, NCES has found that there were average differences of about one scale point due to administration, which was a much smaller difference than was anticipated.

While NCES was working through the details of the state assessments, a report was released by John J. Cannell that caught the government's attention. In his report, titled *Nationally Normed*

*Elementary Achievement Testing in America's Public Schools: How All Fifty States Are Above the National Average*, Cannell argued that all 50 states and 90% of the school districts used nationally norm-referenced tests to report that they were above the national average (p. ix). This "Lake Wobegon" problem was precisely what we were trying to avoid in the Trial State Assessment.

The technical solution was to augment the state sample of schools in order to embed a small, nationally representative sample of schools within the state sample. That embedded sample was used to equate the state scores to the national scores.

*Sample Sizes*. Another big design issue was what should be the size of the samples used for each state assessment? The sample size would be the same for each state so that the precision of the estimates would be roughly the same for each state. In addition, the precision of the estimates for each state needed to be about the same as for the four regions that had long been reported for NAEP in the national samples. This led to requiring 100 schools, with at least 30 students per school, for each subject and grade covered by the state assessment. These sample sizes would yield standard errors for each state that would be roughly comparable to those for each region of the country.

In the 1988 reauthorization of NAEP there was a restriction against the use of NAEP for district comparisons. This restriction was removed in 1994. States were given the option of increasing their sample size so that more within-state analyses could be undertaken. For example, states were encouraged to add to their sample so they could get estimates of within-state regional differences or more precise estimates of racial/ethnic breakdowns. However, no states participated in this option, primarily because NCES required the states to pay for the increase in sample size. At least one school district (Milwaukee) did participate in 1996 at its own expense.

Another decision made by NCES was the minimum sample size needed to report on a cell in any table. Currently the minimum sample size is 62 students (this has been referred to as the rule of 62), and NAEP does not report the results for any table cell (such as Asian males) unless the minimum sample size is met. This number was arrived at by calculating the sample size needed to detect an effect size of 0.50, with a power of 0.50, a 5% level of significance, and a design effect of approximately 2.00. This standard has served the project well over the years and has prevented many researchers from over-interpreting NAEP data when sample sizes are too small.

*Private Schools.* During the 1990s, NAEP made a major effort to report more data about private school students. Nationally, private schools were oversampled at a rate of 300% in order to include enough private school students for analysis. Also, there was an effort to provide private school breakdowns in the state samples. However, only about 50% of the participating states had sufficient numbers of private schools that were willing to participate in the NAEP test. In 2000, NAGB, NCES, and the states agreed that it would be more useful to further expand the national sample of private schools and discontinue the effort to provide state-by-state data on private schools. NAEP continues to look for better ways to gather data on private schools.

*Item Response Theory (IRT) Scaling.* Item response theory models were introduced into the NAEP project by the Educational Testing Service. In its five-year contract for NAEP, awarded in 1983, ETS promised several important changes to make NAEP more useful to policy makers. Several design proposals were adopted by the government and are still in use today.

ETS suggested the use of item-response models to improve how data were reported. Rather than reporting item-by-item, as had been done in the past, ETS suggested the use of IRT to place items on a scale that policy makers would understand.

IRT scaling was a huge advance for NAEP. Not only did it help create a useful summary of achievement independent of the specific items, but it also facilitated the analysis of how background items relate to student achievement.

*Plausible Values.* Following the award of the NAEP contract to ETS, a seemingly intractable technical problem arose. The IRT method that ETS initially used was developed for individual student testing. From a statistical point of view, this meant that the IRT estimation provided observed scores, rather than true scores, for students. Estimates of observed scores (that is, the students' actual test score obtained from the test items) gave unbiased estimates for individuals, but it biased estimates for groups of individuals. However, NAEP's primary function was to report on groups, not individuals. When aggregated for the nation, the score distributions had so much error as to be unusable, especially in the tails of the distribution.

This problem was solved by Robert Mislevy, who adapted developments in multiple imputation to psychometrics (Mislevy 1985, 1991). Mislevy's approach provided a marginal estimate of the true-score distribution for groups of students without a need to first estimate observed scores for individual students. The marginal estimates allowed NAEP to monitor trends over time even though the error in the test was substantial and varied for individuals.

Unfortunately, most secondary researchers were trained to aggregate up from individual values and did not have the knowledge or software to conduct marginal analyses. In order to give secondary researchers a way to analyze NAEP data, ETS provided "plausible values." These were random draws from the student's posterior distribution of achievement scores. When properly aggregated, they allowed analysts to replicate the ETS marginal analysis.

Multiple imputed data were very difficult for most researchers to analyze. They not only had to incorporate the sampling weights required by the complex nature of the NAEP sample, but they also had to deal with multiple imputations of the dependent variable. NCES later funded the development of user-friendly software that would allow analysts with typical university training to analyze NAEP data without having to understand the statistical underpinnings of plausible values.

## Future Methodological Issues

NAEP still has unresolved methodological issues. For example, because NAEP was developed for assessing large populations, its current procedures require very large samples for stable results. However, there is considerable need and continuing political pressure to have NAEP assess smaller populations, such as districts and schools. Before NAEP attempts to assess these smaller populations, it will need to be redesigned so that it uses less complex procedures that produce faster and more easily understood results.

Another issue is that various policy makers would like to use NAEP for different purposes. For example, some would like to use NAEP as a national monitor to hold states and districts accountable for student progress. Others would like to use NAEP to evaluate federal or state programs. The validity issues for NAEP associated with these and other purposes need to be evaluated.

Finally, almost everyone wants NAEP to report results more quickly. Currently NAEP is capable of releasing its results in about one year. Although there are good reasons why it takes this long, those reasons are not convincing to the policy makers who need good information fast. They do not want to know what students learned last year, they want to know what they learned this year. Today this is the most immediate and pressing challenge to the NAEP project, and it is the most critical issue that the government is addressing.

# CHAPTER 10

# Interviews

## *An Interview with Chester E. Finn Jr.*

This interview with Chester Finn was held 11 October 2001 at the Thomas B. Fordham Foundation in Washington, D.C., conducted by Ingram Olkin.

**Olkin:** How were you selected by Secretary (William) Bennett to lead NAGB? Can you review this history?

**Finn**: Well, the history goes back a lot further than the beginning of NAGB. There are at least two relevant prior events. The first one is really only of anecdotal interest. I was a graduate student at Harvard, where David Patrick Moynihan was a professor of education and urban affairs and was my advisor. Shortly thereafter, Moynihan became assistant to President Nixon on urban affairs at the White House, and I followed as a junior staff. After joining Moynihan when he was ambassador to India, as a junior education aide in 1969 in the Nixon White House, one of the first people who insisted on coming to see me was the head of ECS, who said to me, "I need to brief you about this thing called the National Assessment of Educational Progress." This was in 1969. ECS had been given the grant to operate NAEP, and I, at the age of 25 or so, was sitting there being briefed by the head of ECS about this new NAEP thing. This was the first I knew about it. I have had a keen interest in NAEP ever since. That's now three decades.

In the Bennett years, as assistant secretary, I tried very hard to strengthen NAEP in at least two ways. One is that Bennett and I came up with the idea of a review of what NAEP was and where it ought to go. The Alexander-James Committee undertook this review. I went to all its meetings and helped ghostwrite its report. I was then involved in the legislative jockeying to try to turn the Alexander-James Report into a statute, which substantially happened.

One of the key people at that time was Terry Hardle, who is now the executive vice president of the American Council on Education, but who in 1987-88 was Senator Ted Kennedy's chief education staffer. He was an old friend and colleague of mine. Kennedy was chairman of the Senate Education Committee at that point, and Terry really carried the ball in the Congress in the 1988 legislation that gave birth to the modern NAEP.

I also had worked real hard as assistant secretary to get both leadership and decent appropriations for NCES in general, and for NAEP in particular, because I thought this was arguably the most important thing that we did in OERI. Bill Bennett agreed.

**Olkin:** Can you clarify the period that you were with Bennett?

**Finn:** I was there from 1985 to 1988 as assistant secretary, and I basically walked out the door from being assistant secretary and sat down as a member of NAGB.

**Olkin:** That was the start of NAGB with you as co-chair.

**Finn:** Yes. At the first meeting of NAGB, I was there as its chair. There had been an antecedent group called the Assessment Policy Committee (APC) that was somewhat of a house organ of ETS, which had its own advisory committee to advise it on how to administer NAEP. There were good people, whom Greg Anrig and others appointed, to be the policy advisory committee for NAEP when ETS was running it.

NAGB was shaped to a considerable extent by Mike Kirst, who functioned as an advisor/consultant to the Alexander-James Committee. I remember several long meetings with Mike Kirst and Emerson Elliott and myself where we actually framed a lot of the structural material that went into the Alexander-James Report. I also helped Bennett decide whom to appoint to NAGB.

**Olkin:** So the two of you, in effect, put the first slate together. What kind of criteria did you use in your choice of members?

**Finn:** The law spelled out the categories of membership, for example, a local superintendent, three teachers, and so forth. So we didn't have total freedom. We looked for people whom we thought shared our view that NAEP needed to become a more vigorous source of policy information at the national and especially the state level.

There were two big events in the early years of NAGB, as far as I am concerned, and both were foreshadowed in the legislation. One was the addition of state NAEP; and the other was the addition of what we called achievement levels, the standard-setting role of NAEP. Those were the two big items that happened under NAGB in its early years. We knew that NAEP needed to move in the general direction of state NAEP and to do a much better job in reporting its results. I don't think we were very clear at the beginning about what form this reporting should take. But it was clear that the traditional mode of reporting NAEP results was of little benefit to those in the policy world.

**Olkin:** So the goal was for lay people to understand what the results meant.

**Finn:** Yes, governors and legislators — lay people. I think it is fair to say in retrospect that the early design of NAEP had been aimed at educators, at helping teachers and educators do better. It was not designed as an accountability measure for policy makers to know how the system is doing in their state, for example, compared to the country. Indeed, it was exactly such comparisons that were assiduously resisted in the early days of NAEP by the state chiefs and others who wanted no part of it. By the mid-1980s, however, the governors wanted this kind of information; and there wasn't any source other than the infamous wall chart where SAT scores were compared by state. Everybody knew that wasn't the best way to do this. But there wasn't any alternative. So NAGB and NAEP became the alternative.

We looked for people we thought had interesting and solid ideas about education, about testing, and were likely to be positive about these kinds of big changes. We also appointed some carryover members from the old Assessment Policy Committee. For example, when I arrived at the first NAGB meeting, the vice chairman was Pat Frank, the Florida ex-legislator who had been chairman of the Assessment Policy Committee under ETS' aegis. We were consciously not trying to throw people out. They were good people, but we felt deeply that the contractor shouldn't be in charge of the policy committee. That was just wrong. What was needed was an independent policy committee, which is what NAGB is. But that didn't mean it couldn't recycle some of the same people who were very good and who had been functioning in a similar role as the old APC.

**Olkin:** Was there general consensus in NAGB on the two important issues that you mentioned?

**Finn:** It took a while; people had to think their way through them. State NAEP was more clearly foreshadowed in the statute in 1988. The phrase in the 1988 statute was, I believe, that this was to be a "trial state assessment," that is, essentially an experiment with state NAEP.

**Olkin:** We almost always referred to it as "Trial State Assessment."

**Finn:** It was viewed at the outset as "let's try this." And the NAGB members all acknowledged that we needed to try this, and then it was a question of how quickly and how much zest there was for making this happen in a timely way.

**Olkin:** What about the achievement levels?

**Finn:** The achievement levels were more complicated because we were in uncharted waters here. The country was beginning to try to set standards in various ways for its education system. Mind you, we're talking about 1988-89, just months before the governors had their Charlottesville meeting — out of which they emerged with six national goals, one of which said that all children should become proficient in challenging subject matter — and they named five subjects. But the governors and the President didn't say who was going to define what it meant to be proficient in challenging subject matter in these five subjects.

We basically said, "Let us do it. We already have this testing instrument. We have permission in the law to set 'achievement levels.' The governors and the President are referring to proficiency in challenging subject matter. The country has no way of knowing when it's there, or how to know when it's there, or who is to say how to know when it's there. So let us do it." And thus began the achievement-level process. As you know, it has led to an infinity of complexities. But I don't think NAGB ever had any doubt that it was a legitimate thing to undertake. And I think history now shows that the country by and large has responded very positively to the fact that these achievement levels are there, and people are glad to have them. All sorts of entities and organizations and policy makers now use them as markers of how their state is doing, which isn't to say that we knew how to do it, but that we felt there was deep legitimacy in making the effort and finding a way.

**Olkin:** In retrospect, to what extent do you feel that the goals that you had in mind when you started as chair of NAGB were accomplished?

**Finn:** I feel very satisfied about this. I've done a lot of things over the years, but I think possibly the most important thing I ever did was to help push NAEP into being a measure of state performance and into telling the country in a clearcut way how it actually is doing. I think if I had to compose my professional epitaph, I might put that first on the list.

**Olkin:** What do you think NAGB should be doing now to ensure that NAEP makes this important contribution? New entities have come into the picture, for example, accountability, confirmation.

**Finn:** Some of this is still a little murky because some of it is still in the hands of Congress. There are several sticky issues still out there, which to the best of my knowledge have not yet been settled by Congress. Whether NAEP will, in fact, be required of every state, whether it will be used for confirmation in a high-stakes sense, where some federal reward or punishment follows upon a NAEP result, as opposed to simply an external audit with a "sunlight" function — basically a second opinion — that's not yet settled. The issue of mandatory participation is not settled, and reportedly a number of members of Congress are digging a little more deeply than I think they probably should into what kinds of questions are on the test and what kinds of background questions are being asked of kids. I'm not absolutely sure right now that this enhanced role that the Administration has sought for NAEP is going to turn out to be a good thing, because I can see some harm coming to the value and reliability of the instrument if it is made to bear too many political burdens.

**Olkin:** That's the essence of my next question. Can we maintain the integrity of NAEP once you start giving it many chores?

**Finn:** A very good question. I don't think we know yet. NAGB has clearly said they are willing to try. Their basic policy stance has been, "We are willing to play this role if you want us to, Congress."

The mandatory participation I'm a little concerned about. Test taking, at the end of the day, is a volitional act. It's hard for me to tell somebody that they are required to take a cognitive test if they don't want to, and then believe that the results of how they do on that test will be trustworthy. You can make someone take a blood test, I suppose, or a DNA test; but I have some doubts about the value of a cognitive test that you take against your will. It is the compulsory aspect that I question, because it's not just compelling a state; states will also have to recruit schools. How are they going to recruit schools if the state didn't want to participate in the first place? So, I've got a concern there.

I do think the federal government should pay for it. I do think that it should be embarrassing for a state not to participate, and I do think that money shouldn't be the excuse for not participating.

The high-stakes aspect also gives me the willies the more I think about it. I really don't want states trying to finagle their NAEP results because of rewards and punishments. Now, you can say the probability is that nobody takes it seriously because it doesn't count and therefore we don't know whether it's really accurate. For example, we have problems like 12th-graders who don't even finish the test because they know it doesn't count, and so the 12th-grade data are not very robust. That's a problem of low stakes. You get a different set of problems if you go toward high stakes for NAEP results.

**Olkin:** One of the problems, of course, with high stakes is that it generates gamesmanship.

**Finn:** Exactly. Yet the absence of stakes generates a different kind of gamesmanship. It leads to kids doodling on their answer sheet instead of bothering to answer the question. So you're stuck either way in this regard. I have these concerns about how NAEP is going to fare under the new regime that I think is being visited upon it. It has acquired respect for being an accurate barometer, and you could jeopardize it by making excessive or inappropriate use of this instrument.

**Olkin:** That's the part about maintaining the integrity of NAEP. Do you have any thoughts on what they should do?

**Finn:** We are within a few weeks of resolving this legislatively, and I've offered some thoughts from time to time to staffers, organizations, and lobbyists. I signed on to a group letter a few days ago, with Bill Bennett and some others, about how to deal with the NAEP issue. We recommended not using it for high-stakes purposes and giving it only every second year in fourth- and eighth-grade reading and math, not every year, because I don't think the annual score fluctuations at the state level are worth much. It's fundamentally a long-term trend measure.

Anyway, I have been weighing in on this issue while it is in Congress; but it is soon going to be out of Congress, and there will almost surely be a stepped up role for NAEP as part of this legislation. How many of these concerns I am voicing will end up being warranted, I don't have any way of knowing yet. But I feel that this is the price of success, almost like the President and his team arrive with such reverence for NAEP that they're now trying to overuse it. It's a curious kind of problem to have. NAGB is going to try heroically and conscientiously to make this work right. They also have some other problems they need to solve.

For two years in a row, the Brown Center at Brookings has done an annual report on education. This year's report, which came out last month, has a whole section on the confusion that results from the fact that there is a main NAEP and a long-term trend NAEP and they operate side by side, yet produce very different results. This shows the degree to which you can reach different policy conclusions depending on which NAEP you are looking at and, of course, which period of time you are looking at. NAEP is no longer a simple, straightforward barometer. It's now as if there are barometer and thermometer versions of NAEP, and you have to look at them both and then figure out which one you are more interested in, the temperature or the air pressure. So that's an issue.

The 12th-grade participation-rate issue that I already alluded to is a problem. I'm not sure we have reliable 12th-grade NAEP data.

Content issues continue to recur in the math framework. NAGB is wrestling with that right now as they try to put together a new framework. And that always carries with it a profound and ultimately unanswerable issue about whether the goal of a NAEP content framework is to mirror what is in the American curriculum or mirror what one would like it to be. This is a very important, deeply unresolveable kind of dilemma.

Last, the government, broadly speaking, is facing some structural issues about the governance, management, and operation of NAEP. NAEP needs to be reauthorized, NAGB needs to be reauthorized, NCES needs to be reauthorized, OERI needs to be reauthorized; and all of these are going to require revisiting the "who is in charge of what" issue. I am one of the people who doesn't think the present balance between NAGB and NCES has been a very satisfactory one in terms of the operation of NAEP.

**Olkin:** Let's discuss this a bit more because there are various aspects. For example, NAGB was involved more with Congress and the legislation that came out, whereas NCES was in a position of not knowing exactly what was going on. Consequently, this would naturally lead to some tension.

**Finn:** There is tension, some of it built into the current structure where, for example, NAGB is supposed to set the policy, but NCES issues the request for proposals for the contract and then manages the contract. A lot of policy is contained in the contract, so that, although NAGB can set policy, NCES need not carry it out. For example, NAGB has been stewing for years about how slowly the data come out after an administration of NAEP, a minimum of a year to obtain the first results. Why is that? It is because the contract is structured in such a way that the handful of people who write these reports at ETS do them one at a time. There's no multi-tasking when it comes to NAEP report writing. So you have to wait until they are free to work on a report, and then you have to wait until it can be released. This makes for very slow data circulation. Why is it set up that way? Because the contract and the funding of this arrangement with ETS were set up that way. For example, there's no bonus payment to get a report out in six months instead of 12, and there's no penalty for taking 15 months instead of eight. These are examples of where NAGB wants to speed up the process, but actually has no control over the means of production.

The greatest conflict has arisen over issues of data release and who's at the press conference telling the world what the data show and spinning the results to make the newspaper reporters happy. The issue there is ultimately whether it's a purely statistical event or a policy event when you report on a new NAEP result. If it's a policy event, then there's a lot of jockeying among policy makers to determine who gets to provide the spin.

**Olkin:** I am confused by your point about timeliness. Can't NAGB discuss this with the contractor?

**Finn:** You're putting your finger on a problem. NAGB has no relationship whatsoever with the contractors.

**Olkin:** NAGB attends the meeting of the technical advisory committee where all the plans are laid out.

**Finn:** The staff of NAGB does, but not the members of NAGB.

**Olkin:** Would it be helpful if some NAGB members did attend?

**Finn:** Well, it would be helpful; but it wouldn't solve the problem. The problem is that the contractor doesn't answer to NAGB. The contractor answers to the commissioner of NCES and to the contract office at the Department of Education, and they don't answer to NAGB. From the contractor's point of view, NAGB is just standing over on the side making pronouncements. The contractor has no obligation at all to NAGB.

**Olkin:** All right. What are other issues on your mind that might improve NAEP?

**Finn:** Well, I'm generally a small-government kind of guy, but the NAEP budget right now is not sufficient to allow enough subjects to be assessed on a sufficiently frequent basis to provide the country with the data that it needs in such fields as history, civics, and science.

Also related to the budget is the fact that not all NAEP administrations go to the state level; some of them remain national only. I think that's a problem. A state might also want to know how its kids are doing in history, say, or civics; and right now we often can't tell them because states don't participate in every part of the assessment.

**Olkin:** One issue that arises is that policy makers are in one domain, and technical-type individuals in education are in another domain. Have there been conflicts between the policy makers and the technical savants in the testing community?

**Finn:** Yes.

**Olkin:** Are these conflicts being resolved?

**Finn:** No, it's continuing.

**Olkin:** Is there a way we can minimize those conflicts?

**Finn:** I lost a lot of respect for the technical types in the course of these conflicts. They so often, it seems to me, turn out to be very effective at criticizing somebody else's decision and totally unable to suggest a viable alternative. This is nowhere more vivid than in the discussion of the modified Angoff method for setting these achievement levels. A large number of technical experts have bitched and moaned about the way this is done, but I have yet to see any of them propose another way to do it. So, I get fed up with technical experts whose only role is to be nay-sayers and critics and who can't come up with viable, constructive alternatives. The long-term result, frankly, has been that, while NAEP has steadily gotten better because of some of the technical criticism and advice it has gotten, overall the critics from the technical community have marginalized themselves by appearing to take an adversarial stance toward some of the things that are most important in the views of those operating NAEP, such as setting standards. That seems to be so unpalatable to just about everybody in the technical community that it has just led to a kind of war of attrition.

**Olkin:** The conflict between policy and technical matters is not unique to education. There's a similar tension in medicine. If there's no clear cut, technical way to say that a treatment is good, and you make a policy statement about the treatment, then there's a loss function in making a mistake. And there's a price to be paid.

**Finn:** Yes, but there's also a loss function in not doing it. That's the tradeoff. You've suggested an analogy to me. My wife is a cardiac pathologist, and she does a lot of research on interventional cardiology. What she frequently discovers is that the latest gizmos and gimmicks that the interventional cardiologists are using turn out, over the long run, not to work very well. So when the pharmaceutical companies come out and say this new stent that we have created has a terrific three-month survival rate, my wife says they're not telling us about the 12-month survival rate. She says it doesn't work nearly as well over the longer haul. So I do see the analogy here. Nevertheless, in the NAEP context, the technical community has mostly positioned itself as kvetching, rather than offering up viable, constructive alternative ways to do things that policy makers clearly want to do.

**Olkin:** You now have just raised an interesting point. Do we offer contracts and grants to technical people to try to resolve policy issues in a solid technical way? A good example would be to say, "What is a good way to confirm high stakes?"

**Finn:** That's a good question. Over the years there have been a nontrivial number of contracts and grants given out — invitational conferences on standards setting. There have been both some grants given out by NAGB itself and some given out by NCES to various technical advisors; some given out by the contractors to various technical advisors; some given out by the Department of Education's planning and evaluation shop, which normally ends up turning to the National Academy of Sciences, which has gotten a lot of money over the years to study NAEP. So there is real money flowing into the watchers and the analysts and the critics and the external reviewers.

**Olkin:** It is important for the tension to diminish because technical aspects are important in the construction of policy.

**Finn:** I don't disagree with that. I don't see the mechanism right now, though.

**Olkin:** There's a general question about federal statistics, more than just about NAEP. I suspect that there's been a slight diminution in terms of how people view federal statistics; they're a lot more skeptical. Do you see this as being true?

**Finn:** Well, I agree with you about the problem. University of Wisconsin Professor Andy Porter and I were at a meeting together a few days ago; and he said, "Can't you do anything to get them to appoint an NCES commissioner? That place is really languishing in the absence of a leader."

The fact of the matter is the Administration seems to have shelved that issue until they decide their structural issue — about what level and reporting to whom do they want NCES to be at — so they are not looking very actively for a commissioner because they have not decided what the job description will be. The upshot is that NCES has for a very long time now had a reasonably competent career bureaucrat running it, but no vivid leadership or direction of any kind, either from the NCES commissioner or from the OERI assistant secretary. This is a big problem.

The integrity issues are also very vivid. These numbers become weapons in all sorts of political and policy battles. Therefore people want to influence the numbers, which numbers are gathered or how they're interpreted. A big issue is protecting the number-gathering function from the many people who would like to shove it around. Yet we ought not preserve it in amber, either, because there are changing needs for data gathering. It is not sufficient to just say, "Let's do it the way we've always done it." But how do you make data adaptable to changing needs without letting it get pushed around by people who want to maneuver their own thing? I don't know how to do that.

**Olkin:** The political aspect is a very interesting point. The Bureau of Labor Statistics has managed not to become political. The Commissioner of BLS for umpteen years never was on either side of the political fence, but just reported the indices, such as the consumer price index or the unemployment index. Why is education so much more political?

**Finn:** Part of it is culture and tradition; part of it is structure, location, and stature. The education data-gathering function is, you know, one unit under one assistant secretary; and it's a unit with very little by way of outside constituents. The number mavens are few and far between in the education field. There's also an almost irresistible push from the reformers and improvers of education to want the data to be used in a more proactive way. This affects the way data are gathered, interpreted, and explained. There's a really strong push in education for the agency reporting the data to offer causal explanations of why things are the way they are.

**Olkin:** Causality is certainly a central part of data reporting.

**Finn:** It's deeply sought by the entire education field. Yet, the instant that the reporting agency jumps into causality, it has jumped into politics. There's just no alternative in this field and so, lo and behold, you discover that fourth-graders are reading not quite as well this year as they were last year. People instantly want to know why. The instant you start offering even a conjecture, you're into politics. Yet to be silent and say, "We don't go there. We will tell you the results and we will not attempt to give you any explanation of why," that gets you into a different kind of trouble. Then you're called irrelevant, etc. And this even turns up, as I alluded to a few minutes ago, in these congressional assaults on background questions, which are deemed to be political.

**Olkin:** There has been a long interplay between background, school variables, and achievement.

**Finn:** One of the NAEP background questions that's been there forever asks the kids whether there's a daily newspaper in their house. This question is not stupid to ask if you're going to try to explain why some of the fourth-graders read better than others, or at least which fourth-graders have which attributes that other fourth-graders don't have. A whole bunch of congressional staff members have concluded that this is an intrusive and inappropriate question for the federal government to ask. And they are such statistical novices that they are saying things like, "Well, the Census Bureau also asks those questions, why does the Education Department have to ask those questions?" Of course, it has never occurred to them that the Census Bureau data don't link up with the education test results, and you don't want them to. Or you get into another whole difficulty having to do with a government linking up all of its data systems with each other, which would be a much worse problem than letting a sample-based study, which doesn't even report individual data, to find out how many kids have newspapers in their homes. And yet that's become politics.

# An Interview with Marshall S. Smith

This interview with Marshall S. Smith was held 29 January 2002 at the William and Flora Hewlett Foundation in Menlo Park, California, conducted by Ingram Olkin.

**Olkin**: When did you begin to work in the Department of Education, what was your capacity there, and can you provide some history?

**Smith**: Actually I go back even earlier with NAEP. I remember talking with Fred Mosteller and the Statistical Advisory Group at one point in Boulder in the early 1970s.

**Olkin**: Was this a technical advisory group?

**Smith**: Yes. We talked about different ways of developing test items, as well as other technical aspects. The first time I came into education in the federal government was in 1973. I was a visiting scholar at the National Institute of Education (NIE), which was then an agency in the Department of Health, Education and Welfare. At that time the national assessment, of course, was with ECS and monitored by NCES; and we at NIE really didn't have much to do with it. NAEP was interesting when results came out; but it was a bit sporadic, and it didn't affect the kinds of activities that we were involved with in the NIE, which was mostly research. When Carter became president, I moved over to be a political appointee; and I ran the policy group at the Office of Education. Then the last year that I was there, I was the chief of staff to Shirley Hufstedler, who was the first secretary of education.

During that period, I was engaged in activities that could have drawn on the national assessment had it actually been policy oriented. But it wasn't intended to be focused on policy. It was intended to assess student academic progress.

During that time, around 1977 to 1980, we discovered that, in fact, some test scores were going down. It was the SAT college entrance test scores we were looking at, and that captured the attention of people who were worried about test scores, about whether or not there was a declining human capital in the United States and whether schools were getting better or worse.

The national assessment didn't enter much into that discussion, nor did the international studies. I actually looked pretty closely into the international studies when I wrote a piece for the National Academy of Sciences, National Research Council, and argued that in that time period, they did not have much effect on policy. The big effects on policy from the international assessments came around 1982-83 when *A Nation at Risk* was released. I had left the government by that time — there was a new administration, the Reagan Administration — but I was still doing quite a bit of work in Washington.

In 1982-83 I worked with Gordon Ambach, when he was president of the Council of Chief State School Officers. The chiefs, under Ambach's leadership, made a decision at that time that they wanted to measure achievement at the state level. This was a difficult decision for states that traditionally had low scores on standardized tests. But they made the decision because they feared the "report card" that compared states that the federal government, under Secretary of Education Terrel Bell, was releasing every year. In effect, they were asking for a state NAEP as early as 1983 or 1984 to be a gold standard that could validly be used to compare states.

**Olkin**: That was fairly early in the evolution of NAEP.

**Smith**: Yes, the federal report card used the SATs as their test score measure. Everybody felt that this was a poor measure for lots of reasons. For example, it wasn't taken as much by students in some states as it was in others. The chiefs felt that if they were going to be measured, they wanted a reasonable measure. They had a long debate, and I wrote a paper for them on indicators. We were at the final meeting of the chiefs when they actually made the vote; the motion passed by one vote for state-to-state comparisons. It was a very important moment, I think, because it indicated the importance that assessments began to have at the state level. Putting NAEP at the state level moved up the ante in terms of people's attention to it, their concerns, and certainly the state governments' concerns.

So that all happened about 1983-84, just after the *Nation at Risk* report appeared. Of course, *A Nation at Risk* moved up the ante at the same time. There were three or four other reports that also came out. We had the council's action to say, "All right. Let the states be compared." We had national direction set in the reports saying that reform should happen. All of this resulted in a momentum that pushed education forward. It ended up, of course, in 1989-90 with the summit that President Bush called with Governor Bill Clinton, who was then the lead governor. The two of them pulled together all the governors and convinced them to have a set of common national goals. NAEP would play a major role in thinking about how to assess progress toward the goals, particularly in the goals around mathematics and reading achievement.

**Olkin:** So NAEP was specifically pinpointed?

**Smith:** Yes, it was definitely thought of during that period. I believe that the chiefs had it in mind as the measure that was going to be used to compare states during their debate. Work was advanced in NCES on how to carry out state NAEP.

There was another issue involving NAEP that I was involved in after I left the government the first time. I was on the committee in 1983 that reviewed the proposals to either keep NAEP at ECS or to put it at ETS. In retrospect, that turned out to be a very big decision, though we did not realize that at the time.

**Olkin:** It set in motion such a major enterprise that you couldn't undo very easily even if you wanted to make a change from one group to another.

**Smith:** Exactly. Definitely. Well, it changed a lot of things. It changed the methodology in really significant ways; and unless you keep the same methodology, you would find it difficult to track results across time in a valid manner. It also moved NAEP from a neutral or passive thermometer to a much more aggressive posture. The reports changed in their style, the approach changed in the vigor of the activities of advertising it and disseminating the information. ETS, far more than ECS, saw the results of the NAEP as important data for policy and deliberately and aggressively interpreted and disseminated the data. ETS brought in Archie Lapointe to lead its NAEP team, and he was aggressive about bringing the results to the press. So you have changes that were not just switching one letter from ECS to ETS, but were really major. If you look at that sweep of time up to 1993 when I entered the government again, there was a lot of activity in the early 1990s about reforms, building on many of those activities that came from the summit.

**Olkin:** Let me interject a point. You mentioned the Council of Chief State School Officers and the National Governors' Association. Did they have any influence in the way NAEP was structured or conducted?

**Smith:** I think the chiefs had a definite influence on the decision to have a state NAEP. So that's a big influence. I know that ETS had some advisory panels, and representatives of those organizations might be on these panels. Other than that, I don't think they had much influence on the way NAEP was structured.

Although I was on advisory panels for ETS, including their research advisory panel, ETS pretty much, as far as I could tell, went its own way with oversight from NCES and later NAGB. The only place where they really took a lot of advice would have been on the questions. I think the structure of NCES during that period and later on was pretty solid; the NCES Advisory Board had a good effect. Then, of course, the evolution of the national assessment governing process was important. NAGB wasn't as strong as they were later on, but it was pretty strong.

I don't know if other people agree with that, but I have always been impressed by its independence. I haven't always been impressed by NAGB and NCES' decisions about NAEP or their reasons for the decisions, but I have been impressed by their independence. That independence continued through the Clinton Administration as well. NAGB had generally strong chairpeople — Mark Musick for years was a very competent and strong chair. That was true also for heads of NCES, though they always wanted to exert more authority over NAEP than they ended up being able to exert.

**Olkin:** Was NAEP important to Congress or the White House? Of course, now it certainly is important.

**Smith:** Yes, now it is. I think it became more and more important during the 1990s. It was very important to us in the Clinton Administration — very important to the people making policy decisions or framing policy issues for the President and the Secretary. NAEP was often referred to in policy discussions. Somewhat earlier, NAEP went through a kind of reformation — perhaps in 1989 or 1990 — and we ended up with three NAEPs: a new NAEP, a state NAEP, and a trend NAEP. The new NAEP is a very high-quality assessment dating from the early 1990s that is used for the national report card. The trend NAEP is a basic assessment that dates from the late 1960s and early 1970s and allows comparisons across three decades. But the fact that it was developed in the late Sixties means that it measures the kinds of curricula that existed then, which are less rigorous than the curricula that now exist and are reflected in the new NAEP and the state NAEP.

The three different NAEPS often created confusion. Policy makers have no idea what you are talking about when you say there are really three NAEPs. They roll their eyes and say "what is all this stuff?" In the Clinton Administration, NAEP was used to make every possible policy argument. This is easier when there are three NAEPs to choose among.

One of the problems that occurs with three NAEPS is that trend NAEP didn't really track with the new NAEP, particularly in mathematics. In mathematics, the new NAEP showed dramatically improving scores between 1990 and 2000, and the trend

NAEP increased only a little. Nobody can explain this difference. This is a problem that needs to be addressed at some point.

But in terms of the effects on policy, I think NAEP since the early 1980s has been continuously important. NAEP was always factored into decisions. As an example, during the Clinton Administration we used 1994 as a baseline because we wanted to give our new legislation, passed in 1993 and 1994, time to be implemented.

**Olkin:** I suspect that every administration uses this maximization principle.

**Smith:** Exactly so. But that means that they are paying attention to NAEP. They are thinking about it and how it affects things. I think the fact that the reading scores had been pretty level for years really influenced the push that the Clinton Administration made on reading over time. This priority is continuously in people's minds now.

It was always frustrating that the tests weren't given on a regular schedule; we would always include in the budgets for the test to be put on a regular schedule, and then Congress would always cut the budget. It's very hard to do, but the new administration is going to try again. They may get it, but I wouldn't count on it now with the deficit spending that's going on.

**Olkin:** Let me go back. There was a new entity, namely NAGB. There also were the NAEP contractors and NCES. So we had three Ns all involved in NAEP in different ways. What were the tensions, the conflicts among these groups, if any, and how were they resolved? Were they serious?

**Smith:** Let's see now. NAGB started in 1988. At that time ETS was the contractor and, of course, we had NCES with Commissioner Emerson Elliott. There was always tension between each of the possible pairs. In the early years, of course, it was NAGB beginning to try to move into its niche.

**Olkin:** To find its role.

**Smith:** Yes, what is its role. ETS had been doing the job for three or four years at that point, and they were pretty well settled in. They knew what they were doing. They had a method to do it. They weren't going to be shaken out of that method. But then along came the reading anomaly, which shook things up a little and probably influenced the balance of authority among NAGB, NCES, and ETS.

I think Emerson Elliott at NCES was very steady. He had his eye clearly on the longer range and wanted to get this worked out. So he wasn't going to get involved in minor disputes very much.

**Olkin:** He never let politics enter into his approach.

**Smith:** Exactly. There was concern over some issues from assistant commissioners. They would feel frustrated that they didn't have control over certain aspects, that somehow NAGB was taking authority away from them. My sense, at least in those early years, was that it wasn't too bad.

I don't really know how much tension there was between ETS and NAGB. However, there is tension on another dimension between NAGB and the Administration. Each of the administrations wanted to have more control over what the content was, and NAGB would negotiate with the administration over how much money was going to go in the budget. Some of the negotiation was with NCES and the assistant secretary. Then later on in the process, another part of the negotiation would come in meetings between NAGB and the secretary. There were fairly regular meetings in the Clinton Administration between NAGB and the secretary, at least twice a year — once around budget development time and probably once during the appropriation process. I suspect the same holds true for other administrations.

**Olkin:** Would you recommend a different mode of control — some alternative management structure — for NAEP? Or perhaps these tensions are intrinsic to the process. That is, no matter how you do the management, there are going to be groups where there is tension.

**Smith:** I think they probably are intrinsic. There will always be tension between the actual hands-on developers, the ETS's, and whoever the governing body is. That will happen because the developers will see themselves as the experts, and efforts to control the design by any other body is going to be seen as an imposition. I think the real question is how do you create a quasi-governmental body that has true independence and, at the same time, has enough clout to get good appropriations. The closer you are to the secretary and the more the secretary makes NAEP a priority, the greater the chance is that OMB and the President will make it a priority, and therefore the greater chance that it will get the appropriation it wants. If NAGB were a totally independent operation, it would not have any political clout or anything to trade off, and the tradeoffs are very important in this game. Under these circumstances, it would be much harder to have a stable budget. We in the Department of Education in the Clinton Administration didn't do a very good job of giving NAEP a stable budget, but I think that it would have had an even harder time had it been out there all alone.

**Olkin:** So there's a fundamental dilemma in running a national assessment, namely, the more independent and apolitical that it tries to be — which is probably good — the harder it is to continue with the appropriation process.

**Smith:** Exactly, unless there is some way of guaranteeing the level of assessments over a long period of time — a "locked box," for example. This hasn't worked, of course, in any other field; and there's no reason it would work here. However, it might be worth trying to explore something like that because money set aside over a sustained period of time to continue NAEP with a good quasi-governmental body to oversee it — so the operation just doesn't run amok — that would be a powerful mixture. But as you say, this tension is substantial. It is created by the dilemma between independence and political clout.

**Olkin:** You see independence as being a very important part of NAEP.

**Smith:** Yes, I see independence as very important; but I also see a regular, predictable appropriation that is large enough to really give you good measures in a regular and rigorous way as also being very important.

**Olkin:** If you start losing independence, and it becomes a political tool, then it's going to be difficult to do anything well. To some degree we see that kind of politicization with the Census.

**Smith:** Yes. We also had some trouble with NAEP when Vice President Gore announced certain results. Of course, he announced the results because it was good news.

**Olkin:** Well, every administration is going to want to take credit for good news.

**Smith:** It is natural to want to take credit if the scores are going up, and not if the scores are going down.

**Olkin:** You and Secretary Richard Riley aggressively supported a national, annual test of reading at grade 4 and math at grade 8. Did you envision a role for NAEP had that proposal been enacted by Congress?

**Smith:** Not a role for NAEP, per se. However, the plan was for the test to be designed to be as close as possible to being an individual NAEP. The problem, of course, is that each test would have been only 55 minutes long, and the statisticians felt that it would end up correlating very highly with NAEP; but it wouldn't, obviously, have the performance items in it that NAEP has. The idea behind the national tests was to be able to give to individual parents and individual teachers a score for each kid that did track NAEP well enough so that they would be able to calibrate it against NAEP. The idea was also to have that test given and then returned within three weeks. Students would receive very quick feedback, and teachers and parents would learn how well the student did. The test also would be put on the Web so that each item would be available and explained, and other items like it would be available. Students would know what the item was supposed to be measuring and how to begin to study for it. So it was really an attempt to create a transparent diagnostic test. NAEP wasn't seen as an integral part of this, but the value of NAEP was recognized.

**Olkin:** As you see it, NAEP really was a phenomenal achievement in many, many ways, given all the political aspects of education. We were very fortunate from the beginning to have it designed so well. In the early years, we could easily have gone off in the wrong direction.

**Smith:** Right. I think it stayed pretty independent, even in the development of frameworks, which could have been much more political than they were. They were constructed in a relatively unbiased fashion. This turned out to be important in a variety of ways. For example, one of the best examples that I know of was the use of state NAEP to understand whether there have been effective reforms in Texas. This has been a recent controversy. And the piece of information that tips the scales in my view is the fact that the NAEP scores have gone up on a regular basis in Texas. This makes it much more credible than just having the Texas test. You could not have practiced against a NAEP given to only a few people. It's not something that the teachers know much about, and yet the scores went up in a fairly dramatic fashion.

**Olkin:** NAEP is the calibration, and it is what we use as the pure calibration.

**Smith:** Right.

**Olkin:** Let me turn to the current Administration's legislation, No Child Left Behind. There are many aspects: the high stakes, NAEP's involvement, confirmation, and so on. Perhaps you can comment about this.

**Smith:** Well, in general, what the bill did was continue the standards movement. It continued the policies instituted by the Clinton Administration in 1994. It emphasizes accountability more and emphasizes testing more. With respect to NAEP, I think what it has done is fine. It will now require NAEP to be taken by states, and NAEP will be given on a regular schedule.

**Olkin:** Do you think NAEP can confirm improvement at the atomic level, namely, schools or districts? And if not, how will we confirm?

**Smith:** No. I don't think we have an independent way of confirming most districts. NAEP could be used with some cities if we oversample them — New York City, Los Angeles, and a few cities. I think that you may find pressure to take a NAEP-like assessment and apply it within a state so that you get estimates within cities and rural areas. But I think for the next few years that won't happen.

**Olkin:** Things will have to settle down for a while?

**Smith:** In the future, there are all sorts of places that NAEP could go. A large part of NAEP could be put on the Web, at least for the eighth-graders and older students — maybe even for the fourth-graders — and the test itself would be much more efficient. A student would not have to spend as much time taking the test, and at the same time you can give students items that are more complex and demanding. So you could give a NAEP to individuals on the Web.

**Olkin:** I think what you are saying is that the new technology permits us to see an expanded version of NAEP that could move in all directions, much more down to an atomic level without necessarily having a trial district NAEP or a trial school NAEP, the way we have a trial state NAEP.

**Smith:** Yes. Exactly.

**Olkin:** That would certainly make NAEP more valuable, in that it would now be not only at a global level but a personal level.

**Smith:** Right. Then we would need to feed information back in a reasonable way. This is a big move and will probably be fought by the publishers because it will interfere with their sales.

**Olkin:** What other thoughts do you have on NAEP and its future?

**Smith:** Well, the standards movement in a lot of states is nearing adolescence. It's now four or five years old and should be producing some results. Texas and North Carolina, for example, have had positive results that NAEP has confirmed, according to a RAND study. I think that you're going to be seeing some changes in many other states and, I hope, positive changes. NAEP will play an important confirming role.

**Olkin:** The word "confirm" has been used. Who's going to do the confirming? NCES, ETS, the state?

**Smith:** No. I think researchers are going to be the confirmers. I think people are going to be looking at these things very closely.

**Olkin:** So there might be panels?

**Smith:** Panels or individuals writing about this. I think you'll find newspaper reporters also confirming. They will look to the NAEP scores and they'll look at their states' test scores to see if there are big differences between the tests. For example, the average scores on the SAT-9 in math and reading in fourth and eighth grades in California are above the national median, but the state NAEP scores are well below the national averages. This raises serious questions about the validity of the SAT-9s.

# An Interview with John F. Jennings

This interview with John F. (Jack) Jennings was held on the telephone on 14 August 2001, conducted by Ingram Olkin.

**Olkin**: Thanks, Jack. You were in the midst of the political process. When did you first learn about NAEP and in what capacity?

**Jennings**: Well, in 1968-69 I was the staff director for the Elementary and Secondary Education Subcommittee in the House of Representatives. And I was aware of what was happening with NAEP at that time, with the origins of NAEP.

**Olkin**: When the law was passed by Congress in 1988 authorizing trial state assessments and creating NAGB, it passed in different forms in the House and Senate. Now, as you recall, what were the major differences and what transpired in the conference committee?

**Jennings**: In 1988 the Congress was considering many of the suggestions from the Alexander-James Commission, if I remember correctly. In the House, we did adopt an extension of NAEP and an expansion of NAEP, but the Senate was much more comprehensive in proposing the creation of the NAGB, including semi-autonomous appointing authority for NAGB. The Senate also put in provisions regarding different achievement levels. All those changes to NAEP were adopted in the Senate as a floor amendment, which I believe was offered by Massachusetts Senator Ted Kennedy. This means that these proposals did not go through hearings or go through the committee. Rather, they were adopted on the Senate floor with almost no discussion. In the House bill, we did not have many of the same provisions. So in conference there was considerable debate about the merits of the Senate amendments dealing with NAGB, as well as with the expansion of NAEP to incorporate these achievement levels.

Unfortunately, because of the way the Congress operated at the time, these were mostly staff discussions that were off the record; and most of what was presented to the public in the conference committee in a public session were things that had already been decided at the staff level.

**Olkin**: What accounted for the apparent conflict between the House Committee on Education and Labor and NAGB?

**Jennings**: Well, you have to look at it more broadly than NAGB. Many of the members in the House, on the House Education Committee, especially the more liberal Democratic members, were very skeptical about testing, the use of testing. And I think they and their staff did not want to have an expansion of the National Assessment of Educational Progress. They were also suspicious of what would happen if the National Assessment Governing Board became more independent.

This was after a period when many of the Democrats, especially the more liberal Democrats, felt that the Reagan Administration had criticized education to an undue degree. They felt that some of the appointments to NAGB were very partisan and very anti-public school, and the appointees would be using an expansion of NAEP and independence for NAGB as a way to push an agenda for privatization and vouchers. So a number of the House Democratic members were reluctant to expand NAEP and were reluctant to expand the role of NAGB.

At the time, the Democrats were in control of both the House and the Senate; but in the Senate there was less reluctance on the part of Senator Kennedy, who was one of the most prominent liberals, to an expansion of NAEP and the creation of NAGB. The other liberals in the Senate, such as Illinois Senator Paul Simon, did not express the same degree of concern about NAEP and NAGB as House Democrats did. On the Republican side in the House, the Republicans were generally in favor of the national assessment, but I don't remember them being strong advocates for an expansion of the national assessment or for NAGB. On the Senate side, I think the Republicans were supportive of an expansion of NAEP and NAGB; but, again, it wasn't a major issue.

You have to remember that in a bill of that complexity, the National Assessment of Educational Progress and the role of NAGB were minor issues. The major issues had to do with whether you ratchet up standards in Title I, the amount of money provided to Title I, who gets the money, how many federal programs do you have, how do you administer those programs. It was a very large, complex bill dealing with most of the federal government's elementary and secondary programs. And the issues involving NAEP and NAGB were not major issues.

**Olkin:** How were decisions made?

**Jennings:** Decisions were made mostly at the staff level and ratified by the members, rather than being decisions which the elected members argued over in public. The way that these things go, the staff is given the task of clearing the underbrush, of trying to resolve the secondary and tertiary issues; and the members of Congress ratify their agreements or reject the staff agreements and debate those smaller issues themselves. But the primary attention of the members of Congress is on the big issues.

The same thing is happening today as the Congress resolves the current reauthorization of the Elementary and Secondary Education Act. The staff members are meeting today, in August 2001, resolving the secondary issues; and the members will meet in September to deal with the 10 or 20 major issues. So it's just a matter of how these things go in terms of the congressional process.

There were disagreements about NAEP and NAGB, but there were disagreements on many issues. This area certainly was not one of the major issues in the conference; it wasn't one of the major disagreements in the conference.

**Olkin**: How were the various conflicts resolved? Was it at the staff level?

**Jennings**: Yes, I don't believe any of the issues dealing with NAEP or NAGB went to the members. I think they were all resolved at the staff level. If I remember correctly, the Senate was pushing for the idea of a separate budget for NAGB and for power for NAGB to appoint its own members so that it would be a self-perpetuating institution; and they were also pushing for these achievement levels, as well as for a general expansion of NAEP. If I remember correctly, we agreed to the general expansion of NAEP. After some arguing, we agreed to the achievement levels; and then we put very modest restraints on the role of NAGB, and its budget was folded into the general NAEP authorization of appropriations. But these were relatively minor changes from what the Alexander-James panel had recommended.

**Olkin**: That changes a lot of the mechanics of how the legislation eventually evolved.

**Jennings**: But I have to tell you, I don't think that the members of Congress or the staff understood fully the extent to which these achievement levels would become important.

It sounded as if it would be a good thing to do, but today these achievement levels are driving much policy discussion. They are the achievement levels that are used in the national press; they are the achievement levels used by the presidential administrations. The Bush Administration is using them right now. They are the achievement levels that governors point to. They assumed a greater importance than anticipated. As you know, the concept was adopted by the Congress, and then there were later controversies about the development of those achievement levels. Those controversies engendered a great deal of confusion and studies and one thing and then another, and they're still somewhat controversial.

**Olkin**: In general, they're words that the lay public and that the media can easily describe, whereas distributions and more sophisticated methods are not that well understood.

**Jennings**: Right, but the problem seems to have been that NAGB decided that they would be high standards. For instance, you have a discrepancy between how American kids are ranked on reading achievement levels used in NAEP as compared to international reading levels. Using international reading standards, it seems that American kids do pretty well. Using the NAEP standards, it seems that they do not do as well. And so it's not so much a problem of the use of achievement levels as it is a problem of what happened after 1988 in terms of how these achievement levels were defined.

**Olkin**: Did NAEP get different attention from the executive officers under different presidents, under different administrations?

**Jennings**: I don't believe so. One key factor in leading to the state-level NAEP was their use. I think it was Secretary of Education Terrel Bell and then Secretary William Bennett who created their own achievement charts. And that led the states to shift their view on whether state-level achievement data was useful.

As to a different use of NAEP, I don't think in general that national results have been used differently. Well, let me back up a minute. Depending on the political agenda of an administration, somebody can read results differently and can cite them differently. If Secretary Lamar Alexander wanted to show that American schools were not doing well, he could point to certain aspects of NAEP. If Secretary Richard Riley wanted to show that American schools were improving, he could point to other aspects of NAEP. Now, they were dealing at different periods in time when NAEP results were different, but still the words they put around the results can have an effect.

I hesitate to say that administrations really looked at NAEP differently, because it is objective data. But an administration, regardless of party, will try to make a case for its agenda. Therefore they will marshal their information or their supporting data in whatever manner they think will help them achieve their objectives. So I wouldn't condemn any administration for how they use NAEP. I don't remember any egregious situation where somebody just totally misinterpreted NAEP. I would say that different administrations may have looked at the results differently; but it was because they had different policy objectives, and test results can be viewed differently. It is an illustration of the old saying, "Is a glass half filled or half empty?" So I wouldn't condemn anybody. It's the way policy is debated.

**Olkin**: During your time on the congressional staff, was the continuation of NAEP ever in any real jeopardy?

**Jennings**: No. The continuation of NAEP was not in jeopardy. But the gradual expansion of NAEP became a cause of debate at different points in time. NAEP, as you know, has grown considerably; and the growth at the national level was less of a concern than the growth at the state level, and then the option to permit local NAEP. The growth at the state level was controversial, and the states changed their positions so gradually that they came to support it. But growth at the local level was also controversial because liberals did not like the idea of a further expansion of testing, and conservatives gradually came to distrust NAEP as a prototype national test. This, in fact, did lead to controversies later. When President Clinton proposed a national test, some of the conservative groups started to look at NAEP in general. And there is one camp on the right which is opposed to NAEP as a national test.

You may want to talk to people at NAGB. They asked me to come down and testify about a year ago on certain aspects of NAEP. At that meeting there was a representative of a group that was opposed to an expansion of NAEP, and he raised questions about NAEP as a prototype national test. Also, in the House-passed ESEA bill, President George W. Bush's proposal that each state administer NAEP was changed at the urging of conservatives to say any nationally used test, because of their fear of a national test.

**Olkin**: Certainly the states were worried about state comparisons?

**Jennings**: Well, the states were worried about that because comparisons can be used so unfairly. The ACT [American College Testing Program] results are coming out tomorrow, I believe; and there's a chart in there on ACT results by state, which is a very unfair comparison because you have different percentages of students in each state taking the ACT. ACT puts out a disclaimer saying you have to be careful in how you use this data, and so forth. But the press picks up the chart and says that in

Massachusetts, ACT scores are such and such, when the percentage of kids taking the ACT in Massachusetts can be very small. So test results have to be used carefully, and unfortunately the press will just look at a chart and duplicate the chart or interpret the results from the chart.

I think this is what the states were concerned about, that once there were national comparisons — or state-by-state comparisons — that the data would be used unfairly. But what is happening in the country is that we are comparing ourselves more and more as we all become more competitive. And what's happening in the world, as the world is developing greater communications, is that we are becoming more comparison-minded and more competitive internationally. So there are problems with use and misuse of comparisons in data, but I believe the trend is toward more and more comparison.

The main problem with tests is that tests are useful indicators of how well people have done in school. You can argue about whether they are the appropriate tests. But the main problem is that test results have to improve instruction eventually. They shouldn't just be used as a judgment on how well schools are doing. And unfortunately, many of the standardized tests used today are not used to improve instruction. They are used as a barometer of how well schools are doing. School people become very resentful because the judgment is passed in the press and by the politicians on the success of schools, and then educators feel that they are not given the help to improve the test results. So we get mixed up between use of tests for accountability and use of tests for diagnosis.

We haven't clarified what use we want to make of tests for each of those reasons. Many of the psychometricians say you cannot use the same tests for both purposes. If that's true, then we have to either find a different way to test and combine the purposes, possibly using computers and technology more, or we have to have clear limits on the use of tests for accountability and try to encourage more testing for diagnosis.

**Olkin**: Where is this dialogue taking place at the present time?

**Jennings**: I do not believe it is taking place, because we are still on a testing kick, partially for the reasons I mentioned, namely, we want to compare ourselves to everybody to see how well we are doing, but partially because the policy makers have become overly enamored of testing. By policy makers, I include the news media, as well as elected politicians and business people and other influential people.

Reaction is setting in against an expansion of standardized testing and standards-based reform to a degree. I hope that the policy makers take note of this reaction and then begin to assess how well they use assessment, and that we have more of a debate about proper use of tests. But I don't think we have even begun that debate yet, and it has to be a national debate that occurs.

**Olkin**: It would really be a move backwards if there's a backlash that in some way jeopardizes NAEP.

**Jennings**: I don't think that will happen. I think NAEP is on very secure political ground for several reasons. It is the only reliable national test. You cannot rely on SAT scores, ACT scores; you cannot rely on commercial tests. So it is a high-quality instrument that gives us consistent data over time, even though there are controversies about different aspects of NAEP.

Second, because it is a high-quality instrument and because the National Assessment Governing Board has done a good job over time in terms of making sure that NAEP is a good instrument, and the National Center for Education Statistics and various secretaries of education and Congress have also done that, I think the business community and political leaders rely on NAEP and will insist that it be continued.

The danger for NAEP and for NAGB comes if NAEP is perceived as being expanded to become a national test for individual students. Then I think the problem will arise from people who are concerned about an expansion of any national or federal role in education. But I don't see that happening. Some of the folks who are advocates for NAEP would like to see an expansion of NAEP to serve that purpose; and if that occurs, I'd say that will create some serious problems for NAEP.

Look at three recent presidents in a row. President George Bush called for a national test for individual students. Bill Clinton called for a national test for individual students. And President George W. Bush is calling for an expansion of state-level testing in grades three through eight for individual students. So you have three presidents in a row, Democrat and Republicans, who are calling for a major expansion of testing to produce data for individual students. Two of them proposed a national test. The third, because of political reaction to the first two proposals, is proposing an expansion of state-level testing.

So we are not at the end of a push toward more testing and more individual test-score data. It's just a matter of how will we decide to do it and whether there is reliance on state-level testing, local-level testing, or some combination. The business community especially is very interested in getting more test data as barometers of how well schools are doing. There is this general interest in comparing ourselves to everybody in that, if we are able to compare ourselves, somehow we will do better, that we will become more competitive.

We shall have to see where things go, but I know that some folks who are proponents of NAEP want NAEP to be first in line if there is a return to an idea of a national test, so that there will not be another national test that is a competitor to NAEP. If that occurs, I think NAEP will become a far different thing.

Unfortunately, if you put consequences in NAEP — real consequences — for individual students, then NAEP becomes a different test. The irony is that it may show a great increase in student achievement. That is because, instead of testing 12th-graders who don't give a darn — a sample of 12th-graders take a test that they don't care about and, in effect, blow it off — you would have 12th-graders who cared a lot about it because there would be individual consequences. You might see 12th-grade scores go up considerably. So it would become a different type of test.

I don't think that's such a good idea. I think it's far better to continue NAEP as what they call a thermometer to gauge achievement over time. Even with all its flaws. Even with testing

12th-graders who shouldn't be tested because they don't care; it should be an earlier grade that's tested. Even with achievement levels being at very high levels, which may be unreasonable in some subject areas. Even with all it flaws, NAEP is a priceless treasure that we have to continue.

**Olkin**: Do you have a view of whether NAEP has become more policy relevant, and should it become so?

**Jennings**: Well without a doubt, NAEP has become more policy relevant. As soon as *USA Today* and the *New York Times* print stories using NAEP data about the number of kids who are at proficiency levels, it has gained policy relevance. As soon as governors start citing the numbers for their states and bemoaning the fact that their student populations are or are not at certain achievement levels, it's a policy instrument. So NAEP is important for policy today.

Before NAEP is even considered — or before any consideration is given to expanding the use of NAEP as a policy instrument — the data that NAEP has already collected, background data, should be mined for policy significance. I am told repeatedly by people who know that there is a vast quantity of data that has been collected through these interviews that are related to NAEP, through the surveys and so on, information that is not being used to draw policy conclusions about the condition of education, about improvements that could be made in education, and so forth. So before we think about a gigantic new step, I think we should use what we already have in the computers.

**Olkin**: You mean that we really need to unleash a lot of research on all the data related to education that we have collected?

**Jennings**: Yes. People in the schools feel that too much data is collected already, and they don't get the feedback on what they've given when they answer all these surveys. If we were to respect the people who are teaching and who are principals and who are asked to fill out all these surveys all the time — from all these different levels of government — the least we can do is use the information they provide to draw out what we can about the enterprise and report back the results to people.

**Olkin**: Could you comment a bit about your relations with NCES, with NAGB, with the National Academy of Education panel?

**Jennings**: These entities don't exist apart from the people who are in them. Over the years, I've dealt with all these entities, and I've dealt with different people in them. But sometimes, depending on the appointees and the composition of these different groups, I've had closer relationships than others.

**Olkin**: Can you give us your perspectives on NAEP or on education in general?

**Jennings**: NAEP is an invaluable instrument, and it is in all our interests that it continue. It should receive adequate funding so that it can assess in more areas and more regularly. I hope, though, that NAEP does not become enmeshed in too many accountability schemes where it's perceived as very important in measuring progress and linked to rewards and punishments, because then NAEP will become a different type of thing.

**Olkin**: There are several key words in the current proposed legislation. One is "confirm improvement" and the other is "improvement" itself. It's not quite clear how NAEP can be used to confirm that there's improvement at the state level or at the school level. That may be a problem that could jeopardize NAEP in its whole, namely, being used for purposes other than what it was originally designed for.

**Jennings**: Right. Well, we're caught between a couple of forces here. Nothing stays the same, and so NAEP may become different than how it was conceived in the 1960s. It already has become different because it has state-level data and it tests in many different areas, but in the beginning it wasn't doing either of those. And so it has become a different type of instrument.

The question is what do we want out of NAEP? Do we want it to be an independent barometer of how well kids are doing nationally and possibly by state, or do we want it enmeshed in other policies and policy changes? And if we do the latter, it means that people look at NAEP differently.

I think that NAEP results in general may be underreporting achievement in American education because of the structure of NAEP; but there are not consequences, because of the way that NAEP is given. If we attach consequences to it, we'll have improvements in NAEP scores; but we won't have continuity in results. If we want to have continuity in results so that we know over time how well we are doing, we have to pick the instrument we have, though there may be problems with it.

The interest in accountability and greater accountability is so great today that people keep searching for anything they can find to pass judgments. I'm sure the Bush Administration looked around, and what they found was that NAEP was the only national measure that could be relied on to give any kind of independent judgment about how well a state was doing; and therefore they brought it into their accountability scheme. But if it's going to be in any accountability scheme, it has to be written in very, very carefully so that the instrument itself doesn't become different and therefore show different results over time.

# CHAPTER 11

# The Influence of External Evaluations

*Robert L. Linn*

The National Assessment of Educational Progress (NAEP) has never lacked critics. Reactions to NAEP began shortly after the first Carnegie conferences were held in the 1960s. The National Education Association and the American Association of School Administrators saw the national assessment as a threat to local autonomy and a step toward a national curriculum. Those concerns were allayed by the ways in which NAEP came to be defined and implemented, but they have resurfaced whenever someone proposed that NAEP's role should be expanded.

During its history, NAEP has been subjected to many evaluations, both formal and informal. Some of the evaluations have been mandated by Congress. Others have been conducted in response to requests from the National Center for Education Statistics (NCES) or the National Assessment Governing Board (NAGB). Still other evaluations have been conducted on the initiative of individual scholars or have been part of the deliberations of advisory committees.

It would be a mistake to conclude that the majority of these evaluations have been negative. Although most of the evaluators have not hesitated to be critical of many aspects of NAEP, the general tenor of the evaluators' conclusions have been quite positive. NAEP has been subjected to close scrutiny and found to be a valuable source of information.

This chapter will review many of the evaluations that have been conducted and the recommendations that have been offered in order to see to what extent they have influenced NAEP. For the most part, this review is limited to external evaluations available in the literature. While there have been many evaluations and recommendations made over the years by the large number of NAEP advisory committees, including those conducted for NCES, NAGB, and the NAEP contractors, these advisory committee evaluations generally are beyond the scope of this chapter. Exceptions to this rule are made when secondary sources refer to committee recommendations.

## The Role and Functions of NAEP

One obvious role of NAEP is that of an indicator. Early discussions suggested that NAEP might produce indices analogous to the Consumer Price Index (Hazlett 1974). Educational indicators prior to NAEP were largely descriptions of input characteristics, such as enrollment, teacher qualifications, and expenditures. One of the fundamental ideas behind the founding of NAEP was that information about student achievement would be useful in identifying segments of the population at greatest educational risk so that, once identified, actions could be taken to enhance their educational opportunities. Ralph Tyler, for example, argued forcefully that better information was needed to make wise decisions about policies and the allocation of resources. He wrote that:

> The great educational tasks we now face require many more resources than have thus far been available, resources which should be wisely used to produce the maximum effect in extending educational opportunity and raising the level of education. To make these decisions, dependable information about the progress of education is essential. . . . Yet we do not have the necessary comprehensive dependable data; instead, personal views, distorted reports, and journalistic impressions are the sources of public opinion. This situation

will be corrected only by a careful, consistent effort to obtain data to provide sound evidence about the progress of American Education. (Tyler 1966, p. 95)

Equal educational opportunity was a major interest of both Tyler and Francis Keppel. However, Keppel had in mind a more focused and precise instrument than Tyler or the other NAEP developers thought possible. In testimony before the Select Committee on Equal Opportunity, chaired by Minnesota Senator Walter Mondale on 1 December 1971, Keppel gave enthusiastic support to NAEP and argued that the assessment movement fostered by NAEP had great potential for enhancing both the quality and equality of educational opportunity.

> There is an extraordinary hopeful possibility that out of this movement we can develop measures by the school — the program within the school building — which will make it possible — not now, sir, but in due course — to rifle-shoot direct funds to improve the performance within a school building.
>
> I am making a contrast here between the school system as a whole — all the primary, junior high, and high schools, treated as a unit — because the important data on equal educational opportunity gets lost in the aggregate. It would seem to me essential that we disaggregate it; get the unit of measure down to the school itself, the place where the individual in charge can be held more responsible, in my judgment, than the superintendent. (U.S. Senate 1971, p. 10950)

The developers clearly had more modest expectations. According to Greenbaum, Garet, and Solomon:

> Census-like data, the planners knew even then, would not be very dramatic. People expecting quick and simple answers to fundamental questions (Why can't Johnny read?) would be disappointed with initial assessment results. (1977, p. 199)

Womer and Mastie were even more circumspect:

> A recurring concern, both among those who support national assessment and those who have reservations about

it, is the ultimate utility of the results. How will they affect education in this country? This is a very difficult question. While national assessment is designed to provide general information, it is not designed to produce answers to specific questions. (1971, p. 118)

There have been various demands on NAEP to meet purposes for which it was not designed or that it could not afford to do. One recurring demand is that NAEP data be changed so that the information can be used by researchers and policy makers to make inferences about cause and effect. The final report of the National Academy of Education (NAE) evaluation summarized the issue:

There is a natural inclination, particularly when there has been substantial investment . . . to relate NAEP achievement results to the instruction factors surveyed in NAEP's teacher and background questionnaires in order to draw inferences about what works and what fails to work in one's state, district or school. Unfortunately, NAEP is not suitable for drawing strong inferences about which factors or variables account for educational achievement. (Glaser, Linn, and Bohrnstedt 1997, p. 19)

During its first years, NAEP's focus was very different than that of standardized tests. The items in the assessment were chosen because they had a clear educational value, not because they could sort individuals. In addition, NAEP assessments were focused on age levels instead of grade levels, so that grade-level comparisons were meaningless. Thus NAEP was not designed to meet the demands of some researchers and many policy makers.

## The ECS Years

On 1 July 1969, the administrative responsibility for NAEP was transferred from the Committee on Assessing the Progress of Education (CAPE) to the Education Commission of the States (ECS). From 1972 to 1983, when the responsibility for the conduct of NAEP was moved to Educational Testing Service (ETS), assessments were conducted in mathematics, science, music, social studies, reading, art, writing, music, citizenship, literature, basic life skills, and career and occupational development. During the ECS tenure, science was assessed four times; reading, mathematics, and social studies (either alone or in combination with citizenship) were assessed three times each; and music, art, literature, and writing were assessed twice each.

The accomplishments of NAEP during the ECS years were impressive. The system produced trustworthy results that were able to document achievement trends in several subjects. However, policy makers and the public had little awareness of NAEP.

Those who were aware of NAEP expressed a number of concerns about the results, especially data about trends. For example, the trend among 17-year-olds on the science assessment showed a decline in performance (Fitzharris 1993, p. 74).

Some educators argued that the assessments failed to reflect current practices in education because items prepared in the 1960s still were used in the late 1970s, though the science curriculum had changed. Indeed, keeping NAEP aligned with a changing curriculum while also measuring trends was a challenge; and it is an issue that has continued to draw the attention of evaluators to the present.

Another issue was that the NAEP reports emphasized student performance on individual items. Although the reporting of results for individual items is straightforward and has the advantage of directly showing what proportion of students can do a particular task, it has limitations. While averages can be computed for a fixed set of items, averages for different collections of items are not comparable. Thus performance trends are meaningful only for individual items or for common sets of items administered in each of the assessments being compared.

The 1982 report by Willard Wirtz and Archie Lapointe, *Measuring the Quality of Education: A Report on Assessing Educational Progress*, made a number of recommendations for changing NAEP. These recommendations included publishing state-by-state results, reporting results by grade level so that the assessment items could be aggregated, and establishing a policy council to over-see NAEP. When NAEP moved to the Educational Testing Service in 1983, these recommendations were adopted.

## The Educational Testing Service

The Educational Testing Service (ETS) won the NAEP contract in February 1983. The successful ETS proposal called for sub-stantial changes in the design, analysis, and reporting of NAEP results. The broad outline for the new design and rationale for the changes were articulated in a report titled *National Assessment of Educational Progress Reconsidered: A New Design for a New Era* (Messick, Beaton, and Lord 1983).

*Reporting by Grade Level.* One of the major changes intro-duced by ETS with the 1984 assessment was the introduction of NAEP scale scores using item response theory (IRT). The scale was defined as a developmental scale that spanned all three age and grade levels assessed by NAEP and was interpreted as esti-mated scores on a hypothetical 500-item test with specified prop-erties. This allowed researchers to track trends on assessments even if all the items were not identical from one assessment to another. This scale also was thought to provide a means of com-paring changes in achievement for a given age or grade level. However, the IRT scale was very abstract and much more diffi-cult to interpret than the scores for individual items.

Several critics challenged the appropriateness of the cross-age scaling (see, for example, Forsyth 1991; Haertel 1989). Thus it was decided to discontinue cross-grade scaling in favor of within-grade and within-age scaling. But scale interpretation is a diffi-cult challenge whether the scaling is done within or between grade levels. Consequently, a variety of other approaches were tried to aid in interpreting the results.

*State-by-State Assessments.* In 1984 the Council of Chief State School Officers (CCSSO) recommended that the law authorizing NAEP be changed to permit the use of NAEP to make state-by-state comparisons (Fitzharris 1993). Then, in January 1987, the

Alexander-James report gave a high priority to changing NAEP to allow state-by-state comparisons. Indeed, the report made state-by-state comparisons its first recommendation.

> The single most important change recommended by the Study Group is that the assessment collect representative data on achievement in each of the fifty states and the District of Columbia. Today state and local school administrators are encountering a rising public demand for thorough information on the quality of their schools, allowing comparison with data from other states and districts and with their own historical records. (Alexander and James 1987, pp. 11-12)

The report acknowledged that there had been concerns in the past about comparing states, but it concluded that those "concerns are less important now than they were previously, and that most can be readily accommodated with a redesigned national assessment" (p. 5).

A National Academy of Education (NAE) panel was formed to comment on the Alexander-James report. The NAE panel, chaired by University of Pittsburgh Professor Robert Glaser, expressed concern that, if the national assessment allowed state-by-state comparisons, the data would be used to rank the states.

> We are concerned about the emphasis in the Alexander-James report on state-by-state comparisons of average test scores. Many factors influence the relative ranking of states, districts, and schools. Simple comparisons are ripe for abuse and are unlikely to inform meaningful school improvement efforts. (Glaser 1987, p. 59)

Despite these reservations, there seemed to be fairly widespread support for using NAEP to obtain state-by-state results.

Congress followed the advice of the Alexander-James Study Group when it enacted Public Law 100-297, the reauthorization of NAEP in 1988. The reauthorization included an option for states to obtain state-level NAEP results by participating in the Trial State Assessment (TSA) as part of the 1990 and 1992 administrations of NAEP. The 1988 reauthorization also included a requirement for the evaluation of the TSA by either the NAE or the National Academy of Sciences (NAS).

The 1990 TSA was limited to the eighth-grade mathematics assessment. State participation was voluntary. Thirty-seven states, the District of Columbia, and two territories participated in the assessment. Unlike the national samples, which include students in both public and private schools, the state samples were limited to public schools.

Responsibility for the evaluation of the Trial State Assessment was given to the National Academy of Education. The NAE formed a panel to conduct the evaluations of the 1990 and the 1992 TSAs. The first NAE panel report, focusing on the evaluation of the 1990 TSA, was issued in 1992 (Glaser, Linn, and Bohrnstedt 1992). The panel report concluded that the 1990 TSA had been carried out successfully. Because the 1990 TSA had been limited to one grade and one subject and because the 1992 TSA was already under way at the time the report was released, the report recommended that the trial be continued in an expanded form as part of the 1994 assessment.

The second administration and reporting of NAEP at the state level was in 1992. In 1992, the TSA again assessed mathematics for the eighth grade. It also assessed reading and mathematics for the first time for the fourth grade. The number of states participating increased from 37 in 1990 to 41 in 1992.

The evaluation of the 1992 TSA by the NAE panel followed up on many of the issues studied in its evaluation of the 1990 TSA. The recommendation of the NAE panel, based on its evaluation of the 1990 and 1992 trials, was "that the Congress authorize a continuation of state NAEP" (Glaser, Linn, and Bohrnstedt 1993*b*, p. 104). The panel also recommended that "Congress mandate ongoing evaluation of state NAEP with ongoing feedback to Congress" (p. 104).

Congress extended the TSA to include the 1994 administration of NAEP, and the NAE panel's evaluation was expanded to include the 1994 TSA of fourth-grade students in reading (Glaser, Linn, and Bohrnstedt 1996). Subsequently, Congress authorized the continuation of state NAEP and mandated an evaluation of the national assessment, as well as the state assessment (Public Law 103-382). That mandated evaluation was conducted by a committee of the National Research Council (NRC) (Pellegrino, Jones, and Mitchell 1999).

*The National Assessment Governing Board.* Throughout the period that NAEP was conducted by ECS and for the initial years of the ETS contract, NAEP was directly controlled by the Department of Education. With input from the contractor, the department appointed a council to address policy issues; and the contractor coordinated the work of the council. Technical advisory bodies were appointed by and provided advice directly to the contractor.

The Alexander-James panel had reservations about the lack of a governance structure that was independent of NCES, the Department of Education, and the contractor.

> In order to undertake such demanding new tasks as state-by-state comparisons, the national assessment will require some important changes in its current governance structure. . . . We recommend the creation of an independent governing agency, the Educational Assessment Council (EAC). The EAC would operate independently of the institution carrying out the actual assessment and would define content areas, assessment procedures, and guidelines for fair comparisons of states and localities. (Alexander and James 1987, p. 13)

The 1988 reauthorization, Public Law 100-297, established a new governance structure for NAEP. NCES retained responsibility for operations and technical aspects of NAEP analyses, but responsibility for governing NAEP was assigned to a newly authorized body, the National Assessment Governing Board (NAGB). Among its responsibilities, NAGB selects the subject areas to be assessed and is responsible for the NAEP frameworks that specify the content of the assessments in each subject area.

*Other Recommendations.* The NAE panel also made a number of recommendations for improving state NAEP. Several of the panel's recommendations were adopted, including:

1. The trial should be continued for one more round in 1994. While this recommendation was adopted, funding limitations required it be conducted on a smaller scale than the panel recommended.
2. State samples should include students attending private schools.
3. The practice of monitoring a random selection of schools participating in the state NAEP should be continued.
4. New reporting devices should be used, and the release of results should be spread throughout the year.

Two other recommendations were followed, at least in part. These were the recommendation that NAEP content be comprehensive and reflect the most up-to-date approaches, as well as current classroom instruction, and that the exclusion of children with disabilities be evaluated. The remaining five recommendations of the panel were not adopted. These included the recommendation that out-of-school 17-year-olds be included in the assessment, as had been the case in the earliest years of NAEP, and that the prohibition against reporting results below the state level be continued. The prohibition was, in fact, lifted; and districts, as well as states, are now allowed to participate in NAEP.

The NAE evaluations of the 1992 and 1994 trials devoted considerable attention to issues of the content and cognitive demands of the assessments, the issue of inclusion of students with disabilities and students with limited English proficiency in the assessments, and ways to make sampling for the state assessments more efficient. A number of recommendations were made for ways to ensure that the content of the assessments be comprehensive, "reflecting the most forward-looking pedagogical approaches, at the same time they reflect the best of current practice" (Glaser, Linn, and Bohrnstedt 1993*b*, p. xxii). Arguably, NAGB, NCES, and the NAEP contractor worked to achieve that recommendation to the extent feasible within the constraints of the resources that are available for NAEP.

Inclusion of students in assessments is a major issue not only for NAEP, but also for state- and district-mandated assessments.

Inclusion of students with disabilities in assessments is a requirement of the 1997 amendments to Public Law 94-142, the Individuals with Disabilities Education Act (IDEA) of 1975. The IDEA requirement to provide students with accommodations so they can meaningfully participate in assessments is clear. Both the desirability of inclusion and the substantial unknowns of including students in meaningful ways that produce valid results were recognized by the NAE panel in its recommendations for NAEP.

> NCES and NAGB should continue efforts to encourage greater participation of students with disabilities or limited English proficiency in the current NAEP. At the same time, they should continue research to identify adaptations or accommodations for each of these groups that would provide more valid measures of subject-area achievement as specified by the NAEP frameworks. (Glaser, Linn, and Bohrnstedt 1996, p. xxiii)

NCES and NAGB have made major efforts both to make NAEP more inclusive and to carry out the data collection and analyses needed to preserve the validity and interpretability of results, particularly trends in achievement.

## Reporting NAEP Results

The ways that NAEP results are reported have received considerable attention from both those responsible for NAEP and those who have evaluated it. The scale scores used by ETS avoided some of the limitations of reporting of results only in terms of individual exercises. But the meaning of the scale was obscure. Consequently, efforts were made to make the results more easily interpretable. One way of doing this was by identifying items that became known as item anchors — items associated with selected locations on the scale. The intent was to give meaning to the scale by showing items that students located at selected points on the scale would be likely to answer correctly and that lower-scoring students could not. Another approach to giving more meaning to the NAEP scale was to identify achievement levels on the scale that corresponded to what students should be able to do.

*Item Anchoring.* The first report of NAEP results under the ETS contract was in 1984. To help nonspecialists interpret those results, ETS associated labels with scale scores at 50-point intervals from 150 to 350. Those labels identified levels from rudimentary (150) to advanced (350). However, "Users did not find this labeling helpful, because of the cross-grade scale" (Shepard et al. 1993, p. 18). Such labeling also was considered to be beyond the purview of the contractor. Hence the practice was discontinued. Instead, item anchoring was used in an effort to give meaning to the scale.

Item-anchoring procedures were developed by Albert Beaton while he was the head of the data-analysis team at ETS. Items were selected as anchors for the scale points of 150, 200, 250, 300, and 350. In order to qualify as an anchor item, an item had to be answered correctly by at least 65% of the students whose overall performance places them at the anchor point. In addition, the item had to be answered correctly by less than half the students at the next lower anchor point.

Once the eligible items had been selected for each anchor point, they were carefully examined by a group of content specialists and used as the basis for writing descriptions of what students scoring at that point or above were able to do on the assessment. Exemplar anchor items also were selected as explicit illustrations of items answered correctly by two-thirds or more of the students at the anchor point, but less than half the students at the next lower anchor point.

When item anchors were shown as exemplars, they were accompanied by a report of the percentage of students who scored above that point. Unfortunately, as noted by Forsyth (1991) and by Linn and Dunbar (1992), media interpretations of the results were frequently erroneous. For example, in one case the media assumed that, because 19% of the 13-year-old students scored above an anchor score of 300, only 19% could correctly answer the anchor item reported to exemplify performance at a score of 300. The actual percentage of students who answered the item correctly in this example was 51%.

Issues about the use of item anchors became largely moot when NAGB decided to set performance standards, called achievement levels, and to use them in reporting NAEP results.

*Achievement Levels.* The idea for reporting NAEP results in terms of a small number of descriptive categories was suggested by the NAE panel that was formed to provide commentary on the Alexander-James report. The NAE panel recommended that:

> to the maximal extent technically feasible, NAEP use descriptive classifications as the principal scheme in future assessment. For each content area NAEP should articulate clear descriptions of performance levels, descriptions that might be analogous to such craft rankings as novice, journeyman, highly competent and expert. (Glaser 1987, p. 58)

The development of performance standards was undertaken soon after the formation of the NAGB; and the first standards, called achievement levels, were used to report the 1990 mathematics assessment.

The decision to report NAEP results in terms of achievement levels was based on the governing board's interpretation of the legislation that reauthorized NAEP. Among other responsibilities, the legislation assigned NAGB the responsibility of "identifying appropriate achievement goals" (Public Law 100-297, Part C, Section 3403 (6) (A)). As was noted by the NAE Panel on the Evaluation of the NAEP Trial State Assessment, the board:

> might have responded in different ways. Given the emerging consensus for establishing national education standards, the fact that the Education Summit was silent on who should set standards, and the fact that NAEP was the only national assessment of achievement based on defensible samples, NAGB interpreted the authorizing legislation as a mandate to set performance standards, which it named "achievement levels," for NAEP. (Shepard et al. 1993, p. xviii)

The achievement levels were important because of the political pressure for national standards, and thus the 1990 achievement levels were subjected to several evaluations (for example, Linn,

Koretz, Baker, and Burstein 1991; Stufflebeam, Jaeger, and Scriven 1991*b*; General Accounting Office 1993). NAGB was responsive to many of the criticisms and undertook another, more extensive, standard-setting effort for the 1992 mathematics and reading assessments. However, the evaluations of the 1992 effort were again quite critical (for example, Burstein et al. 1993; Burstein et al. 1995/1996; Shepard et al. 1993; Shepard 1995). The NAE panel concluded that the achievement levels might reduce, rather than enhance, the validity of interpretations of NAEP results.

Not all evaluators agreed with the negative evaluations. Indeed, there were strong defenders of the 1992 mathematics achievement levels, the process used to set them, and the interpretations they were intended to support (see, for example, American College Testing Program 1993; Cizek 1993; Kane 1993*a*).

Much of the debate about achievement levels has focused on the method for setting standards. That is hardly surprising given that the NAE panel recommended against the use of "the Angoff method or any other item-judgment method to set achievement levels" because the panel concluded that such methods were "fundamentally flawed" (Shepard et al. 1993, p. 132).

There is broad agreement in the technical community that different methods of setting standards lead to different cut-scores, but there is not general agreement that one particular method is best. Also, there is agreement that standards ultimately involve policy judgments. Thus NAGB has continued to rely on achievement levels that use techniques considered flawed by some evaluators.

The most recent evaluations of NAEP, conducted by a committee of the National Research Council (NRC), have continued to find fault with the NAEP achievement levels. The NRC committee's recommendation was:

> Summary Recommendation 5. The current process for setting achievement levels should be replaced. New models for setting achievement levels should be developed in which the judgmental process and data are made clearer to NAEP users. (Pellegrino, Jones, and Mitchell 1999, p. 162)

This NRC recommendation, like similar ones before it from other evaluators, was rejected by NAGB.

## Other NRC Recommendations

The analysis of the NAEP achievement levels is one of the few areas in which the conclusions of evaluators of NAEP have been uniformly and consistently negative without having any effect on practice. The recommendations of evaluators have been ignored or rejected. An unfortunate effect of this impasse is that it has overshadowed other aspects of evaluation reports. Thus some of the other conclusions and recommendations of evaluation panels may have had less effect than they otherwise might have had.

This appears to be the case for the report of the NRC Committee on the Evaluation of the National and State Assessments of Educational Progress (Pellegrino, Jones, and Mitchell 1999). The NRC committee reached five broad summary conclusions and made broad recommendations for each of those conclusions, only one of which dealt with achievement levels. But it was the conclusion and associated recommendation on achievement levels that received the most attention when the report was presented. The other four summary conclusions and associated recommendations are potentially important ones for the future of NAEP.

*Coordinated System of Indicators.* The NRC committee's first summary conclusion concerned the limitations of any single method for collecting data, such as NAEP, for measuring all the aspects of student achievement. Associated with this conclusion was the committee's first summary recommendation.

> The nation's educational progress should be portrayed by a broad array of education indicators that includes but goes beyond NAEP's achievement results. The U.S. Department of Education should integrate and supplement the current collections of data about education inputs, practices, and outcomes to provide a more comprehensive picture of education in America. In this system, the measurement of student achievement should be reconfigured so that large-scale surveys are but one of several methods used to collect infor-

mation about student achievement. (Pellegrino, Jones, and Mitchell 1999, p. 22)

The earlier NAE panel argued for better integration with other sources of information and for NAEP to serve as a resource for other data-collection systems (Glaser, Linn, and Bohrnstedt 1997, pp. 108-109). The NRC committee developed this idea more fully. The coordinated system envisioned by the NRC committee would include information on financial resources, school organization and governance, teacher and professional development, instructional practice, content standards and curricula, school climate, home and community support for learning, and student background, in addition to student achievement. In addition to NAEP, the student-achievement component of the coordinated system also would include such international assessments as the Third International Mathematics and Science Study and such longitudinal studies as the National Education Longitudinal Study and the Early Childhood Longitudinal Study.

*Redesign.* In its second summary recommendation, the NRC committee proposed a significant reconfiguration of NAEP:

> Summary Recommendation 2. NAEP should reduce the number of independent large-scale data collections while maintaining trends lines, periodically updating frameworks, and providing accurate national and state-level estimates of academic achievement. (Pellegrino, Jones, and Mitchell 1999, p. 56)

The committee argued that the reduction of independent large-scale data collections could be accomplished, in part, by merging the main NAEP with the trend NAEP. As noted in the committee report, this recommendation is consistent with suggestions for redesign offered by NAGB (1997*d*), the NAGB Design Feasibility Team (Forsyth et al. 1996), and the NAE panel's final report (Glaser, Linn, and Bohrnstedt 1997). In addition, some steps toward that goal already had been taken.

The NRC committee also argued that the national and state designs could be streamlined by combining them. This suggestion also had been made by other groups, but operational obstacles prevented any clear action in this direction.

In addition to recommending streamlining and combining the large-scale survey functions of NAEP, the NRC committee concluded that the "collection of meaningful NAEP data in the twelfth grade is problematic given the insufficient motivation of high school seniors and their highly variable curricula and dropout rates" (Pellegrino, Jones, and Mitchell 1999, p. 84). Therefore the committee recommended that assessing students in grades 10 or 11 be explored.

*Inclusion.* The NRC committee's third summary conclusion focused on the assessment of students with disabilities and of English-language learners.

> Summary Conclusion 3. NAEP has the goal of reporting results that reflect the achievement of all students in the nation. However, many students with disabilities and English-language learners have been excluded from the assessments. Some steps have been taken recently to expand the participation of these students in NAEP, but their performance remains largely invisible. (Pellegrino, Jones, and Mitchell 1999, p. 87)

The NRC committee also recommended that "the proposed system of education indicators should include measures that improve understanding of the performance and educational needs of these populations" (p. 87).

The NAGB and NCES have consistently responded to calls for greater inclusion of students with special needs. However, the field of education measurement has not been very successful in finding valid ways to include such students in assessments so that their results can be combined with, or meaningfully be compared with, the results of other students. The challenges in this area of assessment are many, and the solid answers are relatively few. Thus the meaningful inclusion of all students in assessments, while required by law and recommended by many different evaluators, remains a substantial challenge not just for NCES and NAGB, but for the field of education assessment generally.

*Content.* The NRC committee's fourth summary conclusion and recommendation echoed a theme found repeatedly in evaluations of NAEP, namely that the content coverage of the national assessment should reflect what is known about learning and achievement. The NRC committee's fourth summary recommendation was:

> The entire assessment development process should be guided by a coherent vision of student learning and by the kinds of inferences and conclusions about student perform-ance that are desired in reports of NAEP results. In this as-sessment development process, multiple conditions need to be met: (a) NAEP frameworks and assessments should reflect subject-matter knowledge; research, theory, and practice regarding what students should understand and how they learn; and more comprehensive goals for schooling; (b) assess-ment instruments and scoring criteria should be designed to capture important differences in the levels and types of stu-dents' knowledge and understanding both through large-scale surveys and multiple alternative assessment methods; and (c) NAEP reports should provide descriptions of student performance that enhance the interpretation and usefulness of summary scores. (Pellegrino, Jones, and Mitchell 1999, p. 114)

The NRC committee's vision of NAEP is ambitious. It is one that NCES and NAGB arguably try to achieve. However, time, cost, and the need to maintain trends inevitably make the assess-ment fall short of the vision.

## Conclusion

NAEP has been subjected to close scrutiny by many evaluation panels and by individual investigators throughout its history. Nu-merous recommendations have come from the many evaluations. Those responsible for NAEP have heeded most of those recom-mendations to the extent feasible within the constraints imposed by the level of authorizations. A few recommendations have been rejected because they were considered inconsistent with desired policy or because they were deemed infeasible.

# CHAPTER 12

# NAEP from Three Different Perspectives

*Wayne Martin*

Over a period of three decades, I have viewed NAEP first as a staff member at the Education Commission of the States, then as a state director of assessments, and most recently as director of the State Assessment Center at the Council of Chief State School Officers. NAEP looked different to me from each of these perspectives.

## Perspective 1: NAEP Staff Member

I joined the NAEP project staff in October 1972. At that time, NAEP was a state-of-the-art measurement project designed specifically to accomplish the charge made to the U.S. Office of Education in its original charter in 1867, to monitor and report on the nation's educational progress. Within measurement and education circles, NAEP was known as "Ralph's Baby" — a reference to a contemporary novel and movie, *Rosemary's Baby*, and to Ralph W. Tyler's tireless efforts to establish NAEP.

NAEP provided a sharp contrast to the standardized, nationally norm-referenced achievement tests of the period. While the standardized tests were limited to multiple-choice items, NAEP included multiple-choice questions, open-ended or free-response items, and performance tasks. Each assessment was constructed to identify what students know and can do. In many ways, it was the model for today's standards-based assessments.

The states feared that national assessment was an attempt by the federal government to take over education. Schools and districts feared that it was an attempt to establish a national curriculum. Conspiracy theorists saw it as a way to establish a national database about American youth to either identify them or to brainwash them.

To the measurement community, NAEP was an elegant design problem to be developed and refined. To the education policy community, it was a means to foster and encourage the improvement of education opportunities, systems, and funding. To the federal government, it was an extremely expensive toy (at an annual funding level of $6 million) with which no one quite knew what to do.

In its early years, NAEP suffered from too much information and no meaningful way to put all of it together. The early assessments reported the $p$-values (percentages correct) for each item, as well as their associated standard errors. In addition to computing these values for the national sample, NAEP also reported them for four regions of the country (Northeast, Southeast, Central, and West), sex (female, male), race (black, white, Hispanic, Asian American, and Native American), size of community (four categories), type of community (four categories), size and type of community (seven categories), and level of parental education (four categories).

After a thorough investigation by the Analysis Advisory Committee (ANAC), mean and median $p$-values for groups of items were reported for the nation and the various subgroups. While this reduced the sheer bulk of the reports, it limited the possible uses of the data.

NAEP began to reach a broader audience when it developed its "focused reports" (for example, Consumer Mathematics) which contained a combination of specific item-level data and summary data across groups of items. The focused reports were further enhanced by adding interpretive comments by educators concerning the implications of the results for instruction. This was done through either contracts with such subject-matter groups as the National Council for the Social Studies and the National Council of Teachers of Mathematics or by establishing learning area committees who worked with an assessment from developing objectives through reporting.

The success of the focused reports led to the development of "probes." A probe was designed to be a limited assessment of a specific topic or area administered to one or more age groups. The probes were done as "contract work" from other funding sources within the federal government. For example, NAEP conducted several "functional literacy" assessments of 17-year-olds for the Right-to-Read Program. It conducted an energy assessment of 13- and 17-year-olds for the Department of Energy. It also contracted with the Department of Defense Dependents Schools (DoDDS) to conduct writing assessments of DoDDS students.

Although the NAEP reports began to reach a broad audience after the first report was released that indicated the change in science knowledge, federal monitors continued to ask whether these reports justified the time and expense of NAEP. As a consequence, the NAEP budget began to shrink, and parts of the program were lost. These losses included the assessment of young adults, the assessment of out-of-school 17-year-olds, the individually administered booklets with the performance tasks, and annual assessments. The percentage of open-ended items, which required hand-scoring, was reduced. Finally, learning areas began to be lost; art, music, and career and occupational development disappeared from the assessment schedule.

The federal monitors also wanted the national assessment to become "policy relevant" and attempted to force the project in that direction. During the "back-to-the-basics" movement, there was a strong push to persuade NAEP to narrow its assessment coverage to monitor the basics. When there was a national furor over the decline in the SAT and ACT scores, the federal monitors wanted to know why NAEP couldn't contribute more to the public debate.

NAEP also had supporters. State departments of education began to look at NAEP as a model for state testing programs. NAEP shared its released items and its expertise with state staff. Indeed, the Annual Large-Scale Assessment Conference began as a vehicle for training state staff. Local districts were intrigued about the possibility of using released assessment items to compare themselves to the nation and to similar types of schools by using the size-and-type of community variable. Public-use data tapes were made available to researchers, and the federal government sponsored secondary analyses of the NAEP database to increase its policy relevance. The use of NAEP reading data, which showed significant improvements in literal comprehension among minority students and other targeted populations, ensured continued congressional support for the national assessment.

The Education Commission of the States (ECS) was successful in fending off potential competitors for the various NAEP grants and contracts until 1982. Though the staff that ECS had hired for NAEP was extremely dedicated to the project, the organization's motivation was much simpler. The organization had become dependent on the overhead received from the NAEP work. However, this dependence was resented by the ECS central staff; and despite the attempts of various NAEP directors, both the project and project staff were treated as "step-children" within the organization.

By 1982, the NAEP staff had done about as much as could be done within the existing design and existing budget. ECS had no financial resources to support or supplement the project. Staff had done more with less, taken on contract work, produced useful and readable reports for a variety of constituents, provided professional development for countless state assessment staff, and survived various political assaults by federal officials, as well as the political right and political left. There was little or no new magic to add when it was time for the 1982 contract bids.

As a result of that competition, in 1983 the contract was transferred from the Education Commission of the States to the Educational Testing Service (ETS). ETS offered an innovative, partial incomplete block design (the BIB-Spiral) for NAEP that allowed for many potential enhancements. In addition, ETS proposed bridge studies to continue the long-term trend lines. ETS also had the financial resources to support and supplement the project.

In retrospect, the transfer of NAEP to ETS was very good for the national assessment. The National Report Card and the current national and state NAEP programs are the result of this transfer. But at the time, it looked like a very bad move — especially to the NAEP staff at ECS.

## Perspective 2: State Assessment Director

In 1984 I joined the Colorado Department of Education as a research/legislative policy analyst within the Planning and Evaluation Unit. Part of my responsibility was to prepare research reports for internal and external use; the other part was to monitor specific legislative issues for the Colorado State Board of Education, so that they could be briefed on the issues and provided with options that they might want to pursue legislatively.

Colorado was — and still is — an education "local-control" state. Most of the authority is vested with the local education agencies and their boards. For example, curricular decisions are the responsibility of the district; districts issue diplomas, not the state; and districts set graduation requirements, not the state. The state board of education has a general oversight and supervisory role that is manifested through its state accreditation and accountability requirements for districts and schools. Whereas other states were adopting minimum competency tests, Colorado allowed each district to decide if it wished to have a minimum competency test for graduation. Similarly, each district was required to have a testing program; but all of the decisions regarding the testing program (test selection, grades to be tested, time of testing during the school year, reporting metric for the test, etc.) were left to the district.

The question of statewide testing was raised by the Colorado General Assembly in 1985, and I was assigned to monitor the issue for the state board of education because of my training and experience with NAEP. The legislature was tired of having a patchwork quilt of student test results. They wanted to be able to compare district and school results.

The Colorado education community managed to seize on several related issues and combined them in a research proposal that gave the state two years to explore a variety of policy options. During the first year, I was assigned by the state board to carry out a legislatively prescribed state testing experience for all students in grades 3, 6, 9, and 12 using a standardized, nationally norm-referenced achievement test. During the second year, I was allowed to explore alternative assessment models.

The first-year report contained results for every school district in the state at the four grades, despite Colorado's strong tradition of local control. The second year allowed for several alternative models for statewide testing to be piloted using samples. Drawing on my NAEP experience, the alternative models included a writing assessment, a school-readiness measure for first-graders, a physical-fitness test, an achievement-and-ability test, and some experimentation with "higher order" thinking measures. The state board liked not being limited to the traditional standardized test and preferred to have state-level results.

Surprisingly, there were few complaints about the results being based on samples, with no results for all districts or all schools. As a result, the state board adopted a statewide assessment program in 1988 that included many NAEP features. Given that the purpose was to produce state results, the state testing program was based on samples of public schools. No district-level results were produced. Schools were the sampling unit, and all students within the school at the selected grade were to be tested. School results and individual student results were sent directly to the schools.

A three-year cycle was established for the tests. In the first year, a standardized, nationally norm-referenced achievement test was to be administered to the sample in grades 4, 8, and 11. In the second year, a writing assessment was to be administered; and a mathematics assessment was to be administered in the third year. Then the cycle began again.

When the Trial State NAEP program was authorized by Congress in 1988, the Colorado Board of Education chose to make state NAEP part of the Colorado assessment program. This meant that schools that were selected for the sample were required to participate.

Districts and schools began to grumble about the state NAEP program. To make it more palatable, Colorado agreed to reimburse districts for two days of a substitute teacher's pay to cover the NAEP training and assessment administration sessions. In addition, the state paid the travel costs of the teacher to attend the training session. However, this did not halt complaints about the "master" state NAEP testing schedule, which assigned a specific date and time for individual schools to administer the assessment. Although the first Trial State NAEP was limited to eighth-grade mathematics, districts that were accustomed to local control now had to deal with both the "heavy-hand" of the state and the even heavier hand of the federal government. If the decision to participate had been left to individual schools and districts, it is doubtful that Colorado could have met the minimum sample participation criteria.

ETS had established the NAEP Network to provide information directly to the states about the state NAEP program. Each state sent one or two representatives to several meetings in Washington, D.C., before the actual administration of the assessment, with the costs covered by ETS under the terms of its contract with the National Center for Education Statistics. Discussions of both the national and state reports were held at almost every meeting. Prototype reports were provided for comment and review. Estimated average scale scores were the main reporting metric.

Several days before the reports were released, participating states were requested to send two representatives to a special two-day NAEP Network meeting, where reporting procedures, details of the news conference, and some results were presented. Most states sent their state assessment director and a senior-level administrator from the state department of education. During that meeting, an argument ensued over the term "grade level." The difference between grades for national average scores was approximately 40 points. Also, the difference between average scale scores for minority and majority eighth-grade students was approximately 40 points. These two comparisons led some to comment that minority students were scoring at the fourth-grade level. Given the controversy and heated debate that this remark generated, it was announced the next day that it had been removed from all release documents.

The meeting closed with attendees being taken to one of the first meetings of the National Education Goals Panel to hear an address by President George Bush. State personnel then went home to prepare for the release the following week.

To facilitate the release of state results, NCES arranged to have each state's copies of both the national report and the state report shipped directly to the state assessment director immediately before the news conference so that the state could use the reports as part of its news release. Unfortunately, delays in the production of the report resulted in the materials having to be sent by Federal Express to the states. While this sounded like a good idea, no one took into account the size and volume of such a shipment.

Both reports suffered from the traditional NAEP reporting problem: how to make the reports readable while still presenting as complete a statistical picture as possible. Also, the reporting function had been moved from the contractor to NCES as a part of the 1988 reauthorization of NAEP, which meant that *all* NAEP reports had to go through the NCES report adjudication process. The adjudication process requirements for NCES were the same as for other federal statistical agencies. This meant that all interpretive and speculative comments could no longer be included in the report. It also meant that virtually every number included in the report had to be accompanied by its associated standard error.

The Colorado reports arrived on a shrink-wrapped wooden pallet, an unusual experience for the Federal Express delivery person. He was even less happy when he found that the Colorado Department of Education was in a building with no loading dock and that he was going to have to park on the street at a meter, unload the shipment from his truck, bring it through the front door, cart it through the lobby to the freight elevator, then take it to my office on the opposite side of the fifth floor. Just as I finished explaining to the delivery person where the pallet needed to go, a pigeon deposited a "gift" on the man's head and shoulders. At that point, I decided the best thing to do was to tell him that I'd meet him on the fifth floor and to get out of his way.

These "secure, embargoed materials" never made it all the way to my office, which was one of the few places in the building where they could be stored in a locked room. The weight of the hand cart, wooden pallet, and reports prevented the original 1920s freight elevator from "leveling" at the fifth floor. Thus, it was necessary to unwrap the pallet and move each carton off the elevator to the hallway. At this point, I thought it best to sign the delivery receipt and let the delivery person leave. Of course, the delivery truck was ticketed because its meter had expired.

While the effort required from state education agency staff for the 1990 state NAEP program was manageable, the 1992 state NAEP program was more difficult. In that year, both fourth- and eighth-grade mathematics were being assessed. That meant maintaining two master NAEP testing schedules, notifying districts of twice as many schools being sampled, training twice as many NAEP test administrators, and spending twice the resources from the state testing budget. By that time, I had delegated the details of state NAEP to a staff member while I concentrated on the state testing program.

The 1994 NAEP program originally scheduled science and mathematics assessments in both the fourth and eighth grade. State NAEP costs were increasing in terms of state education agency staff time and expenses, even in states where participation by schools was required. State staff began grumbling about this burden, and states began to look for ways to cover these costs. The Statewide Systemic Initiative (SSI) program for science and mathematics education, funded by the National Science Foundation (NSF), appeared to be such a resource for Colorado. The five-year NSF proposal outlined how the state would use the 1994 state NAEP results and committed the state to participate in the 1998 state NAEP program during the last year of the SSI grant. By this time, the "trial" aspect of state NAEP was completed; and the program was considered successful enough to be carried forward.

A federal funding shortfall forced NCES and NAGB to cancel the 1994 mathematics and science assessments and replace them with a reading assessment. For states such as Colorado that tried to build state NAEP into their overall state assessment plans, this switch was a strong blow. Chief state school officers and state assessment directors began to lobby both NAGB and NCES for a regular, dependable assessment schedule, at least for the state NAEP program. If state NAEP were to become a regular part of state plans, it must have a predictable schedule that could meet planning and budgeting purposes. NAGB agreed and eventually established a 10-year master schedule for the state NAEP program.

During the early 1990s a number of events affected state assessment policy. Colorado joined the New Standards Project, and I became the Colorado New Standards Team Leader. Colorado Governor Roy Romer was selected to be the co-chair of the National Education Goals Panel and the National Commission of Education Standards and Tests (NCEST). Colorado Commissioner of Education Bill Randall was appointed to the National Assessment Governing Board, where he eventually served as chair of the Achievement Levels Committee and NAGB. He also was elected to the board of directors of the Council of Chief State School Officers and eventually became that organization's president. I was appointed to the Permanent Standing Assessment Task Force and the Assessment Subcommittee of the Education Information Advisory Committee (EIAC) for the CCSSO and became chair of both two years later. Obviously, this convergence was instrumental in Colorado's decision to launch itself into standards-based reform. It also gave Colorado a vested interest in the state NAEP program.

EIAC is a forum where state and local education agency staff meet with federal government staff and federal contractors to discuss data-collection issues. Its mission is to reduce the burden on state and local staff by ensuring that duplicate data collections are avoided and by establishing common definitions across various federal offices and agencies. If issues cannot be resolved through face-to-face discussions at EIAC, EIAC concerns are conveyed to the CCSSO, the secretary of education, the appropriate assistant secretaries, and the Office of Management and Budget, which conducts a review of all government forms used to collect data.

The Permanent Standing Assessment Task Force, which is part of the EIAC Assessment Subcommittee, is funded by NCES to gain input from states on assessment and evaluation issues, especially national assessment and the state NAEP program. It meets four times during the year.

The first major issue faced by the task force was the controversy over the achievement levels for the 1990 mathematics assessment. Though the wording of the 1988 reauthorization was vague and somewhat ambiguous, the National Assessment Governing Board felt that it justified establishing achievement levels for the 1990 mathematics assessment. Their first attempt at setting achievement levels was quite controversial, to say the least. Both the procedures and the levels themselves were challenged. As a statistical agency, NCES felt strongly that achievement levels should *not* be included in any of their NAEP reports because the levels represented judgments that might not be replicated and because achievement levels were still in a developmental stage. The EIAC Assessment Task Force chose to support the NCES position.

A report containing the achievement levels probably would not have survived the NCES adjudication process. As a result, NAGB published the 1990 national and state NAEP mathematics achievement levels in a separate report. The NAGB achievement levels — both the process for setting them and the levels themselves — were subjected to a number of reviews and studies, including a special study by the National Academy of Education that found that the achievement levels were "fundamentally flawed."

Meanwhile, the New Standards Project was pushing the concept of performance standards or performance levels; and states were beginning to consider performance levels as an alternative method of reporting student achievement. The Goals 2000 legislation, and the Improving America's Schools Act the following year, advocated a standards-based system that included performance levels. As a result, the EIAC Assessment Subcommittee, as well as the Permanent Standing Task Force, went on record to support achievement levels as the preferred reporting metric for the national and state NAEP reports.

The EIAC Assessment Subcommittee and the Permanent Standing Assessment Task Force continued to study the NAEP achievement-levels methodology, with cooperation from both NAGB and NCES. However, NCES and NAGB were sharply divided over the issue of achievement levels, including how and where they should be reported. Indeed, the assessment subcommittee periodically had to attempt to broker agreements between the two to get state NAEP reports released in a more timely manner.

Budget shortfalls continued to plague NAEP. The 1996 state NAEP program was scheduled to be the assessment of science and mathematics at grades four and eight. But because of a budget problem, the science assessment was limited to only one grade, though mathematics was assessed at both grades.

By this point, most state assessment directors had appointed other staff members to serve as the state NAEP coordinator, if they had any staff within their agency to whom it could be assigned. Thus state NAEP became a less critical concern for most state assessment directors. The assessment requirements of the 1994 Improving America's Schools Act became a much bigger concern, and state assessment directors focused on those issues. As a result, state assessment directors were not always "up to date" about state NAEP plans.

The budget shortfall also affected some of the technical aspects of NAEP. It had been planned to link the 1996 state NAEP mathematics assessments to the Third International Mathematics and Science Study (TIMSS), which was conducted in 1995. The goal was to use the state's NAEP mathematics scores to estimate a state's performance on TIMSS. But the funding to have some students take both assessments was not available. Instead, there was enough funding to attempt a "statistical equating," based on a common population estimation approach. Because several states, including Colorado, had chosen to participate in TIMSS at state expense, the actual results for these states would serve as a check on how well the linking worked. The approach appeared to work well at the eighth-grade level; it did not work at the fourth-grade level. As a result, the estimated TIMSS scores were never released formally.

## Perspective 3: National Observer

In fall 1996, I became director of the State Education Assessment Center (SEAC) at the Council of Chief State School Officers; and my view of NAEP changed once again. First, I had to stop thinking in terms of how a particular NCES or NAGB decision would affect "my state" and start thinking about how it would affect all states. While this sounds like a subtle distinction, it has the potential effect of changing one's position on a particular issue.

For example, I opposed the inclusion of private schools in state NAEP as the Colorado state assessment director. Private schools represented a small proportion of Colorado students (around 5%), the state education board had no jurisdiction over private schools, and I was prohibited by the state constitution from spending any public funds on private schools. Thus, from that perspective, including private schools was a major problem. As SEAC director, I could see the value of including private schools in state NAEP. The private-school population is a much larger proportion of students in some states. State boards and state education agencies do have limited jurisdiction over private schools in some states. And in some states, the private-school population represents the "cream of the crop." For those states, the more complete picture provided by including private schools in state NAEP is very important.

Second, I had to again focus on the national program (known jokingly as "Mother NAEP") and not just state NAEP. As a state assessment director, the national NAEP results were important to me only as a point of reference for the Colorado results. Results for subjects assessed at only the national level were of mild interest, but had little importance. Now I had to think about the effect of national NAEP results in the context of education policy "within the Beltway," that is, at the U.S. Department of Education, the National Science Foundation, and Congress.

Finally, I had to adjust to two particular attitudes within national discussions. The first attitude is that people take themselves and the issues being discussed very seriously. During similar discussions at the state level, it had been possible to make jokes and use humor to relieve tension. When I tried this at the national level, I discovered that few people, if any, laughed, and that most tried to take my comment seriously.

The second attitude was much more troubling from my perspective. That attitude was an assumption that all states were equal or equivalent in terms of education and that, if something worked in one state, it should be applied to all states. There was little or no recognition of the differences among states in terms of public education, from governance issues and locus of control to state funding and state political dynamics, especially the relationship between the governor, chief state school officer, the state board, and the state legislature. Though I had been fortunate enough to work in a state where these political dynamics were positive, I knew the effects of a negative political dynamic from a number of other state assessment directors. It is very difficult to convey to many within the Capital Beltway that state assessment programs are established to meet state needs, not federal needs; that they are subject to the dictates of state legislatures; and that they change to meet the shifting political needs of the state.

The unique aspects of each of the states and jurisdictions are often overlooked when legislation is crafted. Then federal and congressional staff are surprised when this results in a multitude of variations on a theme, rather than the single theme they envisioned. The accountability sections of the Higher Education Act of 1998, which called for a state report card on teacher-training institutions, is a prime example. It assumed that there was a single model for the preparation and induction of new teachers and that it was appropriate that new teachers be tested at about the same time in every jurisdiction. This assumption drove the reporting requirements.

From the CCSSO perspective, NAEP's most pressing need was to establish a fixed schedule for the state NAEP program. Once NAGB adopted the schedule, states became much more comfortable with the program. Now state NAEP could be included in state plans and budget building. Increasingly, states began to look at their state NAEP results for confirmation of their state reform efforts. State NAEP began to serve as an independent, external validation of state assessment results in many states.

In spring 1997, the Clinton Administration began its push for a national test. While the Administration had seriously considered trying for "common, national goals" in reading and mathematics, initial reaction led it instead to propose a "voluntary national test" of fourth-grade reading and eighth-grade mathematics. To side-step the issue of national standards for such an assessment, it was decided that the tests would be based on the NAEP assessment frameworks for eighth-grade mathematics and fourth-grade reading. The goal was to build an individual NAEP score for each student whose school, district, state, and parent "volunteered" the student to be tested. A student report would provide the total score and the score in terms of the NAEP achievement levels (advanced, proficient, basic, and below basic). For mathematics, it also would provide scores in terms of the TIMSS percentiles. Testing was to be limited to under two hours total, and every item was to be released after the test was administered.

The proposed Voluntary National Test (VNT) quickly became the "hot" education topic across the country. States were divided about the VNT. Some could see its potential usefulness; others opposed it as a federal intrusion on the state's responsibility for education. Many of the original arguments raised when NAEP was launched in the late 1960s resurfaced. Congress was divided on the issue. The Senate was neutral to mildly supportive; the House of Representatives took a very dim view of the proposal. In some ways, the VNT became almost a surrogate for standards-based reform as embodied in the Goals 2000 legislation and the Improving America's Schools Act of 1994. NAEP, of course, stood at the base of the debate.

As a part of its reauthorization, the prohibition on reporting NAEP below the state level was changed to allow reporting for districts, but district participation would be at the expense of the districts that participated. The prohibition on reporting school or student results remained in place. Interestingly, the National Assessment Governing Board was not actively involved with the proposal, nor was the National Center for Education Statistics, the federal agency with fiscal and operational control over NAEP. Both were kept on the sideline; and the Office of Educational Research and Improvement (OERI) assumed responsibility for the VNT, though direction often came from the Department of Education's highest management.

The individual chiefs were split on the VNT issue, but the CCSSO was able to develop a consensus position supporting its development, with the understanding that this was necessary before each state could choose whether to participate. The CCSSO did not take a position, pro or con, on the VNT. However, because of its prior work on various NAEP assessment frameworks, the CCSSO was asked — in conjunction with MPR Associates — to take on the development of the test and the item specifications for the test in the late spring. The work needed to be done quickly; the final report was due in October. And the work had to be conducted openly to allow for public scrutiny. NAGB staff and NCES staff attended most of the VNT meetings of the steering committee, the planning committees, and the technical advisory committee, but only in the role of observers and never as participants.

Awarding the contract to implement the specifications also was done hurriedly. Before the specifications were completed, a contract was awarded to a consortium of contractors put together by the American Institutes for Research (AIR). Consortium staff began attending the meetings as observers.

The political dynamic around the VNT became explosive within the Beltway. The House asserted itself and attempted to bring the VNT to a halt. The Clinton Administration responded by trying to generate political support among states and major urban school districts. While these efforts did generate some support, the support came at a cost. In some states, the VNT exacerbated a tense political dynamic between the governor, the chief state school officer, and the state board of education. In addition, it heightened tension between the state and urban districts in several states. It also raised several thorny issues about NAEP: the descriptive power of the achievement levels, the high percentage of students below the basic level, and the inclusion of limited-English-proficient students.

To prevent events from escalating any further, Secretary of Education Richard Riley halted work on the VNT by the AIR consortium to allow for time to work out a compromise with Congress. The test and item specifications were the only aspects allowed to continue. As a part of the compromise, responsibility for the VNT was transferred to the National Assessment Governing Board, the National Academy of Science conducted studies on the VNT and alternatives to a national test, and future work on the VNT was limited strictly to development aspects and could not include large-scale pilot testing. The voluntary national test was not dead, but it was definitely on life support. It would continue to linger in this condition until spring 2001, when the contract with the AIR consortium was completed and ended by NAGB.

The enactment of Goals 2000, the Improving America's Schools Act (IASA), and the Individuals with Disabilities Education Act (IDEA) brought a huge change to state and local assessment programs. Until then, large-scale assessment programs excluded limited-English-proficient and special education students. Most programs allowed limited-English-proficient students a two- or three-year exemption from testing. Similarly, special education students often were exempted, either by the provisions of their individualized education plan (IEP) or by a lack of needed testing accommodations. Indeed, most commercial standardized tests excluded such students from the standardization or norming samples and stated that such students should not be tested by the instruments for that reason. With the legislation came the requirement for large-scale assessment programs to include these students. Thus states began developing appropriate accommodations, modifications, and alternative measures to meet these new requirements.

NAEP was exempt from this legislation, though it began to be pressured by advocacy groups and the Office of Civil Rights to be more inclusive. To that end, NAEP began using "split samples" (generally, half-samples) to explore the effects of attempting to become more inclusive. Part of the sample would be administered using traditional student criteria while the other part of the sample would be administered using new criteria that offered specific accommodations. This allowed NAEP to maintain short-term trend lines, as the portion of the sample using traditional criteria was used for reporting trends. However, this was limited to the national sample until 1998.

For the 1998 reading assessment, both the national samples at grades 4, 8, and 12 and the state samples at grades 4 and 8 were designed to be "half samples." One half used the traditional criteria; the other half used new criteria that included accommodations that NAEP felt reasonably comfortable offering, both in terms of administrative logistics and construct validity. The 1998 Reading National Report Card, which included the state NAEP data, presented short-term trend results based on the half-samples using the traditional criteria. Given the increasing attention focused on NAEP results, much was made of the states that had shown significant growth between the 1994 and 1998 reading assessments.

While all states were working to modify their state assessment programs to become more inclusive, progress across the states was uneven. Some states had just begun; others were implementing a large number of student accommodations within their program. In states where more rapid progress was being made, students were tested only if such accommodations were allowed in the assessment. As a result, those states generally had a higher student exclusion rate for the half-sample using the traditional NAEP criteria.

When a subsequent NAEP reading report presented results from the "accommodated" half-sample for the nation and the states, which allowed for comparing the two half-samples, a public furor developed over the previously released trend results. Results from the traditional half-sample and the accommodated half-sample not only were different at the individual state level, but the relative position of states was different. Were the gains "real" for those states that had the largest reported gains, or were the gains a result of having excluded more students from the assessment? Unfortunately, there was no way to answer the question, though NCES commissioned a number of studies using various assumptions about the potential "scores" of the excluded students from certain states.

States felt somewhat victimized by this experience. States that had made great strides in being inclusive felt that their trend results were called into question. States that were just beginning their inclusion adjustments felt that their real achievement gains were underestimated by the trend data because more special education students were included in their results. NAGB, the NCES project staff, and the contractors felt confused and abused for taking steps to report trend data as accurately as possible and for making the transition to be more inclusive.

The 2000 national and state NAEP mathematics assessment also was conducted using half-samples. Given the reading experience, the EIAC Assessment Subcommittee and Permanent Standing Assessment Task Force requested that NAGB delay the report of the trend data until the data for the accommodated sample were ready and both sets of data could be released in a single report. It was hoped that this would prevent the furor raised with the reading results. Following some deliberations with NCES staff and the contractors, NAGB agreed to report the 2000 Mathematics National Report Card in this manner.

At its May 2001 meeting, the National Assessment Governing Board adopted a policy, beginning with the 2002 assessment of reading, that all future assessments be conducted using only the inclusive samples. No future assessments would be administered using the traditional NAEP criteria.

However, there is a cost to this transition. Both national and state short-term trend lines will have a "one-time discontinuity" for each of the subject areas. For mathematics, this means that there will be a short-term trend line from 1990 at grade 8 (1992 at grade 4) to the 2000 results. These results will be based on the traditional criteria. Beginning with the next mathematics assessment (currently scheduled for 2004), there will be a new trend line from 2000 to subsequent assessments, based on the inclusive criteria, though the national trend line may be extended back to the 1996 mathematics assessment because the split-sample approach was tried at the national level in 1996. Similarly, the 2002 reading assessment will have a trend line going back to 1994 and a new trend line running from 1998 to 2002 and subsequent assessments.

The NAEP short-term trend lines have become increasingly important to states. The state trend lines are considered to be external evidence that state reforms are effective. Standards-based reform is a long-term effort that must span political terms. The Nation's Report Card, with its national and state components, has the ability to document the progress of reform. Disrupting these valuable trend data must not be undertaken lightly.

"Ralph's baby" has come a long way from its start. Along the way, it has:

- Provoked public debate over state versus federal control of education.
- Raised fears of a national curriculum.
- Been accused of being just another expensive, irrelevant, government study.
- Provided evidence that American public education was failing or succeeding, depending on one's point of view.
- Grown from being "state of the art" to being a "desired model" for standards-based assessments.
- Withstood numerous efforts to make it something it was not, including an individual test.

The question today is whether it will continue to monitor education reform in the 21st century or whether it will be used to drive education reform.

# CHAPTER 13

# What NAEP Really Could Do

*Frederic A. Mosher*

While it is not reasonable to expect NAEP to provide definitive evidence about what does or does not work in American education, it is quite reasonable to ask it to do a much better job than it currently does of defining and measuring our common goals for education and of reporting on our progress toward attaining them. Those goals have changed radically in the last decades of the 20th century, and it now is time for NAEP to recognize that the technology of testing also must change.

Ralph Tyler knew that norm-referenced, standardized tests were developed to sort students. His vision was an assessment that would support teaching and learning, rather than select and sort students. Tyler was pretty scathing about a system focused primarily on grading and sorting. "These policies and practices have existed for so long that we rarely note how sharply they differ from those of an institution devoted wholly to teaching and learning. For example, if you or I want to learn to play golf, we go to a 'pro' whose job it is to teach us. We do not expect that after a few practice periods he will say, 'You are getting a "D" in your work. I may have to fail you if you don't improve.' Instead we expect him to say, 'You are making progress on your drive, but you need to bring your full body into the swing. A little later I'll give you further practice on your putting to increase accuracy and decrease power'" (Tyler 1974, p. 5).

Tyler pointed out that the kinds of assessments that would be appropriate for measuring these changing goals would have to report what students actually had learned. It should report what the population, and sub-groups of the population, know and can do. The reports should be easily interpretable by the lay public and not be couched in terms of mysterious scale scores or percentiles, as conventional tests are. If the assessment's items or "exercises" were written so that, on their face, they reflected important aspects of core school subjects, he felt that reporting the results in terms of the proportions of the relevant demographic groups who succeeded on each exercise would provide evidence to the public that could be interpreted easily.

It turned out that Tyler was wrong about how easy it would be to interpret item-by-item pass-fail percentages. It proved, not surprisingly, to be hard for any individual observers to sum in their heads the item-by-item percentages across the released items in order to make a judgment about how they felt about the result: Was this result good or bad? Are American students doing as well as we would hope? Of course, it didn't help that only a subset of the actual items were released each time, so there always was uncertainty about how well the released items represented the rest. NAEP devoutly refused to make such judgments itself, and no one else could find a firm footing to justify taking a stand.

NAEP could, of course, report differential performance between or among groups for each item; and after it had done a second assessment on a particular subject, it could begin to report changes in performance over time. Nevertheless, being able to report group differences or changes in the percent succeeding on the items did not establish a basis for judging the importance of the differences or the degree of change.

In some ways, the history of NAEP could be written as the story of the struggle to find a way to report the assessment's results so that people could understand them and form some judgment of their significance. For a time, there was reporting of group means or medians for clusters of items that seemed to be tapping the same construct or objective. Whereas that compensated somewhat for the vagaries of individual items, it didn't seem to help public understanding.

When ETS took over responsibility for the NAEP contract from ECS in the early 1980s, there was a major shift to reporting the results for different subjects in terms of scores on a common scale. The scales represented a radical shift from reporting individual items or exercises. It was accomplished by using Item Response Theory (IRT) techniques to place the items on a common dimension. Attempts were made to interpret the scores by identifying various "anchor" points along the scale. Each of these anchor points included a set of items that were answered correctly by a much larger proportion of the students who "scored" at that point than by the proportion of the students at the next lower anchor point. Those items could be inspected to see what a student would have to know and be able to do to answer them, and that extrapolation was used to suggest what a student who scored at that anchor point would know and be able to do.

These interpretations helped a bit, but they soon were superseded by the move to report results in terms of the proportions of each group who exceeded one of three "achievement levels" (basic, proficient, or advanced). The National Assessment Governing Board took responsibility for defining and reporting these levels after Congress established the board in the 1988 reauthorization of NAEP. The idea of reporting this way had been suggested in the National Academy of Education's (Glaser 1987) review of its own Alexander-James report on NAEP (Alexander and James 1987). That NAGB could make this shift to reporting in terms of standards for what was desirable for students to do, as opposed to reporting only in terms of what they actually could do, implied that Congress and NAGB sensed there had been a major change in American education. That change reflected the accountability and standards movement, which swept the states and shaped the rhetoric of federal education policy.

What had been feared when the assessment first was proposed seemed now to be welcomed. In addition, when NAEP asserted an authoritative judgment about what levels of performance should be considered basic, proficient, or advanced, it suddenly found itself the center of attention. The need to know where we stood seemed to have trumped the traditional assertion of local responsibility for making such judgments, as well as the need to understand how the judgments were being made.

Undoubtedly there were observers who wished the schools to be seen to be doing badly, but even the many, more friendly observers seem to have been perversely reassured by the fact that the report card showed failing grades. If everything had been rosy, there might have been skepticism; but the willingness to report bad news clearly seems to have enhanced NAEP's credibility. Even though most expert reviews of the process used by NAGB to set these achievement levels have judged that process to be "fatally flawed" (see Chapter 11), this perceived credibility made it easy for NAGB to ignore the criticism or to dismiss them as defensive pleading by the education establishment.

Defining and reporting performance standards is necessary if the reports are to be meaningful to the public. Conventional norm-referenced tests provide a basis for such interpretations in terms of the performance of the student's peers. That is, if you know a score, you know where it ranks against the scores of others in the norming population, even if you can't tell exactly what it means. Because the structure of most school subjects and skills is complex and probably not well understood by most adults, the most accessible way to report information about a student's or a group's performance is to sum up the assessment results and say whether they are good, good enough, excellent, and so on.

Because the goal of schooling has shifted toward helping every student reach proficiency in the core subjects, it obviously is important to define those proficiencies in terms of performance standards. However, many students will exceed whatever standards are set as being proficient; and so it seems wise to report in terms of one or more levels of performance above proficiency, as NAGB had done with the advanced level in order to recognize and encourage talent and effort. It probably also would be useful to define and report on important stages of progress below proficiency as a basis both for providing encouragement and for assessing whether instruction is producing progress. Thus standards-based reporting seems to be appealing and useful.

The problems with standards-based reporting are rooted in the fact that such reporting presupposes that whoever sets the standards has a structured concept of the relevant domain of knowledge or skill and is able to make a judgment about how much of that structure has to be known in order to meet the standard. Also, those to whom such judgments are reported must believe that such judgments have been made authoritatively and in good faith.

At their simplest, such standards might be just a list of facts that should be known about the domain, or perhaps what proportion of those facts should be known. But that is a highly unsatisfactory way to think about most school subjects. Most subjects involve a complex structure of content, understanding, and skills in using and reasoning with the content; and they are developed and learned over time with experience in school and out. They may be learned in particular sequences, and those sequences may be based on what new knowledge can be built on what students already know; but they also might be a matter of arbitrary choice or stylistic differences in schools, or even just a serendipitous function of variations in life experiences.

The point is that the possible structures underlying standards go well beyond something that can be represented on a simple, single, numerical scale. A case ought to be made for why a particular set of choices is made, and that case ought to reflect a serious understanding of the nature of the domain and its structure.

Understanding the structure of the domains of school learning is important not only for setting standards, but also for designing tests and assessments. In fact, achievement tests that generate a single, ordered set of scores are an assertion that it is appropriate to represent the structure of performance and understanding in the domain in terms of a single, numerical dimension.

Ralph Tyler's original specifications for NAEP reflected a "bits and pieces" concept of the structure of school subjects. He rejected tests with scale scores and emphasized developing a wider range of assessment items and exercises keyed to objectives that experts and practitioners thought were important. At the beginning, he was not concerned with setting standards for what students ought to know; rather, he wanted to report what they did know. He thought that reporting the proportions of students who answered each item correctly would be sufficient. The implied structure of knowledge seems to be a flat array of facts and skills that are either known or not.

But Tyler wasn't that naive. He knew that school objectives or frameworks would be more complex, and he certainly had a more complex understanding of the relevant subjects. He and John Tukey may have thought that the curriculum in American schools was so diffuse that it would not be possible to order student performances with reference to an expected order in which aspects of the subject were likely to be introduced in the schools. Perhaps Tyler opted for item-by-item reporting on the assumption that each reader would bring to a NAEP report his or her own conception of the structure of the subject and be able to impose his or her own judgments on the outcomes. Or perhaps, in a somewhat more calculating way, he realized that readers were not likely to be able to bring their own conceptions to bear on, and to interpret, the item-by-item information and that the frustrating effort to make sense of all the data might eventually motivate more serious attention to how the structure of performance ought to be understood. Perhaps he thought that starting that search from the individual items might keep it closer to the complexity of the subject than would be likely if the need to make sense of the information got sidetracked by superficially plausible reporting in terms of scales. I'd like to think that he was that calculating and prescient, but I'm not sure.

In any case, the early NAEP and its later variants have failed to invest in developing the kind of understanding of subject matter that would provide a basis for developing sound standards. In spite of NAEP's many innovations, it shares that particular failure with most conventional tests. Just like conventional tests, NAEP seems to have relied on a theory of subject matter that was really a "theory" of item types.

This reliance on items is a product of classical psychometric theory. Psychometric theory assumes that one is trying to measure individuals on some dimension on which individuals differ in quantitative terms. This dimension could tap some underlying construct, such as "general academic ability" or "intelligence," but it also could tap "knowledge of mathematics" or "ability to read and comprehend text."

Assume that such a construct and dimension exists and that there is a large set of test items that appear to reflect what the construct is about. That is, for the construct of "reading comprehension ability," there are items that ask questions that require understanding the text by reading it. If the pool of items is given to students who vary in how much knowledge or skill they have acquired in the relevant domain, then it is reasonable to expect that those who have acquired more of that knowledge or skill should answer correctly more of such items than would those who have acquired less knowledge or skill.

Consider the correlation of each item with the overall performance of individuals on the total pool of items. The items that show a high correlation with the total number correct on the item pool (or that "discriminate" between the high- and low-scorers) and that also correlate strongly with each other are arguably revealing the existence of an underlying dimension. Because they were all written to be "about" a particular construct, it is reasonable to think that the dimension they reflect is the one that they were designed to tap. In conventional test development, the items that "discriminate" in this way are the ones that become strong candidates for inclusion in the final test. Those that don't work are discarded.

When items are chosen in this way, and they ask about content that is connected with the target construct, there generally has not been much additional attention paid to whether the items distinguish among the component elements or skills that a good theory of the subject might suggest are important. The items that work as though they lie on a common dimension are selected from the item pool and formed into one or more candidate tests to be used for measuring the construct. Those tests will be named to imply that they measure the ability or achievement represented by that construct. Candidate tests developed in this way may be evaluated further in at least three ways. First, these tests must be shown to have reasonable reliability; that is, they should give consistent results for individuals over relevant periods of time. Second, if the test is reasonably reliable, then it becomes worthwhile to evaluate what it is measuring, that is, its validity.

The third test evaluation process, in most cases, involves assigning quantitative meaning to the test's "raw scores." Usually these raw scores are the numbers of items that test-takers answer correctly. In the case of standardized, norm-referenced tests, this process is usually grounded in the assumption, based on a strong extrapolation from the variation in many human physical characteristics, that the underlying distribution of individual differences on the target construct will resemble the Gaussian, or normal, probability distribution. If the raw scores are mathematically transformed in a way that adjusts the score distribution so that it resembles the normal distribution, the resulting transformed scores should directly reflect the quantitative relationships in the underlying construct dimension. Those relationships can arguably then be characterized as meeting the criteria for an interval scale. This is the strongest interpretation of the label "norm-referenced," though the label could be used in any case in which scores take their meaning from reference to one or more parameters of the score distribution.

In the case of NAEP, its scores are not meant to be interpreted directly in terms of parameters of the score distributions; rather, they are interpreted according to concepts of what students know and can do. However, once NAEP shifted to reporting in terms of scale scores — and then to making achievement-level judgments with reference to those scales — the quantitative relationship among those scores was determined by techniques based on "Item Response Theory" that are close statistical relatives of norm-referencing in that they rely in a nontheoretical way on the statistical behavior of the individual items.

Another problem is that psychometric methods may produce scales that confound content knowledge or skill with dispositions and aptitudes. For example, a person taking a test in a particular subject can be characterized as having both knowledge of the content domain and a general academic ability or aptitude. Any particular test item can require the relevant knowledge to get it right, but it also may require some level of academic aptitude. Students can differ in both these constructs.

Content that everyone has learned will produce little variation, so items that assess that content are likely to be excluded from the test. And for content that few or none have been taught, items that tap that also will not show much variation. The items that are used are likely to tap both content and relevant aptitudes, and the extent to which they tap either one is uncertain.

NAEP's assessments and levels probably confound the two constructs and thus may provide ambiguous or misleading information. One way to see this is to look at the items NAEP has released that illustrate what students at the "advanced" achievement level are able to do. Taking 12th-grade mathematics as an example, the most difficult items reported for the 1996 mathematics assessment (ones that students who would score in the advanced range are more likely to get right than are students who score at lower levels) are hardly "advanced" by world standards (Takahira et al. 1998). This probably is because more advanced items would not "work" statistically because too few students, whatever their ability, have been taught that content. In recognition of this problem, the 1996 mathematics assessment included a special "advanced study" designed to measure the performance of specially selected students who had taken or were taking more advanced courses, at least Algebra I by the eighth grade and pre-calculus or beyond by the 12th grade (Mitchell et al. 1999). The students who had taken these more advanced courses were marginally more advantaged in background than the students in the overall NAEP population, and they performed marginally better on the regular NAEP scales. They nonetheless did not perform well on the more advanced items in the special study.

Both this special study and the main NAEP appear to be influenced by the mathematics standards of the National Council of Teachers of Mathematics (1989). Among other things, the NCTM standards emphasized that students should develop "mathematical power," meaning that they should be able to apply their mathematical knowledge to the solution of real-world problems, and that they should be able to communicate what they are doing and to "make connections" between mathematical ideas and situations. The NAEP mathematics frameworks have adopted that language, and the items used in the assessment have tried to tap the capabilities that are implied by the new language. The problem is that these capabilities seem to be exactly the ones that in the past have not been explicitly taught by the schools and that therefore have probably been among the key "stealth factors" influencing variability in performance on standardized tests.

NAEP does not seem to recognize fully that its items, and thus the reporting scales based on them, may confound subject matter with the students' aptitudes. The aspects of the items that tap the latter could account for a great deal of the variation in performance on the NAEP scales. Thus NAEP may characterize students as "advanced" and to imply that they are advanced with respect to content when that is not necessarily true. And, when students fail to meet standards at the basic or proficient level, NAEP reports imply that it is because they have not been taught "the basics," when perhaps that also is not completely true.

Thus the current NAEP results are not really adequate as an indicator of the effectiveness of instruction in American schools or as an indicator of what American students know and can do. This is not a problem just with NAEP, but with testing generally. However, NAEP could help disentangle the constructs in its reporting, and doing so may be crucial in guiding the education system toward success in helping all students to meet significant standards

Ralph Tyler and the founders of NAEP understood the limitations of using conventional tests to give feedback on what students specifically knew and were able to do. Tyler recognized that standardized achievement tests were closely related to aptitude tests. What Tyler did not consider is that aptitudes might themselves be teachable and that they too should be distinguished and measured as potential outcomes of instruction. We do not currently know how to teach aptitudes, and we cannot be sure that all such aptitudes are amenable to instruction. However, if the hopes of enabling most students to reach or exceed much higher standards are to be realized, it will be essential to find ways both to teach and to test the the requisite abilities.

It would be unreasonable to expect NAEP to solve this problem on its own. But it could play a crucial role. A National Research Council evaluation of NAEP (Pellegrino, Jones, and Mitchell 1999) recommended that it consider exploring a "New-Paradigm" NAEP, which would be devoted to elaborating and experimenting with new approaches that would be truer to the complexity of actual student knowledge and skills. The results of such work might be incorporated into the main NAEP assessments, or they might constitute a parallel set of more specific studies to illuminate particular issues.

It is important for NAEP to focus on developing ways of reporting its results in terms of an elaborated concept of the development and structure of knowledge and skill in the subjects it is assessing. That concept should include an attempt to distinguish between the aspects of content that currently are the explicit focus of instruction in the schools and the content-relevant dispositions and aptitudes that are not explicitly taught, but that could be taught. Regular NAEP could contribute to this exploration by making a much more systematic attempt to reflect these issues in the design of its assessment instruments. The importance of NAEP is that it has the flexibility, the scale, and the potential resources to do the job right.

If U.S. education has truly become committed to the goal of leaving no child behind, it should recognize that reaching that goal is not simply a matter of will. It also requires new knowledge. NAEP could play a crucial role in achieving this goal. It could provide improved feedback on the degree to which there is progress toward attainment of the goal, and it could set a framework for designing more targeted assessments to be used by schools and teachers to guide instruction and by researchers to learn how to help make instruction more effective.

If NAEP is trapped into playing the role of certifying state and local accountability systems that assign rewards and punishments on a year-to-year basis, it is likely to be destroyed by association with an impossible fantasy. But NAEP could be an indispensable asset for ensuring accountability for fundamental change on a time scale that respects the realities of the ways in which human beings and human societies actually learn.

# PART II

# DEVELOPING ASSESSMENT MATERIALS

# CHAPTER 14

# Assessing Citizenship

*Vincent Campbell and Daryl Nichols*

Nearly all objectives of public education are too broad in purpose to be defined exhaustively, let alone *measured* exhaustively. The purposes of K-12 education are just too diverse, not only because of the breadth of competencies addressed, but also because the real-life situations in which these competencies will be demonstrated vary so greatly. This is especially true in science, social studies, and citizenship, but also to a large degree in the other academic areas.

In the 1960s the National Assessment of Educational Progress established citizenship objectives that looked at much more than the students' knowledge of civics. The early objectives were focused on students' skills, life habits, and attitudes. Whereas traditional achievement tests rely heavily on multiple-choice items, NAEP's citizenship objectives required a variety of kinds of assessment, including constructed responses, self-reports, and observed behavior in group settings.

The Exploratory Committee on Assessing the Progress of Education (ECAPE) sought to identify objectives for a national assessment that were considered important by scholars, accepted as an educational task by the school, and considered desirable by thoughtful lay citizens (Tyler 1969). However, the committee decided that the national assessment objectives would not be limited by school curricula that were in place at the time of the assessment. This gave NAEP the role of identifying important public objectives that are given too little attention in schools, as well as assessing how well students are achieving the objectives schools currently emphasize.

ECAPE selected the American Institutes for Research (AIR) to plan and implement the first assessment of citizenship for NAEP. The AIR team defined the citizenship objectives comprehensively, without regard to what was taught in the schools, and developed exercises to assess the objectives as completely as possible within the limits of available resources. The 32 specific objectives were grouped under the following nine goals, which expect students to:

- Show concern for the welfare and dignity of others.
- Support rights and freedoms of all individuals.
- Help maintain law and order.
- Know the main structure and functions of our governments.
- Seek community improvement through active democratic participation.
- Understand problems of international relations.
- Support rationality in communication, thought, and action on social problems.
- Take responsibility for own personal development and obligations.
- Help and respect their own families (Committee on Assessing the Progress of Education 1969*b*).

These objectives broadened the scope of citizenship considerably beyond what most schools were teaching explicitly, the assumption being that responsibility for teaching students to be good citizens is a joint responsibility of parents, community, schools, and the student, rather than a responsibility of only the schools.

Each of these objectives can be demonstrated within a very large domain. Unless these domains are mapped as completely as possible, there will be problems with any assessment. For example, if tests are built by sampling haphazardly from a vaguely defined domain, the results of one test do not predict those of another very well, even if both are nominally measuring the same subject. This can cause what has been called the Lake Wobegon effect (Cannell

1984). Grade-level groups in a school system take the same test for several years, with better and better results. Then the test is changed and performance falls back to the original level, rising again year by year until the test is changed again. This effect has been noted especially with the use of standardized, norm-referenced tests, which historically have not always specified what objectives were being addressed within a subject area.

Mapping the domain requires spelling out the different skills, knowledge, and areas of application included in that domain. If some aspects are more important than others, either because they are more important in real life or because they are prerequisite to learning others, these too should be spelled out.

Even if parts of the domain are not assessed, as will usually be the case, everyone can still get a clearer picture of which aspects of each objective are being measured, provided the domain has been mapped comprehensively. More important, instruction and assessment can be planned jointly in a way that honestly takes account of which parts are being taught and assessed.

For the NAEP citizenship assessment, the AIR team spelled out specific behaviors that illustrated achievement of each of the 32 objectives. These behaviors were intended to be a comprehensive, though not exhaustive, description of the domain of each objective. A typical sample for one objective is shown below.

> Goal: Seek community improvement through active democratic participation.
>
> Objective: Apply democratic procedures on a practical level when working in a group.
>
> Age 9: Group situations in which nine-year-olds might be involved include classroom activities, clubs, and recreation teams. In such situations, students try to help the group move toward its goals. They encourage the hearing of different viewpoints before voting on an issue. They abide by democratically determined decisions and follow established procedures for trying to change a decision (persuasion, petition, etc.). They mediate or seek compromise when others disagree. They are willing to give in when the situation calls for some immediate action and

their own objections are unimportant. They explore and take turns with various leader and follower roles.

Age 13: In addition to the objectives that nine-year-olds are expected to meet, 13-year-olds should understand that a leader must use his or her authority responsibly.

Age 17: Group situations in which 17-year-olds might be involved include student council, committees, clubs, and athletic teams. In such situations students try to help the group move toward its goals. They support the right of dissenting views to be voiced and encourage adequate discussion before voting. They abide by democratically determined decisions but know the established procedures for trying to change a decision (persuasion, argument, petition, etc.). They mediate and seek compromise and common ground when others disagree. They are willing to give in when the situation calls for some immediate action or when their objection is relatively unimportant. They understand the responsibilities involved in accepting leadership (for example, to keep informed on relevant matters; to clarify issues, sum up discussions, and present suggestions to the group; to direct the execution of an agreed-on plan of action; and to coordinate activities with other groups). They understand that a leader's greater responsibility makes it necessary for the leader to exercise authority; but they understand that subordinates also have responsibilities to the group.

Adult: The objectives are the same as those for 17-year-olds, except "group situations" refers to meetings of public or private civic groups.

The paragraph format used above to map the domain is not recommended for mathematics, science, language arts, and some other subjects. Especially in mathematics, some concepts and skills are prerequisite to learning others. In such cases a diagram or list format showing such relationships is a better tool for mapping the domain.

## Developing the Exercises

The method of explicit rationales provided a loose framework for exercise development. That method was developed mainly in such settings as occupational skill measurement, where the domain is narrower and more is known about specific causes of success and failure. The key elements of the approach are:

1. Systematic and precise statement of the objective . . . accompanied with specific examples and delimitation of the specific behavior or other goal.
2. Analysis of the nature, causes, and conditions of the behavior defined in the specific objective, based on the experience with this type of behavior by experts in the area. It includes insights, inferences, and hypotheses.
3. Design of evaluation procedures that reflect the reasoning in the analysis. (Flanagan and Jung 1970)

The first item above is what we have called mapping the domain.

The method of explicit rationales was adapted to meet the needs of developing exercises to assess citizenship with its broad domains. Steps 2 and 3 below were often merged and often resembled brainstorming more than they did the execution of an orderly procedure.

1. Map the domain.
2. Select or sample part of the domain for assessment. Think of an example of a behavior that demonstrates an important achievement of this kind, one that gets to the heart of the objective. Usually examples were drawn from actual experiences of staff and consultants. Create several such examples as sources of ideas for different assessments.
3. Explore alternative types of assessments. This was a creative search for ideas.
4. Critically evaluate the assessment ideas, mainly in terms of: a) validity as indicators of the percentage of an age group achieving the specific objective, b) administrative feasibility, c) standardization problems, and d) reportability to the lay public.
5. For each promising assessment idea, construct a draft and pilot test it on a few students. Refine the exercise, pilot testing it repeatedly if necessary, and ready it for expert review.

For each NAEP target age group, a book of rationales summarizing the above process and the resulting assessment ideas was submitted to NAEP (see, for example, Nichols et al. 1965). Intensive joint review by the Technical Advisory Committee, NAEP staff, and the AIR team resulted in most exercises being accepted, often with revisions, and a few items getting rejected. The exercises then were field tested and refined further.

This development process resulted in the exercises that were used in the first national assessment of citizenship (Campbell et al. 1970). There were several types of exercise used in that assessment.

Paper-and-pencil questions were most numerous. When they were given at ages 9, 13, and 17, the text was presented aloud by tape recording while the respondent followed the text in his booklet. This procedure was of considerable help to poor readers, and it increased the likelihood that any inadequate response reflected achievement, rather than reading ability. Further simplification for the respondent was achieved by grouping exercises within packages according to format (all multiple-choice exercises, for example, were grouped in a single section) and using sample or practice exercises to introduce each new format. This method of packaging was intended to minimize the effects of varying degrees of test sophistication among respondents.

No citizenship exercise called for lengthy, organized writing because this would have depended too much on writing skill. A few exercises called for listing up to five words or phrases, and occasionally for writing a short sentence.

Individual interviews were used extensively for adults. They also were used for younger ages in exercises that called for lengthy responses or for dialogue between administrator and respondent. For some of these exercises, the respondent was able to follow the question in printed form as the interview proceeded. A number of paper-and-pencil exercises were converted to interview format after tryouts indicated that a respondent might not understand the exact intent of a question, so that further probes and paraphrasing were needed.

Responses to open-ended exercises were categorized and scored by trained persons in accordance with previously written instructions. For many exercises, these categories of answers are of some interest in themselves and are reported in the examples below.

Perhaps the most difficult and controversial type of measure was the self-report, in which the respondent was asked a series of questions about his or her own past experiences. For example, questions about membership in civic organizations or about past instances of helping a friend were of this type. These questions were nearly always presented in interviews. To maximize validity, questions were put in a neutral context or worded in such a way that the "desired" or right answer was not obvious. Respondents were asked to support answers with factual details about the time, place, or content in order to verify that the alleged incident actually took place. For example, if a respondent said he wrote a letter to his congressman, he was asked to tell what the letter was about. (In this particular case the exercise appeared on paper so that the respondent could see the need for verifying the answer before he answered "yes" in the first place.)

One type of self-report exercise calls for special explanation. In this type we sought to learn *how often* the respondent does something that is obviously good citizenship. We chose not to ask outright how often some obviously desirable action had been performed, because this approach seemed to rely too much on untrustworthy memory and to invite exaggeration. Instead, respondents were asked if they had ever acted this way; and if the answer was "yes," they were asked to recall the most recent time of such action and to provide a few details. The details were intended to verify the story and also to get the respondent's memory fixed on a particular event. Finally, almost incidentally, the respondent was asked how long ago it happened. The more people who report having performed the action in the recent past (for example, within the past month), the greater the indication that the behavior occurs with substantial frequency in the general population.

Some exercises examined values. Respondents were asked what they ought to do or whether they would or would not be willing to perform a certain act. To bring what a person *says* he or she would be willing to do closer to what actually might be done, the context of such questions was made as neutral as possible, for example, by suggesting that differing opinions were quite acceptable. We do not know how close the match is between what people say they are willing to do and what they actually do. However, stated willingness to engage in a desirable act is a civic goal in itself because it tends to encourage sound policies and practices.

Effective citizenship involves working well with other people. To measure the skills of interaction and willingness to participate and communicate, it seemed necessary to observe the behavior of respondents in group situations. Paper-and-pencil exercises are less expensive, and so are interviews; but neither provide convincing measures of group-interaction skills.

For each group-interaction exercise actually used in the first assessment, many cycles of development, tryout, and revision were necessary before behavior could be perceived and scored reliably by different scorers. Administrators of group-interaction exercises were given about three days of special training to prepare them for the assessment. Students accepted the group tasks and topics as relevant and took part with serious interest.

Below is a sample of exercises measuring several different objectives, exercises that survived expert review and field testing and were used in the first assessment. In the report (Campbell et al. 1970), exercises and results were grouped by goal, and each goal began with a summary and analysis of all results for that goal. Then each released exercise (only half were released) was presented with its results.

### Exercise for ages 13, 17, and adult. Interview

*Objective:* Understand and oppose unequal opportunity in the areas of education, housing, employment, and recreation.

*Targeted Behaviors*: They know of obvious and subtle forms of discrimination against minorities. They are aware of the extent of unequal opportunity in their own communities.

A. Is there any place in the world where people are not treated fairly because of their religion? ("Yes," "No," "I don't know")
B. (If "Yes" to A) Where is that?
C. What kind of unfair treatment happens there?
D. Does it ever happen in the United States? ("Yes," "No," "I don't know")
E. (If "Yes" to D) Where is that?
F. What kind of unfair treatment happens there?

*Acceptable Answers to C and F:* Any plausible answers that indicated the respondents were aware of some actual kind of religious discrimination were accepted. Categories of acceptable answers: government restriction on where to worship, governmental suppression of any kind of worship, restrictions on beliefs, physical punishment for religious activities, loss of rights or property, place of living or movement restricted, and social discrimination. In some circumstances any of these types of unfair treatment could be scored as unacceptable answers. For example, governmental restrictions or suppression was an acceptable answer concerning Russia (at that time), but it was not acceptable concerning the United States because it would be an extremely rare occurrence in this country.

### Exercise for adult. Interview
*Objective:* Actively work for community improvement.
A. In the past year have you performed any unpaid civic activities, such as doing volunteer work in a school or library or helping with a project to improve the community? ("Yes," "No")
B. (If "Yes" to A) What activities have you performed? (Used to verify response to A and to elicit up to five activities from respondent.)

### Exercise for ages 13 and 17. Observed group interaction
*Objective:* Apply democratic procedures on a practical level when working in a group.
*Targeted Behaviors:* Try to inform themselves on socially important matters and to understand alternative viewpoints. Weigh alternatives and consequences carefully, then make decisions and

carry them out without undue delay. Have good ideas for solutions. Support free communication (encourage the hearing of different viewpoints) and communicate honestly with others (willingly express their own views on civic and social matters, however controversial the issue; encourage the hearing of dissenting viewpoints).

*Exercise Description:* The purpose of this exercise was to provide a standard situation in which to measure effective cooperation on a group task. At each age, groups of eight students were asked to choose, from a list of issues (see below), the five most important issues between teenagers and adults; to rank them in order of importance; and to write a recommendation for at least the two most important problems. They were asked to write recommendations for all five problems if they had time. They had 30 minutes to complete the task. The only rule was that a majority of the group must agree on anything they wrote.

Two observers recorded individual acts of group members as they discussed the issues, each observer recording different types of behavior. At no time did the observers participate in the discussion. Observers were specially trained in recognizing the individual actions they were responsible for recording.

The task seemed appropriate and interesting to all groups, and some groups tackled it with enthusiasm. The types of behavior measured included cooperation, organization, contribution of substance, and defending a viewpoint.

## List of Issues

| *Age 13* | *Age 17* |
|---|---|
| Time limits (for being home, being in bed, etc.) | Censorship |
| Home Duties | Curfew |
| School Assignments | Voting Age |
| Adult Books and Movies | Drinking |
| Sports and Other Activities | Smoking |
| Dating and Parties | Working Rules and Laws |
| Parents' Approval of Friends | Marriage |

| | |
|---|---|
| Money (where from and how spent) | Auto Insurance |
| Dress and Appearance | Dress and Appearance |
| Smoking | Military Service |
| Swearing | School Attendance |
| Being Talked to Like an Adult | Civil Liability |
| Criminal Liability | |

### Exercise for age 13. Interview

*Objective:* Help younger brothers and sisters to develop into good citizens.

*Targeted Behaviors:* Answer questions patiently and describe and interpret their own experiences for the benefit of younger siblings.

A. Do you have any younger brothers or sisters? ("Yes," "No")

B. (If "Yes" to A) What are their ages; how old are they? (Select the sibling between the ages of 3 and 9 whose age is nearest 6 and ask the remaining questions about this sibling. If no sibling between the ages of 3 and 9, go to the next exercise.)

C. What is the name of your brother or sister who is _____ years old? (In asking the remaining questions, refer to sibling by name.)

D. As you know, smaller children often come up with some questions which even adults have a difficult time answering. Has (name) asked you a tough question of this sort in the past month? ("Yes," "No")

E. (If "Yes" to D) What was the question about? (If student hesitates, say, "You don't have to tell me if it is personal.")

F. Were you able to satisfy (name) with your answer? ("Yes," "No") (If student hesitates) That is, was he/she happy with your answer?"

*Comment.* This exercise assumes that children tend to ask older siblings for help to the extent they perceive them as willing to help. Thus being asked a tough question indicates being seen as a helpful person. For siblings, it is assumed this perception is based on past experience.

## Advantages of Nontraditional Assessment

*Validity for Important Objectives:* It is widely accepted that multiple-choice questions often are not as valid as other methods of assessing education outcomes. This has been a major impetus for the shift toward "performance" assessments. In part, this is an effect of standardized-test makers using low-cost, multiple-choice questions excessively and targeting broad subjects, rather than specific standards.

Despite this weakness of norm-referenced tests, multiple-choice test items can validly measure certain standards. Unfortunately, what most such items measure well is not very important to society. Most multiple-choice questions measure the recognition of facts and relationships. Although such recognition-level knowledge has its uses, it is not what employers and policy experts claim is deficient in high school and college graduates.

Problem solving is one such critical deficiency, and it is not well addressed by traditional testing. Multiple-choice tests that address problem solving nearly always focus on a single right answer, even though most real-life problems involve a range of acceptable solutions that can be compared and traded off using multiple criteria. This "one-answer" mental set inevitably leads many students to try to "reverse engineer" the answer by trying tricks (for example, "Are there two numbers in the problem statement I can combine to get this exact number?"), rather than by demonstrating important problem-solving skills. The most critical deficiency in problem solving is in setting up or structuring a problem, especially where essential variables are either unstated or have unknown values. For this, an assessment that examines the student's initial view of the problem, and perhaps solution strategies, is essential. Open-ended, constructed responses from the student seem to be required.

In divergent problem solving, where many approaches might work, multiple-choice items are even less appropriate. An open-ended performance assessment is clearly a more valid way to assess such an objective, as it gives each respondent the opportunity to pursue a different strategy.

In addition to problem solving, many other important objectives of public education can be achieved in a variety of alternative ways, and seldom is one particular way required. Examples are constructing a plan of action or a work of art, or almost any task that requires integrating many elements into a total product.

"Metacognitive" skills, which refer to thinking about one's own thinking, represent another class of objectives that seldom can be assessed well by multiple-choice items. There is evidence that such skills are essential to problem solving, and in particular to the selection and monitoring of strategies for addressing a problem (Pellegrino, Chudowsky, and Glaser 2001, pp. 69, 267). Researchers in this area have concluded that formative assessments of multiple types are needed by students and teachers if they are to monitor what is being learned about the use of strategies. For example, assessments in the form of probing interviews can reveal what a student is thinking as she or he confronts a problem and tries one approach or another to solve it.

Valid measures of constructive, proactive skills need to accommodate a diversity of possible approaches to the task or problem. The self-report interviews we used in NAEP citizenship assessment allowed the student or adult to select pertinent events from his or her own life. The group interaction exercises imposed a standard situation on the students but allowed them to pursue divergent problem solving in a variety of ways, using their own ideas. Thus one strength of the nontraditional assessments is their flexibility for measuring different alternative ways of achieving a given objective.

Another strength of such nontraditional measures is that they can either report actual achievements that are valued by the lay public or simulate what people recognize as an important achievement in real life. The group problem-solving situation described in one of the exercises above closely resembles many real-life group problem-solving situations in which adults take part, including conflict resolution, policy planning meetings, and public hearings on proposed legislation. If students can show they are effective in a simulation, people can reasonably infer that such competencies will carry over to real-life situations.

Of course, simulations of real-life problems are valid measures only to the extent that success in the exercise depends on the targeted skill, rather than on some peripheral trait, such as glibness or a pleasing personality. This demands considerable effort in developing the exercise and scoring it. Self-reports have weaknesses, too. They are always vulnerable to fabrication and exaggeration. This weakness can be minimized, as described earlier, though it is not likely to be eliminated.

If traditional and nontraditional methods are of about equal validity for a given set of objectives, and if both are at least moderately valid, the current practice in large-scale assessments of using mostly multiple-choice items might be justified. But for many objectives, especially the most important ones, one cannot accept the assumption of equal validity. Large-scale assessments, such as NAEP, are criticized because they currently neglect such skills as problem representation, use of strategies and self-monitoring, and explaining and interpreting, all of which are skills that are poorly assessed by multiple-choice items. The National Academy of Education (Glaser, Linn, and Bohrnstedt 1997) recommended that NAEP revise its frameworks and assessments to include such objectives. A committee of the National Research Council (Elmore and Rothman 1999) agreed and proposed that NAEP regularly assess these objectives using in-depth instruments with smaller student samples.

*Types of Validity:* Alternative assessment methods seem necessary if we are to select the most valid ways to measure contrasting types of objectives, including skills, higher-order thinking, and habits. Alternative methods appear to have greater *face validity* than multiple-choice items for such objectives. Alternative assessment methods also are more convincing in a substantive, cognitive way regarding the relation of the assessment task to the kinds of real-life performance desired.

Studies of *predictive validity*, showing the extent to which exercise results correlate with later civic behavior, have not yet been conducted in citizenship, nor for most other real-life skills.

*Construct validity* examines the logical connections between theory and evidence (see, for example, Shepard 1993). National assessment objectives represent diverse social goals, most of them not yet analyzed in formal theory; thus little can be said about construct validity. But the points raised above about performance on a test and similarities to real-life performance represent beginning steps toward construct validity.

*Reporting to the Lay Public:* Nontraditional exercises that stand on their own have the added advantage that lay persons can understand the reported results. An exercise is described, and the percent of students who demonstrated specific types of behavior is reported. No mathematics or psychometric knowledge is required of the audience, as is the case with normative tests.

A multiple-choice test item, by itself, usually is not as impressive as a demonstration of achieving an objective. Results of multiple-choice tests typically are aggregated from a number of similar items, and some quantitative level of success on the aggregate is reported. People are becoming more accepting of such aggregate indices, such as SAT scores and percentiles; but the abstract index obscures the behavioral basis by which achievement is measured, and quantitative errors of interpretation abound.

## Challenges in Nontraditional Assessment

*Uniformity of Administration:* Paper-and-pencil tests, whether multiple-choice or open-ended, typically can be administered by a standard procedure that requires less training than that required for nontraditional assessments. On the other hand, interviews and simulations usually require considerable training, not only because the use of materials and procedures is more complex, but because the sequence of events may be highly variable from one administration to another, depending on how the students respond. Such variation does not necessarily make the measure less valid, but it raises the validity question, "Does the likelihood of success for a given student change with variations in the administration?"

This raises a larger question of whether achievement level depends on administration mode. It does, whether the tests are traditional multiple-choice or whether they use some alternative format.

In state assessments, students with language or other handicaps commonly are given accommodations, such as reading the question aloud to the student, rather than requiring the student to read it only from print, with the expectation that students will score higher and the measure still will be valid. The fly in the ointment is that students without such handicaps also tend to score higher with the use of accommodations, causing proficiency level results to depend on mode of administration. In our field tests of citizenship exercises, for example, 25% more students succeeded on the average if a given exercise was given in an individual interview, rather than in a group administration.

*Scoring:* A clear advantage of multiple-choice items is the objectivity of scoring. Open-ended, constructed-response measures can be administered as objectively as multiple-choice items can in paper-and-pencil mode, but scoring them in a uniform way is more challenging. In an interview mode, where oral responses are captured on the fly, the demand on the interviewer for instant categorization of responses requires significant training.

Scoring guides to standardize the scoring of open-ended responses have been elaborated extensively in recent years by states and school districts as they developed performance measures. Often the guide is presented as a two-dimensional array, a "rubric," in which one dimension is the level of proficiency and the second is a listing of content, behaviors, or other aspects of the response to be scored. The rubric can reduce a very complex scoring situation to manageable proportions.

The more successful rubrics simplify the judgmental task by arranging the content of the response into a few criteria that can be scored separately, one criterion at a time. For example, scoring on a writing standard might be separated into "communication" and "mechanics." The scorer then can compare the proficiency-level definitions for mechanics alone and score the student's response in that more limited domain. The criteria are weighted or combined in some other logical way to obtain an overall proficiency level, for example, meeting two of three criteria qualifies the student for that proficiency level.

The less successful rubrics tend to describe in a list or paragraph the performance of students at a given proficiency level, but they do not specify how all the described items are to be combined. Some scorers may use a modal approach, choosing the proficiency level where the most items are checked, while others may use a conjoint model, scoring at a given proficiency level only if all the items at that level are achieved.

*Cost Considerations:* The higher cost of administering and scoring nontraditional exercises naturally raises the question, Are they worth it? The issues are somewhat different for large-scale assessments than for assessment in ordinary classroom use. For large-scale assessment, a useful perspective may be to ask which is the better use of money. For the same money, one could use multiple-choice items and either assess a much larger sample or assess more often, or both.

If nontraditional methods of assessment have greater validity for many important objectives, then getting more data on a less valid measure (multiple-choice test) may not be worthwhile. A more valid measure surely provides the public and the schools with more useful information for improving curricula and teaching methods, even if a fixed budget allows assessment only half as often. Costs could be contained by using smaller samples for more costly measures, increasing the margin of error from, say, 5% to 10%. For high-stakes decisions based on large-scale assessments, such as evaluating and accrediting schools, the difference in validity seems even more critical. With so much at stake, surely a more expensive measure is justified if it is more valid for assessing the important standards.

Knowing that any measure has weaknesses, having two or more different types of measures has advantages over using a single measure. This advantage is quite important to principals and teachers at a time when standardized tests are being viewed more critically.

Funding research on predictive validity of education assessments is another big challenge. But what could be more important than knowing whether what we measure in our assessments relates to real-life accomplishments. This is especially critical in view of the findings that multiple-choice tests do *not* predict real-life achievements well.

One important difference between traditional assessment and real life is that, in real life, experts use a rich context, both environmental and social, to understand a situation and to act wisely (Pellegrino, Chudowsky, and Glaser 2001, p. 77). Students likewise learn better when a task is placed in a physical context (for example, manipulative objects in math or a familiar neighborhood problem) so they can bring to bear all the knowledge they have. It follows that situational or performance measures that provide a rich context will enable students to demonstrate their skills better than will context-free multiple-choice tests. The extra cost of such measures may be well worthwhile if they provide the most valid way for students to demonstrate key skills, especially if the assessments themselves are valuable learning experiences.

## Summary

The citizenship objectives established by the National Assessment of Educational Progress in the 1960s covered much more than the academic knowledge of civics. NAEP also assessed students' skills, life habits, and attitudes about citizenship. For such objectives, a variety of different kinds of assessment were developed by the AIR team, and results on such assessments were reported in the first national assessment of citizenship.

To assess such objectives, NAEP and the AIR team did not rely on multiple-choice tests but, instead, used a variety of nontraditional exercises, including interviews and observed group interactions. For most citizenship objectives, and for many objectives in other areas, nontraditional exercises can be more valid measurement tools than are the standardized, multiple-choice tests that now dominate large-scale assessments.

# CHAPTER 15

# Assessing Writing and Mathematics

*Ina V.S. Mullis*

When NAEP began in the 1960s, there were no guidelines for what should be tested. Before NAEP could begin to write exercises for the assessments, it had to define sets of goals or objectives for each subject area. To meet this challenge, NAEP developed what has come to be known as the consensus process for developing objectives.

NAEP developed assessment objectives in behavioral terms. The objectives were designed to reflect learning goals or outcomes that students would be expected to achieve in the course of their schooling. In addition, the objectives for each subject had to be:

- Considered authentic by scholars in the discipline.
- Accepted as an educational task by schools.
- Regarded as desirable by thoughtful lay citizens.

For the first assessments, the objectives and exercises for each subject area were put into final form by organizations under contract to the Exploratory Committee for Assessing the Progress of Education (ECAPE), such as the Educational Testing Service and the American Institutes for Research. However, by 1975 NAEP was facing dramatic budget reductions, from approximately $6 million annually down to approximately $3 million. Thus NAEP switched from using contractors to having its own staff manage the compli-cated consensus process used to develop assessment objectives.

A second era in development procedures occurred in 1983, when the Educational Testing Service (ETS) was awarded the grant for administering NAEP. The move to ETS necessitated modifications to align NAEP development procedures with policies long estab-lished at ETS to govern decisions about test development and use. It also involved developing procedures consistent with *A New Design for a New Era,* as envisioned by Samuel Messick, Albert Beaton, and Frederic Lord (1983). This included developing "blocks" of items suitable for a Balanced Incomplete Block BIB-spiraled design, implementing scoring procedures suitable for Item Response Theory (IRT) scaling, and designing long-range plans for determining which items would be kept secure for meas-uring trends and which would be released for public use.

The third big change in development procedures occurred at the end of the 1980s. Because the 1990 mathematics assessment included the first trial state-by-state assessment, the objectives for that assessment were developed through a specially funded project called the National Assessment Planning Project.

Managed by the Council of Chief State School Officers (CCSSO), the development process for the 1990 mathematics objectives was greatly expanded to ensure careful attention to the goals and practices at the state level. A steering committee repre-senting 18 national organizations provided guidance for the process; and subject-matter expertise was provided by a Mathematics Objec-tives Committee consisting of specialists from states, universities, and local groups, well buttressed with extensive mail reviews.

The National Assessment Planning Project served as the forerunner to the procedures used since 1992 by the National Assessment Governing Board (NAGB) in fulfilling its responsi-bilities for developing NAEP objectives and test specifications.

## Objectives for the Second Writing Assessment

Preparation for the second assessment of each subject spanned approximately six to seven years, beginning in 1969. Because writing, together with science and citizenship, was one of the subject areas included in the very first year of NAEP assessments in 1969-70, it was scheduled for reassessment in 1973-74. Thus some of the earliest work on objectives redevelopment was done in writing.

The task of redeveloping objectives for the second writing assessment was awarded in 1969 to ETS, the same contractor that developed the objectives for the first writing assessment. Work on redeveloping those objectives was begun while data from the first writing assessment were being gathered and analyzed.

Redeveloping the writing objectives for the second assessment commenced with a mail review by 30 individuals, including educators, subject-matter specialists, and representatives of the lay public, primarily members of local and state boards of education, PTA officers, and others involved in education and community service. In the summer of 1969, ETS convened a conference of writing specialists, educators, and concerned lay citizens to revise the 1965 objectives, taking into account the comments of the mail reviewers, as well as the findings of current scholarship, research, and professional opinion. That conference outlined three major objectives for the writing assessment:

1. To demonstrate ability in writing to reveal personal feelings and ideas.
2. To demonstrate the ability to write in response to a wide range of societal demands and obligations.
3. To appreciate the value of writing.

Following the conference, ETS developed descriptions of the objectives and had them reviewed by panels of lay persons. The greatest concern of the reviewers was that there was not enough specific attention to grammar and punctuation and that the objectives should be made more detailed and explicit. ETS then revised the objectives and conducted two final mail reviews, resulting in the finished objectives outlined below. Because of restricted funding in the mid-1970s, the 1973-74 writing objectives served as the basis for developing exercises for both the second and third assessments.

The outline of writing objectives for 1973-74 sets forth three primary objectives, each with two or more subobjectives:

I. Demonstrates ability in writing to reveal personal feelings and ideas.
   A. Through free expression
   B. Through the use of conventional modes of discourse

II. Demonstrates ability to write in response to a wide range of societal demands and obligations. Ability is defined to include correctness in usage, punctuation, spelling, and form or convention as appropriate to particular writing tasks, e.g., manuscripts, letters.
   A. Social
   B. Personal
   C. Organizational
   D. Community
   E. Business/Vocational
   F. Scholastic

III. Indicates the importance attached to writing skills.
   A. Recognizes the necessity of writing for a variety of needs (as in I and II)
   B. Writes to fulfill those needs
   C. Gets satisfaction, even enjoyment, from having written something well. (NAEP 1972)

In the writing objectives booklet for the second assessment, each objective was described in both general terms and in more detail, including writing samples produced by students at each of the ages assessed by NAEP at the time (9, 13, 17, and adult). By the time the second writing assessment was conducted, NAEP resources no longer supported assessing students not attending school (adults and some 17-year-olds).

One recurring concern was the difficulty and appropriateness of measuring an objective that requested students to reveal personal feelings. NAEP elected to interpret Objective I broadly, as the ability to engage in writing for expressive purposes. It also was decided that writing of the sort described in Objective II is done for particular audience and should be evaluated in view of its intended effect on that audience. Thus, for the second and third assessments of writing, NAEP developed Objective II writing tasks that measured either explanatory or persuasive writing appropriate to specific social, business, or scholastic situations.

Generally, the second (1973-74) and third (1978-79) NAEP writing assessments were relatively limited in scope. In particular, the 1978-79 assessment was one of three conducted that year, so it contained only four essay or letter-writing tasks for each age: 9, 13, and 17.

Beginning with the second writing assessment, the student responses were scored in several ways (NAEP 1981*a*). Almost all of the essays and letters were evaluated using the "primary trait" system of scoring. This system, developed especially for NAEP, described a respondent's ability to choose and effectively carry out appropriate rhetorical strategies. NAEP used a four-point scale to describe levels of proficiency in the primary skill being assessed. Generally, level 1 indicated little or no evidence of the skill, level 2 indicated minimal evidence, level 3 indicated solid performance or competence, and level 4 indicated very good performance. Particular essays also were judged for overall quality using holistic scoring or were examined for specific elements of coherence, mechanics, and syntax. Since the latter types of scoring were very time-consuming and expensive, NAEP generally applied these types of scoring to only one or two writing tasks at an age level.

The basic measure of achievement reported by NAEP during its tenure at ECS was the percentage of respondents answering a given item acceptably. For writing, however, exact definitions of "correct" or "acceptable" performance is debatable. Thus the general procedure was to report percentages for each response category. To help determine whether performance had changed over time, percentages of better papers from each assessment were totaled and compared for each writing task.

## Mathematics Assessment in the 1970s

The objectives for the second mathematics assessment were developed through conferences organized by NAEP staff. As explained in *Mathematics Objectives: Second Assessment* (NAEP 1978), the conference procedure was intended to give the assessment greater flexibility, involve more mathematics and education professionals, and be more efficient in cost and time. Several types of consultants participated in development conferences, including college or university mathematics educators, mathematicians, classroom teachers, and interested lay citizens.

Consistent with the criteria used to develop NAEP objectives, the mathematics experts generally had to agree that the objectives were worthwhile and important to assess. The classroom teachers had to consider the objectives to be desirable teaching objectives in most schools. Finally, the lay group had to agree that an objective was important for America's youth to achieve and that it was of value in society.

Development of the second cycle of mathematics objectives began with two conferences of mathematics educators, mathematicians, and teachers, with each group independently asked to list objectives they thought were important. The result was two outlines of objectives with different formats, but 80% agreement in content. A subcommittee from each group met during a third conference to synthesize the two outlines.

The content domain for the second assessment encompassed mathematics up to, but not including, calculus. It drew primarily from the curriculum current at the time in elementary and secondary schools, though a nod to the future was made through greater use of metric measures and an earlier introduction to decimals and calculator computation. Even for the assessment at age 17, very few exercises depended on material taught in Algebra 2 and trigonometry. Because many of the 17-year-olds assessed were no longer taking mathematics courses, most of the items assessed material typically learned in eighth-, ninth-, and 10th-grade mathematics courses.

Each process category suggested a type of mental process, though it was emphasized that neither objectives nor exercises were likely to fall neatly in a single category, because different people may use different processes or different combinations of processes. However, the system was meant to ensure consideration of the diversity possible within a given content category.

Most interesting, and a giant step forward for NAEP, was the idea of the mathematics advisory board that the objectives should constitute a plan or framework for both exercise development and for reporting. The board members thought the second assessment would be better organized and more comprehensive than the first assessment if a reporting scheme existed before the exercises were developed. To provide a reporting plan, the advisory board developed a series of questions intended to be addressed by the results of sets of assessment exercises. The questions parallel those still asked nearly three decades later. For example, some of the questions were: "How well can students read graphs and tables?" "How well can students translate a verbal statement into symbols or a figure, and vice versa?" "How well can students solve typical textbook problems?" and "How well can students use mathematics in reasoning and making judgments?"

Based on the firm foundation provided in the mid-1970s by NAEP's mathematics advisory board for the second assessment, the third mathematics assessment built on the previous objectives, with some revisions reflecting changes in content and trends in school mathematics. Using a process very similar to that used for the second assessment, the objectives for the third mathematics assessment, conducted in 1981-82, were developed under the guidance of NAEP staff at ECS. Attitudes toward mathematics, ability to use the calculator, and computer literacy, considered "special topics" in the second assessment, were incorporated into the matrix for the third assessment. A nine-member advisory committee was instrumental in reviewing the objectives and providing guidance throughout the development process.

While under the auspices of ECS, NAEP developed and reported results for three mathematics assessments, 1972-73,

1977-78, and 1981-82. Besides providing the percentage of students responding correctly to individual items, NAEP reported the average performance (mean) across groups of similar mathematics items, for example, by objective or topic. This arithmetic average, the estimate of performance on a group of items, was termed the average percentage acceptable or the mean performance level.

The most interesting aspect for mathematics education was the ability to report trends across three cycles. Based on a large development effort for the 1977-78 assessment, identical item sets — 233 items at age 9 and 383 items each at ages 13 and 17 — were used to measure changes in achievement from the 1977-78 assessment to the 1981-82 assessment (NAEP 1983). However, these trend sets were not the same for all assessments. Only some items — 23 at age 9, 43 at age 13, and 61 at age 17 — were used in all three mathematics assessments.

About half of the exercises used to measure change from the second to the third assessment were multiple-choice; and about half were open-ended, with students having to supply the correct answer. There were four major exercise clusters, including exercises measuring knowledge, skills, understanding, and applications.

To present a general picture of changes in mathematics achievement, NAEP reported the gains and losses for groups of exercises in terms of the differences in the average percentages of acceptable responses. Across the three assessments, mean performance for nine-year-olds was relatively stable. At age 13, students performed similarly between the first two assessments but improved dramatically between 1972-73 and 1981-82, particularly on rather routine items, such as computation and figure recognition. At age 17, performance declined between the first two assessments and then stabilized.

## The Move to ETS

With the move to ETS in 1983, NAEP objectives continued to be developed through a nationally representative consensus process. In fact, the consensus process was described in Public

Law 98-511, Section 405 (E) (19 October 1984), which author-ized NAEP through 30 June 1988. The law stated that "each learn-ing area assessment shall have goal statements devised through a national consensus approach, providing for active participation of teachers, curriculum specialists, subject matter specialists, local school administrators, parents, and members of the general public."

True to the fundamentals established for the initial assessments in the 1960s, subject-area specialists were involved to ensure that the objectives reflected current practice, as well as new directions in theory. Parents active in school-related organizations and other concerned citizens were included to ensure that the objectives were free from bias and met with their expectations for achieve-ment. Teachers participated to be certain that the objectives were appropriate and realistic from the classroom perspective, and school superintendents and curriculum specialists were involved to represent the perspectives of school administrators.

ETS had guidelines and procedures for most activities, so one of the first development tasks at ETS was to document the proce-dures that would be used to develop NAEP objectives and items and have the procedures approved by NAEP's Assessment Policy Committee (Mullis, MacDonald, and Mead 1988). From the early years, NAEP had periodically convened its Assessment Policy Committee, composed of policy makers, educators, and business leaders, to consider matters of general policy. In order to increase public understanding of NAEP, ETS greatly enhanced the size and scope of NAEP's Assessment Policy Committee. From 1983 until Congress established NAGB in 1988, the Assessment Policy Committee had the responsibility for guiding NAEP policies, including the subject areas to be assessed and the development procedures.

Early in 1984, the Assessment Policy Committee approved the following procedures for setting NAEP objectives in each cur-riculum area.

1. Conduct a mail review of the objectives used in the previous assessment, involving about 25 educators and specialists to

represent differing points of view, geographic locations, backgrounds, and constituencies.

2. Establish a Learning Area Committee to help guide assessment development procedures, composed of approximately eight members representing differing perspectives and backgrounds.

3. Convene the Learning Area Committee to review and revise the objectives from the previous assessment, based on the results of the mail review and their own judgment.

4. Conduct a mail review of the updated objectives by practitioners from around the country, including school administrators, teachers, and teacher trainers.

5. Convene the Learning Area Committee to revise the objectives in light of the comments made by the practitioners.

6. Conduct a mail review of the final draft of the objectives by members of the lay public for their reactions and opinions, and modify the objectives as necessary.

7. Send the objectives to the Learning Area Committee for final review.

8. Publish, print, and disseminate the objectives.

Even more than before, the contributors to the NAEP objectives-development process were chosen to reflect perspectives of people in various sizes and types of communities, from many geographic regions, and from various racial and ethnic groups. Of course, it was not possible for the final objectives to reflect the views of every individual who participated; but every effort was made to have the objectives represent, as nearly as possible, the consensus of opinions obtained from the development and review groups.

In October 1981 the ETS Board of Trustees adopted and publicly announced as corporate policy the *ETS Standards for Quality and Fairness*. To quote from the preface: "Compliance with the Standards is taken seriously at ETS. The Standards are applied to all ETS-administered programs." In particular, the standards required substantive contributions to the test-development process from qualified persons not on the ETS staff. This development approach was not new to NAEP, but it took on a new standardized form at ETS, with each subject-area development being carried out under the guidance of the Learning Area Committee.

In addition, the standards required that individual items be reviewed to ensure that language, symbols, words, phrases, and content that are generally regarded as sexist, racist, negative toward population subgroups, or otherwise potentially offensive are eliminated except when judged to be necessary for adequate representation of the domain.

Beyond attention to representation by diverse groups, ETS had a specific sensitivity-review process for its tests. The ETS Test Sensitivity Review Process was developed in 1980 and revised in 1986 (Educational Testing Service 1986, 1987*a*). According to the guidelines and procedures, each pretest and test needed to have a sensitivity review by reviewers trained in two-day workshops. Later in the 1980s, the sensitivity-review process began to be further informed by the empirical results of analyses for differential item functioning.

In addition to the ETS sensitivity review, item development at ETS involved a series of in-house reviews conducted in accordance with the standards. During the period under discussion in this chapter, the major reviews were:

- Subject-matter specialist reviews for accuracy, content appropriateness, suitability of language, difficulty, and adequacy of domain sampling.
- Test-development specialist reviews to ensure that appropriate technical standards were met, such as those contained in the ETS item writers' manuals.
- Editorial reviews to meet standards for clarity, accuracy, and consistency and to check the directions, typography, and test-book layout.

For NAEP, all items also were submitted for a complex clearance process conducted by the Office of Management and Budget and involving staff from the National Center for Education Statistics.

The Assessment Policy Committee approved the following carefully developed and tested series of steps for NAEP to use in creating test items:

1. Convene the Learning Area Committee to determine the specific types of items to be developed.
2. Draft a development and analysis plan for review by the Learning Area Committee, the NAEP staff at large, and selected external reviewers.
3. Review the existing pool of trend items in detail.
4. Develop item specifications and prototype items, keeping in mind the selection of trend items.
5. Arrange for skilled and experienced item writers to develop the items.
6. Conduct subject-area specialist reviews of the newly developed items both internally and externally.
7. Conduct ETS editorial reviews.
8. Conduct ETS sensitivity reviews.
9. Prepare the field-test materials and obtain clearance from the Office of Management and Budget.
10. Conduct the field test with a representative group of students.
11. Score and analyze field-test results.
12. Make any necessary revisions based on the field test and have items re-edited.
13. Conduct the final ETS sensitivity review.
14. Convene the Learning Area Committee to select the items for the assessment.
15. Assemble the items into blocks according to the analysis plan and statistical guidelines established at the beginning of the process.
16. Conduct a final review to ensure that each assessment block and booklet meets the overall guidelines for the assessment, and print the booklets.

It is worth noting that during the mid-1980s, NAEP, together with the rest of the test-development programs at ETS, made the switch from paper-and-pencil to computerized test documentation and assembly. When NAEP arrived at ETS in 1983, index cards and colored "stickies" were the backbone of test creation, review, and assembly. By the beginning of the Trial State Assessment in 1990, the ETS test-development process was completely computerized. This evolution in documentation, development, assembly, and printing procedures greatly facilitated NAEP's ability to accommodate the growth of the state assessment program.

## Writing Assessment During the 1980s

By 1988 NAEP was conducting the fifth national assessment of writing. Previous assessments were in 1969-70, 1973-74, 1978-79, and 1983-84. With each successive assessment and set of writing objectives, NAEP attempted to reflect forward thinking about effective teaching and learning in writing.

Many educators, including university professors, writing researchers, classroom teachers, school administrators, and curriculum specialists, as well as concerned parents and lay persons, participated in developing and reviewing successive drafts of the 1988 writing objectives. These objectives, outlined below, were based on the premise that individuals write for a purpose to an audience (Educational Testing Service 1987*a*). The purpose of the writing affects the ideas that are included, the way they are organized, and the manner in which they are expressed. The writing objectives for the 1988 assessment were:

I. Students Use Writing to Accomplish a Variety of Purposes
   A. Informative Writing
   B. Persuasive Writing
   C. Personal/Imaginative Narrative Writing

II. Students Manage the Writing Process: Generating, Drafting, Revising, and Editing

III. Students Control the Forms of Written Language
   A. Genre
   B. Organization and Elaboration
   C. Conventions (Usage and Mechanics)

IV. Students Value Writing and What Has Been Written
   A. Value for Interpersonal Communication
   B. Value for Society
   C. Value for Self

The writing objectives booklet for the fifth assessment described each objective in detail and included a section for teachers on putting the writing objectives into practice. It is important to note that in the years before widespread availability of state-developed curriculum frameworks, the NAEP objectives booklets for all the subject areas were in considerable demand. Because the objectives defined what a national consensus of subject experts, educators, and lay persons felt were important learning goals for students, they were useful to a variety of audiences. Although the NAEP consensus process tended to result in broad guidelines, rather than specific goals, they provided an excellent foundation for building and refining objectives appropriate to particular situations.

For the 1983-84 assessment, NAEP worked, first at ECS and subsequently at ETS, to broaden the coverage of the types of writing assessed. Using an iterative series of item-writing conferences and pilot testing, NAEP at ECS developed and field tested 90 booklets of writing tasks for students, 30 for each of the three ages assessed. Subsequently, NAEP was transferred to ETS; and the writing tasks and scoring guides were further reviewed by subject-matter specialists and editors, as well as for bias according to the ETS Standards. ETS submitted the final set of writing tasks to OMB clearance, including 15 tasks for each age/grade. In 1983-84, to begin the shift from age-based to grade-based assessment, ETS assessed students aged 9, 13, and 17, and students in the corresponding modal grades 4, 8, and 11.

For the fourth and fifth writing assessments in 1984 and 1988, ETS introduced the Average Response Method (ARM) for scaling writing (Applebee et al.1990). In 1988, based on the primary trait scores for each of approximately eight tasks per grade, the ARM was generalized to provide performance comparisons across grades, based on a linking subset of items, and to allow the inclusion of new writing tasks on the scale. While modest in its beginnings, these pioneering efforts led to the more ambitious writing assessments of NAEP in the 1990s. More recently in the 1998 assessment, NAEP administered approximately 20 prompts at each grade and used IRT methods to develop an independent overall scale for each of the grades (Greenwald et al. 1999).

To complement "test" writing with "best" writing, ETS conducted the Writing Portfolio Study in 1992. NAEP asked nationally representative subgroups of fourth- and eighth-graders who participated in the writing assessment to work with their teachers and submit three pieces of writing from their language arts or English classes that represented their *best* writing efforts (Gentile, Martin-Rehrmann, and Kennedy 1995). Students were asked to give special preference to pieces developed using writing-process strategies, such as pre-writing, peer review, and revising successive drafts, and to select different kinds of writing (that is, narrative, informative, and persuasive). The NAEP procedure of investigating classroom writing showed a smaller difference between assessment and classroom than might have been anticipated. The results reported in *Windows into the Classroom* indicated that even at eighth grade, only 4% of the informative papers were organized and developed. However, the majority of the informative portfolio papers (53%) did have at least one coherent and developed section.

## Mathematics Objectives During the 1980s

The mathematics objectives for the fourth assessment in 1985-86 were developed under the auspices of ETS. Following the procedures established by the Assessment Policy Committee, ETS staff managed the objectives-development process with the guidance of the Mathematics Learning Area Committee. The process involved iterative mail and committee reviews and revision similar to previous assessments.

As reproduced below from *Math Objectives: 1985-86 Assessment* (NAEP, no date) the framework included five process areas (Problem Solving/Reasoning, Routine Application, Understanding/Comprehension, Skill, and Knowledge) and seven content areas (Mathematics Methods; Discrete Mathematics; Data Organization and Interpretation; Measurement; Geometry; Relations, Functions, etc.; and Numbers and Operations). In response to a request by the Assessment Policy Committee, the Mathematics Learning Area Committee revised the process areas to focus on higher-level, critical-thinking skills. In general, however, the mathematics objectives framework did not change dramatically across the second, third, and fourth assessments.

Starting with the fifth mathematics assessment conducted in 1990, NAEP began using an updated and more elaborate consensus process to develop objectives.

In 1988 Congress passed the Hawkins-Stafford Amendments, Public Law 100-297, which added a new dimension to NAEP, a voluntary Trial State Assessment in 1990 and 1992. The first Trial State Assessment was conducted in mathematics at grade 8, with 40 states and territories participating. The Trial State Assessments continued in 1992 in mathematics at grades 4 and 8 and reading at grade 4. Beginning in 1994, the trial program was deemed successful and state assessments became a regular part of NAEP.

Anticipating the new legislation, in mid-1987 the federal government arranged for a special grant from the National Science Foundation and the Department of Education to the Council of Chief State School Officers (CCSSO) to lay the groundwork for the 1990 Trial State Assessment in mathematics at grade 8. The CCSSO established the National Assessment Planning Project to oversee the work for the Trial State Assessment. To provide for continuity between 1990 and 1992, as well as between the state and national programs, the project developed new mathematics objectives for all three grades to be assessed in 1990 (grades 4, 8, and 12). The National Assessment Planning Project involved a steering committee, whose members included policy makers, practitioners, and citizens nominated by 18 national organizations, to make overall recommendations about assessment development and reporting. A Mathematics Objectives Committee of teachers, school administrators, state-level mathematics specialists, mathematicians, parents, and citizens was created to recommend the mathematics objectives for the assessment.

In creating the draft objectives framework, the Mathematics Objectives Committee gave attention to several frames of reference (Foertsch, Jones, and Koffler 1992). For example, the assessment was intended to reflect many of the states' curricular emphases and objectives without being geared to the lowest common denominator; be inclusive of what various scholars, practitioners, and interested citizens felt should be included in the curriculum; and be aligned with the draft of the *Curriculum and Evaluation Standards for School Mathematics*, developed by the National Council of Teachers of Mathematics.

The draft framework was sent for review by the mathematics supervisor in each of the 50 state education agencies and to 25 mathematics educators and scholars. After making revisions to address the extensive reviews, the framework was approved with refinements by the steering committee, the Assessment Policy Committee, and a special Task Force on State Comparisons.

Since 1992, the process of developing the NAEP frameworks has been carried out under the direction of NAGB. Created by Congress in 1988, NAGB is responsible for setting policy for NAEP. Among its responsibilities, the board is specifically charged with selecting subject areas to be assessed and developing assessment objectives and test specifications by use of a national consensus approach. The mathematics objectives framework developed under the auspices of the CCSSO through the special NAEP Planning Project was endorsed by NAGB for 1992.

Because the mathematics objectives were relatively similar from assessment to assessment through the years of development managed by ECS and ETS, so were the assessment items. With each new assessment, mathematics items were developed by external item writers, staff, and the advisory committee. Beginning with the 1985-86 assessment, all items were subjected to the stringent, multi-step ETS internal review. The Learning Area Committee worked with NAEP staff to prepare the items for OMB clearance and field testing. After field testing, the Learning Area Committee recommended the items for the final assessment. These final blocks and booklets were subjected to the ETS and NAEP review processes and eventually submitted for OMB clearance.

Each mathematics assessment contained a range of open-ended and multiple-choice questions. Generally, several hundred items were included at each age or grade assessed, primarily in the multiple-choice format. Although changes were made from assessment to assessment, a small set of exercises was kept constant in order to anchor the results across time. Consistent with the transfer from ECS to ETS, the method of reporting shifted from percentage correct to scaling between the 1981-82 and the 1985-86 assessments. In 1985-86, the mathematics assessment was assembled according to a BIB design and analyzed using IRT to estimate levels of mathematics achievement for the nation and for various subpopulations of students.

The juxtaposition of the beginning of the Trial State Assessment program with the availability of the NCTM's *Curriculum and Evaluation Standards for School Mathematics* (1989) signaled a new era for NAEP mathematics assessment. According to the NCTM evaluation standards, the following were among assessment practices that needed to receive more attention:

- Assessing what students know and how they think about mathematics.
- Developing problem situations that require the applications of a number of mathematical ideas.
- Using calculators, computers, and manipulatives in assessment.

By NAEP's 1992 mathematics assessment, about one-third of the questions and approximately half of the students' response time was devoted to questions asking students to construct their own responses (Dossey, Mullis, and Jones 1993). These questions continued the previous practice of supplying students with protractor/rulers and calculators for portions of the assessment. For 1990, the calculators provided to students were upgraded from four-function to scientific calculators at grades 8 and 12, including for the Trial State Assessment. For 1990 and 1992, the assessment also included an estimation portion that was administered with a paced audiotape timed to encourage students to estimate, rather than "work out," their answers.

New for the 1992 assessment were extended-response questions that allowed students five minutes or so to demonstrate — in writing, by giving examples, or by drawing diagrams — their mathematical reasoning and problem-solving abilities. Also, the assessment was expanded to include manipulable geometric shapes and spinners.

## Summary

Although NAEP development has always been rooted in a consensus process involving diverse groups of people, management of the consensus process and its goals have changed in major ways since the first round of data collection in 1969-70. At ECS during the 1970s, NAEP grew from being conducted largely through contractors to being managed by its own staff guided by subject-matter and technical committees.

In 1983, ETS was awarded the grant for managing NAEP. At ETS, NAEP operated within the environment of a testing organization with well-established procedures and guidelines. Development procedures also needed to be aligned with the major change in NAEP's approach to analysis and reporting under ETS. NAEP changed from the percentage-correct technology to IRT scaling and routinized rigorous approaches to measuring trends in achievement. Also during the 1980s, test development changed from being a paper-based endeavor to one that was computerized from initial item development through printing.

In 1988 Congress added state-by-state assessments to NAEP. Thus, for the 1990 and 1992 Trial State Assessments in mathematics, NAEP enjoyed new challenges in developing objectives and items responsive to the needs of states. At the same time, NAGB assumed responsibility for managing NAEP's consensus process for developing the frameworks and objectives underlying assessment in each subject area.

# PART III

# SAMPLING AND SCORING

# CHAPTER 16

# Survey Design Issues

*James R. Chromy, Alva L. Finkner,*
*and Daniel G. Horvitz*

The Research Triangle Institute (RTI) was responsible for conducting and administering NAEP from February 1969 to 1983. As Charles X. Larrabee, public information officer, explains, "for nearly 15 years the National Assessment of Educational Progress (NAEP) devoured the time and energies of a major segment of RTI's sampling statisticians and survey specialists, of several dozen regional and district supervisors around the country, and of up to 500 and more temporary field personnel who might be needed at any given time" (1991, p. 129).

RTI's association with NAEP began in 1966 when Gertrude Cox and Dan Horvitz met with Ralph Tyler and other members of the Exploratory Committee on Assessing the Progress of Education (ECAPE) to discuss the survey methods that would make NAEP possible. Following the initial planning stages, RTI became the contractor for sampling and administration.

Following Cox and Horvitz's early meetings with ECAPE, RTI became involved in two sets of planning activities. The first, led by Cox and senior social scientist William C. Eckerman, involved experimental studies on the possible effects of interviewing mode and environment; the second, led by Horvitz, pertained to development of sample and survey designs.

Gertrude Cox had already retired from heading the University of North Carolina Institute of Statistics in 1960 and from directing RTI's Statistics Research Division in 1965; but she continued to teach and consult, and she had a strong interest in the early development of NAEP. Cox designed and analyzed an experiment to investigate two issues important to administering NAEP exercises. The first study was to determine whether performance on exercises was likely to be affected by the assessment environment. This was important because 17-year-olds would be assessed both in a school environment and, if not attending school, in a home environment. And because the NAEP planners planned to use both group and individual administration modes, Cox conducted a study to determine how performance was likely to be influenced by the mode of administration (Cox 1968).

Cox's report to the Technical Advisory Committee (TAC) focused on administration methods. Among her conclusions were:

- There is some indication that poorer results are obtained in the social science assessments in out-of-school administration. Only random variation exists between administration methods in the other subjects.
- The effect of method of administration did not differ across regions.
- Given adequate time to make arrangements, in-school administrators can be hired locally and successfully supervised by one RTI staff member.
- An RTI staff member was needed at each school to make decisions about substitutions and rescheduling.
- In large schools, a school official should be on call to help locate students who are tardy for appointments.
- Monday is the poorest day for group administration.
- Group sessions should not be scheduled for first period in schools using busing.
- A letter to parents explaining the project and requesting permission to test their children could improve response rates and reduce the number of questions students have when reporting for testing.

- Do not use school counselors to help conduct individual in-school administrations.

Cox also noted that individual items were too variable in their responses and suggested combining three or four items within the same objective for reporting purposes. She recommended that reported results include confidence limits. She also initiated some item analysis and located possible regional biases in a question on weather-pattern movement.

The item-packaging plan employed in Cox's experiment was quite complex and well ahead of its time. Within each form, multiple subjects were assessed in the same booklet. Ordering effects were controlled by randomization. The design did not guarantee that all pairs of items would be administered to the same student subsample as proposed by Tom Knapp. Knapp (1968) proposed adoption of a partially balanced incomplete block design (PBIBD) to control the number of times each pair of exercises is administered. Neither Cox's nor Knapp's packaging approaches were employed in the early assessment years due to their added complexity, limitations imposed by tape pacing of group sessions, and limitations in the ability to produce the required numbers of automatically scored assessment packages.

## Planning the Sample and Survey Design

ECAPE and TAC established many general guidelines at the outset of the sample and survey design process; others were established as the discussions progressed. A few of these guidelines are listed below:

- Assessment target populations were to be defined by age, rather than by grade. Age groups were nine-year-olds, 13-year-olds, 17-year-olds, and young adults aged 26 to 35.
- Several different subjects were to be assessed, perhaps as many as 10.
- Rather than focusing on student scores, statistical estimates were to measure the performance of populations and defined subpopulations on individual exercises.

- Sample size requirements were to be based on the ability to detect meaningful progress over time.
- No single survey participant would be required to spend more than about one hour in answering a subset of the total set of assessment items.
- A matrix sampling approach was to be used to group the total set of exercises into booklets that conform to the time limitation.
- Both group and individual administration of booklets were planned.
- Group-administered booklets would be packaged with one exercise to a page and paced with a tape recording.
- Except for measuring reading ability, the audiotape-paced presentation would read the exercise material to the respondents to ensure that the ability in the subject matter, rather than reading ability, was being measured.
- A limited number of performance exercises would be administered individually.
- Assessment of nine-year-olds and 13-year-olds would be limited to an in-school setting because these age groups are required to attend school.
- Both public and private schools were to be included.
- Pending the outcome of experimental studies on school versus home administration, 17-year-olds would be sampled in school and, if not attending school, at home.
- Estimates were to be developed for national and regional populations and subpopulations only. No results would ever be released for a student, a school, a district, or a state.
- Young adults aged 26 to 35 would be surveyed using a household sample. The same sample would be used to screen for out-of-school 17-year-olds.
- Progress would be measured by repeating the assessment at regular intervals.

The list of requirements for assessments seems extensive, but few of the details were actually provided. To help guide the sample size and allocation issues, subpopulation definitions needed to be more specific. The size of the exercise pool and the number of exercises to be available for the first round of assessment were largely hypothetical. Sample size requirements had to be developed at the exercise level and then expanded to all-package coverage. Unique optimal sample allocation problems were introduced because geographic primary sampling unit and school cost components were shared across packages (exercises); similar cost sharing occurred for the household sample.

Statisticians and social scientists from RTI often were invited to attend TAC meetings or to present intermediate results on sample and survey design development to the TAC. The RTI staff members attending these meetings during the planning phases included Jim Chromy, Bill Eckerman, Al Finkner, George Herbert, and Dan Horvitz.

One problem faced in the early years was getting the cooperation of schools. In a presentation to the RTI Board of Governors' Executive Committee concerning RTI's involvement, Al Finkner noted the positions that some national organizations took toward a national assessment. Also, RTI's own experience in getting cooperation for the Cox and Eckerman experimental studies demonstrated the mixed feelings that education leaders had about the project. The North Carolina Superintendent of Schools wrote a cordial letter to school administrators that said he would look "with favor upon participation by any local schools administrative units that might desire to do so." However, he added, "We would not want the cooperation of this Department and our local school administrative units in this research effort to be construed as connoting acceptance or approval of National assessment of education in principle or in fact."

One local school system contacted about participating in the research study declined after review, citing "risk in maintaining relationships with our professional organizations which have taken a stand in opposition to national assessment in the form they perceive it is likely to take." Cooperation eventually was obtained for the research studies in North Carolina and in other public school systems, but this early experience in obtaining school cooperation led to serious reconsideration of the "top down" approach to obtaining school system cooperation when NAEP became operational.

Failures to obtain endorsements at state and district levels continued to be a problem in early NAEP surveys, but they were not nearly as severe as these early experiences indicated.

Another topic discussed at the TAC meetings was a plan for the decision-making process. One of the items prepared by RTI and presented by Jim Chromy at the June 1968 meeting of TAC was a draft set of Operational Flow Charts (RTI 1968). The flow charts had been prepared by Gipsie Ranney at RTI with inputs from other RTI staff, Daryl Nichols of AIR, John Johnstone of the National Opinion Research Center, Burdette Hansen of the Measurement Research Center, and Scarvia Anderson, Arlene Barron, Charles Barr, and Jerry Weisbrodt of ETS. Daryl Nichols had provided a copy of a February 1968 AIR proposal that contained detailed flow charts of the first year operations. The development phase included general issues, including the designation of a coordinating agency, universe definition and sampling design, test item development, and operations planning, all leading to an operations phase.

The operations phase showed three related components of field work; scoring, tabulation, and analysis; and evaluation. These operational components were linked back to the coordinating agency and to continuing development activities. This concept of a never-ending process of adjusting and moving forward from survey to survey, with continuing redevelopment, pretty well describes NAEP to this day.

Item development was a major component of the survey planning process. As opposed to conventional norm-referenced tests used to evaluate individual students, the national assessment focused on group evaluation. These criterion-referenced measures could be readily understood by a layman. Repetition of the assessment after a few years would trace the growth of knowledge over time. Two principles set the stage for the statistical issues relating to required sample sizes.

- Most measures would be simple proportions of subpopulations responding a certain way.
- Emphasis would be placed on measurement of change, particularly on progress (increasing percent with the correct response).

The extended coverage of many subjects and the subpopulations to be assessed were another sample and survey design issue because they established the total size of the study. It was clear from the earliest planning stages that no individual would ever take the entire set of test items and that different individuals could be selected into the sample for each repetition of the survey (Carnegie Corporation 1966). Other test development issues that affected the sample and survey design included:

- Subject cycling from year to year.
- The total number of items by age group and year.
- Scoring methods.
- Security required to avoid revealing current year items expected to be repeated in subsequent assessments.
- Presentation formats.
- Time requirements.

Because cost generally is traded off with precision in survey design, all of these item development issues were crucial to the sample and survey design.

Test items came to be called exercises or assessment exercises. Even though no formal sampling process was followed, the set of exercises finally appearing in an assessment was viewed as a sample from a larger universe of potentially available exercises (Womer 1970, p. 20).

Defining the survey universe and key subpopulations occupied a large part of the planning process. The Technical Advisory Committee was interested in defining meaningful subpopulations or variables for analysis and reporting purposes. Thus, over time, variables such as TOC (type of community), SOC (size of community), and SES (socioeconomic status) were discussed in some depth with respect to their definitions and their measurement. Exploratory tabulations to show relative sizes of subpopulations and U.S. Census maps showing county distributions of variables related to type of community and SES were presented to TAC at several sessions. Even though many other ways of partitioning the total population for reporting purposes evolved over time, the partitioning of the initial subpopulation focused on 256 groups defined by:

- Four age groups
- Two sexes
- Four types of community
- Two SES groups
- Four regions

Except for sex, some decisions had to be reached to define these subpopulations. For sex, it was decided that both sexes would be represented in the sample about equally.

At the universe level, it was decided to exclude institutionalized persons (for example, persons attending schools for the mentally or physically handicapped and those in penal institutions). Geographically, the target population included all 50 states and the District of Columbia. After some consideration, Puerto Rico and other territories or possessions were excluded.

Age, rather than grade, was used to define the major subpopulations in NAEP with the general definitions being nine-year-old, 13-year-old, 17-year-old, and young adults. Although the Carnegie Corporation article (1966, p. 2) defined the young adult population as 30-year-olds, it was judged that a broader young-adult age group, 26 to 35, would be acceptable and would require fewer screening interviews. Similarly, the 17-year-old out-of-school definition was broadened to two years (16½ to 18½). Finally, operational definitions were based on year and month of birth and coordinated with timing of the particular age-group assessment periods.

Regional definitions seemed straightforward, but a good deal of discussion occurred concerning whether to use regions as defined by the U.S. Census or the Office of Business Economics.

For example, the Office of Business Economics places Texas and Oklahoma in the West, while the U.S. Census places those states in the South. Texas did not seem to fit neatly into the West or the Southeast; West Virginia did not fit neatly into the Central or Southeast region. Potential regional definitions by county for these two states were considered but dropped in favor of a strictly state-based regional classification, with Texas becoming part of the West and West Virginia part of the Southeast. The Office of Business Economics definitions for Northeast, Central, Southeast, and West were considered more appropriate for education issues and adopted for sampling purposes. For reporting purposes, Womer (1970) defines regions with west Texas included with the West and east Texas included with the Southeast.

Type of community target populations were conceptually defined as: large city, suburban, small city, and rural and small town. However, these general definitions needed considerable work in order to become specific in terms of what constitutes large, what units are to be measured (for example, cities, counties, central cities, or metropolitan areas), and what the source of the population count should be. With the national assessment beginning near the end of a decade, the most recent U.S. Census data were almost 10 years old.

RTI presented some alternative definitions to TAC in September 1967 and in a revised memorandum in December 1967. The more specific definitions were:

- Large city: Central cities of 200,000 or more in 1960.
- Suburban: Remainder of SMSAs containing the large central cities.
- Small city: Counties that were more than 50% urban in 1960.
- Rural and small town: Counties that were less than 50% urban in 1960.

Type of community reporting population definitions continued to be refined in the early assessment years.

Socioeconomic status or socioeducational status was a well-understood concept, but one that was difficult to apply operationally when collecting data from young school children. The intent was to be able to report results separately for examinees from disadvantaged homes (Womer 1970, p. 40). Results would be reported for the low-SES group and the remainder. Two issues arose as a result of this general intent:

- How should SES be defined so that examinees at all ages could be classified into the two categories?
- What sampling strategies could be applied to ensure a large enough sample of the low-SES group to provide adequate precision for separately reporting results for that group?

Considerable effort was devoted to answering these questions, but those efforts did not lead to definitive answers. For example, at a May 1968 TAC meeting in Chapel Hill, North Carolina, the discussion focused on family income as a prime indicator of SES. The committee felt strongly that person-level, rather than school-level, classification was appropriate for SES. In the school population, Title I eligibility data maintained at the school might be an initial option. Dan Horvitz suggested a three-step sequential procedure involving 1) school-records information when available, 2) questionnaires sent to the parents when school records were not available, and 3) an interviewer visit to the home when the first two methods failed. The committee decided to request more information from RTI, ETS, and AIR.

The discussion of SES continued later in the month at a format and packaging conference held in St. Paul, Minnesota. A poverty line defined by family annual incomes of less than $3,000 was considered, but it was recognized that this was an oversimplification. Refinements were available that take account of family size and source of income (farm versus nonfarm). Both RTI and AIR reported on contacts with local school district personnel supporting the existence, but not necessarily the availability, of school data to classify students by poverty level. In addition, the sources of school data varied widely and included considerable judgment exercised by the school administrative staff. The field studies also identified serious concerns about privacy that might prevent schools from sharing income data even when they possessed it. Daryl Nichols proposed an income-indicator approach previously used in Project Talent; indicators included father's occupation, father's education, and mother's education.

RTI subsequently reported to TAC on a mail survey of schools across all four regions. That survey inquired about the availability of income or income indicator data. Based on the approximately 200 responses received, 93% had information on Title I, ESEA participation; 58% on parent's education; and 92% on father's occupation. In a small sample, AIR found a correlation of about 0.61 between teacher's estimates of father's income (low, medium, and high) and independent home appraisals (Lehmann 1968).

The approach to SES classification and sampling was explored further at a specifications conference held 2-3 August 1968. The minutes of the conference summarize the SES discussion:

> Measuring SES is a difficult task due to the sensitivity of some of the acceptable measures as well as the difficulty in obtaining accurate measures of the indicants that are not sensitive. It was the feeling of the conferees that family income must not be used as a measure of SES. Most people consider this an invasion of privacy and those who don't seldom report an accurate figure anyway.

A long list of indicators was considered at the conference, including parents' occupation and education, housing, items found in the home (automobiles, telephones, televisions, and flush toilets), census tract data, and school data. It was felt that some combination of these variables would successfully define the extremes for the first year.

The August 1968 specifications conference also addressed options for oversampling low-SES students and adults. Morris Hansen (then at the Census Bureau) felt that the most common oversampling is by a factor of two or three. Oversampling could be achieved at the school level by sampling more low-SES schools when these schools had predominantly low-SES students. Oversampling in most schools would rely on teacher preclassification of students; for example, if the school's percent poverty was

10%, teachers would identify the lowest 10% of students based on available information. The low-SES students would then be sampled at the higher rate. It was recognized that more research on both classification and sampling methods was needed and that methods might change after the first year.

SES still was an issue when the first assessments were finished. Two SES Tail-Sheet Meetings were held in February and March 1970 to refine plans for the second year of assessments. Representatives of OPAC, the Operations Advisory Committee, and ANAC, the Analysis Advisory Committee (the successor committee to TAC) participated in the meetings.

The term "tail-sheet" refers to the background questions used to classify students into reporting groups because these questions were presented on a separate page or pages following the cognitive-response sections of each assessment booklet. The first-year tail sheet had included questions about parental education and six home characteristics. Dan Horvitz reported $p$-values (in this case, the proportions of students who could respond correctly to NAEP exercises). The $p$-values were tabulated by highest education in the home, by a socioeconomic variable based on tail-sheet questions about family autos and telephones, and by a family reading-materials index based on tail-sheet questions about newspapers, encyclopedia, magazines, and books in the home. His results showed a consistent pattern of increased $p$-values associated with highest education level in the home, with ownership of both a telephone and an auto, and with having more reading materials in the home. Somewhat stronger relationships (more significantly different $p$-values) were found for the family reading index and the family auto and telephone status than for highest education level, but all three showed substantial significant effects.

Horvitz found that observed performance improves with parental education when the family reading index is at higher levels but shows little improvement with parental education if the family reading index is at its lower levels. In contrast, performance increases with increasing family reading material index regardless of the parents' education level. Students from homes with neither parent having completed high school, but with a higher family reading material index, performed better than did students from homes with some education beyond high school but with a low family reading material index. As of this writing, both the parental education variable and the family reading material index continue to be used as background variables.

Cal Stephenson of Measurement Research Center (MRC) reported on a study of the accuracy of 13-year-olds' responses regarding parental education. Approximately two-thirds of 13-year-olds reported parental education measures consistent with parent reports or school records. The accuracy of student reports improved with increasing education level of parents. Concern was expressed about the accuracy of data based on nine-year-olds' reports.

ANAC was concerned that the public would not accept measures of SES other than parental education. Other participants (Herbert Conrad of the U.S. Office of Education and Morris Hansen of Westat) doubted that SES based on the six home characteristics would be misinterpreted by the public. It was finally recommended that both parental education and home characteristic questions be retained on the tail-sheet for the second year (31 March 1970 meeting minutes).

Race was not one of the characteristics initially defining the 256 NAEP subpopulations, but it was incorporated into the reporting scheme later. Because of the small sample size at the package level, the smallest separately reportable racial minority group was blacks (Womer 1970, p. 41).

## Packaging, Session Types, and Administration Methods

Other issues, which weren't entirely sample or survey design issues, are discussed here because they helped establish bounds on the sample and survey design.

The Technical Advisory Committee still was working with contractors and consultants to determine the specifics of the overall assessment plan in the spring and summer of 1968, though the assessment was scheduled to begin in the fall. In March 1968, TAC held a contractor/consultant meeting at Chicago's O'Hare airport. The Friday-Saturday meeting included representatives of American Institutes for Research, Audits and Surveys, Educational Testing Service, National Opinion Research Center, Opinion Research Associates, and Research Triangle Institute. Steve Withey and Morris Hansen attended as consultants to ECAPE and TAC. Many of the contractors, including Research Triangle Institute, already had submitted proposals or concept papers for conducting various components of the assessment, but many additional decisions became "near final" at a subsequent specifications conference held in August 1968. By that time, the starting date for the national assessment was postponed to spring 1969 because of uncertain funding from the Office of Education.

Several packaging issues were resolved during this period. Machine-scorable packages were to be used. The format would be only one item per page, which would force respondents to focus on one item at a time and would work well with the taped administration. Because there was no focus on individual scores, packages could contain any combination of exercises as long as the expected time to complete the exercises was in the range of 40 to 50 minutes. Packages were not limited to a single subject.

Taped administration or pacing was chosen for all group sessions except those in reading. This early use of accommodation was an attempt to measure the respondent's knowledge in the subject being tested, rather than the respondent's ability to read. Early research had shown that a taped presentation increased the performance of poor readers and did not adversely affect the performance of average and above-average readers (Womer 1970, p. 31).

Most exercises could be administered in group sessions. The size of group sessions was limited to no more than 12 students so that all participants could hear the tape recording. Some exercises could be administered only in an individual session with monitoring by a trained test administrator. A few planned exercises assessed the performance of students working as a group, which required a special group administration method.

The first three age groups would be sampled through schools, and the test exercises were to be administered in school. Adults and out-of-school 17-year-olds were to be selected using a household sample and would be assessed at their homes. Rather than using tape recorders, interviewers would read exercises to adult and out-of-school 17-year-old respondents.

During this planning process, many other options for administering the assessment were explored. For example, Daryl Nichols of AIR advocated using vans to control the testing environment and to minimize demands on school facilities.

Another issue at the May 1968 TAC meeting was scheduling the in-school and out-of-school assessments. Several options were considered, including concurrent testing of all age groups and continuous testing throughout the school year. The scheduling of out-of-school assessment was less of a concern.

The participants in that meeting decided to assess nine-year-olds in January and February, 13-year-olds in October and November, and 17-year-olds in April and May. Womer documented the reasoning for this sequence in a 1969 memorandum that discussed other sequencing options that still were being considered while the first assessment was in progress. The assessment of 17-year-olds was placed in the spring in order to bring them close to the end of their high school career. The assessment of nine-year-olds was placed away from the fall to give the youngest group a few more months' exposure to school. These periods were adjusted only slightly to accommodate school schedules.

The varying dates of assessment created some concern about reference dates for defining age. Using January 1 of the current school year was considered desirable. Defining 17-year-olds as 16½ to 17½ was also proposed as a means of avoiding problems with students attending college at a young age. Using this age definition for 17-year-olds suggested that out-of-school 17-year-olds would be mostly dropouts. To increase the sample yield for out-of-school 17-year-olds, the out-of-school definition could include persons 16½ to 18½ as long as they were out of school when they were 16½ to 17½ and were properly weighted to represent a single year of eligibility.

## Frame Choices and Sample Design

In order to carry out an assessment, the sampling unit (for example, household or school) needs to be determined. The *frame* or *sampling frame* consists of the information needed to generate a list of sampling units or elements to be sampled. In the United States, no complete registry of persons is available, so direct sampling from a person frame was not possible. Multistage sampling permits the use of frames of other types (for example, land areas or schools) at early stages of the design so that the final list of persons can be limited to the next to final stage of sampling. For area household survey frames, the next to final stage is the household; for school survey frames, the next to final stage is the school.

At the March contractors' meeting, Morris Hansen suggested contacting the U.S. Census Bureau to investigate the feasibility of coordinating the assessment of out-of-school 17-year-olds with the bureau's Current Population Survey (CPS). A meeting of ECAPE, RTI, and U.S. Census staff took place on April 5 to explore the potential uses of the CPS or other census data for the national assessment. Some tentative options were developed to use expired CPS households as a screening sample for a 17-year-old out-of-school assessment. A second meeting was held with census staff in July 1968 to consider these options. Based on using all 449 primary sampling units in the CPS, a rough estimate of 1,600 to 2,000 out-of-school 17-year-olds could be identified over the period of one year. It would be necessary to get a signed release from these CPS sample members before they could participate in assessment. Womer subsequently outlined a census task and requested a contract for sample selection, but the U.S. Census screening option never developed.

The possible need to sample colleges or other institutions to identify early high school graduates or dropouts not living in the household population also was considered. Defining the target population as being 16½ to 17½ decreased the need for screening college populations.

Ultimately the mixed-frame approach was prescribed. This frame specified sampling nine-year-olds, 13-year-olds, and in-school 17-year-olds through a school frame and sampling out-of-school 17-year-olds and young adults through a household frame. More work on out-of-school 17-year-old sampling continued during the early NAEP years.

In early 1967, it was assumed that all 10 subjects might be assessed in a single year and then again periodically, for example, every five years. This assumption not only would have required precision at the single-exercise level for each of 256 subpopulations, it also would have required exceedingly large sample sizes. Exercise development could not occur fast enough to consider such a "one shot" design, and more reasonable sample design approaches developed over time.

In October 1967, RTI working papers developed cost and variance models for evaluating alternative designs (RTI 1967a, b). The models generally assumed a three-stage design for either a household frame or a school frame. Primary sampling units (PSUs) were defined as contiguous land areas for both frames. The models allowed consideration of PSUs with populations of 10,000, 50,000, 100,000, and 1,000,000 persons. Population densities of 10, 50, and 100 persons per square mile were used to develop travel-cost functions based on land area. Secondary sampling units (SSUs) were conceptualized simply as clusters of persons within the PSU; the cluster could be groups of students in school or groups of persons residing in a small land area. The third-stage sampling units were the persons actually selected to participate in the assessment.

Both cost and variance models still assumed that estimates would be required for 256 populations. The cost models assumed eight populations defined by sex and four age groups, so that certain costs (for example, PSU and SSU costs) could be shared across age groups. The models did not attempt to share costs across SES or type of community populations, though some PSUs might contain more than one level of these population-defining factors. Also, no sharing of costs across packages was introduced at this time; but this additional concept of "dilution" of costs due to multiple packages was pointed out later by John Tukey. These early models assumed that a PSU supervisor would be hired for each PSU so that there was no travel among PSUs. Within a PSU, travel costs were based on an average round-trip mileage to any point in the PSU from the center of the PSU. This turned out to be a multiple of the square root of the area of the PSU, which could be determined based on population size and density assumptions.

The model for screening costs in the household frame used the ratio of the total population to the target population. Based on these assumptions, 630 persons would have to be screened in the household frame in order to identify one out-of-school person aged 16½ to 17½ (assuming 20% were out of school). About 65 persons would have to be screened in the household frame to identify an in-school nine- or 13-year-old, and about 80 to identify an in-school 17-year-old. About 10 persons would have to be screened to identify one adult aged 26 to 35. These models gave an early indication of the high cost of screening for the out-of-school 17-year-old population.

Separate cost models were developed for individual- and group-administered packages. Salary costs for administrators were included in the cluster cost component for group-administered packages so that the cost per person for group-administered sessions was under $2.00, with $1.50 associated with scoring. The person-level variable cost for individually administered packages was modeled at just under $6.00 for both in-school and out-of-school testing environments, though these were optimistic estimates at 1960s price levels that covered only the parts of the cost that were believed to vary with changes in sample sizes. The final cost models had parameters associated both with frame sizes and sample sizes at three stages of sampling.

The variance models also had components for frame and sample sizes at each stage and fully incorporated finite population correction factors. The models allowed assumptions about the intracluster correlation at the second stage and then used an exponential modeling approach outlined by Cochran (1963, p. 244) based on work by Jessen (1942), Hendricks (1944), and Mahalanobis (1944). Assumptions of intracluster correlations of 0.025, 0.05, and 0.10 were used. The exponential models and assumptions about the population size at each stage allowed development of model variance components at all three stages of sampling.

Intracluster correlation is a measure associated with cluster sampling and measures how clustered samples would compare to simple random samples drawn from a complete population frame (if one existed). Efficient designs generally apply clustered sampling to control costs but limit the cluster size in order to control the effect of clustering on the precision of estimates. Generally, persons selected in clusters (schools or households) are more similar to each other or more homogeneous than are persons drawn in a simple random sample. A positive intracluster correlation coefficient indicates this homogeneity. A coefficient of 1.00 would indicate that all members of every cluster are identical

Some possible scenarios were outlined in the working paper. At $20,000 per age-sex group, optimum designs for nine- and 13-year-olds led to age-sex group sample sizes of about 2,500 for the group administration in school, about 725 for individual administrations in school, and about 500 for individual administrations using a household frame.

Shortly after this, draft proposals were requested from RTI and other subcontractors for all or parts of the assessment task. RTI submitted draft proposals covering four activities: 1) design, selection, and specification of a national sample; 2) design of the testing procedure; 3) administration of the tests; and 4) tabulation of the results. RTI submitted proposals for both a household and mixed (school and household) frame.

RTI's draft proposals for the household frame (RTI 1968) proposed a sample of 100 primary sampling units and 1,600 second-stage sampling units consisting of smaller land areas. The survey plans were designed to yield 102,400 persons equally allocated among the four age groups (25,600 per age group). One notable adjustment to the requirements incorporated in the mixed-frame proposal was that screening for out-of-school 17-year-olds would be limited to the number of households required to obtain the sample of adults 26 to 35; this led to a planned yield of 25,600 persons 26 to 35, and 800 to 850 out-of-school 17-year-olds. Clustering effects on the variance of estimates were considered a more serious problem in the school portion of the sample, so in-school age-group samples were increased by 25% to 32,000 per age group. The in-school component assumed only group admin-istrations with session sizes of 25 students.

## Transition from Planning to Doing

Although many details remained to be developed, the planning process was successful in resolving the large issues about the nature of NAEP for several years to come. The mode of adminis-tration was established; and cooperation from school systems, while not guaranteed, had been demonstrated with some of the planning studies. The general schedule for the assessments was established, and exercises for the first year's assessment were under development. Target populations and reporting subgroups were defined. A general approach to packaging NAEP exercises into booklets for group or individual administration was in place. Decisions were reached about the scheduling of in-school assess-ments by age group across the school year. General sample-size guidelines were established. The stage was set for moving into a new phase.

Research Triangle Institute was awarded the contract for sam-pling and data collection. William C. Eckerman became the first project director, with James R. Chromy serving as assistant direc-tor for sampling and William K. Grogan, a senior survey special-ist, serving as assistant director for administration. Finkner and Horvitz continued to provide close oversight and guidance to the NAEP contract because it represented the largest survey effort yet undertaken by RTI. The staffing and supervision of field staff in the central and west region was subcontracted to Measurement Research Center (MRC) of Iowa City, with overall central coor-dination from RTI. MRC also was awarded the contract for printing and scoring the NAEP packages. MRC activities were led by Calvin Stephenson and John O'Neill, with corporate support provided by Burdette Hansen. The first year's data collection also included a group-participation package in citizenship, which was administered in 32 PSUs by AIR of Palo Alto, California. The overall coordination of funding and subcontracting, the development of objectives and final exercises, and the analysis of the data remained the responsibility of a growing NAEP staff, organized under the Education Commission of the States (ECS) in Denver, Colorado. Stanley Ahmann became the NAEP director following the transition from ECAPE to CAPE to NAEP and the staff's move to Denver.

Rather than starting in fall 1968 as had been planned, the first year's survey activities began with the assessment of 17-year-olds in spring 1969. Out-of-school 17-year-olds and young adults were assessed in summer 1969. During the following school year (1969-70), 13-year-olds were assessed in the fall and nine-year-olds were assessed in the winter. No assessment was conducted in spring 1970, so that the second year's in-school assessment could begin in the fall and conform to the normal school year for 1970-71.

Writing, science, and citizenship were assessed in the first year. With the exception of the special group-participation packages in citizenship, most packages contained a mix of exercises from all three subjects. The general objectives for the design were:

- To represent adequately certain subpopulations specified by NAEP, including the oversampling of some of these populations to obtain a more nearly balanced sample.
- To allow the administration of several packages of exercises, with each package constituting a single survey in the usual sample design sense.
- To obtain sufficiently precise estimates at the lowest possible cost.
- To allow the data to be analyzed to obtain subpopulation estimates on a post-definitional basis.

- To facilitate smooth field-operating procedures and to control the workload at any single PSU.
- To the extent possible within the above objectives, to provide for relatively simple estimation procedures (Chromy and Horvitz 1970).

The mixed-frame approach was adopted with close coordination of the school and household designs. Multistage stratified samples were used for both frames, with one set of PSUs selected to serve subsequent stages of sampling for both frames. A sample of about 2,000 responses was considered adequate for precise estimates at the national and regional levels. To allow for the greater clustering effect on the group-administered packages, a sample size of about 2,500 was planned for the in-school group-administered packages. To further control the clustering effect on variances, the group sessions were limited to 12 students.

Focusing on precision for national and regional estimates, the sample was equally allocated to the four regions. The final primary sampling design consisted of 208 PSUs allocated to four regions and four sizes of community (SOC), as shown in Table 1. The final PSU identification within a count unit (an identifiable land area with size data) was based on different units for each age group. For the in-school sample, PSUs were defined in terms of schools with nine-year-olds, schools with 13-year-olds, and schools with 17-year-olds. For the young adult and out-of-school 17-year-old samples, PSUs were defined in terms of households within area segments.

To keep the estimation process simple and to achieve the gains normally associated with maintaining equal probability sampling, sampling units were defined to be approximately equal in size and were associated with larger count units. The size (population) of the count units was known from the past U.S. Census. The count unit/ultimate sampling unit method requires that the count of sampling units in each count unit be specified in advance; sampling units are fully identified only when selected following a

Table 1. First-year primary sampling allocation of PSUs.

| Size of Community (SOC) Stratum | Region | | | | SOC Total |
|---|---|---|---|---|---|
| | Northeast | Southeast | Central | West | |
| Central cities of 180,000 or more | 15 | 8 | 12 | 15 | 50 |
| Surrounding metropolitan areas | 15 | 6 | 12 | 14 | 47 |
| Other metropolitan areas and counties with a city of 15,000 | 15 | 15 | 12 | 12 | 54 |
| All remaining areas | 7 | 23 | 16 | 11 | 57 |
| Regional totals | 52 | 52 | 52 | 52 | 208 |

rule for partitioning the count unit into sampling units (Monroe and Finkner 1959).

Additional stratification within the region-SOC strata was based on the count unit percent of families earning less than $3,000 and on geographic location within region. In most cases, the final primary sample strata were sized to receive an allocation of two PSUs; when the region-SOC stratum was allocated an odd number of PSUs, one final primary sample stratum was allocated only one PSU. PSUs were selected with equal probability and without replacement. Actual identification of the PSU was required only in count units that contained one or more selected PSUs, then a separate determination of the sample PSUs was made for each of the main three age groups surveyed in schools and for the household sample. The general rules for PSU formation were to form heterogeneous clusters with particular emphasis on representing some high and some low socioeconomic areas in each PSU.

Each PSU was required to be large enough to yield the required sample size for each package assigned to the particular age group. Table 2 shows the first-year package counts by age and type. Each PSU had to be large enough to allow for selection of a subsample of 12 students per group package and nine students per individual package; this required at least 114 students at age nine, 135 at age 13, and 150 at age 17. A target PSU size of 250 to 350 students in each age group was used in constructing the primary sampling frame and associated counts of PSUs with each primary count unit. This allowed for subsampling and non-response. It also allowed for selection of an additional sample for the special group participation package in 32 PSUs.

Table 2. First-year number of packages by age and type.

| Type | Age 9 | Age 13 | Age 17 | Adults |
|------|-------|--------|--------|--------|
| Individually administered | 2 | 3 | 2 | 10 |
| Group administered | 8 | 9 | 11 | 0 |
| Special group participation | 1 | 1 | 1 | 0 |

In the school frame, PSUs were identified as all or portions of two or more schools. A list of all public and private schools in the count unit was compiled from state government and private school directories. Preliminary estimates of the number of students by age group were developed based on average age-to-grade ratios applied to reported grade enrollment, allocation to grades based on reported total enrollment and grade range, or pupil-teacher ratios applied to reported teacher counts allocated to grade range. If a count unit contained only one PSU, all schools were in that PSU. Most count units contained more than one PSU. Based on the number of PSUs assigned to a count unit, school age enrollments were allocated to PSU membership to form the required number of PSUs. Large schools could contribute age enrollments to more than one PSU. By listing schools and partitioning their age enrollments systematically, we identified the ultimate PSU by the initial random PSU selection. The final definitions of a school-frame PSU for an age group consisted of a list of schools contributing to the PSU and a school factor that indicated the proportion of that school belonging to the PSU.

After initial visits to each PSU, better estimates of age enrollment and data to develop an SES index were obtained for the selected schools. These revised estimates of age-specific enrollments were then used to allocate group package sessions to the schools in the PSU. It often was possible to subsample the schools and to allocate the required sessions to a subset of those associated with the PSU.

As an intermediate step, the sample of schools in each PSU consisted of a list of schools and an assigned number of group sessions. The next step was to randomly assign the group sessions to the schools. The selected schools were ordered by an SES index, and group packages were assigned based on a random permutation of the package numbers. In a paired PSU also ordered by the SES index, the same random permutation was reversed, thus providing some distribution of each group package sample across varying levels of SES. Individual package sessions were assigned based on a predetermined association with group package sessions. For example, if age 13 had nine group packages and three individual packages, each of three individual packages was administered once at a school for each group package assigned to that school.

Given the package assignments at each school, the total student sample was specified. Schools, often assisted by field staff, developed complete lists of all age eligible students. The default procedure was to enter names and limited demographic information on cards. A random sample was selected for each group package session and its associated individual package sessions. Schools were asked to sort the 17-year-old students into the lowest third on SES and the remainder. When schools were willing to do this, the low-SES students were sampled at twice the rate of the high-SES students.

The PSUs for the household frame were identified in the same count units as those for the school frame. Each PSU represented about 16,000 persons. Secondary sampling units (SSUs) were defined in terms of clusters of 35 to 40 housing units, with an expected yield of 12½ eligible adult respondents; the count unit/ultimate sampling unit method also was applied at the second stage of sampling. Stratification of the second-stage frame was achieved by ordering the second-stage count units by percent of families earning less than $3,000.

The SSUs were first associated with the selected PSU as a systematic sample with the start number specified by the selected PSU order within the primary count unit. This PSU subset of SSUs was then eligible to be selected at the second stage. The poorest 25% were sampled at twice the rate of the remainder. This was achieved by forming five strata, with each of the first two containing one-eighth of the SSUs and the remaining three strata each containing one-fourth of the SSUs. Two SSUs were selected from each secondary stratum with equal probabilities and without replacement. All households in the SSU were included in the sample, but the SSU itself was defined as a systematic subsample of a larger count unit that had predetermined boundaries.

All eligible adults and out-of-school 17-year-olds identified during administration of a household-screening interview were included in the sample and asked to participate.

## Survey Protocol

Finkner (1969) described the procedures for in-school and out-of-school assessments as they had been developed through fall 1969. RTI and MRC employed a combined staff of 27 district supervisors, four regional supervisors, and two field coordinators. District supervisors all had academic training at least at the bachelor's level. For the in-school assessment, two exercise administrators were recruited at each PSU to conduct the assessment under the direction of a district supervisor. Exercise administrators were substitute teachers recommended by school officials, by state employment agencies, and by personal contacts.

Finkner outlined these steps for in-school data collection:

- Letters outlining the project and requesting support were mailed to each governor, each chief state school officer, and to the executive officers of the state branches of other education organizations where they were organized.
- After the school sample was identified, chief state school officers were notified of the counties selected for national assessment.

- Local school superintendents were notified of their selection and were provided background material and a list of selected schools. A date for the initial district supervisor's visit was suggested.
- District supervisors conducted highly structured telephone calls with each superintendent, confirming a meeting date. (This had been done once for the 17-year-old sample in the spring and once for combined meetings for the nine- and 13-year-old samples in the fall.)
- Principals received explanatory material and an invitation to attend an orientation meeting with the district supervisor. They also were asked to complete a principal's questionnaire with current enrollment information and proxy measures for SES classification.
- Field manuals for regional supervisors, district supervisors, and exercise administrators were prepared.
- A full-week session for supervisor training was held in Iowa City in mid-February 1969 for the 17-year-old assessment and at Ann Arbor in mid-August for the other two in-school age groups.
- Exercises were packaged, and booklets were printed by MRC.
- District supervisors spent about 2½ days in each PSU to meet with school officials and to recruit and train exercise administrators.
- A district supervisor and two exercise administrators selected the sample and conducted the assessment over a one-week period at each PSU for each age group.
- Completed packages were sent to MRC for scoring and tabulating.

No student names were ever removed from the schools. An arbitrary identification number identified completed packages and could be associated with the PSU and the school. Schools maintained student sample lists for a limited time following the assessment.

The field protocol for the out-of-school assessment included the following steps:

- Exercises were packaged and booklets printed by MRC.
- Field manuals were prepared for regional supervisors, district supervisors, and exercise administrators.
- By the end of May, district supervisors hired three exercise administrators per PSU, with one designated as a coordinator and liaison between the district supervisor and the other two.
- Supervisors attended a training session at RTI during the first week in June.
- Over the next two weeks, district supervisors held four training sessions with six exercise administrators at each session.
- Out-of-school assessment was conducted from June 23 to mid-August.
- During the assessment, district supervisors visited each PSU to check on progress and the quality of the work.

## Response Rates

It is somewhat difficult to reconstruct response rates for the first year, though Finkner (1969) reports on the response to the 17-year-old in-school assessment. Nonresponse was encountered at all stages of the sample design. One state with five PSUs decided early not to participate, and replacements were selected from other states in the region. Three other PSUs refused early in the process and were replaced with supplements resulting in a cooperating sample of 193 PSUs out of a target sample of 208 PSUs, or about 92.8% allowing for replacements. If we don't allow for replacements, 185 out of 208 initially selected PSUs participated for a response rate of 88.9% at the PSU level. Within the 193 participating PSUs, 673 schools were initially invited to participate and 20, or 3%, failed to respond. As a result of the package allocation scheme, subsampling left 513 schools that indicated they would participate, eliminating 140 schools. Assessment was conducted in all 513 of these schools. The overall school response rate was computed on an unweighted basis as 86% to 90%, depending on how initial PSU nonrespondents are treated.

If some selected schools refused to participate, the student sample usually was re-allocated to the remaining participating schools. Group sessions were designed for 12 students, but four standby selections were asked to come to each session; if some of the original 12 selected students did not participate, students in the standby sample were asked to participate. For individual sessions, one standby student was selected for each scheduled session and asked to participate if the originally selected student did not keep the appointment.

Table 3 shows the student and adult achieved-sample sizes by package type. The substitution policy makes it impossible to compute a precise response rate without additional information. Assuming 12 students per group package and 193 PSUs at age 17, the target sample for in-school only would have been 2,316 students.

Table 3. First-year achieved-sample sizes by age and package type.

| Package Type | Age 9 | Age 13 | Age 17* | Adults |
|---|---|---|---|---|
| Group administrations | 19,478 | 21,725 | 23,961 | |
| Per package | 2,435 | 2,414 | 2,178 | |
| Individual administrations | 3,715 | 5,582 | 3,568 | 8,634 |
| Per package | 1,858 | 1,861 | 1,784 | 863 |
| Special group package | 1,438 | 1,412 | 1,315 | |
| Total sample | 24,631 | 28,719 | 28,884 | 8,634 |

*Includes both in-school and out-of-school respondents.

At age 9 and age 13, samples were drawn in 208 PSUs, yielding a target sample size of 2,496 students per group package and 1,872 per individual package. The actual group package responding samples were 97.6% of target at age 9 and 96.7% of target at age 13. For individually administered packages, the responding samples were 99.2% of target for age 9 and 99.4% of target for age 13. Because substitutions at both the school and the student levels were not identified in the information available, overall response rates could not be computed.

Because most exercises were administered using a paced-tape presentation, exercise-level nonresponse was minimal. However, state and local authorities requested that some exercises not be given in their schools. As a result, one exercise at age 9, four exercises at age 13, and three exercises at age 17 had reduced sample sizes (Abelson et al. 1970, p. F-1).

Achtermann (1974) provided an excellent summary of out-of-school procedures and response rates. The district supervisors who conducted the in-school assessment through May also were in charge of the out-of-school assessment conducted in the 208 PSUs. Each adult identified in the screening process was asked to complete only one adult package, and no incentives were paid. Adult packages contained a mixture of interviewer-administered and self-administered exercises. Screening was performed to identify eligible adults born between July 1933 and June 1943. Out-of-school 17-year olds were asked to participate in a set of four or five packages and were paid $10 for participation. To increase the yield, the age eligibility criterion was expanded to include two groups:

- Persons born between October 1950 and September 1951 who were not enrolled in school in March 1968.
- Persons born between October of 1951 and September 1952 who were not enrolled in school in March 1969.

Paced taping was used for the comparable in-school group packages. No group participation package was administered to the out-of-school 17-year-olds.

Achtermann also provided data on screening and interviewing rates for the first four years of out-of-school assessment. Data for years 01 and 02 are summarized in Table 4.

The first-year out-of-school survey was clearly not a success. The overall response rates, computed as the product of the screening response rate and the package administration rate, were 44.4% for adults and 37.3% for out-of-school 17-year-olds. An analysis of the nonresponse at the screening level revealed that noncontacts were a more severe problem than refusals; screening nonresponse was 9.2% refusals and 13.4% not contacted or not at home. For package participation, refusals were a more serious problem, with 20.1% of selected eligibles refusing and 15.9% not at home or not contacted.

Table 4. Out-of-school Eligibility and Response Rates (Years 01-02).

| Item | Year 01 | Year 02 |
|---|---|---|
| Area segments | 2,080 | 520 |
| Sample housing units listed | 64,506 | 9,150 |
| Occupied housing units (number) | 59,265 | 8,203 |
| Occupied housing units (as a percent of listed) | 91.9 | 89.6 |
| Completed screening interviews (number) | 45,849 | 8,131 |
| Completed screening interviews (as a percent of occupied) | 77.4 | 99.1 |
| Age-eligible adults | 14,676 | 2,660 |
| Language barrier | 203 | 44 |
| Handicapped | 98 | 39 |
| NAEP-eligible adults (number) | 14,375 | 2,577 |
| NAEP-eligible adults (as a percent of age-eligible adults) | 97.9 | 96.9 |
| Adult respondents (number) | 8,257 | 1,935 |
| Adult respondents (as a percent of NAEP-eligible adults | 57.4 | 75.1 |
| Adult packages completed | 8,257 | 7,473 |
| Overall adult response rate (screening rate times interviewing rate | 44.4 | 74.4 |
| Age-eligible OOS 17-year-olds | 504 | 91 |
| Language barrier | 5 | 0 |
| Handicapped | 16 | 4 |
| NAEP-eligible OOS 17-year-olds | 483 | 87 |
| Package respondents (number) | 233 | 84 |
| Package respondents (as a percent of NAEP-eligible | 48.2 | 96.6 |
| Age 17 packages completed | About 1,000 | 329 |
| Overall age 17 response rate | 37.3 | 95.7 |

## Analysis Issues

Design-based weights were calculated and used to compute national and subgroup estimates for each exercise, based on each package sample. Most estimates could be constructed as combined ratio estimates reflecting the proportion of a population subgroup that correctly answered a specific NAEP exercise. The design-based Horvitz-Thompson estimator (Horvitz and Thompson 1952) was used to estimate the numerator and denominator of the ratio estimator.

One of the initial problems encountered in the weighted analysis was the treatment of large weights. Chromy (1970) reports on an examination of large weights, particularly in the household sample used for adults and out-of-school 17-year-olds. Use of 1960 U.S. Census data to obtain size measures for a 1969 survey naturally led to large weights for samples selected from small areas that had experienced major growth in population over the decade. While a check of sampling and weight calculation procedures showed that the weights were technically correct for producing unbiased estimates, the unequal weighting effect would produce unacceptably high variances. Searls (1962) considered a similar problem with outliers in small samples. He proposed a censoring method that arbitrarily reduced extreme values to some prespecified level. This method introduced some bias into the estimate, but it was shown to be effective in controlling the mean squared error, which incorporates both bias and variance. The general treatment of outliers by Searls was adapted to the treatment of weight outliers in the NAEP samples.

The estimation of sampling error for the nonlinear ratio estimators, and potentially for other more complex analytic measures, also was addressed with first-year data. Shah (1970) examined variance estimation procedures for complex estimators using either jackknife or replicated half-sample procedures for samples with two observations (PSUs) per stratum. With guidance from the Technical Advisory Committee and, in particular, from John Tukey, jackknife variance estimation procedures were implemented for NAEP analysis. Folsom (1974, Chapter 2) presents a detailed review of the first-year variance estimation procedures for ratios and for balanced effects (adjusted for comparable mix on other specified factors).

Chromy, Moore, and Clemmer (1972) examined the design effects from the first-year sample based on 149 selected exercises. Unequal weighting effects ranged from 1.3 to 1.6. Overall design effect estimates, which reflect stratification, clustering, and unequal weighting, ranged from less than one to more than five, with a median value for national estimates of 2.38.

## Design Adjustments

The disappointing overall response rates obtained in the out-of-school survey in the first year called for a reevaluation of the overall household survey design used to sample young adults and out-of-school 17-year-olds. The delayed start of the first-year survey and a one-time schedule adjustment to put the second year back on a school year basis allowed some time for a field test of alternate procedures, which incorporated an imbedded experiment to evaluate alternative monetary incentives. The sample for the field test was selected from the nonrespondents to the first-year sample in a subsample of area segments showing particularly poor initial response rates. Rather than employing the same types of staff used for the in-school assessment, experienced household interviewers were recruited and trained and supervised by senior field supervisory personnel. Other procedures included newspaper releases with local newspapers to be used by interviewers, advance contacts with police departments and Better Business Bureaus, timing of screening calls at different times of the day, use of escorts in tough inner-city neighborhoods, referral of all refusals to team leaders for possible follow-up, contacts with neighbors to determine better times to visit in order to contact persons not at home, minimum numbers of callbacks for both screening and interviewing, neighbor questionnaires after four callbacks, and telephone and personal follow-up of refusals by team leaders or by a second interviewer. Persons previously participating were not recontacted; it was assumed that they would participate at any incentive level since they had previously participated without the use of incentives.

Each of the four monetary incentives listed below was assigned and tested in a randomly selected quarter of the sample segments included in the experiment:

- No incentive
- $5 for one package
- $10 for one package
- A variable incentive for up to four packages.

The variable incentive plan gave the respondent an option to complete one package for no reimbursement, two packages for $10, three packages for $15, and four packages for $20. By randomly ordering the package subset offered to each respondent, unbiased estimates could be obtained for exercises from each package, regardless of the number of packages completed by individual respondents.

Chromy and Horvitz (1978) showed that even in the no-incentive segments, response rates were brought up to 91.0% for screening and 70.5% for package participation. The monetary incentive options increased package response rates to 80.4%, 85.3%, and 83.3%, respectively for the $5, $10, and variable incentive treatments. An analysis of costs associated with each option demonstrated that the variable incentive option not only increased response rates, but also decreased average costs per completed package, primarily because the respondents under the variable incentive option completed an average of 3.67 packages.

The variable incentive procedure was adopted for the second-year household survey. In addition, a separate, specially qualified, interviewing and supervisory staff was used; and a smaller sample size was implemented in the second year to phase in the improved procedures on a manageable basis.

The other major problem identified in the first year was the high cost of identifying and collecting data from out-of-school 17-year-olds. Plans were developed to test alternative sampling frames during the second year.

## Changes for the Second Year

Major changes in the basic sample and survey design were implemented in the second year of assessments, which included reading and literature. George Duntemann assumed the role of RTI project director. Separate supervisory and field staffs were assigned to the in-school and out-of-school surveys. The mixed school and household frame approach continued, but the separation between the two was increased.

The preponderance of group administration packages and the fact that each package was administered in only one school per PSU in the first year seemed to be a poor way of controlling the distribution of the sample by SES. It appeared that good control on SES could be achieved by doubling the sample in each PSU so that each package was administered twice: once at the high end of SES ranked schools and once at the low end. This option also would reduce overall cost by saving on some of the setup costs associated with adding new PSUs. This meant that in the typical PSU, the number of packages assigned would require a district supervisor and his local team of exercise administrators to conduct the assessment over a two-week period. This type of PSU was termed a "two-week" PSU, as opposed to the few "one-week" PSUs that were allocated to achieve all-state sample representation while trying to maintain a more nearly proportional allocation to states and to other stratification dimensions.

A special design requirement was imposed in the second year requiring each state to be included in the sample, even though no state estimates would be required. In order to maintain control over the sample both by state and by major strata designed to represent region, community type, and SES, a controlled selection scheme was employed to select the primary sample. A newly developed approach to the controlled selection method (Jessen 1970) was adapted to the primary sample selection process. Jessen's method allows one to construct a limited set of feasible samples, which control the distribution of the sample in two dimensions while preserving the cell selection probabilities for all cells in the two-dimensional array created by the joint sample allocation requirements. This allowed the selection of a probability proportional to size (PPS) sample of PSUs, with each state represented at least once while maintaining the distribution of the sample by region, community type, and SES.

With the adoption of Jessen's method for controlled PPS selection, some of the simplicity of the ultimate cluster method employed in the first year was lost, but targeted overall sampling rates and the oversampling of low SES could be achieved in an equivalent manner. Some additional unequal weighting effects were induced by the state allocation requirement. In addition, the controlled selection approach did not ensure that all pairs of PSUs had a positive pairwise probability of selection; as a result, unbiased variance estimation was not possible.

A *Sampling Error Monograph* (Folsom 1974, Chapters 3 and 4) dealt with the specific issue of evaluating approximate variance estimators for the controlled selection design. He employed Monte Carlo simulation methods to evaluate several alternatives. Although his simulation results favored a Taylor-series linearization approach, he concluded that the gain over the jackknife procedure already programmed for NAEP analysis purposes did not justify the expense of reprogramming the analysis software. This early work by Folsom became a basis for developing the SUDAAN software products for the analysis of survey and clustered data.

The PSU selection scheme for the in-school sample allocated 216 weeks of assessment to 116 PSUs, as shown in Table 5. Note that the allocation was 54 weeks of assessment per region, or 216 weeks of assessment nationally. This also can be expressed as 216 group administrations of each group package nationally.

Table 5. Allocation of PSUs by region and workload for the second year.

| Region | 2-week PSUs | 1-week PSUs |
|--------|-------------|-------------|
| Northeast | 24 | 6 |
| Southeast | 27 | 0 |
| Central | 26 | 2 |
| West | 23 | 8 |
| Total | 100 | 16 |

Size of community (SOC) strata were defined in terms of whole counties as:

- SOC 1: All counties containing a central city with a population of 180,000 or more.

- SOC 2: All counties in the same standard metropolitan statistical area (SMSA) as an SOC 1 county.
- All other SMSA counties or non-SMSA counties with at least one city of 25,000 or more.
- The remainder.

The oversampling of low SES was applied at the PSU level or at the school level within PSUs, depending on the SOC stratum. Up to eight primary strata were defined in each region as:

- SOC 1, self-representing
- SOC 1, other
- SOC 2, self-representing
- SOC 2, other
- SOC 3, low SES
- SOC 3, high SES
- SOC 4, low SES
- SOC 4, high SES.

Some large PSUs in SOC strata 1 and 2 were sampled with probability 1.0 and were called self-representing PSUs. Other PSUs were sampled with probabilities less than 1.0.

In SOC strata 1 and 2, oversampling was achieved by oversampling low-SES schools within each PSU. SOC 1 and 2 PSUs were generally two-week PSUs. Schools within all two-week PSUs were first ordered by SES using local area data. In SOC 1 and 2 PSUs, approximately one-third of the schools with the lowest SES formed one stratum, and the remaining two-thirds of the schools formed the other stratum. By allocating equal school samples to both strata, low-SES schools were sampled at twice the rate of high-SES schools.

In SOC strata 3 and 4, oversampling of low SES was achieved by allocation to the low and high SES strata at the primary sampling stage; low-SES PSUs were sampled at twice the rate of high-SES PSUs. Within SOC 3 and 4 PSUs, two school strata of equal size were used, and half the sample was selected from each. The oversampling of low-SES students within schools was not attempted in the second year of assessments.

Schools participating in the first-year assessment were arbitrarily excluded from the second-year sample whenever possible. In later years, improved procedures were developed to coordinate multiyear samples so that schools would not be asked to participate in two successive years. A procedure for supplementing the sample with a sample of new schools (not on the original school sampling frame) was followed in the second year.

The in-school sample involved nine group and three individual packages at age 9, thirteen group and two individual packages at age 13, and ten group and two individual packages at age 17. Package counts were allocated to schools (to achieve the SES oversampling when applicable) and group packages were assigned based on a random permutation. The same permutation was repeated twice in two-week PSUs so that each package was administered once in a low-SES and once in a high-SES school. Individual packages were assigned by pre-association with group package numbers. No group participation packages were used in the second year.

One package was randomly selected to serve as a supplemental sample to be allocated to schools with very small enrollments in the target age group. Because these schools sometimes had no students in the target age but were included only to ensure that almost all students in the target age had a chance to be selected, the use of a supplemental sample package, to be administered if needed, usually avoided the need for split sessions or the possible loss of sample size by assigning a regular session to these schools.

Student selection procedures were similar to those used in the first year, except that no attempt was made to identify and oversample low-SES students.

All states cooperated in the second year. Two 2-week PSUs refused early; and after efforts to secure cooperation were exhausted, replacement PSUs were selected. Lack of school cooperation in one selected PSU reduced the sample by about one-half; a one-week replacement PSU was selected to supplement the sample. In terms of weeks of assessment, the PSU response rate (before sample replacement) could be computed as 97.7%. School cooperation rates (including schools that had no eligibles or were determined to be closed) were 93.0%, 93.1%, and 91.7% at ages 9, 13, and 17, respectively. The number of schools in which some assessment was conducted was 1,007, 1,029, and 631 at ages 9, 13, and 17, respectively.

Exact student response rates from among those initially selected could not be determined because of inadequate data, but more information was preserved about the use of alternatives. The percent of group sessions completed was very high at all age groups; and the group session sample sizes were 96.0%, 95.9%, and 90.1% of planned sizes at ages 9, 13, and 17, respectively. For individual packages, percent of planned administrations was 99.4%, 99.7%, and 98.9%, respectively. The more liberal alternative policy for individual packages (one alternative per one-person session) accounted for the difference. Group sessions were rescheduled if fewer than eight students, including original and alternative selections, were available. The percentage of completed assessments by original selections was 91.1%, 89.6%, and 82.2% for ages 9, 13, and 17 for group packages, and 90.0%, 88.0%, and 76.1% for individual packages.

Overall response rates — based on the original sample of PSUs, schools, and students and assuming that all sessions could have been scheduled — can be approximated roughly as the product of PSU cooperation rates, school cooperation rates, session completion rates, and proportions of assessments done by original selections. These approximations would be 79.5%, 81.3%, and 66.2% for group packages by age group and 81.3%, 79.8%, and 67.4% for individual packages by age group. These approximations could be high or low depending on whether the failure to achieve planned sample sizes was due to nonresponse or due to inadequate numbers of eligible students in the selected schools. If low-SES schools also have lower response rates, then weighting of response rates to reflect the total population would tend to increase these overall measures because low-SES schools were oversampled.

The data collection from the household frame was scheduled for March through July 1971. Screening was conducted for both young adults and out-of-school 17-year-olds. Both groups were given the opportunity to participate in up to four packages using the variable incentive approach developed in the field test.

As noted above, the household sample was scaled down in the second year, and it was viewed as an opportunity to implement improved procedures on a more limited basis than had been attempted in the first year of assessments. Only six packages were used for the adult sample, with a planned sample size of 1,040 responses per package. The number of housing units included in the sample was based on the need to achieve the prescribed young-adult sample size. The out-of-school 17-year-olds were assigned the same 12 packages used in the school frame. The expected yield of out-of-school 17-year-olds under this alternative plan was much too low (about 15 responses per package) without supplements from other sampling frames.

The all-state participation requirement was not imposed on the out-of-school sample, so the sample was limited to 52 PSUs selected to be nationally representative. A larger initial sample of 208 PSUs was selected so that a coordinated primary sample design could be used over several years. The 52 PSUs were a subset of the larger sample of 208 PSUs held for possible use in subsequent assessments.

The PSU selection for the household sample was similar to that used for the school sample. Controlled selection was used to select the sample of 208 PSUs; but in the state dimension, grouping states was allowed in order to avoid disproportionate allocation. Region and SOC-SES strata were the same as for the school frame. Preliminary county population estimates from the 1970 U.S. Census were used as size measures at the PSU level.

Ten area segments were selected per PSU, with about 18 housing unit addresses listed per segment. The overall expected yield was 6,306 completed adult packages. The actual response was 7,473 completed adult packages. Household eligibility (92.2%), screening response rates (99.1%), and packages completed per respondent (3.86) were all higher than projected. The proportion of persons agreeing to participate in at least one package (75.1%) was somewhat lower than projected. The overall response of 74.4% was a resounding success when compared to the first-year experience and validated the findings of the incentive response experiments conducted earlier.

The household sampling frame produced 325 package responses. This was more than initially projected, but still only about 27 responses per package. A special pilot study was undertaken in the second year of assessments to develop other frames for selecting out-of-school 17-year-olds. The main focus was on following dropouts identified through the school frame, but approaches using Neighborhood Youth Corps and Job Corps programs also were tested. Moore and Jones (1973) report on the results of the pilot study.

The general approach was to use several frames (including the household frame) to select samples and then to apply multiple frame estimation theory to produce a combined estimate whose coverage exceeded that of any of the individual frames. The most successful approach was the one using school dropout lists and lists of early graduates from schools with any of grades 9, 10, 11, or 12. A subsample of 58 of the 116 school-frame PSUs was selected to test the dropout frame procedures. In these 58 PSUs, 173 schools were asked to provide dropout lists from the current year and two prior years; 147 schools, or 85%, provided lists. Dropout dates and birth dates also were obtained whenever possible, so that age eligibility and out-of-school status could be verified. A sample of 957 potential eligibles was selected based on the information provided with the lists. Field interviewers were assigned to locate the sampled dropouts, ascertain their eligibility, and administer assessment packages to those located and determined to be eligible. Eligibility status was determined for 701, or 73.2%, of those selected through contacts with the selected person or a family member. Of the 701 person or family contacts, 476 identified selected persons who were age-eligible and out of school at the target date; and 345, or 72.4%, agreed to complete assessment packages. The variable incentive procedure was used to encourage participation in more than one package; 1,317 package responses, or 3.82 per respondent, were obtained.

As a result of this pilot study, the multiple-frame approach and the area household sample was adopted for future years. Moore and Jones (1973) reported on some expansion of the school list procedures in third year to include age-eligible dropouts from schools with grades 7 or 8, but not higher grades.

## Design Adjustments in the Early Years

Searls (1974) summarized the design adjustments incorporated through the fourth year of the assessments. PSU size measures were based on 1970 census data. Federal tax return data on the percent of returns with adjusted gross income of less than $3,000 by zip code area were used to help determine SES for schools. The in-school sampling in the third year closely resembled the second-year approach. Size of community strata were revised for the fourth year to be more nearly equal in size. Equal probability school selection procedures were used for low age-enrollment schools because all or most of the eligible students usually were selected in such schools. Some of the intermediate subsampling procedures for schools were eliminated. Schools selected in either of two prior years of assessment were not re-assessed whenever this was feasible. A new PSU sample for the fourth year achieved the all-state representation requirement with an approach that guaranteed that all pairs of PSUs had positive inclusion probabilities; this change resolved the problem with biased variance estimation in the second-year design.

In the third year of assessments, the household frame sample was expanded to 104 of the selected 208 PSUs, and the target sample size was increased to 2,000 adult respondents per package. Data at the census block group and census enumeration district level, rather than minor civil division and census tract levels, were used to stratify and select household samples within PSUs.

The household survey was discontinued after the fifth year of assessments (1973-74). The 17-year-old out-of-school survey was discontinued after the seventh year (1975-76). The schedule was revised to be an every-other-year assessment beginning with the 12th year (1981-82). Over these 12 surveys, three cycles were completed for several subjects.

RTI continued as the contractor for sampling and administration as long as NAEP remained a project of ECS. RTI project directors included Paul Homeyer (1972-73), Al Finkner (1974), Dan Horvitz (1974-77), and Jim Chromy (1977-83). Eventually, RTI assumed sole responsibility for the administration of the assessment in all regions. MRC continued to be the printing and scoring contractor. Close coordination among NAEP staff at ECS, print and scoring staff at MRC, and sampling and administration staff at RTI continued throughout the period, with quarterly management meetings being held at Research Triangle Park, Iowa City, Denver, and occasionally at other locations.

Al Finkner, Bill Grogan, and Jim Chromy attended a final management meeting and the last ECS/NAEP Assessment Policy Committee meeting in Denver in May 1983. The meetings were followed by a "wake/party" marking the closing down of the ECS/NAEP staff operations in Denver. Many of the NAEP staff had found other employment, but most were still looking for positions in the Denver area.

# CHAPTER 17

# Sampling and Field Operations at Westat, 1983 to 2001

*Keith Rust*

Westat was a subcontractor to Educational Testing Service when ETS was awarded the NAEP grant in 1983. Westat was responsible for sample design and selection, data collection and field operations, survey weighting, and, in collaboration with ETS, the estimation of sampling error. Since that time, Westat has continued to be responsible for these activities as NAEP has passed through phases of being a grant, to a contract, to a cooperative agreement. At times Westat has been under subcontract to ETS, and at other times Westat has contracted directly with the National Center for Education Statistics (NCES).

NAEP has continued to evolve throughout the 18 years in which Westat has been actively involved in conducting the program. At the technical and operational level, one can distinguish four phases: 1) the initial transition, 2) national assessment with scaling and balanced incomplete block (BIB) spiraling of assessment booklets, 3) state assessment, and 4) the era of accommodations for special needs students. NAEP appears to be entering a new phase, in which it will be used for state and school accountability, following the recent passage of the federal No Child Left Behind legislation. The exact implications of this for NAEP are not clear at present.

The rest of this chapter will cover each of the four phases in turn, and under each I will discuss both the sampling, weighting, and variance-estimation features, as well as the field-operations procedures for data collection. This is not a description of everything NAEP has ever done in these areas; rather, it is a history of changes and innovations and the reasons that they came about.

The details of the various issues and procedures described in what follows are published in NAEP technical reports, which have been published by NCES and ETS for every assessment from 1984 to 2000.

## The Transition: 1983 to 1985

ETS proposed several innovative features when it was awarded the NAEP grant. These innovations were primarily in the areas of test design and reporting results, not sampling and weighting. Indeed, because of the timing of the grant award, the previous grantee, the Education Commission of the States (ECS), and its sampling subcontractor, Research Triangle Institute (RTI), selected the school sample and designed the assessment instrument for the 1984 assessment. The 1984 assessment was carried out by ETS and Westat by following the plan established by ECS and RTI.

Morris Hansen headed Westat's sampling and weighting activities for NAEP from the outset, with Renee Slobasky in charge of field operations. Morris worked very closely with Ben Tepping, who worked on the technical challenges in sampling, weighting, and variance estimation; and for the rest of the decade they headed NAEP's efforts in these areas. But their innovations did not begin to come into effect until the 1986 assessment.

*The Jackknife:* One aspect of the existing NAEP procedures that immediately attracted the attention of Hansen and Tepping was the use of the jackknife procedure for estimating sampling errors. The use of the jackknife in NAEP can be traced to the influence of John Tukey at the beginning of the program. Tukey had been the first to suggest the jackknife technique as a multipurpose tool for variance estimation in sample surveys (Tukey 1958) and over the succeeding 25 years several authors had elaborated on both its method and its theoretical properties.

At the same time that the jackknife was becoming an accepted and established procedure for variance estimation in complex surveys, another, operationally similar, technique known as balanced half-sampling or balanced repeated replication (BRR) was developed. The initial origins of this technique are less clear, but one possibility is that an unbalanced version of this procedure was used in a somewhat ad-hoc fashion at the Institute for Social Research (ISR) at the University of Michigan from about the early 1960s. Today such a procedure would be called a bootstrap, but that term had not been coined then. McCarthy (1966) showed how the efficiency of this procedure could be greatly enhanced through a procedure for selecting balanced half-samples.

In 1974 Kish and Frankel of the ISR published a paper that presented extensive simulation comparisons of the performance of BRR, the jackknife, and Taylor-series linearization for estimating variances from multistage samples. Taylor-series linearization was the most widely known technique at that time for estimating sampling variances from sample surveys, and it remains in widespread use. The main finding in the paper was the similarity of the results from the three methods, though Kish and Frankel argued that there was evidence that BRR performed a little better with respect to the behavior of large-sample-theory-based confidence intervals constructed from the variance estimates.

For the kind of projects that Westat carried out, the replication techniques of BRR and the jackknife had a strong appeal. Once the sampling statistician has performed the initial set-up, the procedure for estimating sampling variances is very straightforward. In particular, it can be carried out by researchers and data analysts who have little grounding (and often little interest) in the theory and practice of survey sampling. In the early days this convenience came at the considerable price of requiring substantially greater computer resources, but over time this drawback has essentially disappeared.

Perhaps influenced by the work of Leslie Kish and Martin Frankel, Hansen and Tepping typically used BRR as the method for estimating sampling variances for the surveys that they conducted. Confronted with the jackknife as the established procedure for NAEP, Tepping and Hansen took on the challenge of finding theoretical or empirical advantages of one of these methods when applied to NAEP. In carrying out this work, Tepping generated a simulated NAEP population and sample design, drawing repeated samples from it.

Hansen and Tepping concluded that the jackknife was just fine for NAEP and, in fact, that the resulting variance estimates were slightly more stable than the variance estimates from BRR. They became converts to the jackknife and advocated its use in other Westat projects. As a result, the jackknife procedure has been used in NAEP ever since.

The jackknife procedure does have one theoretical "Achilles heel," though it seems likely that this is not a big problem for NAEP. Brillinger (1977) showed that, when applied to simple random samples, the standard jackknife (these days referred to as the delete-1 jackknife) was statistically inconsistent when used to estimate variances for sample quantiles, such as the median. The variances are not biased *per se*, but they remain quite unstable for large sample sizes and thus can be very misleading if used to form confidence intervals and to conduct hypothesis tests.

Medians and other quantiles are estimated using NAEP data, so this posed a dilemma. However, the jackknife variances derived for medians for NAEP data appeared to be well behaved and consistently bore the expected relationships to the variances of corresponding mean estimates. Hansen and Tepping investigated this problem in the late 1980s and concluded that it was likely that the use of the jackknife with a stratified multistage sample design, as opposed to a simple random sample, meant that the theoretical limitation of the jackknife was largely mitigated. However, this proved difficult to demonstrate conclusively.

J.N.K. (Jon) Rao of Carleton University previously published much research on the asymptotic properties of variance estimators in complex surveys. Colleagues of Rao's had demonstrated that BRR did not suffer from the same theoretical drawback as did the jackknife (Shao and Wu 1992). Therefore Hansen challenged Rao to come up with evidence about the consistency and other asymptotic behavior of the jackknife when used with stratified multistage designs for estimating the variances of quantiles. With these designs and estimators, however, the term "as the sample size increases" is not easy to define unambiguously; and to date no definitive results on the asymptotic behavior of the delete-1 jackknife in these circumstances have been published.

## A New Design for a New Era: 1985 to 1989

The ETS design for NAEP in 1986 ushered in the era of BIB-spiraling, scale scores, "plausible values," and grade-based populations. These changes had some implications for sample design, weighting, variance estimation, and field operations, though in practice the effects on these activities were not as extensive as one might at first imagine. There were innovations in these areas, but many were orthogonal to innovations in test design and reporting.

*Sample Design:* The 1986 NAEP assessment involved several subjects, but the test design was a BIB-spiral design that included all subjects in the BIB. This meant that a single sample of students could be selected for each population, and the BIB-spiraling took care of the assignment of assessment material to individual students. In addition to being operationally more convenient, this approach reduced the clustering of the samples for individual subjects, especially in small schools. In turn, this reduced the design effect, increasing the efficiency of the sample design. The "NAEP Reading Anomaly" of 1986 (Beaton and Zwick 1990) and, more significantly, diverging test specifications for the different subjects led to the demise of BIB-spiraling across subjects. In recent NAEP assessments this has been reduced to spiraling together the history and geography assessments and the writing and civics assessments, but even in these cases an individual student works in only one subject. Spiraling across subjects within test booklets lives on in international assessments, such as the Third International Mathematics and Science Study and the Programme for International Student Assessment (Martin and Kelly 1997).

The major sample-design change that Hansen and Tepping and their colleagues at Westat instituted at this time was to change the definitions of the geographic primary sampling units (PSUs) that NAEP used. In the past, the first-stage sampling units had been individual counties. Working with Slobasky and her colleagues in the field operations area at Westat, Hansen reasoned that counties were too small to serve as efficient first-stage sampling units. In addition, sample-size requirements, especially at the high-school level, meant that a design with counties as PSUs would have required many more counties than traditionally had been selected.

The primary stratification variables were NAEP region (the definitions of NAEP's four regions have been maintained since the beginning of NAEP), and metropolitan/nonmetropolitan status. Metropolitan areas were those counties that were included within a Metropolitan Statistical Area (MSA), as defined by the Office of Management and Budget. Within metropolitan areas, rather than using individual counties as PSUs, Westat used individual MSAs. This meant that, within each sampled MSA, the school sample could represent the different types of communities within the MSA, thus reducing the design effect. At the same time, the travel requirements for the field staff conducting the assessments remained manageable and cost effective. The 20 largest MSAs in the country (based on 1980 census data) were selected with certainty under this design and thus were included in the national NAEP sample each year from 1986 to 1992. From 1994 to 2000, the 22 largest MSAs (based on 1990 census data) were selected with certainty.

In the non-MSA strata, individual counties continued to constitute the PSUs, provided that they were large enough. But most of these counties were too small to give an efficient design. So PSUs were formed by grouping contiguous counties within a region so that each had a minimum 1980 population size of 60,000.

Some PSUs in the western and central regions of the United States covered a very large area with this definition; so in the redesign for 1994 to 2000, this minimum size for a PSU was reduced to 45,000 in these two regions.

The second sampling innovation introduced was designed to effect some moderate oversampling of black and Hispanic students so that NAEP results for these two minority groups would be reported with sufficient reliability. Because only a moderate amount of oversampling was required, Hansen and Tepping developed the plan to oversample, by a factor of two, schools that had more than a specified minimum percentage of minority students. Thus there was no need to involve field operations staff, who selected the student samples within each school, as these staff were not required to select oversamples of any groups of students within a school.

Hansen and Tepping set 10% minority enrollment as the cut-off. That is, a school with more than 10% black and Hispanic students was selected with twice the probability of a school of the same size having less than 10% of students in these two groups. I am not sure how this figure was arrived at; but when I began to work on NAEP in 1987, with Morris' blessing I undertook a systematic analysis to determine what the "correct" figure should be. Most people have the initial reaction that surely 10% is too low because these two groups constitute more than 20% of the student population; thus one would not consider a school with 10% black and Hispanic students as "high minority." I made the breathtaking breakthrough that the correct number was 10% for nine- and 13-year-olds and 15% for 17-year-olds, though for age 17 the difference between using 15% and 10% as the cutoff was trivial. These cutoffs make good choices because the great majority of minority students are in such schools, so that for black and Hispanic students the sample design is close to self-weighting. This makes the design an efficient one for these subgroups without being unduly inefficient for the remainder of the population.

*Field Operations:* During this period the Westat national field operations force was consolidated. Procedures were developed to enable field staff to select samples and administer the assessments. The staff developed procedures for selecting the combined grade and age samples and for carrying out special studies in addition to the more standard NAEP assessments. Procedures were refined for assisting schools in the process of identifying students who were eligible for exclusion from the assessment. Procedures were developed for selecting appropriate samples of teachers and obtaining the information to link the data that they provided to that of their students in the sample.

*Sample Weighting:* Two innovations in weighting were introduced by Hansen and Tepping with the 1986 assessment. The first was a process known as weight trimming. The second was to poststratify NAEP weights to population totals obtained from estimates from the October Education Supplement of the Current Population Survey (CPS). This procedure is described below.

With a three-stage sampling process (PSUs, schools, and students) and with the potential for nonresponse at the last two stages (so that two levels of nonresponse adjustment are required), it sometimes happens that some individual students can receive disproportionately large weights after accounting for these five weighting components. This happens most frequently when a school that is indicated on the sampling frame as being "small" turns out to be "large." Thus, regardless of the number of students selected within the school, the total combined weight of the students from within the school will be very much larger than for other schools in the sample. This can lead to an increase in the design effect, and this can be severe for population subgroups that are well represented in the school in question.

Survey-sampling practitioners understand that, in theory, one can improve the accuracy of the survey estimates by reducing the size of these outlying weights. However, reducing these weights introduces a bias into the estimates. If done appropriately, the size of this bias is far more than compensated for by the reduction in sampling variance that occurs, thus resulting in a reduced mean-square error. The difficulty is in finding a procedure for carrying out this weight trimming, using a defensible and repeatable algorithm, while ensuring that mean-square error reduction is very likely to occur.

Tepping worked on this problem and developed an algorithm still used today for national NAEP samples. It remains one of the few such procedures that is clearly documented and, as a result, has been widely cited. The practice of weight trimming remains more of an art than a science, at least in comparison to other procedures used in survey sampling. Thus, even though the algorithm developed by Tepping is applicable only to multistage sampling designs, it is noteworthy that it has stood the test of time and is one of the few formal weight-trimming algorithms that can be readily cited.

One innovation introduced in 1986 was to survey student populations defined by grade, as well as by age. Thus in 1986 NAEP surveyed students in grades 4, 8, and 11, as well as at ages 9, 13, and 17. Of course, at each age level there was a lot of overlap with the corresponding grade-based population, with about three-quarters of each group being in common (that is, three-quarters of nine-year-olds were in grade 4, and vice versa).

Each year the October CPS supplement obtains information about the age and grade distribution of students, as well as such demographic characteristics as region and race/ethnicity. These estimates are derived from the survey responses, benchmarked to reliable population projections by age, race, and sex. Hansen and Tepping realized that by poststratifying NAEP data to subpopulation estimates obtained from the CPS, the reliability of the estimates could be enhanced. Since 1986 national NAEP estimates have been stratified to the CPS figures by age, grade, region, and race/ethnicity. In the intervening years there have been several studies of the effectiveness of this poststratification. It is clear that poststratification results in up to 50% reductions in sampling variance for some highly aggregated groups. It also is evident that the major gain results from the race/ethnicity stratification, with the age-by-grade distribution also contributing significantly to the gains.

About the time of the 1988 assessment, NAEP changed the way in which it obtained data about the race and Hispanic ethnicity of students. Instead of relying primarily on school reports of individual student's race and ethnicity, since 1988 NAEP has relied primarily on the students' reports. It has become evident that this leads to a problem with the poststratification procedure because substantially more students identify themselves as Hispanic on NAEP questionnaires than are so identified in CPS data and in school records, especially at grade 4. Analysis of this phenomenon has shown that this results from a problem with the student reporting. NAEP asks two questions. The first asks the student to identify to which race/ethnic group the student belongs (with Hispanic being one option). The second asks the student to indicate to which Hispanic subgroup the student belongs (with "not Hispanic" as the first option). This approach evidently confuses many fourth-graders into reporting that they are Hispanic when the evidence from other sources suggests that they are not.

At first it might seem that this finding would dictate that poststratification by race/ethnicity be abandoned. But it has not, for three reasons: 1) eliminating this step would artifactually affect trend results, 2) the great reductions in sampling errors for aggregate estimates clearly outweigh the bias introduced by poststratification, and 3) the poststratification by race/ethnicity does not affect the results for the individual race/ethnicity subgroups that NAEP reports. In particular, results for Hispanic students are not affected by this poststratification procedure because all Hispanic students at a given grade receive the same weight adjustment as a result of poststratification.

A further complication in the poststratification procedure arose during the 1988 assessment. In 1986 NAEP assessed grade 11, and 17-year-olds, where the definition of 17-year-olds meant that most were in grade 11. In 1988 this was changed. For that year and ever since, 17-year-olds were defined to be nine months older, relatively, than they had been in 1986, because this revised definition meant that 17-year-olds were exactly four years older than the 13-year-olds. This also meant that the appropriate grade was grade 12. When it came time to conduct the poststratification for this assessment, the Westat statisticians discovered that the CPS figures showed far more grade-12 students who were 18 and older than were being realized in the NAEP samples. This was determined to be a result of the fact that the CPS figures for grade 12 included persons who were endeavoring to complete a General Education Diploma. This meant that certain adjustments had to be made to the poststratification procedures.

Poststratification has never been used as part of the state assessment program that began in 1990. That is because no reliable, independent source of the population size, broken down by major subgroups, is available. Thus there is no corresponding way to improve the precision of the state NAEP estimates. The samples in state NAEP are two-stage stratified samples, rather than the three-stage design used for national samples. These state samples typically include a sizable proportion of the schools in the state so that, even if a reliable independent source for these population counts existed, it is unlikely that there would be many gains from poststratification.

During this period the only significant forum for the discussion of technical issues in NAEP was the Design and Analysis Committee (earlier called the Technical Advisory Committee) that ETS had established under its grant. A great many of the ideas for innovation and refinement of NAEP came from this group. Particularly enlightening and entertaining were the philosophical and technical debates between John Tukey and Morris Hansen. The two did not always agree with each other on such issues; but this did not matter, because the rest of us learned so much from listening to the discussion.

## The State of Education: 1989 to 1995

In 1988 the decision was made that NAEP would offer an assessment program to the states and other jurisdictions. During the first several years that it was conducted, this was known as the Trial State Assessment. An eighth-grade mathematics assessment was offered in 1990, and the long-term plan was to assess two subjects at grades 4 and 8 every two years. In fact, it was not until the 2000 assessment that this full scope was introduced. Important sample design and data-collection questions quickly arose. The relevant legislation dictated that each state must bear the cost of collecting the data, and this had implications for both of these aspects of the program.

*Sample Design for State Assessments:* The two issues that first arose were: What should be the sample size in a typical state? and How should the sample size be related to the size of the state? NCES made the decision that the precision of the results of the assessment should be the same for each participating state, regardless of size. This dictated that the student and school sample sizes should be about the same in each state, especially in the absence of any design information suggesting that there were significant state-to-state variations in population variance, either within or between schools.

Morris Hansen believed that it would have been more rational to have a minimum size for each state, but with large and diverse states, such as California, having bigger samples. This would permit geographic breakdowns that would be neither possible nor necessary in smaller states. The program did offer each state the possibility to supplement the basic sample; but as states have had to bear the full cost of such supplements, this option has never been exercised by a state. With increasing interest in district-level NAEP results for large school districts, perhaps this aspect of the program will come to fruition during this decade.

Having established that each state would receive the same size sample, the question remained as to what size sample that should be for each grade and subject. I am sure that many NAEP observers assume that there were many careful iterations of power analyses, complex cost models, and full consideration of subgroup analyses, with all of these carefully documented and leading to a precise decision about the sample size required in each state. Perhaps someone did do such calculations, but I believe that the answer evolved in a much more pragmatic fashion. ETS and

Westat staff considered the results that NAEP had produced from the national samples during the 1980s. They observed that typical samples for each grade and subject were about 8,000 students, with about 2,000 in each NAEP region. They judged that precision of these regional results seemed at about the right level to be useful for state results that would be used in making state-by-state comparisons and in monitoring important subgroups within each state. This meant that the student sample in each state should be about 2,000. Because each school in the sample was likely to have to conduct its own assessment sessions, it seemed that a session of 25 or so students per school per subject would be the most workable. Thus this led to a design with about 100 schools selected per state, a number that could ensure a good representation of different kinds of schools within the state and would permit the reliable estimation of sampling variances. Other technical advisors concurred with this approach, and this must have met budgetary constraints because this plan was readily adopted by NCES.

When selecting the sample for the 1990 assessment, Westat and ETS wanted to be very sure that no state with a reasonably good response rate of schools and students would end up with fewer than 2,000 students assessed. Thus we implemented a rather conservative sample design; but we selected enough schools so that, with at most 30 students from each school, there would be 3,000 students in the sample. This meant that, in practice, most states in 1990 actually achieved a sample of 2,500 assessed students. Everyone apparently liked the results from these samples; so when the 1992 sample was designed, the decision was made, and subsequently incorporated in NAGB policy, that the sample sizes from 1990 should be continued. Thus it came about that the state-NAEP sample sizes are "100 schools and 2,500 students" per grade per subject per state (the same schools are largely used for each of the two subjects at a grade). It is interesting to note the level of concern that is expressed whenever there are suggestions that the state assessment sample sizes might be reduced, considering that the original determination was, to some extent, arbitrary.

When the state assessment program was introduced, there was considerable concern about the implications for the quality and integrity of the program arising from the fact that the states, and therefore the schools, were responsible for conducting the assessments and collecting the data. This was addressed in part by continuing to have a separate sample for the national assessment administered by Westat staff. This was also a necessity because no one knew for sure how many states would sign up for the program. I believe that it was decided that there would have to be 10 participants for the state trial program to proceed, and a lot of planning was based on the assumption that there would be 20 participants, without much idea as to which they would be. The deadline for the states to sign up for the 1990 assessment was 1 December 1988. In May 1989 New York signed on as the 38th and last participant.

The major step for ensuring the validity of the results of the assessments was a very extensive quality monitoring and assurance program. A simple experimental design was used as a means to detect incompetent administration and malfeasance and to provide usable data if the presence of either were detected even on a wide scale.

Within each state, a random subsample of one half of the selected schools was chosen, each to be visited during the assessment by a trained quality-control monitor (QCM). The sampled schools were paired to be similar in terms of key sampling characteristics, and one member of each pair was selected to be visited by a QCM. The identity of the schools to be visited was not revealed to the state or the school until an hour or so before the assessment was to begin. The QCM was instructed to observe and record all breaches of the testing protocol and to intervene in the assessment should major breaches be evident. There were three main features that the QCM was to look for: 1) Were the test materials secure until shortly before the assessment session? 2) Did the administrator follow the instructions for conducting the assessment, especially with regards to timing? and 3) Was any inappropriate assistance given to the students during the testing?

Assuming that few violations occurred in which the testing materials were inappropriately opened early, the principle was that the 50% of the sessions that were monitored would provide assessment data of adequate quality. Intentional "cheating" could be ruled out in these schools, and the interventions meant that, even if administrators were incompetent at their task, this would be corrected by the QCMs after recording the offense. It was reasoned that incompetence would be as prevalent in monitored schools as in unmonitored ones and that it could be assumed that the kinds of problems of this nature observed by the QCMs in the 50 schools that they visited within a state would be about equally prevalent (but uncorrected) in the other 50 schools. (Representatives of these other 50 schools were interviewed by telephone after the assessment to monitor problems.) It also was assumed that, other than opening the materials early, participants would not intentionally violate procedures in monitored schools; but there could be no direct observation of this in unmonitored schools. However, the controlled random assignment of schools to be monitored meant that there was substantial statistical power to detect consistent differences between the monitored and unmonitored schools. Had these been detected, the plan was to discard the data from the unmonitored schools, leaving a 50% sample that was fully adequate to represent the state. Finally, having the QCM visits unannounced provided a very strong incentive to schools not to open the testing materials before the assessment session was to be conducted.

In any case, no quality problems of any significance were observed; and in the following years the level of monitoring was reduced to 25% of the schools. The design of the quality-monitoring program provides an effective example of the integration of complex sample-survey design with experimental design, though of an admittedly simple form.

A key feature of the design for 1990, which has been repeated with every state assessment through 2000, is that a national assessment has been conducted in the same grades at the same time, testing the same subjects, and often additional subjects as well. This has led to the operational requirement that the state and national samples be in different schools. As most states do participate in the state assessment program and as more than 100 schools are selected in each grade and state, this means that a large proportion of the fourth- and eighth-grade schools in the country are included in the state assessment samples, especially at grade 8. Thus controlling the overlap between the state and national samples has not been trivial.

To ensure the integrity of both the state and national components, probability-sampling methods have been used to select these samples with minimum overlap. It is not merely a matter of selecting one sample first and then dropping the selected schools from the sampling frame for selecting the second sample. Because the schools are selected with probability proportional to size in both the state and national samples, such an approach would lead to the results from the second sample underrepresenting larger schools. This leaves the potential for significant bias in the statistics derived from the sample. Thus the two samples are selected jointly, using a procedure that gives each school the appropriate probability of being selected in each sample but that minimizes the probability for each school that it will be selected for both samples (for most schools this probability is zero). This procedure is described in Rust and Johnson (1992) and has been applied to all assessments from 1990 to 2000.

In October 1990, a few months after the data collection for the first state assessment but before the results were released, Morris Hansen passed away. Although his guidance was missed as NAEP evolved in future years, Morris helped to set the state assessment program on such a sound footing that no major overhaul of the design proved necessary in the ensuing decade. The national NAEP samples also still bear much resemblance to those he designed.

*Field Operations and Data Collection for the State Assessment Program:* The advent of the Trial State Assessment Program meant that not only were the field operations considerably expanded, but also the nature of the activities changed greatly. For the continuing national assessment components, the operations proceeded as they had in previous years. For the state program, however, a considerably different approach was required.

The authorizing legislation for the state assessment program required that the individual states be responsible for collecting their own data. Not surprisingly, the states chose to do this by having staff members from each participating school conduct the assessment within their own schools, though occasionally a district staff member would conduct the assessment in several schools within the district. In order to maintain high standards for administration procedures, both an extensive training program and rigorous quality-control procedures were implemented.

The training sessions were organized so that each person who was to administer one or more assessment sessions in the state program attended a full-day training session, without the need for overnight travel. This meant that several training sites, typically about 10, were located within each state. For each assessment since 1990, several hundred of these training sessions have been conducted in the month before the assessments.

There was a very large quality-control component for the initial trial state assessment, with half of the participating schools in each state receiving a visit during the assessment administration. A high level of visits has been maintained, with a quarter of the schools being visited. This intensive program has required a well-developed procedure for recruiting and training the quality-control monitors and for recording the results of the quality-control visits.

Throughout the 1990s, the overall standard of the assessment administrations has been uniformly high across states, and it is now taken for granted that these administrations are of a uniformly high quality.

## Including More Students While Maintaining Trends: 1995 to 2001

In the mid-1990s, laws were passed that required individual states to provide accommodations in their assessment programs for students with disabilities (SD) and those of limited English proficiency (LEP). Failure to comply would lead to loss of federal funds.

Because NAEP is a federal program, it came under scrutiny to ensure that its practices were in compliance with what states were required to do with their own testing programs. On the one hand, one could argue that NAEP is not a testing program; instead, it is a survey of student knowledge. No student has ever been educationally disadvantaged because of not being able to take the NAEP assessment under standard conditions. This distinction appears not to have been recognized in the Department of Education. In any case, it became clear that if NAEP were to remain relevant as a measure of achievement and to be an example of best practice in assessment programs, the program would have to provide reasonable accommodations for assessing SD and LEP students.

Aside from the operational costs and difficulties that introducing a program of accommodations in NAEP presented, this idea raised major issues about the validity of NAEP as a measure of achievement, especially for measuring trends over time. A cornerstone of NAEP's validity had always been the use of the same set of standard procedures for assessing every student and that these procedures did not vary over time.

The design of the 1996 national assessment confronted head-on the problem of introducing student accommodations into NAEP assessments while preserving important trend lines. In addition to dealing with the presence of accommodations, it was clear that NAEP needed to revise its rules concerning exclusion. The existing rules were increasingly irrelevant to the way in which information about SD and LEP students was stored and evaluated within schools.

*Sample Designs for Accommodations:* The design of the 1996 national assessment was perhaps the most complex design yet undertaken in NAEP. Three different experimental conditions were established, and each school in the sample was assigned to one of these. In addition, none of these three conditions applied to all parts of the assessment.

To further complicate the sample-design challenge, at grades 8 and 12 a new kind of assessment was introduced that covered only certain students, depending on the courses they had taken. All previous (and subsequent, with the exception of one portion of the 1997 arts assessment) assessments have applied to all students within a grade.

The three experimental conditions, to which sampled schools were assigned randomly, were: 1) exclusion criteria that applied in prior assessments, with no accommodations offered to SD and LEP students; 2) a revised set of exclusion criteria, with no accommodations offered to SD and LEP students; and 3) the revised set of exclusion criteria, with accommodations offered to SD and LEP students.

The subjects assessed in 1996 were mathematics and science. For the main mathematics assessment, one-third of the total sample was assigned to each of the three experimental conditions. For the main science assessment, no students were assigned to Condition 1, two-thirds to Condition 2, and one-third to Condition 3. For the advanced mathematics and science assessments, given only to students meeting certain course-taking requirements in these subjects, half of the samples were assigned to Condition 2 and half to Condition 3. Finally, for two special, additional mathematics assessments, the samples were assigned half to Condition 1 and half to Condition 2.

Condition 1 was designed to guarantee that trends to the past could be measured. It was envisaged that either Condition 2 or Condition 3 would be the standard procedure in future assessments, but it could not be determined which of them would be used until the results from the 1996 assessments and other special studies were analyzed to ascertain the effects, if any, of accommodations on the validity of NAEP assessment results.

Although complex to design and implement, the 1996 national assessment provided invaluable information and paved the way for NAEP to introduce both the revised exclusion criteria and the provision of accommodations in the state assessment program.

In the 1998 assessment, the concept of using a simple experimental design in conjunction with a complex sample design was simplified and extended. Condition 1 was not used, because the results from 1996 showed negligible differences in actual exclusion rates under Condition 1 compared with Condition 2. In the reading assessment, Conditions 2 and 3 were used, with the sample split evenly between the two conditions. This was extended to the state assessment program at both grades.

In the 1998, 2000, and 2001 assessments, the sample was split equally between conditions 2 and 3 for subjects in which trend results were expected to date back to assessments in 1996 or earlier. For assessments with no such expectations for trend results, all students were assessed under Condition 3.

The application of this approach for the four assessment years of 1996, 1998, 2000, and 2001 meant that each of the NAEP subjects of reading, mathematics, science, history, and geography had been assessed at least once under this dual system for both national and state assessments. This approach was not necessary for writing because a change in the assessment framework meant that it was not necessary to maintain trends. Subsequently, the National Assessment Governing Board adopted the policy that, from the 2002 assessments forward, accommodations would be offered routinely as part of NAEP assessments. There is no further need for offering accommodations in some schools and not in others.

*Technology in Field Operations:* The period from 1995 to 2001 also saw a steady increase in the use of technology for conducting field operations. Increasingly sophisticated computerized management-control systems were developed to keep track of recruitment, delivery of materials, and conduct of the assessment.

In the 2001 assessment, NAEP contractors endeavored, on a limited basis (but including several hundred schools), to automate the process of assigning test booklets to individual students, with student identification and the assigned booklet number precoded on the administration schedule. The schools submitted electronic lists of eligible students, and the appropriate student samples were drawn from these, rather than being selected by Westat field staff at the school. This meant that assessment booklets could be sent to the schools, each linked to the student who was to use that booklet. However, NAEP procedures still ensure that no completed assessment booklet leaves a school with the student's identity attached.

Also in 2001, NAEP used computers to administer the assessments of fourth- and eighth-grade students in mathematics. Where possible, the assessment data were collected over the Internet using the school's own computers. In other cases, NAEP field staff brought laptop computers into the school and used them to conduct the assessments.

The 1997 arts assessment perhaps demonstrated the pinnacle of innovation and flexibility in administering assessments. Among the tools and methods used during the assessment were: videotaping student performance, conducting group performances in theater, having students reproduce musical rhythms, having students play their musical instruments, using videotaped displays and slide shows, and having students perform choreographed dance movements.

## Conclusion

The history of Westat's involvement with NAEP since 1983 has seen a continuous expanding and refining of the procedures and operations. Designs and operations that would have been considered impossible in the early years are now implemented routinely.

It seems that another change is about to occur in the NAEP program. Two forces are at work that are dictating the need for change. The first is the interest of the federal administration and Congress in having NAEP play a significant, albeit indirect, role in determining the accountability of states for improvements in education in the elementary and middle school years. The second is the increasing burden that testing programs, including NAEP, are placing on states, districts, and especially schools.

It seems inevitable that NAEP will change in response to these combined forces. For the 2002 assessment, two major operational and design changes have been implemented. The first is to have the NAEP state assessment program administered in schools by Westat field operations staff, rather than by local personnel employed by the school district. The second, made attractive and probably inevitable by this change in administration mode, is that state and national samples will be combined, with no distinction at the school and student level between these two program aspects. It seems likely that these developments foreshadow NAEP's future direction for at least the next decade.

# CHAPTER 18

# Emerging Technical Innovations in NAEP

*Albert E. Beaton and Eugene G. Johnson*

Since its inception, the National Assessment of Educational Progress has been a visionary project. This also has been true of NAEP's use of technology. The technological history divides conveniently into two periods. The first period was from the mid-1960s until 1983. The second period spanned from 1983, when the administration of NAEP passed to the Educational Testing Service (ETS), to the present. During these periods, many advanced techniques were applied for the first time and, in many instances, new techniques were created.

## NAEP from 1969 to 1982

In 1969 an institutional home for NAEP was established at the Education Commission of the States (ECS) in Denver. NAEP remained at ECS until 1983. During this time, NAEP developed and administered assessments in science, reading, literature, music, social studies, mathematics, career and occupational development, writing, art, basic skills, citizenship, consumer skills, and music. Some of these required intensive performance assessments that, due to budgetary constraints, would be dropped.

NAEP was designed to report the achievement of students in the United States as a whole and in subpopulations defined by geographic region of the country, ethnicity, gender, size and type of community, and level of parental education. It was designed specifically to prevent reporting at smaller geographic levels, such as states.

An integral part of the initial NAEP design was the notion that the assessment would measure knowledge and skills that could be gathered from any source, not just from formal school courses. Consensus panels consisting of a broad spectrum of stakeholders with widely differing views were charged with determining the spectrum of learning objectives and sub-objectives for each age. The result was a set of very broad frameworks. Individual items were then written to address each of the individual objectives and sub-objectives, and the results were reported on an individual item basis.

Satisfying the consensus process in assessment development requires a very broad framework and thus a very large number of assessment items, enough so that an individual student would have to spend several hours to answer them all. However, an early insight of NAEP was that, just as it is not necessary to assess all of the students in the country to obtain a measure of the mean country-level performance on any item, it is not necessary to have every assessed student respond to every item. This is certainly true if the object of inference is the average performance on a given item. But further, even if the object of inference is the average performance across a series of items, it is more statistically efficient if different students take different sets of items. This led to the NAEP procedure of assigning different subsets of exercises to different subgroups of students.

Assessment exercises were assigned to different students using a procedure called "multiple matrix sampling." In this procedure, the entire pool of exercises is divided into nonoverlapping booklets, each booklet taking about 45 minutes to administer. Thus an exercise pool of 400 items, each taking 45 seconds to answer, might be divided into nine booklets of about 45 items each (allowing some time for page turning and other administrative tasks). Each student would be presented with only one booklet of items, thereby reducing the burden on the student.

In addition, it was believed that a student's performance on mathematics, for example, should not be confounded with that student's reading ability. Accordingly, in the assessment of most subjects, the assessments were administered using a tape player to play the text of the questions in order to minimize the effect of a student's reading ability on performance. For reading, no text was recorded; but the tape provided timing cues to pace the student through the assessment. The result was that all students within an assessment session had to be given the same assessment booklet. However, the students to be assessed were selected randomly from a list of eligible students within the school, as opposed to the selection of intact classrooms as is done in the Third International Mathematics and Science Study (TIMSS). This sample of students was then randomly divided into sessions, where each session was given a different assessment booklet. The result is that the students responding to any given book (and hence item) were randomly equivalent to the sample of students responding to any other book and item. Consequently, information about student achievement could be based on item-level information, each item based on a representative sample of the population.

In initial NAEP reports, the mode of presentation of the achievement results was on an item-by-item basis. Thus, for example, the first science reports (Abelson et al. 1970; Abelson et al. 1971; Tukey et al., 1973) tell that in 1970, 62% of nine-year-olds correctly identified that "putting sand and salt together makes a mixture." The various reports go on to report similar statistics for nine-year-old students in the Southeast and other regions, as well as by sex, ethnicity, parental education, and size and type of community. This mode of reporting follows the type of reporting of many government agencies, in which each question is of individual interest. However, such a level of reporting provides a vast quantity of information; and there tends to be a large amount of information about student ability common among many items. Item-by-item reporting ignores overarching similarities in trends and subgroup comparisons that are common across items, and thus it hinders the comparison of general performance in the population.

Realizing this, the NAEP architects tried a variety of ways both to provide item information and to present a picture of overall trends in the data. One innovative procedure was to use a variant of the stem-and-leaf display developed by Tukey (1977). This display vaguely resembles a histogram, with one small box representing each item and with the box located along a number line with the ordinate corresponding to the item's percent correct statistic. Two or more items with the same percent correct statistic are stacked on top of each other (if the plot is horizontal) or next to each other (if the plot is vertical). The result is a visual display of the distribution of percents correct across all items within the assessment, or within some subset of the assessment (such as a particular learning objective). Comparisons between subgroups were accomplished by having a series of these plots, one per subgroup (for example, by region). However, though it is a brilliant display device, it left it to the reader to develop his or her own opinions about what the overall summary of the data should be.

A variety of ways to summarize item performance were considered, including medians, means, and some exotic summaries based on the statistical robustness. (These latter statistics were essentially weighted means, where the weights for each item were chosen to optimize some statistical measure, such as resistance to extreme observations or maximum information.) In the end, it was decided that the most useful summary measure would be the mean (NAEP 1979). The grounds for this decision were that the mean is readily understandable to the general public and that the (properly weighted) average of the item means for each of a number of nonoverlapping subgroups of items will equal the overall mean of all the items going into the subgroups. The advantage of averaging is that it tends to cancel out the effects of peculiarities in items that can affect item difficulty in unpredictable ways (making an item surprisingly difficult, for example). Furthermore, averaging makes it possible to compare more easily the general performances of populations.

Despite their advantages, there are a number of significant problems with average item scores. First, their interpretation depends on the selection of the items; the selection of easy or difficult items could make the student performance appear overly high or low. In fact, the early NAEP reports had to repeatedly warn readers about this (see, for example, NAEP 1975). Second, the average score relates to the particular items that contribute to the average, so that direct comparisons between subpopulations require that those subpopulations have been administered the same set of items. This is not a problem within a year, because all items are given to randomly equivalent samples. However, this requirement that the same items be used for comparisons is a major problem for the measurement of trends over time. NAEP releases a portion of its item pool after each assessment so that the public can understand what is being assessed. This means that the pool must be refreshed each time by the inclusion of perhaps one-fourth to one-third new items. The result is that trend comparisons using means must be based only on the overlapping items. The consequence is that, as the number of years being compared increases, the number of items that form the basis of the comparison decreases to the extent that the trend comparisons become unstable. Alternatively, the trends over time must be pieced together through a series of two-point trends over adjacent years (see, for example, NAEP 1979).

An additional problem with the use of means is that there is no way to develop any other measure of the distribution of ability in the population. For example, it is impossible to estimate the proportion of nine-year-olds who would score above a given point if one were to give the students the entire test.

These various problems with means had caused a number of individuals to begin to think of other ways of analyzing NAEP data (Bock, Mislevy, and Woodson 1982; Messick, Beaton, and Lord 1983). This set the scene for the next major phase of NAEP, the model-based era.

## NAEP from 1983 to 2001

In 1982 Gregory Anrig, president of Educational Testing Service, decided that ETS should compete aggressively for the NAEP project. The new grant was to be awarded for five years beginning in 1983 and included the 1983-84 and 1985-86 assessments. He assigned ETS vice president Samuel Messick to be in charge of developing the proposal and brought Archie Lapointe to ETS to be executive director of NAEP if the award was won. The full resources of ETS were available for the proposal development.

ETS did win the competition, and Archie Lapointe became the first executive director under the ETS stewardship of NAEP. Since 1983, other executive directors have been Ina Mullis, Paul Williams, and Stephen Lazer, the current director.

The ETS plan for NAEP was to bring the best available psychometrics to bear and to make NAEP as useful as possible to policy makers and the general public. The key idea was to use item response theory (IRT) to summarize the answers to NAEP questions in scales that could be readily understood. If several items require similar skills, the regularities observed in response patterns often can be exploited to characterize both respondents and items in terms of a relatively small number of variables. These variables include a response-specific variable, called proficiency, which quantifies a respondent's tendency to answer items in a particular way (that is, correctly for right/wrong items) and item-specific variables measuring characteristics of the individual items, such as difficulty.

IRT scales solve the various problems with means discussed previously. All students can be placed on a common scale, even though none of the respondents take all of the items. This permits a direct comparison of scores from the many different booklets that are generated by multiple matrix sampling. More important, the measurement of trends over time does not require the same items to be used each time (a relatively small number of items do have to be repeated). Finally, using the common scale, it becomes possible to discuss distributions of scale scores in the population or subpopulations, estimate the proportions of students scoring above defined levels, and estimate the relationships between background variables and scale scores.

There are several competing IRT models used in item response theory. The Rasch model, named after the Danish psychometrician Georg Rasch, uses one item parameter that characterizes the difficulty of an item; the three-parameter logistic model uses separate parameters to characterize the difficulty, discrimination, and the "guessing" properties of an item. In 1983 ETS had developed the LOGIST program (Wingersky, Barton, and Lord 1982) for fitting the three-parameter logistic model to right/wrong item responses using maximum likelihood methods. ETS intended to use that program for the NAEP data. The BILOG computer program (Mislevy and Bock 1982) also was available for fitting the same model but using marginal maximum likelihood methods. The challenge became adapting the NAEP assessment in order to collect appropriate data to fit these models without disrupting the trend data that had been collected since the beginning of NAEP. The main features of the proposal are recorded in *National Assessment of Educational Progress Reconsidered: A New Design for a New Era* (Messick, Beaton, and Lord 1983). Beaton and Zwick (1992) and Johnson (1992) provide overviews of the design. The characteristics of the NAEP scaling models are documented in Beaton and Johnson (1992) and Mislevy, Johnson, and Muraki (1992).

The new design involved some changes in the area of sampling. In the earlier design, the first stage of sampling for NAEP consisted of primary sampling units (PSUs) that were counties or metropolitan statistical areas. Within the PSUs, all schools, both public and private, were listed; and a sample of schools was selected with probability proportional to their estimated enrollments. Finally, lists of all students at the appropriate ages were constructed, and students who were deemed unable to participate because of limited English proficiency or disabilities were excluded. A sample of students was selected randomly from the final list.

The ETS plan proposed that both age groups and school grades be sampled, not age groups alone. NAEP had sampled ages 9, 13, and 17 in the past; and this approach laid a solid foundation for comparisons over time. However, school decisions are made largely on the basis of grades; and to make the results more relevant, grades 4, 8, and 11 were sampled as well. The general approach to selecting a sample was similar to past assessments, but SDs (Students with Disabilities) and LEPs (students with Limited English Proficiency) were left on the student lists during student sampling. If selected for the sample, the SD and LEP students were then excluded, and a short questionnaire was filled out about the reason for exclusion. In this way, some data could be collected on a national probability sample of SD and LEP students. Other changes, such as the assessment dates, also were made.

A major modification of the NAEP data collection design was the introduction of Balanced Incomplete Block (BIB) spiraling. As mentioned above, NAEP had used matrix sampling to extend the item pool from which assessment items were sampled. In the early NAEP design, all students responded to the same assessment items in an assessment session within a school. Except for reading assessments, the items were delivered orally by a tape recorder, as well as by print. In BIB spiraling, the assessment items are placed in blocks so that all blocks take about the same amount of time for a student to complete. The blocks are placed in assessment booklets so that each block is paired with every other block in some assessment booklet. In this way, data are collected on the correlations among NAEP items. The booklets then are spiraled so that many different booklets are used in an assessment session. BIB spiraling improved the sample design by reducing the design effect. The correlations were intended to allow for studies of the homogeneity of items within subject areas. However, because many booklets were used within a session, the oral administration could not be continued.

In the 1983-84 year, NAEP assessed reading and writing. The assessment items were supplied by the Education Commission of the States (ECS) from past assessments and recent item development. Both reading and writing were to be scaled on a developmental scale, that is, a scale that ran continuously through the different age groups. The scale was developed by administering a sample of items to both the fourth-grade/nine-year-old students and the eighth-grade/13-year-old students, and another sample to both the eighth-grade/13-year-old and the 11th-grade/17-year-old students. Both reading and writing were scaled separately.

However, in order to estimate the correlation between reading and writing performance, reading and writing blocks were spiraled together in the same booklets. Each booklet had three blocks, so a student might be asked to respond to one, two, or three blocks of reading items or, perhaps, no reading items at all. The students who were assigned no reading items were a random subsample and could be ignored for the scaling of reading. The students who were assigned only one or two reading blocks were not measured reliably and thus would affect the reading report. Worse, using the estimation method of maximum likelihood, students who answered all items correctly and those who did less well than answering at random would not have scores at all. The inability to obtain scores for these students threatened a severe bias in the assessment results.

This fact brought about the development of new techniques for analyzing education data. The key insight was that NAEP did not need — in fact, could not report — individual student scores. NAEP was intended to estimate the performance of large groups of students, such as eighth-graders or students in the western section of the United States. Taking advantage of this limitation, Mislevy (1985) applied the missing data techniques developed by Rubin (1987). Instead of computing each student's score, he estimated the distribution of "plausible" scores given the way that the student responded to the assessment items (these missing data imputations are called "plausible values"). A student who was assigned three blocks of reading items would be measured with reasonable accuracy, and the variance of the distribution of plausible values would be small. On the other hand, a student who had been assigned just one block would be poorly measured, and the variance of the plausible values would be large. To represent the proficiency of a student, five random draws from the distribution of plausible values were taken. These were used to estimate the population distributions and the parameters that NAEP sought.

It quickly became apparent that the accuracy of an estimate of a population parameter could be improved by including other information about a student. If a number of variables are known to be associated with student performance, then that information can be used to improve the estimates. Essentially, this means using regression procedures to improve the student's plausible value distributions and the population parameter estimates. This process is known as "conditioning" and should be used whenever population parameters or distributions are to be reported. The failure to use conditioning may result in biased parameter estimates. We note that this procedure would never be appropriate for individual scores intended for student decisions because students with identical item responses may have different plausible distributions because of the associated variables

The methods of item response theory proposed for the reading assessment and future assessments were not appropriate for the writing assessment. At that time, IRT was developed for right/wrong questions, not for items with responses that might be graded as 1, 2, 3, or 4. The few graded responses in the reading assignment were handled by declaring a certain score as passing and thus producing a correct or incorrect response. To handle the writing data, Beaton and Johnson (1990) developed the Average Response Method (ARM) of scaling that extends the plausible value technology to linear models.

Another innovation at this time was the introduction of "scale anchoring." It was a matter of concern that the policy makers and the public would not understand the NAEP scales in the sense of knowing what students at a certain proficiency level would know and be able to do. To answer this concern, several scale points were selected as anchor points. The data files were searched for items that a large proportion of students at a level could answer correctly and that a majority of students at the next lower anchor point could not. These items were presented to expert panels for interpretation of what students at different levels knew and were able to do (Beaton and Allen 1992).

NAEP continued to place special emphasis on the estimation of population parameters and their standard errors. Using the sampling frame, sampling weights were computed and then adjusted for nonresponse and for agreement with available data from the Census Bureau. The jackknife method was used for estimating the standard errors.

The computation of weights is not necessarily straightforward. In the course of trend analyses, particularly in the early years, NAEP analysts occasionally discovered anomalous findings. In one trend analysis in the late 1970s, performance in the Northeast and performance for black students plummeted, accompanied by a massive increase in the standard error. Extensive analysis of the data diagnosed the problem as due to a single small school in a predominantly black area being selected in the sample. This school had a very low probability of selection and consequently had a very large sampling weight. Coupled with this was a high level of nonresponse, leading to enormous weights being attached to each of these students. Essentially, these students were driving the estimates for the Northeast and for blacks. This led NAEP to institute various procedures for restricting the sizes of weights. These included weight smoothing (NAEP 1979; Johnson 1980), in which the weights are adjusted so that trends in estimated subpopulation proportions are smooth, thus damping extreme fluctuations caused by aberrantly large weights. Currently, NAEP dampens extreme weights by weight trimming (Rust and Johnson 1992), in which very large weights are truncated, and adjusts for excessive variability in the sampling weights through poststratification (see Chapter 16).

Because making multiple inferences from a single set of data can lead to spuriously significant results, NAEP has employed procedures to guard against such errors. Until recently, the Bonferroni method was used; but that has been replaced by a method to control for the false discovery rate (FDR). Beginning in 1998, the FDR approach has been used exclusively. For details, see Williams, Jones, and Tukey (1999) as well as Benjamini and Hochberg (1994).

The ETS staff was concerned with maintaining the trends from the past history of NAEP while also introducing innovative methods. To do this, it designed and implemented a number of "bridge studies" to measure the effect of the changes and, if possible, to make the past and present results comparable.

The NAEP procedures have been documented carefully in a series of technical reports (see for example: Beaton 1987, 1988*a*; Johnson and Zwick 1990; Johnson and Allen 1992; Johnson, Carlson, and Kline 1994; Allen, Kline, and Zelenak 1996; Allen, Jenkins, Kulick, and Zelenak 1997; Allen, Carlson, and Zelenak 1999; Allen, Donoghue, and Schoeps 2001). These procedures also are published in separate issues of the *Journal of Educational Measurement* (1992) and the *Journal of Educational Statistics* (1992). The NAEP data have been made available for reanalysis and research by interested researchers.

The next assessment, in 1985-86, was quite ambitious, assessing reading, mathematics, science, and computer competency. In addition, it continued the long-term trends in reading, mathematics, and science. Long-term trends were measured using a separate sample of students and some of the same items and booklets that were used in past assessments. Different bridge samples were used to measure the effect of regularizing the time of year of assessment.

The results of the long-term trend analysis in reading were anomalous. There were seemingly large drops in performance at the 11th and fourth grades but little change at the eighth-grade level. The results were anomalous enough to generate a series of research studies into possible causes of such changes in performance. Many seemingly minor changes in the format and procedures were identified. The final report on the anomaly succinctly summarized the lesson from this exercise: "When measuring change, do not change the measure" (Beaton and Zwick 1990, p. 10). The 1986 reading trend data never were published for the general public (but see Zwick 1991 for further discussion).

Despite the problems involved in changing the measurement, some changes were deemed necessary to keep the assessment up to date and relevant. An assessment system must continually improve itself while preserving what is useful from the past. The 1983-84 assessment introduced many major changes.

The technical innovations in NAEP have continued. IRT methods were expanded using the PARSCALE program (Muraki and Bock 1991), which allowed partially correct responses as well as the right/wrong answers required by the BILOG program. The introduction of PARSCALE ended the need for the Average Response Method, which was replaced.

In 1988, the enabling legislation for NAEP included the formation of a nonpartisan National Assessment Governing Board (NAGB) to control the policy decisions for NAEP. NAGB called for a review of the objectives and specifications in several subject areas, and these led to changes in the assessment design. To avoid anomalous results, separate samples that are administered using booklets and procedures from the past will be used for long-term trends. The newer assessment specifications will be used for describing the current state of student performance. It is expected that both long-term trend samples and the newer assessments will run in parallel until it is clear how the two assessments are related.

The 1988 enabling legislation also included the Trial State Assessment. This policy change required substantial changes in the NAEP sampling designs and administrative procedures. One major difference is that private schools are not included in the state samples, though they are included in the national sample. The sampling design had to allow for a national public school sample even though not all states participated in the assessment. Furthermore, instead of having NAEP staff administer the assessment, the state samples were administered by state staffs that were trained by Westat. The results of the states' assessments are equated to the national assessment to adjust for the small differences that result from the differences between state and national NAEPs.

There has been interest in reporting at levels below the state level. Legislative approval was granted toward the end of the 1990s for a trial to report NAEP results at a district level for those districts that choose to participate and are large enough to support a sufficiently large sample. There also has been interest in reporting results for individual schools, though law currently forbids such reporting. However, a direct application of NAEP assessment methods (in particular, BIB spiraling) to school-level reporting leads to very unstable school-level results for all but the largest schools (Johnson 1994).

Several other technical challenges now are affecting NAEP. The definitions of minority membership have changed to conform to those required by the Office of Management and Budget (OMB). Also, students with disabilities and students with limited English proficiency are included in the assessment. Changes are being made to both the criteria used to include students in the assessment and in the accommodations employed to allow students with disabilities to participate, and the NAEP Design and Analysis Committee currently is addressing problems associated with changes in the populations of students being measured.

With regard to the increased inclusion of students with disabilities and English language learners into the assessment, NAEP has developed a three-sample approach to allow inclusion and accommodation criteria while still maintaining trends. The first of these samples, denoted S1, uses the inclusion criteria that have been in place for NAEP since the outset. This sample maintains a direct means of measuring trends. The second sample, S2, refines the inclusion criteria to make them more standard and to allow for more students to participate in the assessment. The final sample, S3, uses the new inclusion criteria and also allows various accommodations to the testing to allow more students to participate. The accommodations include one-on-one administration, extended time, large print and Braille, and, for English language learners in assessments other than reading and writing in English, test forms in both English and Spanish. The S3 sample represents the procedure that NAEP will use in the future. The psychometric challenges in comparing the results from the three samples have been daunting.

Another major change was NAGB's decision to report results in terms of achievement levels instead of scale anchor points. The scale anchoring procedure describes what students at various scale points know and can do, whereas the achievement levels describe what students *ought* to be able to do. Using definitions of "basic," "proficient," and "advanced" performance, groups of judges examined the NAEP assessment items to determine which items should be answerable at each achievement level. The method is described by Hambleton and Bourque (1991) and Bourque and Byrd (2000).

The NAGB achievement levels have been controversial. Both the National Academy of Education (Shepard et al. 1993) and the National Academy of Sciences (Pellegrino, Jones, and Mitchell 1999) were charged with conducting technical evaluations of NAEP. Both evaluations were critical of the achievement levels. Nevertheless, the achievement levels have been accepted by the public and policy makers as providing useful information about what students should be able to do.

The use of achievement levels brought the issue of student motivation and absenteeism to the fore. Achievement levels are designed to indicate what students should be able to do. Although the panelists have not explicitly said so, it is likely that the word "should" means under circumstances where students are trying their best. There is considerable evidence that high levels of motivation are not being exhibited in the NAEP assessment, particularly at grade 12 (O'Neil et al. 1997). It is both a reporting and analysis challenge to accounting for this lowered motivation. Another problem, which appears to be worsening, is increasing levels of student absenteeism from the assessment, again more so at grade 12. The problem is that the absent students may not have the same performance characteristics as the assessed students, though the nonresponse weighting adjustments assume that absent students can be replaced by the assessed students within certain weighting classes. A study conducted by NAEP in the mid-1970s (Rogers et al. 1989) suggested that many of the students absent from the assessment were, in fact, like the assessed students and that most of the remainder had essentially dropped out of school. Thus the nonresponse adjustments were justified at that time. Whether this still is true is unknown.

Another issue that is still an open question is the best way to interpret trend results. Suppose that the overall average performance for a particular subject for all fourth-grade students decreased by three points between two assessment years (Year 1 and Year 2). Is this decrease due to a real decrease in ability of students in Year 2 relative to matching students in Year 1, or is it due to a change in the population of the students between the two years? For example, there may have been relatively more students of lower ability in the Year 2 grade-4 population than in the Year 1 grade-4 population. All other things being equal, this alone would be sufficient to lead to an overall drop in mean achievement. NAEP experimented for a time with a procedure called "balancing" to address this question (Tukey et al. 1973). Balancing decomposes the performance difference between Year 1 and Year 2 into two additive components. The first component estimates how much of the change in performance would be expected to occur if the demographic composition of the Year 2 population was identical to that of the Year 1 population, but the subgroup achievement measures were as observed (thus measuring the effect of change in achievement for matched populations). The second component measures the change in overall achievement if all subgroups achieved at their Year 2 levels in both years, but the relative proportions of the subgroups in the population in each year were as observed (thus measuring the effect of subpopulation drift for equally able subpopulations). Although very informative, this type of analysis has not been used lately in NAEP analysis and reporting.

Additional analyses have added additional insight into the NAEP data. There is an active Secondary Analysis Grant program to encourage such analyses, and other analyses have been conducted using other funding. Examples of these analyses include: *The NAEP Primer* (Beaton and Gonzalez 1995), which provides a hands-on introduction to the use of plausible values; Hierarchical Linear Models (HLM) (Mullis, Johnson, and Jenkins 1994; Sedlacek 1995), which decompose NAEP results into effects due to schools and students; generalizability theory studies (Brennan and Johnson 1995), which established that the particular performance task given a student has a major effect on the performance measurement for that student; and the two-dimensional jackknife (Cohen, Johnson, and Angeles 2000), which established that NAEP scales are not unidimensional and that the subset of items included in the scale has a major effect on ultimate estimates of proficiency distributions.

NAEP is entering a third era. There is considerable pressure to speed up the reporting timeline from the current 12 to 18 months to six months. Accomplishing such a change will require a radical reengineering of NAEP, including changes in how and when items are calibrated, what is reported, potential item types, and how often the frameworks can be changed (see, for example, Johnson, Lazer, and O'Sullivan 1997). One suggestion is preequating, where field test items are embedded into the main assessment, item parameter estimates for those items are developed from the field test data, and those parameters are used to develop score distributions for students in the next operational assessment. This single change would reduce analysis time by several months, though at some risk to the stability of the pre-equated items.

Another change in the third generation of NAEP is the use of targeted assessments, whereby each assessed individual receives an assessment booklet with the difficulty targeted to that person's predicted level of ability. The current NAEP essentially has books of roughly equal difficulty, which are distributed at random. Targeted assessment allows for the efficient measurement of a wider range of abilities and avoids such unfortunate occurrences as giving a low-ability person a test with many very difficult items. This type of assessment has been tried in mathematics, where some students taking more advanced mathematics classes received a more difficult form; and it will be an integral part of the upcoming foreign language NAEP, an assessment primarily in Spanish with an easier form for beginning Spanish language learners and a harder form for individuals with considerable Spanish background.

The foreign language NAEP also includes an experiment with computer administration, as did the 2000 assessment of mathematics. The mathematics assessment is experimenting with the use of a short form of NAEP, designed to allow for NAEP-like reporting on a metric, which corresponds to a total test score. If successful, such a short form potentially could be used by states and other jurisdictions, such as districts, to develop estimated NAEP scores for years when NAEP is not in the field for that subject. However, there are considerable technical challenges to making such a scheme work successfully (DeVito and Koenig 2001).

Finally, NAEP is moving toward helping interested members of the measurement and policy community conduct their own analyses. The NAEP website now includes a variety of applications that allow the user to search published tables and to create customized extracts of those tables that can be imported into their own reports. Soon to be on the site is the powerful AM analysis system (Cohen and Jiang 2001), which will allow the user to conduct her or his own analysis of the NAEP data in a way that respects the sample design and measurement properties of the data while not burdening the user with the statistical details needed to accomplish this.

# PART IV
# RECENT CHALLENGES

# CHAPTER 19

# Innovations in Instrumentation and Dissemination

*Stephen Lazer*

The National Assessment of Educational Progress has been marked by major redesigns, challenges, and innovations throughout its history. The 1980s and early 1990s were periods of psychometric and policy innovation. Item Response Theory (IRT) scales were introduced in the 1980s, and scaling methodology was revised in the early 1990s to incorporate questions for which partial credit could be assigned. Statistical methods and computer programs (conditioning/plausible values) were developed that allowed NAEP to estimate and report the performance of population groups on the new IRT scales; and these analysis models were improved in the early 1990s. During this era, the National Assessment Governing Board (NAGB) was created. NAGB, in turn, produced new assessment frameworks for the reading, mathematics, science, writing, U.S. history, and geography assessments. Finally — and perhaps, in the end, most significant — the state assessment program became a part of NAEP, with concomitant increases in volume and complexity.

After this era of substantial and major change, it would be easy to view the mid- to late-1990s and the early years of the 21st century as a period of consolidation. Such a view, however, belies the important innovations and successes of this period. It also underestimates the challenges the program faced.

The innovations and changes that occurred during the period loosely bounded by the 1992 and 2002 NAEP assessments issued from three sources. First, the program was called on to implement many of the new ideas first called for in earlier years. In the late 1980s and early 1990s, for example, NAGB created a series of new assessment frameworks that required the developers at Educational Testing Service (ETS) to craft path-breaking instruments. In reading and mathematics, extended and short constructed-response questions, together with multiple-choice items, became the norm. In addition, the reading assessment needed to base sets of items on authentic and complete reading materials, whereas the mathematics assessment needed to incorporate calculator-based and "manipulative-based" (for example, rulers, protractors, and items involving geometric shapes) questions. Framework-mandated change in other subjects was even more profound. The geography assessment was to include "production items," in which children would be asked to produce their own maps and graphics, and "atlas blocks," in which students would be assessed on their ability to use the basic reference tool of the field, an atlas. In science, the framework directed that portions of the assessment be composed of hands-on experiments. In the arts assessment, true performance assessment became the centerpiece of an entire operational measure.

In addition, the psychometric innovations of the previous period themselves necessitated other changes. The "partial-credit" (or graded-response) model for IRT scaling meant that assessment developers needed to develop short constructed-response items that loaned themselves to scoring with polytomous, rather than dichotomous, scoring rubrics. Whereas NAEP extended-answer questions during earlier periods had always had multipoint scoring guides, shorter questions had been scored "right/wrong."

The second source of change in the period between the mid-1990s and the early 21st century was the development of new and powerful computing technologies, in particular the Internet. The enhancement of computing power and speed made it possible to distribute a new range of analysis tools for expert users. New storage media allowed for the distribution of entire data sets on CD, rather than on data tape. Perhaps most important, the Internet made it possible to markedly expand and simplify the dissemination of NAEP reports, data, and released items. Information that had been available to only a few became widely accessible.

Technology had implications for NAEP beyond the dissemination of data. Beginning in 2000, NAEP began systematic studies of computer-delivered assessment. In 2000 and 2001, school questionnaires were made available on the Internet. In 2001 and 2002, electronic file transfer between participating schools and Westat was used to streamline the sampling process.

The third major source of innovation during this period included developments in the broader education and policy world. Perhaps the most profound issue NAEP faced derived from the Individuals with Disabilities in Education Act (IDEA). Until 1996 NAEP had no systematic policy to allow accommodations for special-needs students. Increasing numbers of students received Individualized Education Programs that mandated accommodations for participation in large-scale assessments; but because such accommodations were not available for NAEP, schools excluded increasing numbers of students from the assessment. This created a serious dilemma for NAEP managers and policy makers. Keeping assessment practices consistent with past years would lead to increasing exclusion and, therefore, might affect the measurement of trends. However, changing assessment practice to allow accommodations would alter the basic testing conditions and the effective samples tested, and thus also might affect trends. To cope with this situation, NAEP adopted a multi-year strategy of testing parallel samples in which accommodations either were allowed (as a bridge to the future) or were not allowed (as a bridge to the past).

Beginning in 2002, NAGB determined that NAEP should be expanded, on an experimental basis, to major urban school districts. Although the future of the Trial Urban Assessment is unclear, it has the potential to represent a program expansion of a magnitude similar to the state assessment in 1990.

The greatest potential effect on NAEP is the inclusion of the program in the No Child Left Behind Act (NCLB, Public Law 107-334, 2002). This act mandates that a condition for states receiving Title I funding is their participation in NAEP reading and mathematics assessments at fourth and eighth grades every other year. This profoundly changed the NAEP assessment schedule; previously, no subject was assessed more frequently than every four years, except in special circumstances. Of equal importance, the new law requires that results in these subjects be released within six months of data collection, a far faster schedule than had been met before. Finally, while the specific role of NAEP data in the NCLB accountability system has yet to be determined (and may be somewhat informal), it is clear that the new law will bring new attention and scrutiny to NAEP results.

The likely passage of NCLB led the National Center for Education Statistics (NCES) to ask its contractors to expedite changes that had been in the planning stages for several years. Steps were taken to restructure the NAEP sampling and administration system to allow for a single, common administration model for all NAEP subjects. Variation in the time required for testing the different subjects and in the structure of assessment booklets had led to the need for subject-specific assessment sessions. This not only caused unnecessary complexity in the field operations, but it also made the sample-weighting process (a key component of the analysis) complicated and time consuming. Streamlining was an absolute necessity if the program was to meet aggressive new reporting goals.

This chapter will focus on two of the many factors that helped define the era between 1992 and 2002: innovations in instrumentation and data dissemination. These clearly are among the aspects of the period that have had a great influence beyond the program itself.

## Innovations in Instrument Development

One responsibility given to NAGB was to set performance standards on NAEP assessments, which caused a great deal of controversy. An equally important assignment, though one that received far less attention, was to determine what subjects should be assessed and to define, through the development of assessment frameworks and specifications, the specific content and skills that should be tested in each of those areas.

NAGB began this process in the late 1980s and early 1990s with the key NAEP subjects of mathematics, reading, and writing. Following these efforts, new frameworks were developed to govern the NAEP assessments in science, geography and U.S. history, the arts, and civics. The framework development for science took place in 1990 and 1991, for geography and U.S. history in 1991 and 1992, for the arts in 1993 and 1994, and for civics in 1995 and 1996. NAGB then proceeded to develop new frameworks for foreign language and for economics. In addition, the mathematics framework and specifications were revised and updated in 1992, and the writing specifications were redone in 1996. The change in mathematics did not result in the breaking of a trend line, whereas the change in writing did.

All of these framework-development efforts involved extensive panels of content experts; and in all cases, they led to the creation of entirely new NAEP assessments. In other words, previous content and skills definitions were different enough that new instruments needed to be crafted and new trend lines begun. These new instruments involved new types of items. Some of these item types had not been used in NAEP previously, whereas others had not appeared in *any* large-scale assessments.

*Innovations in Reading Assessment:* Reading tests, perhaps more than assessments in most other areas, face a fundamental tension between the two basic tenets of good measurement, validity and reliability. In "real life," readers tend to deal with extensive texts that have identifiable beginnings, middles, and ends. However, it proved impossible to use such texts for testing reading when individual scores are required. Reading such passages takes too long and therefore led to tests based on a limited number of reading materials and items. These tests would tend, of course, to have low reliability. In other words, measuring reading in an "authentic" manner and having trustworthy test scores are not fully and easily reconcilable. Most reading comprehension measures have adopted a compromise structure in which a moderately large number of reading passages are used and in which these passages represent a sample of a broader domain (a student might get a science passage, a literary passage, and a history passage, for example). The passages used were almost universally short excerpts from longer pieces.

Although NAEP was never concerned with individual scores, NAEP reading assessments before 1992 had the same general form of most reading comprehension tests. Students would read and answer questions about a variety of short passages. The questions tended to look similar to those in other reading assessments, focusing on "main ideas" and "vocabulary in context." In fairness, there were differences — NAEP used a number of constructed-response questions, while most assessments used only multiple-choice items — but these were outweighed by the similarities.

This changed with the 1992 reading assessment. The developers of the new NAGB framework realized that because NAEP did not need to produce individual scores, it could afford to do a more authentic job of measuring reading. The framework called for authentic and complete passages from materials that students would encounter in their regular reading activities; these materials were to be unedited in any way before being used on the assessment.

This change had a profound effect on the assessment. Rather than reading and answering questions about several different materials, in a 50-minute assessment period students read and responded to questions about only two passages. The passages markedly increased in length. Previous reading passages had ranged from a single sentence to, in one case, 600 words. Most were 250 words or shorter. The 1992 passages ranged in length from 400 words (the shortest grade-4 stimulus) to 1,000 words (at grade 12).

With the use of more authentic and complete reading materials came the possibility of assessing students' understandings of the structures of texts and their abilities to relate what they had read to external knowledge or experiences. The measurement of these new outcomes led to a marked expansion in the proportion of the assessment devoted to constructed-response questions. In the earlier reading assessments, about 6% of the items were open-ended. After 1992 more than half the items are constructed-response.

Several examples illustrate the new NAEP reading instruments. Students read a 792-word article about the Anasazi cliff dwellers in Mesa Verde, Colorado, that included pictures and figures showing Anasazi crafts. The question below (from the NCES/NAEP website, nces.ed.gov/nationsreportcard) asks for a fairly standard critical judgment:

> The Anasazi's life before 1200 A.D. was portrayed by the author as being
> A) dangerous and warlike
> B) busy and exciting
> C) difficult and dreary
> D) productive and peaceful

Other questions ask students to make critical judgments that move beyond straightforward interpretation and decoding of text. For example:

> If you could talk to the author of this article, what is one question you could ask her about the Anasazi that is not already answered in the article? Explain why you would want to know this information.

The result of these changes was a reading assessment that looked quite different from both previous NAEP instruments and from other assessments. These innovations were to have analogs in other NAEP subject areas.

*Innovations in Mathematics Assessment:* The mathematics framework was the first of those revised by NAGB. In 1990 it became the first of the "new assessments" put online. It underwent substantial evolution in its early years. Extended constructed-response questions, focusing on problem-solving skills, were added in the 1992 assessment; and short constructed-response questions amenable to partial-credit scoring were added in 1996. As was the case in reading, the new mathematics assessment called for exercises substantially different than in the previous NAEP assessments.

The NAEP mathematics framework called for a composite scale based on measurement of five subscales: numbers and operations, algebra and functions, geometry, data analysis and statistics, and measurement. A sixth scale — estimation — was to be measured periodically but was not part of the main composite scale. The need for multiple subscales placed substantial demands on the ability-estimation systems, which needed to be redeveloped during the 1980s and 1990s. In addition, by 1992 the framework called for a number of exercise types that had not been part of NAEP assessments.

Unlike the case in reading, constructed-response questions had played a role in earlier NAEP mathematics assessments. In the long-term trend mathematics assessments, for example, 35% of the questions are open-ended (compared to roughly 40% in the main assessment). However, the nature of the items differs substantially. In the long-term trend, the constructed-response questions involve straightforward calculation and have numeric answers that are scored as right or wrong. In the main assessment, questions ask students to show work, to explain their mathematical reasoning, and to solve multistep problems.

This move to improve the quality of even the short-answer questions is shown by the fourth-grade question below (from the NCES/NAEP website):

> The lowest point of the St. Lawrence River is 294 feet
> below sea level. The top of Mt. Jacques Cartier is 1,277 feet
> above sea level. How many feet higher is the top of Mt.

Jacques Cartier than the lowest point of the St. Lawrence River? Show your work.

Short answer questions, such as the one above, proved to be strong additions to the program for a number of reasons. At the student level, students were far less likely to skip such questions than they had been to skip the longer and more complex extended-answer questions. These questions also proved to be excellent and efficient sources of statistical information (Mazzeo, Yamamoto, and Kulick 1993).

The ways in which the program assessed multistep problem solving can be seen in the extended-answer questions, first used in 1992. In these questions, students are walked through complex problems and asked to show their work. Examples of such questions can be seen on the NAEP website (nces.ed.gov/nations reportcard).

A "hands-on" component also was added to the mathematics assessment. Geometric shapes were given students, who then were asked to solve a range of problems.

Hands-on features — geometric shapes, rulers, or protractors — are used on discrete portions of the assessment. In 1992, for example, about 22% of sampled students answered a family of questions based on the geometric shapes. In this way, the shapes could contribute to the composite mathematics scale without taking up too large a place in the assessment. This is an efficient and effective way of administering tasks that might otherwise either take up too much assessment space or prove prohibitively expensive. It is made possible by NAEP's matrix sampling approach.

NAEP adopted a similar approach to one of the most potentially controversial issues facing mathematics assessment in the 1990s: using calculators. Many pitched battles have been fought in testing programs over allowing calculators. In NAEP, there was no need to fight that battle. Framework developers simply defined the mathematics domain as involving *both* the ability to do basic calculations without a calculator *and* the ability to use a tool (a calculator) for solving problems. Thus calculators (supplied by NAEP) were allowed on a portion of the assessment.

Some students received no calculator blocks, whereas others received two.

*Innovations in Science Assessment:* Perhaps no new NAGB design placed as many demands on NAEP instrumentation as did the science framework, created in 1990 and 1991. The long-term trend science assessments were entirely multiple-choice. The 1990 "main" science assessment (developed before the NAGB framework) was a combination of multiple-choice and a small number of figural-response questions. The new assessment was to be entirely different. For budgetary reasons, the new science assessment was not administered until 1996.

There were several types of blocks in the new assessment. "Concept/problem solving" blocks were designed to provide the broad content coverage required by the assessment specifications. Made up of a combination of multiple-choice, short-answer, and extended-answer questions, these blocks would be designed to assess students' knowledge and skills across a content domain. In addition, "theme blocks," in-depth questions in a given topical area, were used. For example, students were asked to answer a series of questions about different models of the solar system to measure their understandings of scientific systems and models.

An even greater challenge was the framework's dictate that roughly one-third of the science assessment be based on hands-on experiments. NAEP had experimented with hands-on science assessment in the 1980s (Educational Testing Service 1987*b*). However, in 1996 hands-on experiments were to be given to all students participating in both the national and state science assessments, a total of more than 150,000 children. This raised new issues. The assessment would need to be administered by Westat field staff and school staff who conducted the state assessment. The "kits" needed to conduct the experiments had to be mass produced, and the cost and safety of these materials became a substantial factor.

Before the actual development of exercises began, a series of key decisions was reached. First, it was decided that all students should receive a hands-on component and that the hands-on items should, if possible, be included in the core science scale. In addition, developers, in consultation with Westat field administration specialists, determined that the only way for the assessment to be administered effectively was for each assessed student to have an individual science kit. "Stations," at which a single kit would be set up for use by multiple students (either in groups or one after the other) were rejected as being inconsistent with the basic method of NAEP measurement and as requiring too much administration time in the schools.

The tasks needed to measure outcomes as described in the framework and specifications. Experiments had to be designed that could be completed, along with their associated assessment questions, within a "normal" assessment period. Materials needed to be safe and relatively inexpensive. Finally, experiments had to be structured so that students could answer a common set of questions. Technological and practical limitations made it impossible to observe and grade the actual conduct of experiments; therefore scoring the hands-on blocks would be based on the grading of student responses to a series of test questions based on the experiment they had conducted.

The development effort began by setting practical limits on the types of materials that could be part of the hands-on kits. The cost of the kits was required to fit budgetary limits. Materials were required to be non-toxic, and no live organisms were allowed.

These seem to be commonsense decisions, but developers had little experience on which to base rules for such large-scale performance assessment, and performance assessments of this sort are rife with unexpected lessons. For example, the program intended to forbid live organisms. However, developers discovered that some of the soil used in a "soil test" experiment had developed mold and that some of the acorns in a "seed sorting" task had developed worms.

The extent and specificity of instructions became a key development issue. Some developers believed that scientific enquiry would be measured best if the tasks were comparatively open. However, prototype tasks showed that test-takers tended to get lost in relatively open tasks and that it was difficult to determine whether they had completed enough of the experiment to answer a fixed set of questions. Therefore tasks were made to resemble "scripts," in which students would perform parts of the experiments, answer related questions, and then be moved, by the printed instructions, to other parts of the experiments and other questions.

That decision has been questioned, and concerns have been raised about the "authenticity" of NAEP hands-on science. It is clearly true that the NAEP hands-on blocks do not allow the degree of free inquiry of much scientific experimentation. However, given other constraints, this was the only practical decision. It is possible that computer-simulated experiments will make it possible to avoid some of these limitations in future assessments.

Normally, as part of the NAEP balanced incomplete block (BIB) design, all blocks are balanced by position (that is, a block occurs in all possible positions in an assessment booklet an equal number of times). Hands-on science could not be placed into this design. It would have been disruptive to students doing other parts of the assessment if some of their classmates were conducting experiments. Therefore it was determined that the hands-on component should be the last block in all assessment booklets. Examples of hands-on tasks can be viewed on the NAEP website (nces.ed.gov/nationsreportcard).

The development of hands-on assessment components for large-scale use represented a radical new direction in NAEP. The development process was revised to include intermediate steps for trying out tasks on children. Operational and development concerns were interwoven as never before. In the end, the effort proved successful: In 1996 hands-on experiments were administered to roughly 150,000 students, and hands-on science items were included in the scale on which results were reported.

The use of the two types of innovative blocks in NAEP science — the hands-on and theme blocks — coupled with the extensive use of constructed-response questions, had several major implications for the assessment. Because it was still important to cover the science domain described in the framework and because theme blocks and hands-on experiments were not effective vehicles for domain coverage, the aggregate assessment became quite long. At grade eight, for example, the 1996 operational science pool contained 450 minutes (seven and one-half hours) of assessment (each student took 90 minutes of this). This compares to 225 minutes in reading and 195 minutes in mathematics at eighth grade. This aggregate length, combined with the extensive use of constructed-response questions and hands-on kits, has rendered the science assessment the most expensive of NAEP's state-level subjects. This was an issue that the program had to contend with in later years.

*Innovations in Geography and U.S. History Assessment:* In 1991-92, NAGB produced new frameworks for the geography and U.S. history assessments to be given in 1994. Previous NAEP assessments in history and geography focused on core knowledge and were composed almost exclusively of multiple-choice questions. The new frameworks envisioned very different assessments. In geography, for example, students were to be assessed not just on their knowledge of places and physical phenomena and on their map-reading skills, but also on their ability to use the basic tools of the discipline, including atlases. In addition to testing students' abilities to interpret maps and graphics, they would be asked to create their own maps.

The U.S. history and geography assessments included multiple-choice, short constructed-response, and extended constructed-response questions. All open-ended items allowed partial-credit scoring. The assessments were composed of two sorts of blocks. "General content and skills" blocks, each taking 25 minutes, made up the bulk of the assessment (and at grade 4 made up the entire assessment). At grades 8 and 12, these were augmented by a 50-minute theme block, in which students worked in depth on a single topic. For example, at grade 12 in the U.S. history assessment, some students spent the entire assessment period reviewing documents about the Great Depression and answering sets of related questions.

Substantial effort was spent finding authentic materials for these assessments. For example, a diary excerpt was used on the fourth-grade U.S. history assessment. Primary historical sources were used throughout. On the geography assessment, students were asked to create maps, charts, and graphs from either sets of instructions or from written descriptions.

The geography assessment also attempted to measure students' ability to use the atlas. One of the blocks at each grade was an atlas-based block, which meant that between one-third and one-fifth of the sampled students in the assessment answered a set of questions that required an atlas. Use of the atlas also allowed for the measurement of other outcomes. Color plays a key role in maps, and the atlas allowed NAEP to use color maps as stimuli. Atlases also allowed the synthesis of information from a variety of maps. One example of an atlas-based question is shown below:

> Study the maps of the Middle East on pages 64 and 65 of the atlas. Using the maps, explain why the Suez Canal is both politically and economically important.

*Innovations in Other Assessments:* Instrument innovation during the 1992 to 2002 period reached its peak in two other subject-areas. In the arts, "true" performance assessment was used. Students created works of visual art, played musical instruments, or acted in theater exercises. The results of their work were, depending on the task, videotaped, audiotaped, or photographed. In the arts, NAEP used multiple scoring guides to measure different traits in a single performance (a music task, for example, might be scored for rhythmic accuracy and tone).

To highlight the innovative nature of the assessment, the *1997 Nation's Report Card in the Arts* was released primarily as a CD-ROM, and exemplary student performances were included. However, because the subject was a bit "off the beaten track," compared to mathematics, reading, science, and the social studies, this assessment may have been less influential than others. In addition, the nature of the tasks led to psychometric compromises not used in other subjects. Items that assessed knowledge of music were not placed in the same scale as those measuring performance.

Another NAEP innovation was computer-delivered assessment. The most forward-looking of the computer-based projects, titled "Problem Solving in Technology Rich Environments," covers some of the same ground as the hands-on science tasks. This model project includes two tasks. In the first, students search the Internet for information about weather balloons. The belief is that searching the Internet for valid data will become a key study skill. In the second task, students use simulated experiments to answer questions about the workings of weather balloons. These simulated experiments give students experimental freedom not available to them on the hands-on component of the science assessment. Such simulations might allow NAEP, some day, to avoid the costs associated with buying science kits for all assessed students. This study was administered in spring 2003.

## Innovations in Data Dissemination

Sharing information with secondary users has long been a central goal of the NAEP program. The use of plausible values, rather than marginal estimates of population performance, originally was intended to provide secondary analysts with a data file that they could use. Since 1983 restricted-use files were available for licensed users of NAEP data; and in some cases, public-use files were created as well.

However, before the mid-1990s the best intentions could not eliminate some basic flaws in the dissemination of data and test material. Released test questions could be obtained; but the process involved completing a Department of Education form, paying a nominal fee, and requesting photocopies of the questions. In the case of assessment data, using NAEP secondary analyses involved substantial skill and computing power, which created a real barrier for analysts. Data files were large and inefficient to store and use; and it was a large job to do even simple analyses, such as cross-tabulations.

In these years, NAEP disseminated printed reports for the non-expert reader and the policy maker. These reports included selected tabular summaries and discussions of differences (whether within-year or over time) that were statistically significant. However, whereas they are easy to use, there are problems with relying on printed reports. Printing realities set limitations on the number of tables and variables that could be included in reports. The information included in the reports represented judgments made by the authors, and readers might be interested in other information. Shipping and printing costs place other limits on the effectiveness of printed reports.

The situation improved in the early and mid-1990s. Data sets could be distributed on CD-ROM. The *NAEPEX* computer program allowed users to easily extract data from the larger files. Modules wrote the control statements needed to do cross-tabulations and regression analyses in the standard SAS and SPSS statistical software packages. Later, the American Institutes for Research (AIR) developed the *AM* system, allowing population estimates to be obtained with or without plausible values. However, these tools were intended for a relatively small number of expert users.

Between the two extremes — the expert statistical analyst and the reader interested in only a small number of main variables — was a huge range of potential users of NAEP data. Their needs might not be sophisticated; for example, they might want simple cross-tabulations of an instructional variable, such as those taking a mathematics course, with key reporting categories, such as sex or ethnicity. In each of these cross-tabulations, people traditionally want to see the percentages ("what percentage of female eighth-graders were taking algebra"), the scaled scores achieved by these populations, and the percentages of these populations that met or exceeded achievement level cut-scores.

There was a data source that would have met most of these needs, but it was used internally at ETS and was impossible to disseminate on a mass basis. After analyses were conducted, "almanacs" would be produced for report writers. These almanacs contained cross-tabulations. In any given table, columns were defined by a NAEP background variable (which might range from course-taking to television watching to teacher qualifications), and rows were defined by the "major reporting groups." While these groups varied over time, they always included sex, ethnicity, school type, region, and geographic location (urban/suburban/rural).

Although invaluable to report writers, these almanacs were not useful to the broader public. There was no systematic way to search the data. The almanacs were designed for ETS use and relied on internal jargon. In the early 1990s ETS and NCES distributed these almanacs (first on paper and then as files on diskette) to participating states, but there is little record of the almanacs being used.

The rise of the Internet created the possibility for far broader dissemination of NAEP data. Beginning in 1995, data almanacs from the 1994 assessments were posted on the Web. However, these were Portable Document Format (PDF) files that represented simple snapshots of the printed almanacs. Whereas the public could now access the almanacs, the limitations inherent in the almanacs remained. In addition, it was not easy to download data in a way that could be used to conduct subsequent analyses, or even to include these data in presentations.

With the release of the 1996 data, PDF almanacs again were released, this time with an improved "front end" that made it possible to search the data in a limited manner. However, the search was designed for people who knew the NAEP system. For example, the first search parameter was assessment year, which only makes sense if a user knows in which years NAEP assessed a given subject. In addition, the PDF files retained their inherent limitations.

For data released in conjunction with the 1998 assessments, ETS designers took a major step forward by restructuring the data files as Hypertext Markup Language (HTML) files. For the first time, users were given some flexibility in determining what data should be included in a table. However, this system also had limitations. The HTML files made it possible to download data, but the single-column format (means and standard errors, for example) made it difficult and cumbersome to conduct calculations in spreadsheet programs. In addition, the parentheses traditionally placed around standard-error estimates were interpreted as negative numbers in spreadsheets. Ability to search the data still was very limited.

Faced with these issues, ETS and NCES determined that an entirely new system was needed. The new system would allow users to search all NAEP data without needing to know in what years an assessment was given. It would use search categories that have intrinsic meaning, rather than refer to the instruments by which data was collected. Users would have control over the contents of tables, and data would be easy to load into common spreadsheet and word-processing programs. Interfaces would be simple to use and would use common web conventions. After a 12-month development effort, the new system was released in conjunction with the 2000 mathematics results and now can be seen on the NAEP website.

One key difference between the new data tool and earlier systems is that users can determine what data are in a table. In addition, all data in the columns easily can be used in spreadsheet programs (in fact, data are "drag and drop" compatible). If data are imported into spreadsheets, all numbers come with full precision and not just at the integer-level shown. Expert users can choose to display subscales, instead of composite scales, and can conduct statistical significance tests to control for the false discovery rate (FDR), the procedure used by NAEP. In fact, the ability to search data online has been as useful for the authors of NAEP reports as it has for the general public.

This system represents a major revolution in data dissemination. Thousands of people visit the web tool each month, and state NAEP coordinators have been trained in its use. In addition, a web-based tool for disseminating released test questions is available and has become the single most visited portion of the NAEP website. Future versions of the tool will have an enhanced graphics capacity and will include the ability to create tables and results not included in the current database of summarized results.

NAEP needed to move beyond standard publishing as the mode of releasing results. Not only are NAEP data now used by more people than ever before, but the new demands on NAEP require results to be issued more quickly. To meet these needs, the assessment will continue to be on the forefront of new technologies.

# REFERENCES

Abelson, R.P.; Coffman, W.E.; Jones, L.V.; Mosteller, F.; and Tukey, J.W. *National Assessment of Educational Progress Report 4, 1969-70: Science: Group Results for Sex, Region, and Size of Community.* Washington, D.C.: U.S. Government Printing Office, 1971.

Abelson, R.P.; Cronbach, L.J.; Jones, L.V.; Tukey, J.W.; and Tyler, R.W. *National Assessment of Educational Progress, Report 1: 1969-1970 Science: National Results and Illustrations of Group Comparisons.* Denver: Education Commission of the States, 1970.

Achtermann, V. *Operations Documentation Report: Adult Assessment, Years 01-04.* Denver: Education Commission of the States, 1974.

Ahmann, J.S. *How Much Are Our Young People Learning? The Story of the National Assessment.* Fastback 68. Bloomington, Ind.: Phi Delta Kappa Educational Foundation, 1976.

Alexander, L., and James, H.T., eds. *The Nation's Report Card: Improving Assessment of Student Achievement. Report of the Study Group, with a Review of the Report by a Committee of the National Academy of Education.* Cambridge, Mass.: National Academy of Education, 1987.

Allen, N.L.; Carlson, J.E.; and Zelenak, C.A. *The NAEP 1996 Technical Report.* NCES 1999-452. Washington, D.C.: National Center for Education Statistics, 1999.

Allen, N.L.; Donoghue, J.R.; and Schoeps, T.L. *The NAEP 1998 Technical Report.* NCES 2001-509. Washington, D.C.: National Center for Education Statistics, 2001.

Allen, N.L.; Jenkins, F.; Kulick, E.; and Zelenak, C.A. *Technical Report of the NAEP 1996 State Assessment Program in Mathematics.* NCES 97-951. Washington, D.C.: National Center for Education Statistics, 1997.

Allen, N.L., and Johnson, E.G. "Overview of Part I: The Design and Implementation of the 1996 NAEP." In *The NAEP 1996 Technical Report*, edited by N.L. Allen, J.E. Carlson, and C.A. Zelenak. Washington, D.C.: National Center for Education Statistics, 1999.

Allen, N.L.; Kline, D.L.; and Zelenak, C.A. *The NAEP 1994 Technical Report*. NCES 97-897. Washington, D.C.: National Center for Education Statistics, 1996.

American College Testing Program. *Setting Achievement Levels on the 1992 National Assessment of Educational Progress in Reading, Mathematics, and Writing: Design Document*. Iowa City, 1992.

American College Testing Program. *Setting Achievement Levels on the 1992 National Assessment of Educational Progress in Mathematics, Reading, and Writing: A Technical Report on Reliability and Validity*. Iowa City, 1993.

Angoff, W.A. Personal communication with NAGB, dated 20 December 1989. Available from the National Assessment Governing Board, 800 N Capitol Street, Suite 825, Washington, DC 20002-4233.

Applebee, A.N.; Langer, J.A.; Jenkins, L.B.; Mullis, I.V.S.; and Foertsch, M.A. *Learning to Write in Our Nation's Schools: Instruction and Achievement in 1988 at Grades 4, 8, and 12*. Princeton, N.J.: Educational Testing Service, 1990.

Beaton, A.E., ed. *Implementing the New Design: The NAEP 1983-84 Technical Report*. Princeton, N.J.: Educational Testing Service, 1987.

Beaton, A.E., ed. *Expanding the New Design: The NAEP 1985-86 Technical Report*. Princeton, N.J.: Educational Testing Service, 1988. a

Beaton, A.E. *The NAEP 1985-86 Reading Anomaly: A Technical Report*. Princeton, N.J.: Educational Testing Service, 1988. b

Beaton, A.E. Personal communication with NAGB, dated 7 November 1989. Available from the National Assessment Governing Board, 800 N Capitol Street, Suite 825, Washington, DC 20002-4233.

Beaton, A.E., and Allen, N.L. "Interpreting Scales Through Scale Anchoring." *Journal of Educational Statistics* 17 (1992): 191-204.

Beaton, A.E., and Gonzalez, E. *The NAEP Primer*. Chestnut Hill, Mass.: Boston College, 1995.

Beaton, A.E., and Johnson, E.G. "The Average Response Method (ARM) of Scaling." *Journal of Educational Statistics* 15 (1990): 9-38.

Beaton, A.E., and Johnson, E.G. "Overview of the Scaling Methodology Used in the National Assessment." *Journal of Educational Measurement* 29 (1992): 163-75.

Beaton, A.E., and Zwick, R. *The Effect of Changes in the National Assessment: Disentangling the NAEP 1985-86 Reading Anomaly.* No. 17-TR-21. Princeton, N.J.: Educational Testing Service, 1990.

Beaton, A.E., and Zwick, R. "Overview of the National Assessment of Educational Progress." *Journal of Educational Statistics* 17 (1992): 95-109.

Benjamini, Y., and Hochberg, Y. "Controlling the False Discovery Rate: A Practical and Powerful Approach to Multiple Testing." *Journal of the Royal Statistical Society Series B* 57, no. 1 (1994): 289-300.

Bock, R.D.; Mislevy, R.J.; and Woodson, C.E. "The Next Stage in Educational Assessment." *Educational Researcher* 11, no. 3 (1982): 4-11, 16.

Bourque, M.L., ed. *Proceedings of the Joint Conference on Standard Setting for Large-Scale Assessment.* Washington, D.C.: National Assessment Governing Board and the National Center for Education Statistics, 1995.

Bourque, M.L. "The Role of the National Assessment of Educational Progress (NAEP) in Setting, Reflecting, and Linking National Education Policy to States' Needs." In *Handbook of Educational Policy*, edited by G.J. Cizek. San Diego: Academic Press, 1999.

Bourque, M.L., and Byrd, S., eds. *Student Performance Standards on the National Assessment of Educational Progress: Affirmations and Improvements.* Washington, D.C.: National Assessment Governing Board, 2000.

Bourque, M.L., and Garrison, H. *The Levels of Mathematics Achievement.* vol. 1. Washington, D.C.: National Assessment Governing Board, 1991. a

Bourque, M.L., and Garrison, H. *The Levels of Mathematics Achievement.* vol. 2. Washington, D.C.: National Assessment Governing Board, 1991. b

Brennan, R.L., and Johnson, E.G. "Generalizability of Performance Assessments." *Educational Measurement: Issues and Practice* 14, no. 4 (1995): 9-12.

Brillinger, D.R. "Approximate Estimation of the Standard Errors of Complex Statistics Based on Sample Surveys." *New Zealand Statistician* 11, no. 2 (1977): 35-41.

Bryant, E.C.; Glaser, E.; Hansen, M.H.; and Kirsch, A. *Associations Between Educational Outcomes and Background Variables: A Review of the Literature.* Rockville, Md.: Westat, 1974.

Burstein, L.; Koretz, D.M.; Linn, R.L.; Baker, E.L.; Sugrue, B.; Novak, J.; and Lewis, E. "Describing Performance Standards: The Validity of the 1992 NAEP Achievement Level Descriptors as Characterizations of Mathematics Performance." *Educational Assessment* 3 (1995/1996): 9-51.

Burstein, L.; Koretz, D.M.; Linn, R.L.; Sugrue, B.; Novak, J.; Lewis, E.; and Baker, E.L. *The Validity of Interpretations of the 1992 NAEP Achievement Levels in Mathematics.* Technical Report. Los Angeles: UCLA Center for the Study of Evaluation, August 1993.

Campbell, V.; Nichols, D.; Ferris, M.; Sawyer, S.; and Bond, R. *National Assessment of Educational Progress, Report 2. Citizenship: National Results.* Denver: Education Commission of the States, 1970.

Cannell, J.J. *Nationally Normed Elementary Achievement Testing in America's Public Schools: How All Fifty States Are Above the National Average.* Albuquerque, N.M.: Friends of Education, 1984.

Carnegie Corporation. "The Gross Educational Product: How Much Are Students Learning?" *Carnegie Quarterly* 14 (Spring 1966): 1-4.

Chromy, J.R. *Some Problems with Large Weights.* Research Triangle Park, N.C.: Research Triangle Institute, 1970.

Chromy, J.R., and Horvitz, D.G. "Appendix C. Structure of Sampling and Weighting." In *National Assessment of Educational Progress Report 1, 1969-70: Science: National Results and Illustrations of Group Comparisons,* edited by R.P Abelson, L.J. Cronbach, L.V. Jones, J.W. Tukey, and R.W. Tyler. Washington, D.C.: U.S. Government Printing Office, 1970.

Chromy, J.R., and Horvitz, D.G. "The Use of Monetary Incentives in National Assessment Household Surveys." *Journal of the American Statistical Association* 73 (1978): 473-78.

Chromy, J.R.; Moore, R.P.; and Clemmer, A.F. "Design Effects in the National Assessment of Educational Progress Study." *Proceedings of the American Statistical Association, Social Statistics Section* (1972): 48-52.

Cizek, G.J. "Reactions to the National Academy of Education Report: Setting Performance Standards for Student Achievement." Report. 1993. Available from the National Assessment Governing Board, 800 N Capitol Street, Suite 825, Washington, DC 20002-4233.

Cochran, W.G. *Sampling Techniques*. 2nd ed. New York: John Wiley & Sons, 1963.

Cohen, A.S.; Kane, M.T.; and Crooks, T.J. "A Generalized Examinee-Centered Method for Setting Standards on Achievement Tests." *Applied Measurement in Education* 14 (1999): 343-66.

Cohen, J., and Jiang, T. *Direct Estimation of Latent Distributions for Large-Scale Assessments with Application to the National Assessment of Educational Progress (NAEP)*. Washington, D.C.: American Institutes for Research, 2001.

Cohen, J.; Johnson, E.G.; and Angeles, J. *Variance Estimation When Sampling in Two Dimensions Via the Jackknife with Application to the National Assessment of Educational Progress*. Washington, D.C.: American Institutes for Research, 2000.

Coleman, J.S., et al. *Equality of Educational Opportunity*. Washington, D.C.: U.S. Department of Health, Education and Welfare, 1966.

Committee on Assessing the Progress of Education. *CAPE Newsletter* 2 (May 1969). a

Committee on Assessing the Progress of Education. *National Assessment of Educational Progress: Citizenship Objectives*. Ann Arbor, Mich., 1969. b

Comptroller General of the United States. *The National Assessment of Educational Progress: Its Results Need to Be Made More Useful*. Washington, D.C.: U.S. General Accounting Office, 1976.

Conant, J.B. *Shaping Educational Policy*. New York: McGraw-Hill, 1964.

Council of Great City Schools. "Proposal to Conduct Trial NAEP Assessment for Large Urban School Districts." Washington, D.C., 17 November 2000.

Cox, G.M. *A Methodological Study of In-School Versus Out-of-School Administration of Test Items*. Research Triangle Park, N.C.: Research Triangle Institute, 1968.

DeVito, P.J., and Koenig, J.A., eds. *NAEP Reporting Practices: Investigating District-Level and Market-Basket Reporting*. Washington, D.C.: Committee on NAEP Reporting Practices, Board on Testing and Assessment, National Research Council, 2001.

Dossey, J.A.; Mullis, I.V.S.; and Jones, C.O. *Can Students Do Mathematical Problem Solving?* Princeton, N.J.: Educational Testing Service, 1993.

Educational Testing Service. *ETS Sensitivity Review Process*. Princeton, N.J., 1986.

Educational Testing Service. *ETS Standards for Quality and Fairness.* Princeton, N.J., 1987. a

Educational Testing Service. *Learning by Doing: A Manual for Teaching and Assessing Higher-Order Thinking in Science and Mathematics.* Princeton, N.J., 1987. b

Elmore, R., and Rothman, R. *Testing, Teaching and Learning: A Guide for States and School Districts.* Washington, D.C.: National Academy Press, 1999.

Feuer, M.J.; Holland, P.W.; Green, B.F.; Bertenthal, M.W.; and Hemphill, F.C., eds. *Uncommon Measures: Equivalence and Linkage Among Educational Tests.* Washington, D.C.: National Academy Press, 1999.

Finkner, A.L. "Presentation to the Executive Committee of the RTI Board of Governors." 1968.

Finkner, A.L. "National Assessment of Educational Progress: The Sample and Assessment Methods." Paper presented at the 1969 Annual Meeting of the American Psychological Association, Washington, D.C., 1969.

Finkner, A.L. "NAEP Winddown." Research Triangle Institute memorandum. 1983.

Finley, C.J., and Berdie, F.S. *The National Assessment Approach to Exercise Development.* Denver: National Assessment of Educational Progress, 1970.

Fitzharris, L.H. "An Historical Review of the National Assessment of Educational Progress from 1963 to 1991." Doctoral dissertation, University of South Carolina, 1993.

Flanagan, J., and Jung, S. "Evaluating a Comprehensive Educational System." Presentation at the American Institutes for Research Seminar, Evaluative Research: Strategies and Methods. Washington, D.C., January 1970.

Foertsch, M.A.; Jones, L.R.; and Koffler, S.L. "Developing the NAEP Objectives, Items, and Background Questions for the 1990 Assessment of Reading, Mathematics, and Science." In *The NAEP 1990 Technical Report*, edited by E.G. Johnson and N. L. Allen. Princeton, N.J.: Educational Testing Service, 1992.

Folsom, R.E., Jr. *Sampling Error Monograph: National Assessment Approach to Sampling Error Estimation.* Research Triangle Park, N.C.: Research Triangle Institute, 1974.

Forsyth, R.A. "Do NAEP Results Yield Valid Criterion-Referenced Interpretations?" *Educational Measurement: Issues and Practice* 10 (1991): 3-9, 16.

Forsyth, R.A.; Hambleton, R.K.; Linn, R.L.; Mislevy, R.J.; and Yen, W. *Design/Feasibility Team: Report to the National Assessment Governing Board*. Washington, D.C., 1996.

Gadway, C.J., and Wilson, H.A. *Functional Literacy: Basic Reading Performance*. Denver: National Assessment of Educational Progress, 1976.

General Accounting Office. *Educational Achievement Standards: NAGB's Approach Yields Misleading Interpretations*. Report No. GAO/PEMD-93-12. Washington, D.C., 1993.

Gentile, C.A.; Martin-Rehrmann, J.; and Kennedy, J.H. *Windows into the Classroom: NAEP's 1992 Writing Portfolio Study*. Washington, D.C.: Educational Testing Service, 1995.

Glaser, R. "Commentary by the National Academy of Education." In *The Nation's Report Card: Improving Assessment of Student Achievement. Report of the Study Group, with a Review of the Report by a Committee of the National Academy of Education*, edited by L. Alexander and H.T. James. Cambridge, Mass.: National Academy of Education, 1987.

Glaser, R.; Linn, R.L.; and Bohrnstedt, G.W. *Assessing Achievement in the States*. Stanford, Calif.: National Academy of Education, 1992.

Glaser, R.; Linn, R.L.; and Bohrnstedt, G.W. *Setting Performance Standards for Student Achievement*. Stanford, Calif.: National Academy of Education, 1993. a

Glaser, R.; Linn, R.L.; and Bohrnstedt, G.W. *The Trial State Assessment: Prospects and Realities*. Stanford, Calif.: National Academy of Education, 1993. b

Glaser, R.; Linn, R.L.; and Bohrnstedt, G.W. *Quality and Utility: The 1994 Trial State Assessment in Reading*. Stanford, Calif.: National Academy of Education, 1996.

Glaser, R.; Linn, R.L.; and Bohrnstedt, G.W. *Assessment in Transition: Monitoring the Nation's Educational Progress*. Stanford, Calif.: National Academy of Education, 1997.

Gordon, G.B. "National Assessment Feasibility Study." Unpublished report to the Exploratory Committee on Assessing the Progress of Education. Princeton, N.J.: Educational Testing Service, June 1967.

Goslin, D.A. *The Search for Ability: Standardized Testing in Social Perspective*. New York: Russell Sage Foundation, 1963.

Greenbaum, W.; Garet, M.S.; and Solomon, E. *Measuring Educational Progress*. New York: McGraw-Hill, 1977.

Greenberg, E.; Stancavage, F.B.; Farr, B.; and Bohrnstedt, G.W. "Making Comparisons: Using Background Information from the Nation's Report Card to Understand Student Achievement." Draft document. Washington, D.C.: American Institutes for Research, January 2001.

Greenwald, E.A.; Persky, H.R.; Campbell, J.R.; and Mazzeo, J. *Writing: NAEP 1998 Report Card for the Nation and the States*. Washington, D.C.: Educational Testing Service, 1999.

Grissmer, D.W., and Flannagan, A. "Improving the NAEP Data for Policy Analysis." Draft prepared for the National Center for Education Statistics. Washington, D.C., 1997.

Haertel, E.H. *Report of the NAEP Technical Review Panel on the 1986 Reading Anomaly, the Accuracy of NAEP Trends, and Issues Raised by State-Level NAEP Comparisons*. National Center for Education Statistics Technical Report CS 89-499. Washington, D.C.: U.S. Department of Education, Office of Educational Research and Improvement, 1989.

Hambleton, R.K. *Technical Proposal*. Amherst, Mass.: Laboratory for Psychometric and Evaluative Research, 1990. Available from the National Assessment Governing Board, 800 N Capitol Street, Suite 825, Washington, DC 20002-4233.

Hambleton, R.K. *Setting Achievement Levels on the 1990 NAEP Mathematics Assessment: Response to Technical Criticisms*. Laboratory of Psychometric and Evaluative Research Report No. 217. Amherst, Mass.: University of Massachusetts, 1993.

Hambleton, R.K. *Setting Achievement Levels for Reporting NAEP Scores: A Look Back to 1990*. Laboratory of Psychometric and Evaluative Research Report No. 380. Amherst, Mass.: University of Massachusetts, 2000.

Hambleton, R.K., and Bourque, M.L. *The Levels of Mathematics Achievement: Technical Report*. Washington, D.C.: National Assessment Governing Board, 1991.

Hambleton, R.K.; Brennan, R.L.; Brown, W.; Dodd, B.; Forsyth, R.A.; Mehrens, W.A.; Nellhaus, J.; Reckase, M.; Ridone, D.; van der Linden, W.; and Zwick, R. "A Response to 'Setting Reasonable and Useful Performance Standards' in the National Academy of Sciences' *Grading the Nation's Report Card." Educational Measurement: Issues and Practice* 19, no. 2 (2000): 5-14.

Hambleton, R.K., and Meara, K. "Newspaper Coverage of NAEP Results, 1990 to 1998." In *Student Performance Standards on the National Assessment of Educational Progress: Affirmation and Improvements*, edited by M.L. Bourque and S. Byrd. Washington, D.C.: National Assessment Governing Board, 2000.

Hambleton, R.K., and Plake, B.S. "Using an Extended Angoff Procedure to Set Standards on Complex Assessments." *Applied Measurement in Education* 8 (1995): 41-56.

Hazlett, J.A. "A History of the National Assessment of Educational Progress, 1963-1973." Doctoral dissertation, University of Kansas, 1974.

Hazlett, J.A.; Ahmann, J.S.; and Johnson, G.H. *National Assessment of Educational Progress: Five Year Plan, Fiscal Years 1975 to 1979.* Denver: Education Commission of the States, 1973.

Hendricks, W.A. "The Relative Efficiencies of Groups of Farms as Sampling Units." *Journal of the American Statistical Association* 39 (1944): 367-76.

Heubert, J.P., and Hauser, R.M. *High Stakes: Testing for Tracking, Promotion, and Graduation.* Washington, D.C.: National Academy Press, 1999.

Horvitz, D.G., and Thompson, D.J. "A Generalization of Sampling Without Replacement from a Finite Universe." *Journal of the American Statistical Association* 47 (1952): 663-85.

House Education and the Workforce Committee. *Fact Sheet: H.R. 1 Conference Report Highlights, Accountability for Student Achievement.* Washington, D.C., 10 December 2001.

Impara, J.C., and Plake, B.S. "Standard Setting: An Alternative Approach." *Journal of Educational Measurement* 34 (1997): 353-66.

Jessen, R.J. "Statistical Investigation of a Sample Survey for Obtaining Farm Facts." *Iowa Agricultural Experiment Station Research Bulletin* 304 (1942).

Jessen, R.J. "Probability Sampling with Marginal Constraints." *Journal of the American Statistical Association* 65 (1970): 776-96.

Johnson, E.G. "Adjustment of Respondent Weights by Smoothing to Reduce Random Variability of Estimated Population Proportions of Reporting Groups." In *General Information Yearbook: 1980.* Denver: National Assessment of Educational Progress, 1980.

Johnson, E.G. "Considerations and Techniques for the Analysis of NAEP Data." *Journal of Educational Statistics* 14 (1989): 303-34.

Johnson, E.G. Memorandum for the Record, dated 13 December 1990. Available from the National Assessment Governing Board, 800 N Capitol Street, Suite 825, Washington, DC 20002-4233.

Johnson, E.G. "The Design of the National Assessment of Educational Progress." *Journal of Educational Measurement* 29 (1992): 95-110.

Johnson, E.G. *Standard Errors for Below-State Reporting of NAEP.* Washington, D.C.: National Assessment Governing Board, 1994.

Johnson, E.G., and Allen, N.L. *The NAEP 1990 Technical Report.* No. 21-TR-20. Princeton, N.J.: Educational Testing Service, National Assessment of Educational Progress, 1992.

Johnson, E.G.; Burke, J.; Braden, J.; Hansen, M.H.; Lago, J.; and Tepping, B. "Weighting Procedures and Variance Estimation." In *Expanding the New Design: The NAEP 1985-86 Technical Report*, edited by A.E. Beaton. Princeton, N.J.: Educational Testing Service, 1988.

Johnson, E.G.; Carlson, J.; and Kline, D.L., eds. *The NAEP 1994 Technical Report.* Washington, D.C.: National Center for Education Statistics, 1994.

Johnson, E.G.; Lazer, S.; and O'Sullivan, C. *NAEP Reconfigured: An Integrated Redesign of the National Assessment of Educational Progress.* Washington, D.C.: National Center for Education Statistics, 1997.

Johnson, E.G., and Rust, K.. "Population Inferences and Variance Estimation for NAEP Data." *Journal of Educational Statistics* 17 (1992): 175-90.

Johnson, E.G., and Zwick, R. *Focusing the New Design: The NAEP 1988 Technical Report.* No. 19-TR-20. Princeton, N.J.: Educational Testing Service, 1990.

Jones, L.V. "A History of the National Assessment of Educational Progress and Some Questions About Its Future." *Educational Researcher* 25, no. 7 (1996): 15-22.

Jones, L.V., and Olkin, I., eds. *NAEP Inclusion Strategies: The Report of a Workshop at the National Institute of Statistical Sciences.* Research Triangle Park, N.C.: National Institute of Statistical Sciences, 2000.

Kane, M. *Comments on the NAE Evaluation of the NAGB Achievement Levels.* Washington, D.C.: National Assessment Governing Board, 1993. a

Kane, M. *The Validity of Performance Standards*. Washington, D.C.: National Assessment Governing Board, 1993. b

Keppel, F. *The Necessary Revolution in American Education*. New York: Harper & Row, 1966.

Kirst, M.W. "Roles, Governance, and Multiple Use for a New NAEP." Paper prepared for the Alexander-James Study Group, 1986. ERIC document ED 279704.

Kish, L., and Frankel, M.R. "Inference from Complex Samples." *Journal of the Royal Statistical Society* B36 (1974): 1-37.

Knapp, T. "Tom Knapp's Packaging Proposal." Notes presented to the Technical Advisory Committee of ECAPE, 1968.

Koretz, D.M.; Bertenthal, M.W.; and Green, B.F., eds. *Embedding Questions: The Pursuit of a Common Measure in Uncommon Tests*. Washington, D.C.: National Academy Press, 1999.

Lagemann, E.C. *The Politics of Knowledge: The Carnegie Corporation, Philanthropy, and Public Policy*. Middletown, Conn.: Wesleyan University Press, 1989.

Larrabee, C.X. *Many Missions: Research Triangle Institute's First 31 Years*. Research Triangle Park, N.C., 1991.

Layton, D.H. "The Education Commission of the States Experiment in Interstate Cooperation." Doctoral dissertation, University of Chicago, 1972.

Layton, D.H. "Tenth Birthday for the Education Commission of the States." *Phi Delta Kappan* 57 (September 1975): 45-47.

Layton, D.H. "ECS at 20: New Vitality and New Possibilities." *Phi Delta Kappan* 67 (December 1985): 272-76.

Lehmann, I.J. "SES Classification." Memorandum to CAPE Consultants and TAC, 18 October 1968.

Lewis, D.M.; Green, D.R.; Mitzel, H.C.; Baum, K.; and Patz, R.J. "The Bookmark Standard Setting Procedure: Methodology and Recent Implementations." Paper presented at the National Council on Measurement in Education Annual Meeting, San Diego, 1998.

Linn, R.L. "State-By-State Comparisons of Achievement: Suggestions for Enhancing Validity." *Educational Researcher* 17, no. 3 (1988): 6-9.

Linn, R.L.; Baker, E.L.; and Burstein, L. *The Validity and Credibility of the Achievement Levels for the 1990 National Assessment of Educational Progress in Mathematics*. Los Angeles: Center for Research on Evaluation, Standards and Student Testing, UCLA, 1991.

Linn, R.L.; Baker, E.L.; and Dunbar, S. "Complex, Performance-Based Assessment: Expectations and Validation Criteria." *Educational Researcher* 20, no. 8 (1991): 15-21.

Linn, R.L., and Dunbar, S.B. "Issues in the Design and Reporting of the National Assessment of Educational Progress." *Journal of Educational Measurement* 29 (1992): 177-94.

Linn, R.L.; Koretz, D.; and Baker, E.L. *Assessing the Validity of the National Assessment of Educational Progress: Final Report of the NAEP Technical Review Panel.* Los Angeles: Center for Research on Evaluation, Standards and Student Testing, UCLA, 1995.

Linn, R.L.; Koretz, D.; Baker, E.L.; and Burstein, L. *The Validity and Reliability of the Achievement Levels for the National Assessment of Educational Progress in Mathematics.* Los Angeles: Center for the Study of Evaluation, UCLA, 1991.

Loomis, S., and Bourque, M.L. "From Tradition to Innovation: Standard Setting on the National Assessment of Educational Progress." In *Standard Setting: Concepts, Methods, and Perspectives,* edited by G. Cizek. Mahwah, N.J.: Lawrence Erlbaum Associates, 2001.

Lutkus, A.D. *Including Special-Needs Students in the NAEP 1998 Reading Assessment.* Washington, D.C.: National Center for Education Statistics, 2003.

Mahalanobis, P.C. "On Large-Scale Sample Surveys." *Philosophical Transactions of the Royal Society of London* B 231 (1944): 329-451.

Martin, M.O., and Kelly, D.L., eds. *The Third International Mathematics and Science Study Technical Report, Volume II: Implementation and Analysis, Primary and Middle School Years.* Chestnut Hill, Mass.: Center for the Study of Testing, Evaluation, and Educational Policy, Boston College, 1997.

Massachusetts Department of Education. *The Massachusetts Comprehensive Assessment System: Summary of District Performance.* Malden, Mass., 1998.

Mazzeo, J.; Carlson, J.E.; Voelkl, K.E.; and Lutkus, A.D. *Increasing the Participation of Special Needs Students in NAEP: A Report on 1996 NAEP Research Activities.* NCES 2000-473. Washington, D.C.: National Center for Education Statistics, 2000.

Mazzeo, J.; Yamamoto, K.; and Kulick, E. "Extended Constructed-Response Items in the 1992 NAEP: Psychometrically Speaking,

Were They Worth the Price?" Paper presented at the annual meeting of the National Council on Measurement in Education, Atlanta, Ga., 1993.

McCarthy, P.J. *Replication. An Approach to the Analysis of Data from Complex Surveys.* U.S. Department of Health, Education and Welfare Vital and Health Statistics Series 2, No. 14. Washington, D.C.: U.S. Government Printing Office, 1966.

Merwin, J.C., and Womer, F.B. "Evaluation in Assessing the Progress of Education to Provide Bases of Public Understanding and Public Policy." In *National Society for the Study of Education Yearbook, Educational Evaluation: New Roles, New Means*, edited by R.W. Tyler. Chicago: University of Chicago Press, 1969.

Messick, S.; Beaton, A.; and Lord, F. *National Assessment of Educational Progress Reconsidered: A New Design for a New Era.* Report 83-10. Princeton, N.J.: Educational Testing Service, 1983.

Mislevy, R.J. "Estimation of Latent Group Effects." *Journal of the American Statistical Association* 80 (1985): 993-97.

Mislevy, R.J. "Randomized-Based Inference About Latent Variables from Complex Samples." *Psychometrika* 56 (1991): 177-96.

Mislevy, R.J., and Bock, R.D. *BILOG: Item Analysis and Test Scoring with Binary Logistic Models.* Computer program. Mooresville, Ind.: Scientific Software, 1982.

Mislevy, R.J.; Johnson, E.G.; and Muraki, E. "Scaling Procedures in NAEP." *Journal of Educational Statistics* 17 (1992): 131-54.

Mitchell, J.H.; Hawkins, E.F.; Stancavage, F.B.; and Dossey, J.A. *Estimation Skills, Mathematics-in-Context, and Advanced Skills in Mathematics: Results from Three Studies of the National Assessment of Educational Progress, 1996 Mathematics Assessment.* Washington, D.C.: U.S. Dept. of Education, Office of Educational Research and Improvement, 1999.

Monroe, J., and Finkner, A.L. *Handbook of Area Sampling.* New York: Chilton, 1959.

Mood, A.M. "National Assessment." *American Education* 3 (1967): 11-12.

Moore, R.P.; Chromy, J.R.; and Rogers, W.T. *The National Assessment Approach to Sampling.* Denver: Education Commission of the States, 1974.

Moore, R.P., and Jones, B.L. "Sampling 17-Year-Olds Not Enrolled in School." *Proceedings of the American Statistical Association* (1973): Social Statistics Section, 359-69.

Mullis, I.V.S.; Johnson, E.G.; and Jenkins, F. *Effective Schools and Instruction in Mathematics*. Washington, D.C.: National Center for Education Statistics, 1994.

Mullis, I.V.S.; MacDonald, W.; and Mead, N.A. "Developing the 1986 National Assessment Objectives, Items, and Background Questions." In *Expanding the New Design: The NAEP 1985-86 Technical Report*, edited by A.E. Beaton. Princeton, N.J.: Educational Testing Service, 1988.

Muraki, E., and Bock, R.D. *PARSCALE: Parameter Scaling of Rating Data*. Computer program. Chicago: Scientific Software, 1991.

Mushkin, S.J. *National Assessment and Social Indicators, January 1973*. Washington D.C.: U.S. Government Printing Office, 1973.

National Assessment Governing Board (NAGB). *Briefing Book, January 27-29, 1989 Meeting*. Washington, D.C., January 1989.

National Assessment Governing Board (NAGB). "Minutes of the August 1990 National Assessment Governing Board Meeting." Washington, D.C., 1990. a

National Assessment Governing Board (NAGB). *Setting Appropriate Achievement Levels for the National Assessment of Educational Progress: Policy Framework and Technical Procedures*. Washington, D.C., 1990. b

National Assessment Governing Board (NAGB). "Report of the Reporting and Dissemination Committee. Minutes of the November 1990 National Assessment Governing Board Meeting." Washington, D.C., November 1990. c

National Assessment Governing Board (NAGB). "Report of the Reporting and Dissemination Committee." Minutes of the March 1991 National Assessment Governing Board Meeting, Washington, D.C., March 1991.

National Assessment Governing Board (NAGB). "Report of the Reporting and Dissemination Committee." Minutes of the March 1992 National Assessment Governing Board Meeting. Washington, D.C., March 1992.

National Assessment Governing Board (NAGB). *Arts Education Assessment and Exercise Specification*. Washington, D.C., 1994. a

National Assessment Governing Board (NAGB). "Report of the Reporting and Dissemination Committee." Minutes of the August 1994 National Assessment Governing Board Meeting. Washington, D.C., August 1994. b

National Assessment Governing Board (NAGB). "Report of the Reporting and Dissemination Committee." Minutes of the November 1994 National Assessment Governing Board Meeting. Washington, D.C., November 1994. c

National Assessment Governing Board (NAGB). "Minutes of the March 1995 National Assessment Governing Board Meeting." Washington, D.C., March 1995. a

National Assessment Governing Board (NAGB). "Report of the Reporting and Dissemination Committee." Minutes of the May 1995 National Assessment Governing Board Meeting. Washington, D.C., May 1995. b

National Assessment Governing Board (NAGB). *Policy Statement on Redesigning the National Assessment of Educational Progress.* Washington, D.C., 1996. a

National Assessment Governing Board (NAGB). "Report of the Reporting and Dissemination Committee." Minutes of the August 1996 National Assessment Governing Board Meeting. Washington, D.C., August 1996. b

National Assessment Governing Board (NAGB). "Report of the Reporting and Dissemination Committee." Minutes of the January 1996 National Assessment Governing Board Meeting. Washington, D.C., January 1996. c

National Assessment Governing Board (NAGB). *Civics Framework for the 1998 National Assessment of Educational Progress.* Washington, D.C., 1997. a

National Assessment Governing Board (NAGB). *Writing Framework and Specifications for the 1998 National Assessment of Educational Progress.* Washington, D.C., 1997. b

National Assessment Governing Board (NAGB). "Minutes of the November 1997 National Assessment Governing Board Meeting." Washington, D.C., 1997. c

National Assessment Governing Board (NAGB). *Bridging Policy to Implementation: A Resolution.* Washington, D.C., 1997. d

National Assessment Governing Board (NAGB). *Briefing Book, January 21, 1998 Meeting.* Washington, D.C., January 1998.

National Assessment Governing Board (NAGB). *Mathematics Framework for the 1992, 1996 and 2000 National Assessment of Educational Progress.* Washington, D.C., 1999. a

National Assessment Governing Board (NAGB). *Reading Framework for the National Assessment of Educational Progress: 1992-2000.* Washington, D.C., 1999. b

National Assessment Governing Board (NAGB). "Report of the Reporting and Dissemination Committee." Minutes of the August 1999 National Assessment Governing Board Meeting. Washington, D.C., August 1999. c

National Assessment Governing Board (NAGB). *Science Framework for the 1996 and 2000 National Assessment of Educational Progress.* Washington, D.C., 1999. d

National Assessment Governing Board (NAGB). *Policy Statement on Reporting and Dissemination of National Assessment Results.* Washington, D.C., 1999. e

National Assessment Governing Board (NAGB). *Briefing Book, November 16-18, 2000 Meeting.* Washington, D.C., November 2000. a

National Assessment Governing Board (NAGB). *Geography Framework for the 1994 and 2001 National Assessment of Educational Progress.* Washington, D.C., 2000. b

National Assessment Governing Board (NAGB). "Report of the Nominations Committee." Minutes of the March 2000 National Assessment Governing Board Meeting. Washington, D.C., 2000. c

National Assessment Governing Board (NAGB). *U.S. History Framework for the 1994 and 2001 National Assessment of Educational Progress.* Washington, D.C., 2000. d

National Assessment Governing Board and National Center for Education Statistics. *Proceedings of the Joint Conference on Standard Setting for Large-Scale Assessments of the National Assessment Governing Board (NAGB) and the National Center for Education Statistics (NCES).* Volume II. Washington, D.C., 1995.

National Assessment of Educational Progress (NAEP). *Writing Objectives: Second Assessment.* Denver: Education Commission of the States, 1972.

National Assessment of Educational Progress (NAEP). "States Incorporating NAEP in Their Assessment Programs." *NAEP Newsletter* 6 (February 1973).

National Assessment of Educational Progress (NAEP). *General Information Yearbook.* Report No. 03/04-GIY. Washington D.C.: U.S. Government Printing Office, 1974.

National Assessment of Educational Progress (NAEP). *Social Studies Technical Report: Summary Volume.* Report 03-SS-21. Denver: Education Commission of the States, 1975.

National Assessment of Educational Progress (NAEP). *Science Technical Report: Summary Volume.* Report 04-S-21. Denver: Education Commission of the States, 1977.

National Assessment of Educational Progress (NAEP). *Mathematics Objectives: Second Assessment.* Denver: Education Commission of the States, 1978.

National Assessment of Educational Progress (NAEP). *Three Assessments of Science, 1969-77: Technical Summary.* Report 08-S-21. Denver: Education Commission of the States, 1979.

National Assessment of Educational Progress (NAEP). *Procedural Handbook: 1978-79 Writing Assessment.* Denver: Education Commission of the States, 1981. a

National Assessment of Educational Progress (NAEP). *Mathematics Objectives: 1981–82 Assessment.* Denver: Education Commission of the States, 1981. b

National Assessment of Educational Progress (NAEP). *The Third National Mathematics Assessment: Results, Trends and Issues.* Denver: Education Commission of the States, 1983.

National Assessment of Educational Progress (NAEP). *Writing Objectives: 1988 Assessment.* Princeton, N.J.: Educational Testing Service, 1987.

National Assessment of Educational Progress (NAEP). *Mathematics Objectives: 1990 Assessment.* Princeton, N.J.: Educational Testing Service, 1988.

National Assessment of Educational Progress (NAEP). *Math Objectives: 1985-86 Assessment.* Princeton, N.J.: Educational Testing Service, n.d.

National Assessment of Educational Progress Staff. "Critique of the Report, The Efficacy of the National Assessment of Educational Progress." Denver, March 1973.

National Center for Education Statistics. *Directory of NAEP Publications.* Office of Educational Research and Improvement, NCES 1999-489. Washington D.C.: U.S. Department of Education, 1999.

National Commission on Excellence in Education. *A Nation at Risk: The Imperative for Educational Reform.* Washington, D.C.: U.S. Government Printing Office, 1983.

National Council of Teachers of Mathematics. *Curriculum and Evaluation Standards for School Mathematics*. Reston, Va., 1989.

National Institute of Education. *Director's Report to the Congress on the National Assessment of Educational Progress*. Washington, D.C.: U.S. Department of Education, 1982.

National Institute of Education. *Director's Report to the Congress on the National Assessment of Educational Progress*. Washington, D.C.: U.S. Department of Education, 1986.

National Science Teachers Association (NSTA). *Recommendations to the National Assessment of Educational Progress*. Washington, D.C., 1973. a

National Science Teachers Association (NSTA). *National Assessment: Findings in Science, 1969-70: What Do They Mean?* Washington, D.C., 1973. b

Nellhaus, J. "States with NAEP-Like Performance Standards." In *Student Performance Standards on the National Assessment of Educational Progress: Affirmations and Improvements*, edited by M.L. Bourque and S. Byrd. Washington, D.C.: National Assessment Governing Board, 2000.

Nichols, D.; Campbell, V.; Baer, J.; Ganley, B.; Lumsdaine, J.; and Willis, M. *Methods for Assessing the Achievement of Citizenship Objectives: Age Seventeen*. Palo Alto, Calif.: American Institutes for Research, 1965.

O'Neil, H.F.; Sugrue, B.; Abedi, J.; Baker, E.L.; and Golan, S. *Final Report of Experimental Studies on Motivation and NAEP Test Performance*. CSE Technical Report 427. Los Angeles: CRESST/University of California, Los Angeles, 1997.

Pellegrino, J.W.; Chudowsky, N.; and Glaser, R., eds. *Knowing What Students Know: The Science and Design of Educational Assessment*. Washington, D.C.: National Academy Press, 2001.

Pellegrino, J.W.; Jones, L.R.; and Mitchell, K.J., eds. *Grading the Nation's Report Card: Evaluating NAEP and Transforming the Assessment of Educational Progress*. Washington, D.C.: National Academy Press, 1999.

Reckase, M. *The Evolution of the NAEP Achievement Level Setting Process: A Summary of the Research and Development Efforts Conducted by ACT*. Iowa City: American College Testing Program, 2000.

Research Triangle Institute (RTI). *On Aspects of the Methodology for Assessing the Progress of Education.* Research Triangle Park, N.C., 1967. a

Research Triangle Institute (RTI). *Sampling Plans for Assessing the Progress of Education.* Research Triangle Park, N.C., 1967. b

Research Triangle Institute (RTI). "Program for Assessing the Progress of Education." Draft proposal. Research Triangle Park, N.C., 1968.

Rogers, W.T.; Folsom, R.E., Jr.; Kalsbeek, W.D.; and Clemmer, A.F. "Assessment of Nonresponse Bias in Sample Surveys: An Example from the National Assessment." *Journal of Educational Measurement* 14 (1977): 297-311.

Rothman, R. "Bush's Early Release of NAEP Data Could Harm Credibility, Board Warns." *Education Week,* 10 June 1992, p. 19.

Rubin, D.B. *Multiple Imputation for Nonresponse in Surveys.* New York: John Wiley & Sons, 1987.

Rust, K.F., and Johnson, E.G. "Sampling and Weighting in the National Assessment." *Journal of Educational Statistics* 17 (1992): 111-29.

Sauls, J.M. *Comparison of Black and White Performance Using National Assessment Data.* Prepared for National Advisory Council on Equal Educational Opportunity. Denver: National Assessment of Educational Progress, 1975.

Searls, D.T. *On the Large Observation Problem.* Raleigh: North Carolina State University, 1962.

Searls, D.T. "Foreword." In *The National Assessment Approach to Sampling,* edited by R.P. Moore, J.R. Chromy, and W.T. Rogers. Denver: Education Commission of the States, 1974.

Sedlacek, D.A. *Using HLM and NAEP Data to Explore School Correlates of 1990 Mathematics and Geometry Achievement in Grades 4, 8, 12: Methodology and Results.* NCES 95697. Washington, D.C.: National Center for Education Statistics, 1995.

Shah, B.V. *A Note on Estimating Variance of the Variance Estimator Using Jack-Knife or Half Samples.* Research Triangle Park, N.C.: Research Triangle Institute, 1970.

Shao, J., and Wu, C.F.J. "Asymptotic Properties of the Balanced Repeated Replication Method for Sample Quantiles." *Annals of Statistics* 20 (1992): 1371-93.

Shepard, L.A. "Evaluating Test Validity." In *Review of Research in Education*, edited by L. Hammond. Washington, D.C.: American Educational Research Association, 1993.

Shepard, L.A. "Implications for Standard Setting of the National Academy of Education Evaluation of the National Assessment of Educational Progress Achievement Levels." In *Proceedings of the Joint Conference on Standard Setting for Large-Scale Assessments of the National Assessment Governing Board (NAGB) and the National Center for Education Statistics (NCES)*. Washington D.C.: National Assessment Governing Board and National Center for Education Statistics, 1995.

Shepard, L.A.; Glaser, R.; Linn, R.L.; and Bohrnstedt, G.W. *Setting Performance Standards for Student Achievement: A Report of the National Academy of Education Panel on the Evaluation of the NAEP Trial State Assessment: An Evaluation of the 1992 Achievement Levels*. Stanford, Calif.: National Academy of Education, 1993.

Smith, E.R.; Tyler, R.W.; and the Evaluation Staff. *Appraising and Recording Student Progress*. New York: Harper & Brothers, 1942.

Stufflebeam, D.L.; Jaeger, R.M.; and Scriven, M. "Summative Evaluation of the National Assessment Governing Board's Inaugural 1990-91 Effort to Set Achievement Levels on the National Assessment of Educational Progress." Draft version. Prepared for the National Assessment Governing Board, 23 August 1991. a

Stufflebeam, D.L.; Jaeger, R.M.; and Scriven, M. *Summative Evaluation of the National Assessment Governing Board's Inaugural Effort to Set Achievement Levels on the National Assessment of Educational Progress*. Kalamazoo, Mich.: Evaluation Center, Western Michigan University, 1991. b

Takahira, S.; Gonzales, G.; Frase, M.; and Salganik, L.H. *Pursuing Excellence: A Study of U.S. Twelfth-Grade Mathematics and Science Achievement in International Context*. Washington, D.C.: National Center for Education Statistics, 1998.

Tukey, J.W. "Bias and Confidence in Not-Quite Large Samples." *Annals of Mathematical Statistics* 29 (1958): 614.

Tukey, J.W. *Exploratory Data Analysis*. Reading, Mass.: Addison-Wesley, 1977.

Tukey, J.W.; Abelson, R.P.; Coffman, W.E.; Gilbert, J.P.; Jones, L.V.; and Mosteller, F. *National Assessment of Educational Progress,*

*Report 7: Science: Group and Balanced Group Results for Color, Parental Education, Size and Type of Community, and Balanced Results for Region of the Country and Sex.* Washington, D.C.: U.S. Government Printing Office, 1973.

Tyler, R.W. *Basic Principles of Curriculum and Instruction.* Chicago: University of Chicago Press, 1949.

Tyler, R.W. "Assessing the Progress of Education." *Phi Delta Kappan* 46 (September 1965): 13-16.

Tyler, R.W. "The Development of Instruments for Assessing Educational Progress." In *Proceedings of the 1965 Invitational Conference on Testing Problems.* Princeton, N.J.: Educational Testing Service, 1966.

Tyler, R.W. "Progress Report on the Tryouts of the Assessment Exercises." Paper presented at the meeting of the Exploratory Committee on Assessing the Progress of Education, St. Paul, Minn., July 1967.

Tyler, R. "Introduction." In *National Assessment of Educational Progress: Citizenship Objectives.* Ann Arbor, Mich.: Committee on Assessing the Progress of Education, 1969.

Tyler, R.W. "Introduction: A Perspective on the Issues." In *Crucial Issues in Testing*, edited by R.W. Tyler and R.M. Wolf. Berkeley, Calif.: McCutchan, 1974.

Tyler, R.W. "Appraising and Recording Student Progress." (1942). In *Educational Evaluation: Classic Works of Ralph W. Tyler*, edited by George F. Madaus and Daniel L. Stufflebeam. Boston: Kluwer Academic Publishers, 1989.

U.S. Department of Health, Education and Welfare. *Toward a Social Report.* Washington D.C.: U.S. Government Printing Office, 1969.

U.S. General Accounting Office. *Educational Achievement Standards: NAGB's Approach Yields Misleading Interpretations.* Report No. GAO/PEMD-93-12. Washington, D.C., 1993.

U.S. Senate. *Hearings Before the Select Committee on Equal Educational Opportunity.* Washington, D.C., 1971.

Vinovskis, M.A. *Overseeing the Nation's Report Card: The Creation and Evolution of the National Assessment Governing Board (NAGB).* Washington, D.C.: National Assessment Governing Board, 1998.

Widmeyer, S., and Blaunstein, P. *Dissemination Strategies for the National Assessment of Educational Progress.* Washington, D.C.: Widmeyer Group, 1993.

Williams, V.S.L.; Jones, L.V.; and Tukey, J.W. "Controlling Error in Multiple Comparisons, with Examples from State-to-State Differences in Educational Achievement." *Journal of Educational Statistics* 24 (1999): 42-69.

Wingersky, M.S.; Barton, M.A.; and Lord, F.M. *LOGIST V User's Guide*. Princeton, N.J.: Educational Testing Service, 1982.

Wirtz, W., and Lapointe, A. *Measuring the Quality of Education: A Report on Assessing Educational Progress*. Washington, D.C., 1982.

Womer, F. "Research Towards National Assessment." In *Western Regional Conference on Testing Programs: Proceedings*. Princeton N.J.: Educational Testing Service, 1968. a

Womer, F. "Administration Sequence." Memorandum. Ann Arbor: National Assessment of Educational Progress, 1968. b

Womer, F.B. *What Is National Assessment?* Denver: Education Commission of the States, 1970.

Womer, F.B., and Mastie, M.M. "How Will National Assessment Change American Education? An Assessment of Assessment by the First NAEP Director." *Phi Delta Kappan* 53 (October 1971): 118-20.

Zwick, R. "Effects of Item Order and Context on Estimation of NAEP Reading Proficiency." *Educational Measurement: Issues and Practice* 10 (1991): 10-16.

# APPENDICES

# APPENDIX A

# Glossary*

The glossary provides definitions of technical terms used in this book. Note that technical usage may differ from common usage. For many of the terms, multiple definitions can be found in the literature. Words set in *italics* are defined elsewhere in the glossary.

**accommodation**: A change in the standard procedure for administering a test or a change in the mode of response required of test takers, and intended to lessen *bias* in the *scores* of individuals with a special need or disability. Examples of accommodations include allotting extra time and providing the test in large type.

**achievement levels**: Descriptions of student or adult competency in a particular subject area, usually defined as ordered categories on a continuum, often labeled from "basic" to "advanced," that constitute broad ranges for classifying performance. The National Assessment of Educational Progress (NAEP) defines three achievement levels for each subject and grade being assessed: basic, proficient, and advanced. The National Assessment Governing Board (NAGB), the governing body for NAEP, describes the knowledge or skills demonstrated by students at or above each of these three levels of achievement and provides exemplars of performance for each. NAGB also reports the percentage of students

*Adapted by L.V. Jones and I. Olkin from D.M. Koretz, M.W. Bertenthal, and B.F. Green, eds., *Embedding Questions: The Pursuit of a Common Measure in Uncommon Tests* (Washington, D.C.: National Academy Press, 1999). Used with permission.

who are in the four categories of achievement defined by the four levels: below basic, basic, proficient, and advanced. NAGB does not provide a description for the below basic category.

**achievement-level percentages**: Values that indicate the percentage of students within the total population, or in a particular subgroup, who meet or exceed expectations for what they should know and be able to do. Specifically, they are the *weighted percentages* of students with NAEP composite scores that are equal to, or exceed, NAGB-specified achievement-level *cut scores.*

**Angoff method**: Used to set a minimum passing score on a test, based on judges' estimates of the probabilities that a person who deserves to pass would correctly answer the items.

**assessment**: Any systematic method of obtaining evidence from tests and collateral sources used to draw inferences about characteristics of people, objects, or programs for a specific purpose; often used interchangeably with *test.*

**background items**: *Items* requesting information about *respondent* demographics and education experiences that may be related to achievement.

**bias**: 1) With respect to statistical inference, the difference between the expected value of an estimator and the population parameter being estimated. If the average value of the estimator across all possible *samples* (the estimator's expected value) equals the parameter being estimated, the estimator is said to be *unbiased*; otherwise, the estimator is *biased.* 2) With respect to a test, a *systematic error* in a *test score.* Bias usually favors one group of test takers over another, even when both groups are equivalent in the construct under assessment.

**BIB (balanced incomplete block) spiraling**: A complex variant of *multiple matrix sampling* in which items are administered so that pairs of items are dispensed uniformly to a *sample* of *respondents.*

**block**: A group of assessment items created by dividing the item pool for an age or grade into subsets. Blocks are used in the implementation of the sampling design.

**booklet**: The assessment instrument created by combining *blocks* of assessment items, often administered intact to each test-taker.

**calibrate, calibration**: 1) With respect to scales, the process of setting a *test score* scale, including the *mean, standard deviation*, and possibly the shape of the *score distribution*, so that scores on the scale have the same relative meaning as scores on a related *score* scale. 2) With respect to *items*, the process of estimating the parameters of a set of items using responses from a *sample* of test-takers.

**clustering**: The process of forming sampling units as groups of other units, for example, students within the same classroom.

**common block**: A group of background items included in every assessment *booklet*.

**common measure**: A scale of measurement that has a single meaning. *Scores* from *tests* that are *calibrated* to this scale support the same inferences about student performance from one locality to another and from one year to the next.

**composite scale**: An overall subject-area scale based on the weighted average of the scales that are used to summarize performance on the primary dimensions of the *content domain* or curricular framework for the subject-area assessment. For example, the mathematics composite scale is a weighted average of five content-area scales: number sense, properties, and operations; measurement; geometry and spatial sense; data analysis, statistics, and probability; and algebra and functions. These five scales correspond to the five content-area dimensions of the NAEP mathematics framework.

**conditioning**: The incorporation of background variables in the process of *imputation* used in NAEP that allows *plausible values* to be drawn at random from a conditional distribution for a NAEP respondent, given his or her responses to cognitive exercises and a specific subset of background variables (*conditioning variables*).

**conditioning variables**: Demographic and other background variables characterizing a *respondent*. These variables are used to construct *plausible values*.

**constructed-response item**: A non-multiple-choice item that requires some type of written or oral response. An exercise for which examinees must create their own responses, rather than having to choose a response from an enumerated set. See *selected-response item*.

**content domain**: The set of behaviors, knowledge, skills, abilities, attitudes, or other characteristics measured by a *test*, represented in a detailed specification and organized into categories by which *items* are classified.

**content validity**: The evidence for validity based on the content of a test. In NAEP it is restricted to how well the test items measure a subject area, such as mathematics or reading, as specified in the framework and test specification.

**criterion-referenced test**: A test that allows its users to make interpretations in relation to a functional preformance level, as distinguished from interpretations that are relative to the performance of others. Examples of criterion-referenced interpretations include comparisons to cut scores, interpretations based on expectancy tables, and domain-referenced score interpretations.

**cut score**: For NAEP, a specific *score* value used to separate one *achievement level* from another.

**design effect**: The ratio of the *variance* for a particular (usually complex) *sampling* design to the *variance* for a *simple random sample* of the same size.

**dichotomous item**: An item that is scored as "correct" or "incorrect." In NAEP, a multiple-choice item or an item that requires a constructed response from the student and is subsequently scored by scorers into two categories.

**distribution**: The number or the percentage of cases having each possible data value on a scale of data values. Distributions often are reported in terms of grouped ranges of data values. In testing, data values are usually *test scores*. A distribution often is characterized by its *mean* and *standard deviation*.

**domain**: The full array of a particular subject matter being addressed by an *assessment*.

**effect size**: A measure of the practical effect of a statistical difference, usually a difference of the *means* of two *distributions*. The *mean* difference between two *distributions*, or an equivalent difference, is expressed in units of the *standard deviation* of the dominant distribution or of some average of the two standard deviations. For example, if two distributions had means of 50 and 54, and both had standard deviations of 10, the effect size of their mean difference would be 4/10, or 0.4. The effect size is sometimes called the standardized mean difference. In other contexts, other ways are sometimes used to express the practical size of an observed statistical difference.

**embedding**: In testing, including all or part of one *test* in another. The embedded *items* may be kept together as a unit or interspersed throughout the test.

**equating**: The process of statistical adjustments by which the *scores* on two or more alternative test *forms* are placed on a common scale. The process assumes that the test forms have been constructed using the same explicit content and statistical specifications and administered under identical procedures.

**estimate, estimator**: A *sample statistic* employed to estimate the value of a *parameter* of the *target population*.

**excluded students**: Sampled students who are judged to be unable to participate in an assessment because they have limited English language proficiency or a disability (and to whom *accommodation* is not provided).

**exercise**: A *test item;* originally in NAEP, "exercise" was the preferred designation, to distinguish creative forms of NAEP items from the typical *multiple-choice items* of conventional *tests*.

**expected value**: The theoretical average of the *sample* estimates given by an *estimator* across all possible samples. If an estimator is *unbiased*, then its expected value will equal the population value being estimated.

**false discovery rate (FDR):** In a set of mean differences, the percentage declared to be *statistically significant* in one direction for which the corresponding population difference is expected to be in the other direction.

**field test**: A pretest of *items* to obtain information regarding clarity, difficulty levels, timing, feasibility, and special administrative situations. The field test is performed before revising and selecting the items to be used in the assessment.

**focused BIB spiraling**: A variation of *BIB spiraling* in which *items* are administered so that each pair is presented in some uniform manner to a *sample* of test-takers.

**form**: A particular *test* in a set of tests, all of which have the same test *specification*s. Forms are often constructed to be reasonably equivalent in content and statistical specifications.

**framework**: The detailed description of the *content domain* of a *test*.

**geographic location:** A NAEP reporting category entailing schools located in extreme urban, suburban, and rural areas; formerly "type of community."

**high-stakes test**: A *test* for which results have important, direct consequences for examinees, programs, or institutions.

**imputation**: Prediction of a missing value (for example, of a *test score*) based on some procedure, using a mathematical model in combination with available information. See *plausible values*.

**imputed values**: Values generated through *imputation*. In NAEP, the imputed values are called *plausible values*.

**item**: The basic scoreable part of an assessment. A generic term used to refer to a question or an exercise on a test or assessment. The test-taker is asked to respond to the item in some way.

**item format**: The form in which an *exercise* is presented on a test and the form in which the response is to be made. The formats include, among others, selected-response (*multiple choice*) items and *constructed-response items*, which may be either short-answer or extended-response items.

**item pool**: The collection of all items from which a subset of items is assembled into a test *form*.

**item response theory (IRT)**: Test analysis procedures that assume a mathematical model for the probability that an examinee with a given ability will choose or provide a response to an *assessment exercise*.

**jackknife**: A procedure that estimates *standard errors* of percentages and other statistics. It is particularly suited to complex *sample* designs.

**limited English proficiency (LEP)**: A term used to identify students whose performance on tests of achievement may be inappropriately low because of their poor proficiency in English.

**linking**: A means for placing two or more tests on the same scale so that scores can be used interchangeably. Linking relates to *equating*.

**matrix sampling**: An *assessment* sampling method in which a large set of test items is organized into a number of relatively short subsets, each of which is randomly assigned to a subsample of test-takers, thereby avoiding the need to administer all items to all examinees.

**mean**: The arithmetic average of a set of numbers.

**measurement error**: An index of variation in a measured value, such as a *score*, due to a variety of unknown factors (fatigue, timing mistakes, etc.). In testing, measurement error is viewed as the difference between an observed score and a corresponding theoretical true score or proficiency.

**metric**: The units in which *scale scores* are expressed.

**metropolitan statistical area (MSA)**: An area defined by the federal government for the purposes of presenting general-purpose statistics for metropolitan areas. Typically, an MSA contains a city with a population of at least 50,000 and includes its adjacent areas.

**multiple-choice item**: An item that consists of one or more introductory sentences followed by a list of response options that include the correct answer and several incorrect alternatives.

**multiple matrix sampling**: A sampling plan in which different *samples* of *respondents* take different samples of items.

**multistage sample design**: Indicates more than one stage of sampling. The following is an example of three-stage sampling:

1) *sample* of counties (*primary sampling units* or PSUs), 2) sample of schools within each sample county, and 3) sample of students within each sample school.

**NAEP scales**: The scales used to report NAEP results in each age or grade level, content area, and assessment year.

**nonresponse**: The failure to obtain responses or measurements for some *sample* elements.

**nonsampling error**: A general term applying to all sources of error, other than *sampling error*, that contribute to *measurement error*. Includes errors from defects in the *sampling frame* and mistakes in processing the data.

**normative score**: A value based on a comparison of a *respondent's* performance to that of others in a reference population, typically a *percentile*. Scores of "others" are adjusted so that their *mean* and *standard deviation* (in the reference population) have some specified values, such as a mean of 500 and a standard deviation of 100 (for example, the SAT normative score scale). NAEP scale scores are examples of normative scores.

**norm-referenced**: Interpreted by comparison to the performance of those in a specified population. A norm-referenced test score is interpreted on the basis of a comparison of a test-taker's performance to the performance of other people in a specified reference population, or by a comparison of a group to other groups.

**norms**: *Statistics* or tabular data that summarize the *distribution* of test performance for one or more specified groups, such as test-takers of various ages or grades, expressed as *percentile* scores. Norms usually are designed to represent some larger population, such as test-takers in a state or in the country.

**objective**: A term sometimes used to describe an education goal established through a consensus approach. The consensus group may be scholars in the field, educators, lay persons, or, in NAEP, a combination of these.

**oversampling**: Deliberately sampling a portion of the population at a higher rate than the remainder of the population.

**parameter**: A value of a characteristic of the *distribution* for the *target population*, for example, its *mean* or *standard deviation*.

**percent correct**: The percent of a sample or an *estimate* of the percent in a *target population* that answers a particular exercise correctly.

**percentile**: A score location below which a specified percentage of the population falls. For example, in 1998, the 10th percentile of fourth-grade NAEP reading scores was 167. This means that in 1998, 10% of fourth-graders had NAEP reading scores below 167, whereas 90% scored at or above 167.

**performance standard**: A definition of a certain level of performance in some domain in terms of a *cut score* or a range of *scale scores* on a *test* measuring proficiency in that *domain*. Also, sometimes, a statement or description of a set of operational tasks exemplifying a level of performance associated with a more general content standard; the statement may be used to guide judgments about the location of a *cut score* on a score scale. In NAEP, performance standards are called *achievement levels*.

**plausible values**: Proficiency values drawn at random from a conditional distribution of an NAEP *respondent*, given his or her response to cognitive exercises and a specified subset of background variables (*conditioning variables*). The selection of a plausible value is a form of *imputation*.

**polytomous item**: An *item* for which there are more than two possible responses (other than missing and off-task).

**poststratification**: An adjustment of *sampling weights* after the *sample* has been selected so that certain sample proportions (for example, the proportion of African Americans) match counterpart population proportions.

**primary sampling unit (PSU)**: The basic geographic sampling unit for NAEP. It can be either a single county or a set of contiguous counties.

**probability sample**: A *sample* in which every element of the population has a known nonzero probability of being selected.

**proficiency levels**: See *achievement levels*.

**pseudoreplicate**: An altered sample used in the calculation of the *jackknife variance* estimator; the final estimate is a combination of values based on a number of pseudoreplicates.

**p value**: In NAEP, the percentage of students scoring above a specified *cut score*. More generally, the term refers to a statistical significance level, for example, .05 or 5%, not to be confused with the NAEP definition.

**region**: One of four geographic areas used in gathering and reporting data: Northeast, Southeast, Central, and West (as defined by the Office of Business Economics, U.S. Department of Commerce). A NAEP *reporting subgroup*.

**reliability**: The degree to which scores are expected to be consistent over repeated applications of a measurement procedure and hence are dependable and replicable; the degree to which scores are free of errors of measurement. Reliability is usually expressed by a unit-free index that either is or resembles a product-moment correlation. In classical test theory, the term represents the ratio of true-score variance to observed score variance for a particular examinee population. The conditions under which the coefficient is estimated may involve variation in test forms, measurement occasions, raters, or scorers and may entail multiple examinee products or performances. These and other variations in conditions give rise to specific types of reliability, such as alternative-forms reliability, internal-consistency reliability, test-retest reliability, etc.

**reporting subgroup**: A group within the national population for which NAEP data are reported; for example, gender, race/ethnicity, grade, age, level of parental education, *region*, and geographic location.

**respondent**: A person who is eligible for NAEP, is in the *sample*, and responds by completing one or more items in an assessment booklet.

**sample**: A portion of a population, or a subset from a set of units, that is selected by some probability mechanism for the purpose of investigating the properties of the population. NAEP does not assess an entire population; rather, it selects a *probability sample* from the group to answer assessment items.

**sampling error**: The error in survey estimates that occurs because only a *sample* of the population is observed.

**sampling frame**: The list of sampling units from which the *sample* is selected.

**sampling weight**: A multiplicative factor equal to the reciprocal of the probability of a *respondent* being selected for assessment with adjustment for *nonresponse* and, perhaps, *poststratification*. The weight provides an estimate of the number of persons in the population represented by the *respondents* in the sample.

**scale score**: A score on a test that is expressed on some defined scale of measurement. A NAEP score, derived from student responses to the NAEP assessment items, that summarizes the overall level of performance attained by that student. NAEP subject area scores typically are expressed on 0-500 (reading, mathematics, history, and geography) or 0-300 (science, writing, and civics) scales. When used in conjunction with interpretive aids, they provide information about what a particular aggregate of students in the population knows and can do.

**scaling**: The process of assigning numbers to reflect students' performance on an assessment. In NAEP, scaling is based on *item response theory* (IRT) and results in a scale score for each subject area that can be used to summarize levels of performance attained by particular groups of students.

**score**: Any specific number resulting from the assessment of an individual; a generic term applied for convenience to such diverse measures as test scores, absence records, course grades, ratings, and so forth.

**selected-response item:** See *multiple-choice item.*

**selection probability**: The probability that a particular sampling unit is selected in the *sample.*

**simple random sample**: A collection of *n* sampling units drawn from a population of sampling units so that each sampling unit has an equal chance of being in the *sample* and every combination of *n* sampling units has the same chance of being in the sample.

**standard deviation**: An index of the degree to which a set of data values is concentrated about its *mean.* Sometimes referred to as "spread." For *tests*, the standard deviation measures the variability in a distribution of scores. Distributions with small standard deviations are relatively concentrated; larger standard deviations signify greater variability. In common distributions, like the mathematically defined "normal distribution," roughly 68% of the quantities are within (plus or minus) 1 standard deviation from the *mean*; about 95% are within (plus or minus) 2 standard deviations; nearly all are within (plus or minus) 3 standard deviations. See *distribution, effect size, variance.*

**standard error**: A measure of sampling variability and *measurement error* for a statistic. Because of NAEP's complex *sample design*, sampling standard errors are estimated by *jackknifing* the *samples* from first-stage sample estimates. Standard errors also may include a component due to the error of measurement of individual scores estimated using *plausible values*.

**standardization**: In test administration, maintaining a uniform testing environment and conducting the test according to detailed rules and specifications so that testing conditions are the same for all test-takers. In statistical analysis, transforming a variable so that its *mean* is zero and its *standard deviation* is 1.0 for some specified population or sample.

**statistic**: A characteristic of a sample *distribution*, such as its *mean* or *standard deviation*, often employed to estimate a *parameter* of the target population.

**statistically significant**: Statistical tests are conducted to determine whether the changes or differences between two observed measures are likely to be associated with *sampling error*. The term "significant" does not imply a judgment about the absolute magnitude or educational relevance of changes in student performance.

**stratification**: The division of a population into parts, or strata.

**stratified sample**: A *sample* selected from a population that has been stratified, with a sample selected independently in each *stratum*. The strata are defined for the purpose of reducing *sampling error*.

**stratum**: A collection of sampled units defined by a characteristic such as age or gender. All sampling units belong to a stratum, and the strata are mutually exclusive.

**subject area**: One of the areas assessed by NAEP; for example, art, civics, computer competence, geography, literature, mathematics, music, reading, science, U.S. history, or writing.

**subgroups**: Groups of the student population identified in terms of certain demographic or background characteristics. Some of the major *reporting subgroups* used for reporting NAEP results include students' sex, race or ethnicity, highest level of parental education, and type of school (public or nonpublic). Information gathered from NAEP background questionnaires also makes it possible to report results based on such variables as course-taking, home discussions of school work, and television viewing habits.

**systematic error**: A score component (often observed indirectly), related neither to the characteristic being measured nor to random errors, that appears to be related to some salient variable or subgrouping of cases in an analysis. See *bias*.

**systematic sample (systematic random sample)**: A *sample* selected by a systematic method, for example, units selected from a list at equally spaced intervals.

**target population:** The population to which inferences (*estimates*) from a *sample* are intended to pertain.

**test**: A set of *items* given under prescribed and standardized conditions for the purpose of measuring knowledge of a content area. The person's responses to the items yield a *score*, which is a numerical evaluation of the person's performance on the test.

**test development**: The process through which a test is planned, constructed, evaluated, and modified, including consideration of the content, format, administration, scoring, item properties, scaling, and technical quality for its intended purpose.

**test specifications**: A *framework* that specifies the proportion of items that assess each content and process or skill area; the format of items, responses, and scoring protocols and procedures; and the desired psychometric properties of the items and test, such as the distribution of item difficulty and discrimination indices.

**Trial State Assessment (TSA)**: A NAEP program authorized by Congress in 1988 and established to provide for a program of voluntary state-by-state assessments on a trial basis.

**unbiased**: See *bias*.

**validity**: An overall evaluation of the degree to which accumulated evidence and theory support specific interpretations of test scores.

**variance**: The squared *standard deviation*. The average of the squared deviations of a variable from the *mean* of the variable. The variance of an estimate is the squared *standard error* of the estimate.

**weighted percentage**: A percentage that has been calculated by differentially weighting cases. It differs from a simple percentage, in which all cases are equally weighted. For example, the simple percentage of students in a NAEP sample who answer an item correctly is calculated by tallying the number of students in the sample who provided correct answers, dividing this number by the total sample size, and multiplying the result by 100. The weighted percentage is calculated by tallying the sum of the weights for students answering the item correctly, dividing by the sum of the weights for the total sample, and multiplying by 100. In NAEP, each sampled student is assigned a weight that makes proper allowances for NAEP's sampling design and reflects adjustments for school and student nonparticipation. Weighted percentages are estimates of the percentages of the total population, or population subgroup, that have a specified characteristic. For example, the weighted percentage of fourth-grade students in the NAEP sample that correctly answered a particular NAEP test item is an estimate of the percentage of fourth-grade students in the nation that can correctly answer that question.

# APPENDIX B

# List of Abbreviations

| | |
|---|---|
| AASA | American Association of School Administrators |
| ACES | Advisory Council on Educational Statistics |
| ACT | American College Testing Program |
| ADA | Americans with Disabilities Act |
| ADAC | Analysis and Design Advisory Committee |
| AIR | American Institutes for Research |
| ANAC | Analysis Advisory Committee |
| APC | Advisory Policy Council |
| ARM | average response method |
| ASCD | Association for Supervision and Curriculum Development |
| BIB | balanced incomplete block |
| BRR | balanced repeated replication |
| CAPE | Committee for the Assessment of Progress in Education |
| CBE | Council for Basic Education |
| CCSSO | Council of Chief State School Officers |
| CGCS | Council of Great City Schools |
| CPS | Current Population Survey |
| DAC | Design and Analysis Committee |
| DoDDS | Department of Defense Dependents Schools |
| ECAPE | Exploratory Committee for the Assessment of Progress in Education |
| ECS | Education Commission of the States |
| EIAC | Education Information Advisory Committee |
| ELL | English Language Learner |

| | |
|---|---|
| ERIC | Education Research Information Center |
| ERIE | Eastern Regional Institute for Education |
| ESEA | Elementary and Secondary Education Act |
| ESSI | Education Statistics Services Institute |
| ETS | Educational Testing Service |
| FDR | false discovery rate |
| FIE | Fund for the Improvement of Education |
| GAO | General Accounting Office |
| GED | General Education Diploma |
| HEW | Health Education and Welfare |
| HLM | hierarchical linear model |
| HTML | hypertext markup language |
| IAEP | International Assessment of Educational Achievement |
| IASA | Improving America's Schools Act |
| IDEA | Individuals with Disabilities Education Act |
| IEA | International Assessment of Educational Achievement |
| IEP | Individual Education Plan |
| IRT | item response theory |
| ISR | Institute for Social Research |
| MC | multiple choice |
| MRC | Measurement Research Center |
| MSA | metropolitan statistical area |
| NAACP | National Association for the Advancement of Colored People |
| NAE | National Academy of Education |
| NAEP | National Assessment of Educational Progress |
| NAGB | National Assessment Governing Board |
| NALS | National Adult Literacy Study |
| NAS | National Academy of Sciences |
| NCES | National Center for Education Statistics |
| NCLB | No Child Left Behind Act |
| NCS | National Computer Systems |
| NCTM | National Council of Teachers of Mathematics |
| NEA | National Education Association |
| NIE | National Institute of Education |
| NISS | National Institute of Statistical Sciences |

| | |
|---|---|
| NORC | National Opinion Research Center |
| NRC | National Research Council |
| NSF | National Science Foundation |
| NSTA | National Science Teachers Association |
| OMB | Office of Management and Budget |
| OE | U.S. Office of Education |
| OERI | Office of Educational Research and Improvement |
| OPAC | Operations Advisory Committee |
| PBIBD | partially balanced incomplete block design |
| PC | Psychological Corporation |
| PDF | portable document format |
| PIRLS | Progress in Reading Literacy Study |
| PISA | Program for International Student Assessment |
| PSU | primary sampling unit |
| QCM | quality-control monitor |
| RFP | Request for Proposals |
| RTI | Research Triangle Institute |
| SD | students with disabilities |
| SEAC | State Education Assessment Center |
| SEL | Southeastern Education Laboratory |
| SES | socioeconomic status |
| SMSA | standard metropolitan statistical area |
| SOC | size of community |
| SPSS | Statistical Packages for the Social Sciences |
| SRA | Science Research Associates |
| SRC | Survey Research Center (at the University of Michigan) |
| SREB | Southern Regional Education Board |
| SSI | Statewide Systemic Initiative |
| SSU | secondary sampling unit |
| TAC | Technical Advisory Committee |
| TIMMS | Third International Mathematics and Science Study |
| TSA | Trial State Assessment |
| UMSRC | University of Michigan Survey Research Center |
| USOE | United States Office of Education |
| VNT | Voluntary National Test |

# APPENDIX C

# U.S. Commissioners and Secretaries of Education

Before 1980 this position was titled Commissioner of Education. The first Secretary of Education was Shirley Mount Hufstedler in 1980.

| | |
|---|---|
| 1962-1966 | Francis Keppel |
| 1966-1968 | Harold Howe II |
| 1969-1970 | James E. Allen Jr. |
| 1970-1972 | Sidney P. Marland |
| 1973-1974 | John R. Ottina |
| 1974-1976 | Terrel H. Bell |
| 1976-1977 | Edward Aguirre |
| 1977-1979 | Ernest L. Boyer |
| 1980 | William L. Smith |
| 1980-1981 | Shirley Mount Hufstedler |
| 1981-1984 | Terrel H. Bell |
| 1985-1988 | William J. Bennett |
| 1988-1990 | Lauro F. Cavazos |
| 1990-1992 | Lamar Alexander |
| 1992-2001 | Richard W. Riley |
| 2001-present | Roderick R. Paige |

# APPENDIX D

# U.S. Commissioners of Education Statistics

Before 1984 this position was titled Assistant Commissioner for Education Statistics. The first Comissioner of Education Statistics was Emerson Elliott.

| | |
|---|---|
| 1964-1968 | Alexander M. Mood |
| 1968-1974 | Dorothy M. Gilford |
| 1975-1976 | Francis C. Nassetta (Acting) |
| 1976-1984 | Marie D. Eldridge |
| 1984-1995 | Emerson J. Elliott |
| 1995-1996 | Jeanne E. Griffith (Acting) |
| 1996-1999 | Pascual D. Forgione |
| 1999-2003 | Gary W. Phillips (Acting) |

# APPENDIX E

# National Assessment Governing Board Members

Phyllis W. Aldrich (1988-92)
Saratoga Springs, New York

Francie Alexander (1988-91)
Sacramento, California

Amanda P. Avallone (2003-06)
Boulder, Colorado

Moses Barnes (1998-2002)
Plantation, Florida

David P. Battini (1988-92)
Cairo, New York

Parris C. Battle (1990-94)
Hallandale, Florida

Evan Bayh (1991-95)
Indianapolis, Indiana

Mary R. Blanton (1990-94, 1994-98)
Salisbury, North Carolina
(Vice Chair 1994-98)

Boyd Boehlje (1990-93)
Pella, Iowa

Richard Boyd (1988-92)
Lakewood, Ohio
(Chair 1990-92)

Bruce Brombacher (1988-90)
Westerville, Ohio

Linda R. Bryant (1990-94)
Pittsburgh, Pennsylvania

Barbara Byrd-Bennett (2003-07)
Cleveland, Ohio

Melanie Campbell (1998-2002)
Topeka, Kansas

Michael Castle (1989-91, 1991-95)
Dover, Delaware

Patsy Cavazos (1994-98)
Brookside, Texas

Wilmer S. Cody (1998-2002)
New Orleans, Louisiana

Naomi Cohen (1990-91, 1991-95)
Hartford, Connecticut

Carl A. Cohn (2003-07)
Los Angeles, California

Saul Cooperman (1988-90)
Rocky Hill, New Jersey

Antonio Cortese (1988-90)
Loudenville, New York

Charlotte Crabtree (1992-95)
Pacific Palisades, California

Catherine Davidson (1994-98)
Silverdale, Washington

Wilhelmina F. Delco (1988-90)
Austin, Texas

Shirley V. Dickson (2003-07)
Denver, Colorado

Daniel A. Domenech (1999-2003)
Fairfax, Virginia

Edward Donley (1995-97, 1997-2000, 2000-04)
Allentown, Pennsylvania

John Q. Easton (2003-07)
Chicago, Illinois

James Edgar (1995-97)
Springfield, Illinois

James Ellingson (1994-98)
Moorhead, Minnesota

John Engler (1998-2000)
Lansing, Michigan

Dwight Evans (2003-06)
Philadelphia, Pennsylvania

Victor H. Ferry (1988-90)
Waterford, Connecticut

Chester E. Finn Jr. (1988-92, 1992-96)
Chevy Chase, Maryland
(Chair 1989-90)

Thomas H. Fisher (1996-99, 1999-2003)
Tallahassee, Florida

Sheila M. Ford (2003-06)
Washington, D.C.

Patricia Frank (1988-89)
Tampa, Florida
(Vice Chair 1988-89)

Michael S. Glode (1989-93)
Saratoga, Wyoming

David W. Gordon (2003-07)
Elk Grove, California

Dale E. Graham (1988-90)
Columbia City, Indiana

Michael J. Guerra (1993-97,
   1997-2000)
Washington, D.C.

Edward H. Haertel (1997-
   99, 1999-2003)
Palo Alto, California

Reese Hammond (1988-89)
Washington, D.C.

Catherine (Katy) M. Harvey
   (2003-06)
Bethesda, Maryland

Juanita Haugen (1998-2000,
   2000-04)
Pleasanton, California

William (Jerry) Hume
   (1991-95)
San Francisco, California

Christine Johnson (1990-94)
Englewood, California

Elton L. Jolly (1988-90)
Philadelphia, Pennsylvania

Carole Kennedy (1998-99)
Columbia, Missouri

Dirk Kempthorne (2000-04)
Boise, Idaho

Kathi King (2003-07)
Oakland, Maine

Nancy K. Kopp (1999-2002)
Bethesda, Maryland

Kim Kozbial-Hess (2003-06)
Toledo, Ohio

John S. Lindley (1990-94)
Port Orchard, Nevada

Jan B. Loveless (1993-97)
Midland, Michigan

Lynn Marmer (1997-98)
Cincinnati, Ohio

Margaret Marston-Lampe
   (1988-89)
Arlington, Virginia

Joseph B. Martin (1989-90)
Charlotte, North Carolina

Marilyn McConachie
   (1993-97)
Northbrook, Illinois

Catherine T. McNamee,
   C.S.J. (1988-89)
Washington, D.C.

Stephen E. Merrill (1991-95)
Manchester, New Hampshire

Jason P. Millman (1992-96)
Ithaca, New York

Richard P. Mills (1992-96)
Albany, New York

William J. Moloney (1996-98)
Denver, Colorado

Annette Morgan (1995-98)
Kansas City, Missouri

Carl J. Moser (1990-93)
St. Charles, Missouri

John A. Murphy (1991-93)
Charlotte, North Carolina

Ronnie Musgrove (2001-04)
Jackson, Mississippi

Mark D. Musick (1988-96,
   1996-99, 1999-2003)
Atlanta, Georgia
(Vice Chair 1990-92; Chair
   1992-94, 1997-2002)

Roy M. Nageak Sr. (2001-03)
Barrow, Alaska

Mitsugi Nakashima (1993-97, 1997-2000)
Kalahoe, Hawaii

Michael Nettles (1992-96,
   1996-99, 1999-2003)
Ann Arbor, Michigan
(Vice Chair 1998-2003)

Robert Orr (1988-91)
Indianapolis, Indiana

Debra Paulson (1998-2002)
El Paso, Texas

Norma Paulus (1996-99)
Salem, Oregon

Carolyn Pollan (1989-93)
Fort Smith, Arkansas

Jo Ann Pottorff (1997-2000,
   2000-04)
Topeka, Kansas
(Vice Chair 2003-04)

Matthew W. Prophet Jr.
   (1988-91)
Portland, Oregon

William T. Randall (1990-94, 1994-98)
Denver, Colorado
(Vice Chair 1992-94; Chair
   1994-97)

Diane Ravitch (1996-2000,
   2000-04)
Brooklyn, New York

Mark D. Reckase (2003-07)
East Lansing, Michigan

Dorothy K. Rich (1988-91)
Washington, D.C.

Richard Riley (1988-91)
Columbia, South Carolina

Roy Romer (1996-99, 1999-
2002)
Denver, Colorado

Edgar Ross (1993-97)
U.S. Virgin Islands

Lourdes Sheehan, R.S.M.
(2000-04)
Washington, D.C.

Fannie Simmons (1994-98)
Columbia, South Carolina

Raymond Simon (2002-03)
Little Rock, Arkansas

John H. Stevens (1998-2002)
Austin, Texas

Thomas Topuzes (1989-93)
El Centro, California

Daniel Towler (1988-89)
Pasadena, California

Adam Urbanski (1995-98,
1998-2002)
Hilton, New York

Migdania D. Vega (2000-02)
Miami, Florida

Deborah Voltz (1996-99,
1999-2003)
Louisville, Kentucky

Herbert Walberg (1988-92)
Oak Park, Illinois

Michael E. Ward (1999-
2003, 2003-07)
Raleigh, North Carolina

Eileen L. Weiser (2003-07)
Lansing, Michigan

Marilyn Whirry (1992-96,
1996-99, 1999-2003)
Torrance, California

Darvin M. Winick (2002-06)
Dickinson, Texas
(Chair 2002-04)

Dennie P. Wolf (1996-97,
1997-2000, 2000-04)
Providence, Rhode Island

# APPENDIX F

# NAEP Executive Directors

| | |
|---|---|
| 1964-1965 | Stephen Withey |
| 1965-1967 | Jack Merwin |
| 1967-1971 | Frank Womer |
| 1971-1975 | Stanley Ahmann |
| 1975-1982 | Roy Forbes |
| 1982-1983 | Beverly Anderson |
| 1983-1997 | Archie Lapointe |
| 1997-1998 | Paul Williams |
| 1998- | Stephen Lazer |

# APPENDIX G

# The Charter Technical Advisory Committee (1965-1969)

Robert P. Abelson
Lee J. Cronbach
Lyle V. Jones
John W. Tukey (chair)

# APPENDIX H

# The Analysis Advisory Committee
# (1969-1983)

Term of service on ANAC varied from one year for James Davis to 15 years for Lyle Jones and John Tukey. Names marked with an asterisk served as chair of ANAC for one or more years.

Robert P. Abelson
R. Darrell Bock
Lloyd Bond
David R. Brillinger
William E. Coffman
James A. Davis
Janet Dixon Elashoff*
John P. Gilbert
Gene V. Glass
Lyle V. Jones
Lincoln E. Moses
Frederick Mosteller*
John W. Tukey*

# APPENDIX I

# Technical Advisory Committee and Design and Analysis Committee, 1987-Present

In 1987 the committee was called the Technical Advisory Committee. The committee name was changed to Design and Analysis Committee in January 1988. Names marked with an asterisk served as chair for one or more years.

| | |
|---|---|
| Albert E. Beaton | 1990- |
| Betsy J. Becker | 2003- |
| Jeri Benson | 1992-1995 |
| Johnny Blair | 1996- |
| John B. Carroll | 1988-1993 |
| T. Anne Cleary | 1991 |
| Clifford C. Clogg | 1991-1995 |
| William W. Cooley | 1992-1993 |
| Jeremy Finn | 1990- |
| Robert Glaser | 1987 |
| Bert F. Green Jr. | 1987-1992 |
| Paul W. Holland | 1995-2000 |
| Huynh Huynh | 1990- |
| Sylvia T. Johnson* | 1987-2001 |
| Brian W. Junker | 2003- |
| Edward W. Kifer | 1996- |
| Gaea Leinhardt | 1994-1996 |
| Robert L. Linn* | 1987-1989 |

| | |
|---|---|
| David F. Lohman | 1993- |
| Serge Madhere | 1996-2002 |
| Sally C. Morton | 2003- |
| Bengt Muthen | 1991-1994 |
| Anthony J. Nitko* | 1992-2001 |
| Ingram Olkin* | 1987- |
| Tej Pandey | 1988- |
| Juliet Shaffer | 1991-1995 |
| Richard E. Snow | 1987-1990 |
| S. Lynne Stokes | 2003- |
| Hariharan Swaminathan | 1995-2001 |
| Sheila D. Thompson | 2003- |
| John W. Tukey | 1988-1991 |
| Rebecca Zwick | 2001- |

# APPENDIX J

# Summary Report:
# Two Conferences on a National
# Assessment of Educational Progress
### David A. Goslin*

## I. Objectives

A. To provide Congress, as well as state and local governments, with *meaningful* data on the strengths and weaknesses of the American educational system — *presumably to be used in the formation of public policies in the field of education.*

1. Subject area deficiencies (for example, mathematics, science, reading) within groups of schools or across all schools

2. General deficiencies in educational attainment by type of school (states, regions, localities, individual school districts)

3. Problems:

   a. If such data were used as the whole basis for the allocation of public funds, they might have a strong leveling effect on the educational system.

   b. There is some question about how much attention legislators really pay to statistics.

*This report was prepared by David A. Goslin for the Carnegie Corporation to describe the conferences of 18-19 December 1963 and 27-28 January 1964. See Chapter 1 for more details.

B. To provide comparative data to stimulate competition among states or communities — the major problem remains one of providing helpful information without making invidious comparisons convenient.

C. To provide a basis for international comparisons, assuming that some of the difficult sampling and testing problems in such a comparison could be handled satisfactorily.

D. To provide data for research on educational problems and processes.
1. Following the model of the Census Bureau and the Bureau of Labor Statistics
2. This would require the collection of auxiliary information on characteristics of the region, community, school, school population, teachers, etc.

E. To forestall less effective or misdirected attempts at assessment by public or private agencies.

## II.  Sampling and Reporting — Major Questions

A. In-school vs. non-school populations (school drop-outs, adults)
1. Expense — it would probably cost 20 to 30 times more per subject to assess non-school populations (unless they could be reached in some captive situation comparable to a school — e.g., union meeting, P.T.A.).
2. Content — it would probably be necessary to develop quite different tests for each non-school population.
3. Assessment of drop-outs and adults might have great significance for:
   a. the development of adequate vocational training programs
   b. a better understanding of adult education needs

B. The in-school population
1. Age vs. grade-level assessment

    a. There are severe administrative problems in attempting to assess an age group in schools.

    b. At the same time since promotion policies vary, assessment by grade provides less accurate comparisons between schools.

    c. An alternative might be the assessment of children who have been in school for a specified number of years.

2. When should assessment take place?

    a. probably at least two or three times prior to age 16

    b. desirability of assessing 13-14 year age group
      i) the curriculum is more uniform up to this point
      ii) there is less of a drop-out problem at this stage

3. Should the assessment include private (including parochial) schools?

    a. The inclusion of the private school population is necessary if the assessment is to be complete.

    b. Participation would probably have to be voluntary.

C. Number and type of units

1. Administrative desirability of sampling schools (or school districts as opposed to individuals

2. Reporting units

    a. states

    b. regions

    c. individual school systems — possibility of permitting school systems to buy into the program on a voluntary basis so that they could get comparable data

3. Report by items — see III below

4. Importance of a sufficiently large sample of schools to represent *all* of the various types of school districts in the state due to the potential use of the data for policy formation, including the distribution of funds

D. Group assessment vs. individual assessment — individuals probably would not complete the entire test since the aim of the program would not be to assess individual acccomplishment.
  1. This would have the advantage of greater flexibility in format than heretofore possible.
  2. It would make possible greater comprehensibility of content with less individual time consumption.
  3. It would require a larger sample.
E. Background data
  1. Characteristics of students and their families (social class, race, religion, ethnic group membership, size of family, relation to siblings, personality, etc.)
  2. Characteristics of schools (administrative structure, per pupil expenditures, physical plant, facilities, program, etc.)
  3. Characteristics of teachers (background, experience, training, etc.)

## III.  Content of Tests

A. Range of subjects to be covered — the tests should fairly reflect the aims of education in the United States, including both the traditional and modern curriculum.
  1. Greater coverage of subject matter would reduce the impact of the program on any one field.
  2. Greater coverage of subject matter might stimulate schools to venture into areas covered by the test, but which would be new to the school.
  3. Greater coverage of subject matter might give more schools an opportunity to excel in something, thereby reducing the possibility of invidious comparisons.
  4. Greater coverage of subject matter leads to a greater danger of harmful impact (or possible lack of local cooperation) in those fields (for example social studies) about which there is less agreement among school people regarding content or approach.

5. At the individual level, greater coverage might lead to more frustration whenever children have not received instruction in a subject covered by the test.

B. Type of items
    1. A major characteristic of the proposed testing program is that the items would be required to have a high degree of face validity.
        a. in order to justify the program to Congress and the public
        b. in order to present meaningful data to the public — this would also make possible the item by item report of findings noted above
    2. Inclusion of "personality" and other non-subject-matter items
        a. What responsibility does the school have for the social adjustment of students?
        b. What responsibility does the school have for motivating students to achieve?
        c. What responsibility does the school have for training students in general problem solving techniques?
        d. Great difficulty in developing reliable, valid items in these areas
        e. However, inclusion of such items might "take the heat off of the subject matter" to some extent.
    3. Problems
        a. how to be fair to all when there are several legitimate approaches to a single topic — for example, mathematics instruction at present
        b. how to decide what range of item difficulty to provide
            i) three levels of accomplishment might be assessed; test would include items that 90%, 50%, and 10% of the population, respectively, would be expected to pass

        ii) or, stress *only* those things that everybody ought to be able to do (However, if nearly everyone *can* do them, one doesn't learn much and may be setting too low a standard. On the other hand if everybody can't do them, then the test begins to resemble existing tests more.)

   c. how to make sure that there will be a relationship between test performance and the "real capabilities" of the population

      i) the lack of relationship between scores on existing tests and non-academic performance, except at the extremes of the distribution, has been repeatedly demonstrated

      ii) special difficulties are encountered in occupational areas where skills as opposed to knowledge are required (for example, performance tests may be required to assess the effectiveness of vocational education)

      iii) special difficulties are encountered in fields that are undergoing rapid technological change

C. Adequacy of existing tests

   1. Many current test items lack face validity.

   2. Most current tests are designed for individual assessment.

   3. The relatively high correlation one finds among the performances of the same individuals on most current ability tests (IQ and achievement) raises the question of whether it is really possible to design anything very new — even if something other than predictive validity is used to evaluate new items.

   4. Tests like the AGC1 and some of the basic tests (including performance tests) used by the Federal Civil Service might provide a starting point since they are pitched at a lower level than, for example, college admissions tests.

5. Answers here would depend to some extent on IIIB3b above.

D. Getting agreement from members of diverse groups on what "everyone in the society ought to know"
   1. This question precedes, but does not take the place of, the technical problems that the psychometricians must solve.
   2 Rapid social and technological change adds to the difficulty in getting agreement.
   3. Relevant and important performance variables are likely to be different in different parts and levels of the society (for example, it may be more important for a lower class boy of below average intelligence to acquire certain manual skills than to be able to read and understand the *New York Times*).
   4. This problem is related to the organizational and political questions discussed in V below.

## IV. Unanticipated Consequences for Education

A. Tests may have the effect of defining the legitimate boundaries of educational concern in the eyes of Congress, the public, and even educators.
   1. A distinction must be made between the following two questions in structuring any assessment
      a. How effective is the existing educational system?
      b. Is the existing system meeting the needs of the country?
   2. It is clear that the group constructing the test would in many respects be setting educational standards.
   3. Financial penalties on some aspects of school programs may result from the omission of a subject matter area (and lobbying to get new areas into the test may result).

B. Tests may inhibit educational innovation, both with respect to content and method, as has been the case in

New York state as a consequence of the Regents' testing program.

C. Inevitably, there will be a tendency on the part of teachers to teach for the test as long as there is any way for teachers to be evaluated, either individually or collectively (as in a school), on the basis of how well their students do on the test.

    1. Items would have to be made public (because of the avowed purpose of an item-by-item report of results), therefore special instruction on the subjects covered by the test would be possible.

    2. Even though the original plan might specifically exclude individual school or teacher comparisons (for example, by staggering the testing schedule, testing only a few students in any school), it is likely that pressure from schools themselves would force permission of at least voluntary and informal participation by individual schools.

D. There is also the more general danger of setting standards too low, either with respect to a desired ultimate goal or with respect to the rate of progress. Thus the program might turn out to have a self-limiting effect on the educational system as a whole. (It should be noted that this would be particularly true if items were generally low in difficulty as would be necessary to avoid some of the other potentially harmful consequences.)

## V.  Organizational Considerations

A. Public auspices vs. Private (or joint effort)

    1. Private support, at least initially, might avoid the "government control over education" labeling. However, a private group could not require school or individual participation without legislative support.

    2. Justification for public support for such a program exists in the Charter of the Office of Education.

B. One-shot vs. a continuing agency

1. Might depend on whether program was to be private or public.
2. Research goals (as well as most of the other aims) could best be achieved with a continuing body.
3. Continuing agency would best fit Office of Education mandate to "report on the condition and progress" of American education.

C. Supervision
   1. It would be necessary for the controlling body to be composed of specialists in education and psychometrics, as well as intelligent laymen who might be in a position to make sure that the items included on the test have some relevance to real life concerns.
   2. Congressional involvement in the item selection process should be avoided.

D. Political considerations
   1. How do you make this program look like you are maximizing local control? In many cases centralization of certain functions aid local units in making intelligent decisions: in effect, increasing the range of local options.
   2. How do you satisfy the individual motives of Congressmen and provide assurances that each area will receive the benefits of the program?
   3. What kind of reaction can be expected from the South?
   4. What are to be the relative roles of the federal government and the respective states in the program?

E. Other problems
   1. Competent technical manpower in the testing field is in short supply.
   2. A considerable length of time is necessary for planning and test development.
   3. It would be desirable to get some useful data the first year.

# APPENDIX K

# NAEP Assessments, 1969-2012

The current schedule for 2002 and beyond assumes continuing legislative authority. The schedule may be augmented, with advance public notice, as resources permit.

NAGB has reexamined the assessment schedule for 2003 and beyond to address the requirements of the No Child Left Behind Act of 2001. According to the new law:

- NAEP must administer reading and mathematics assessments for grades 4 and 8 every other year in all states.
- In addition, NAEP must test these subjects on a nationally representative basis at grade 12 at least as often as it has done in the past, or every four years.
- Whereas NAEP is required to administer long-term trend assessments in reading and mathematics at ages 9, 13, and 17, there is no requirement that the science and writing trend assessments be continued. NAGB will formulate policy for the long-term trend assessments.
- Provided funds are available, NAEP may conduct national and state assessments at grades 4, 8, and 12 in "additional subject matter, including writing, science, history, geography, civics, economics, foreign languages, and arts."

This assessment schedule is based on conservative estimates of costs and anticipated appropriations.

| Year | National | Long-Term Trend | State |
|------|----------|-----------------|-------|
| 1969-70 | citizenship<br>science<br>writing | science[1] | State assessments began in 1990 |
| 1970-71 | literature<br>reading | reading[1] | |
| 1971-72 | music<br>social studies | | |
| 1972-73 | mathematics<br>science | mathematics[1], science[1] | |
| 1973-74 | career & occupational development writing | | |
| 1974-75 | art<br>index of basic skills<br>reading | reading[1] | |
| 1975-76 | citzenship/social studies<br>mathematics[2] | citizenship/social studies[1] | |
| 1976-77 | basic life skills[2]<br>science | science[1] | |
| 1977-78 | consumer skills[2]<br>mathematics | mathematics[1] | |
| 1978-79 | art<br>music<br>writing | | |
| 1979-80 | reading<br>literature<br>art | reading[1] | |
| 1981-82[3] | mathematics<br>science<br>citizenship<br>social studies | mathematics[1], science[1] | |
| 1984 | reading<br>writing | reading, writing | |
| 1986 | computer competence<br>U.S. history [2]<br>literature[2]<br>mathematics<br>science<br>reading | mathematics, science, reading[4] | |
| 1988 | civics<br>document literacy[2]<br>geography[2]<br>U.S. history<br>reading<br>writing | civics[1], mathematics, science, reading, writing | |
| 1990 | mathematics<br>science<br>reading | mathematics, science, reading, writing | mathematics[5] (8) |
| 1992 | mathematics<br>reading<br>writing | mathematics, science reading, writing | mathematics[5] (4, 8)<br>reading[5] (4) |
| 1994 | geography<br>U.S. history<br>reading | mathematics, science, reading, writing | reading[5] (4) |

| Year | | | |
|------|--------------------------------------------|--------------------------------|--------------------------------------------|
| 1996 | mathematics<br>science                     | reading, writing,<br>mathematics, science | mathematics (4, 8)<br>science (8)          |
| 1997 | arts (8)                                    |                                |                                            |
| 1998 | reading<br>writing<br>civics               |                                | reading (4, 8)<br>writing (8)              |
| 1999 |                                            | reading, mathematics,<br>science |                                            |
| 2000 | mathematics<br>science<br>reading (4)      |                                | mathematics (4, 8)<br>science (4, 8)       |
| 2001 | U.S. history<br>geography                   |                                |                                            |
| 2002 | reading<br>writing                          |                                | reading (4, 8)<br>writing (4, 8)           |
| 2003 | reading<br>mathematics                      |                                | reading (4, 8)<br>mathematics (4, 8)       |
| 2004 | foreign language (12)[6]<br>writing         | reading, mathematics           |                                            |
| 2005 | reading<br>mathematics[7]<br>science        |                                | reading (4, 8)<br>mathematics (4, 8)[7]<br>science (4, 8) |
| 2006 | world history (12)[6]<br>economics (12)[6]<br>civics |                        |                                            |
| 2007 | reading[7]<br>mathematics<br>writing        |                                | reading (4, 8)[7]<br>mathematics (4, 8)<br>writing (4, 8) |
| 2008 | arts[7]                                     | reading, mathematics           |                                            |
| 2009 | reading<br>mathematics<br>science[7]        |                                | reading (4, 8)<br>mathematics (4, 8)<br>science (4, 8)[7] |
| 2010 | U.S. history[7]<br>geography[7]             |                                |                                            |
| 2011 | reading<br>mathematics<br>writing[7]        |                                | reading (4, 8)<br>mathematics (4, 8)<br>writing (4, 8)[7] |
| 2012 | civics[7]<br>foreign language               | reading, mathematics           |                                            |

1. This assessment appears in reports as part of long-term trend. Note that the civics assessment in 1988 is the third point in the trend with citizenship/social studies in 1981-82 and in 1975-76. There are no points on the trend line for writing before 1984.

2. This was a small, special-interest assessment administered to limited national samples at specific grades or ages and was not part of a main assessment. Note that this chart includes only assessments administered to in-school samples; not shown are several special NAEP assessments of adults.

3. Explanation of format for year column: Before 1984, the main NAEP assessments were administered in fall of one year through spring of the next. Beginning with 1984, the main NAEP was administered after the new year in winter, though the assessments to measure long-term trend continued with their traditional administration in fall, winter, and spring. Because the main assessment is the largest component of NAEP, beginning with 1984 we have listed its administration year, rather than the two years over which the trend continued to be administered. Note also that the state component is administered at essentially the same time as the main NAEP.

4. The 1986 long-term trend reading assessment is not included on the trend line in reports because the results for this assessment were unusual. Further information on this reading anomaly is available in Beaton and Zwick (1990).

5. State assessments in 1990-94 were referred to as trial state assessments (TSA).

6. A new framework is planned for implementation for this subject.

7. NAGB will decide whether a new or updated framework is needed.

# APPENDIX L

# Name Index

Numerals in italics signify that the item is an entry in the References section.

# ABOUT THE AUTHORS

**Clay Allison** is a *nom de plume* for a well-known freelance writer formerly associated with *Time* magazine. Mr. Allison is author of numerous books, has contributed articles to national magazines, and is a consultant in the writing field.

**Albert E. Beaton** is a professor of education in the Lynch School of Education at Boston College and a Senior Research Fellow at the American Institutes for Research. He has specialized in large-scale national and international assessment, including positions as director of data analysis for the Equality of Educational Opportunity Survey (the Coleman Report), the National Longitudinal Study of the Class of 1972, the National Assessment of Educational Progress (NAEP), and as the international study director of the Third International Study of Mathematics and Science (TIMSS). He has served on many advisory committees, including the NAEP Design and Analysis Committee and the IEA Technical Advisory Committee. Beaton received his Ed.D. in educational measurement and statistics from Harvard University, where he was director of its Statistical Laboratory. Before moving to Boston College, he was at the Educational Testing Service, where he held many professional and management positions and where he authored many books and articles. He was a co-recipient (with John W. Tukey) of the Wilcoxon Award for the best paper in *Technometrics* in 1974; in 1987 he won the ETS Senior Scientist Award; and in 1988 he was a co-recipient of the NCME Triennial Award for technical contributions to educational measurement (with Robert Mislevy, Eugene Johnson, and Kathy Sheehan). He is a member of the International Academy of Education.

**Mary Lyn Bourque** was chief psychometrician for the National Assessment Governing Board, where she was responsible for policy-related technical issues, particularly setting standards on the National Assessment from 1989 to 2001. Currently, she provides consulting services to local and state departments of education and foreign ministries of education, as well as professional development for teachers and administrators in applied measurement topics. A former secondary school science teacher, she served as director of testing for the school district of Providence, Rhode Island, and directed scoring and evaluation for Cooperative Education Services in Norwalk, Connecticut. Bourque received a doctorate in education from the University of Massachusetts in 1979. She is a member of the National Council for Measurement in Education and the American Educational Research Association, and she has authored numerous technical reports and articles on applied measurement issues. She has published in *Reading Research Quarterly, Educational Measurement: Issues and Practices, Education,* and was a contributor to recent publications including the *Handbook of Educational Policy* and *Monitoring the Standards of Education*, an international publication sponsored by the International Academy of Education. Her research interests focus on large-scale assessment, standard setting, and applied measurement issues.

**Vincent Campbell** has conducted research on self-directed learning, problem solving, character education, and community involvement in public education. His recent focus has been standards-based assessment and learning. He led the development of the Student Achievement Management Information System, designed to support accountability and to help improve learning in the classroom. For some years he consulted for government and industry as a decision analyst, and he was a visiting professor at George Washington University for two years in the field of decision-support systems. He conducted pioneering research on citizen participation in civic decisions and has since implemented direct democracy experiments in several communities. At the

American Institutes for Research (AIR), he and Daryl Nichols co-directed AIR's citizenship assessment for NAEP, leading the AIR team in exercise development, administration, and reporting results for the first national assessment in citizenship. He received his Ph.D. in social psychology from the University of Colorado. He was elected twice to the school board of Portola Valley, California.

**Peggy G. Carr** is the associate commissioner of assessment for the National Center for Education Statistics (NCES), U.S. Department of Education, where she is responsible for national large-scale assessments. Her primary responsibility is for the National Assessment of Educational Progress (NAEP). Carr received her B.S. in Psychology in 1976 from North Carolina Central University in Durham, North Carolina, and both her M.S. in 1978 and Ph.D. in 1982 in developmental psychology from Howard University. Before coming to NCES, Carr served as the chief statistician for the Office of Civil Rights, where she was engaged in the application of statistics and survey methods in the field of discrimination and legislative compliance reviews. Earlier, she served as the director of Howard University's statistical and research computer laboratory, as well as an adjunct faculty member. Carr has published in a variety of areas in the psychosocial field and has a particular interest in issues concerning racial and gender differences in achievement and assessment.

**James R. Chromy** is chief scientist for sampling methodology at RTI, Research Triangle Park, N.C. He first became involved with the national assessment in 1967, working with Daniel Horvitz during the sample planning activities. He subsequently served as associate project director for sampling (1968 to 1970), senior advisor for sampling and weighting (1970 to 1977), and project director (1977 to 1983) for the NAEP Sampling and Administration contracts. He is currently a member of the NAEP Validity Studies Panel and has served on a number of National Institute of Statistical Sciences advisory panels on NAEP statistical issues. He received his B.S. in agriculture from the University of Nebraska and his master's and Ph.D. degrees in statistics from North Carolina State University. He worked as a field office agricultural statistician for the Department of Agriculture before beginning his career with RTI in 1966. At RTI, he held a series of research administrative positions, including center director and research vice president before assuming the chief scientist role in 1994. His research focus has been on sample design and survey methodology issues applied to wide variety of population surveys. He is a Fellow of the American Statistical Association and holds an adjunct professor appointment at North Carolina State University.

**Lee J. Cronbach** (1916-2001) was recognized as "gifted" by Lewis Terman and became a member of the gifted group in the Terman Study. He taught mathematics in high school for two years, attended the University of California at Berkeley, and later earned a Ph.D. at the University of Chicago, where he studied with Ralph Tyler. He was on the faculty of Washington State University when WWII started. He became a research psychologist at the U.S. Navy's sonar school in San Diego and in 1946 joined the faculty of the University of Chicago. From 1948 until 1963 he was a faculty member at the University of Illinois and subsequently at Stanford University until his retirement in 1980. His main research area was psychometrics, particularly psychological measurement. His 1957 book (with Goldine Gleser), *Psychological Tests and Personnel Decisions*, became a classic. His two books on generalizability and aptitude-treatment interactions are major research accomplishments. Cronbach participated in the first Carnegie conference that ultimately led to a national assessment, and from 1965 to 1969 he was a charter member of the Technical Advisory Committee that developed the design for NAEP.

**Emerson J. Elliott** is the director of program standards and evaluation at the National Council for Accreditation of Teacher

Education. He was Commissioner of Education Statistics at the U.S. Department of Education from 1984 to 1995 and deputy director of the National Institute of Education from 1972 to 1977. Previously he was the senior education examiner at the Office of Management and Budget. Elliott currently advises the National Center for Public Policy in Higher Education on state indicators and is a member of the National Academies of Science Board on International Comparative Studies in Education. He has been a consultant to the National Education Research Policy and Priorities Board and was a member of National Academies of Science panel on a Strategic Education Research Program. He received a Presidential Rank Award for distinguished performance in the Senior Executive Service of the federal government and was elected an American Statistical Association Fellow in 1996. His academic preparation was at Albion College (physics) and the University of Michigan (public administration).

**Alva L. Finkner** received his B.S. from Colorado State College, his M.S. from Kansas State College, and his Ph.D. from North Carolina State College. Finkner began his career with the Statistical Reporting Service of the U.S. Department of Agriculture, was associate professor of experimental statistics at North Carolina State University from 1950 to 1955, professor from 1955 to 1960, and adjunct professor from 1960 to 1983. He joined the Research Triangle Institute in 1960 and was associated with the national assessment in various capacities from 1967 to 1983, except for a leave of absence in 1974 to 1977 to accept the position of associate director for statistical standards and methodology at the U.S. Bureau of the Census. He served in the U.S. Army from 1942 to 1946, with two of those years in the Pacific Theater. He was a member of the Operations Analysis Standby Unit of the U.S. Air Force from 1950 to 1970 and a member of the National Defense Executive Reserve from 1967 to 1970. He is a Fellow of the American Statistical Association, a member of the International Statistical Institute, an Associate of the Inter-American Statistical Institute, and a charter member of the International Association of Survey Statisticians. He retired as senior vice president of Research Triangle Institute in 1983.

**Chester E. Finn Jr.** is the John M. Olin Fellow at the Manhattan Institute and president of the Thomas B. Fordham Foundation. His primary focus has been the reform of primary and secondary schooling. Finn is also a Fellow at the International Academy of Education, a Distinguished Visiting Fellow at Stanford's Hoover Institution, and an Adjunct Fellow at the Hudson Institute. He has been professor of education and public policy at Vanderbilt University since 1981. From 1985 to 1988 he served as assistant secretary for research and improvement and counselor to the secretary at the U.S. Department of Education. From 1988 until 1996 he served on the National Assessment Governing Board, including two years (1988-90) as its first chairman. Earlier positions include staff assistant to the President of the United States, special assistant to the governor of Massachusetts, counsel to the American ambassador to India, research associate at the Brookings Institution, and legislative director for Senator Daniel Patrick Moynihan. He is the author or co-author of 13 books and several hundred articles.

**John W. Gardner** (1912-2002), writer, educator, and public servant, was a consulting professor in the School of Education at Stanford University at the time of his death in 2002. A graduate of Stanford (A.B., 1935; M.A., 1936) and the University of California (Ph.D., 1938), he taught psychology at the University of California, Connecticut College, and Mount Holyoke College. During World War II he was a captain in the Marine Corps assigned to the Office of Strategic Services in Italy and Austria. While president of the Carnegie Corporation and the Carnegie Foundation for the Advancement of Teaching in the mid-1960s, Gardner fostered the initial impetus for a national education assessment. He served on President Kennedy's Task Force on Education and was chairman of President Kennedy's Commission on International Educational and Cultural Affairs. He was Secretary of Health, Education and Welfare (1965-68) in the Johnson Administration during HEW's most active period, was involved in developing Medicare and implementing civil rights laws, and was chairman of President Johnson's Task Force on Education and of the White House Conference on Education (1965). After riots devastated American cities in 1968, Gardner became chairman of the National Urban Coalition (1968-1970). He then founded and became the first chairman of Common Cause (1970-77), and later a co-founder of Independent Sector. He was a member of President Carter's Commission on an Agenda for the Eighties and chairman (1976-1980) of the President's Commission on White House Fellowships. During 1981-82 he served as a member of President Reagan's Task Force on Private Sector Initiatives. Gardner was the editor of President Kennedy's book, *To Turn The Tide*, and authored eight books, including *Excellence*, *Self-Renewal*, and *On Leadership*. In 1964 he was awarded the Presidential Medal of Freedom, the highest civil honor in the United States.

**Dorothy Morrow Gilford** served as director of the National Center for Educational Statistics and assistant commissioner for education statistics of the U.S. Office of Education from 1968 to 1974. She had administrative responsibility for the USOE grant to the Education Commission of the States for the NAEP project from 1971 to 1974. Earlier she had been director of the Division of Mathematical Sciences of the Office of Naval Research. From 1974 to 1994 she served as study director for various National Academy of Sciences studies and most recently as director of the Board on International Comparative Studies of Education. In these capacities she was author or editor of NAS reports recommending policy-relevant statistical systems for programs on women and minority Ph.D.s; rural development; family assistance; teacher supply, demand, and quality; the aging population; and international comparative studies in education. She is a member of the International Statistics Institute and the American Educational Research Association, and she is a Fellow and past vice president of the American Statistical Association. In 1965 she received the Federal Woman's Award from the U.S. Civil Service Commission. She received B.S. and M.S. degrees in mathematics from the University of Washington.

**David A. Goslin** received his M.A. and Ph.D. in sociology from Yale University in 1962, following an undergraduate degree in psychology from Swarthmore College. He joined the staff of Russell Sage Foundation in 1962, with responsibility for conceptualizing a program of research on the social consequences of standardized testing in American society. His first book, *The Search for Ability: Standardized Testing in Social Perspective* (1962), provided the background for this research program, which subsequently was funded by Russell Sage Foundation and the Carnegie Corporation of New York. In 1963-64, he served as recorder for the two conferences organized by the Carnegie Corporation to explore the feasibility and desirability of establishing a national assessment of educational attainment, which led to the creation of NAEP. From 1974 to 1987 he served as executive director of the Commission on Behavioral and Social Sciences and Education of the National Research Council, National Academy of Sciences, and from 1987 to 2001 as president and CEO of the American Institutes for Research in the Behavioral Sciences. His publications also include *Teachers and Testing* (1965), *The School in Contemporary Society* (1967), and *The Handbook of Socialization Theory and Research* (1969). Currently, he is working on a new book, tentatively titled, *Rules of Engagement: Motivation and Learning in America's Schools.*

**Daniel G. Horvitz** received his B.S. from the University of Massachusetts at Amherst and his Ph.D. from Iowa State University in 1953. Prior to joining the Research Triangle Institute (RTI) in 1962, he held several academic positions. He first became involved with NAEP in 1966 when he and Gertrude Cox began collaboration on sampling and methodology issues with the Exploratory Committee on Assessing the Progress of Education. He maintained an interest in RTI's NAEP-related projects and served as the project director for sampling and administration from 1974 to 1977. From 1974 to 1989 he held leadership positions at RTI, including vice president for statistical sciences and executive vice president. He retired from RTI in 1991. Horvitz was instrumental in establishing the National Institute for Statistical Sciences (NISS) in the Research Triangle Park and served as its interim director in 1990 and 1991. He is a Fellow of the American Statistical Association, for which he served as vice president (1985-87) and as chair of the Committee on Fellows (1992). He is also a Fellow of the American Association for the Advancement of Science and an elected member of the International Statistical Institute. His research interests have focused on sampling theory and survey design and methods, with emphasis on improving data quality.

**John F. "Jack" Jennings** founded the Center on Education Policy, the national independent advocate for public education and for more effective public schools, in 1995. The center works to help Americans better understand the role of public education in a democracy and the need to improve the academic quality of public schools. Jennings served as director and president of the center since its founding. From 1967 to 1994, Jennings worked in the area of federal aid to education for the U.S. Congress and was involved in nearly every major education debate held at the national level. He participated in the reauthorizations of the Elementary and Secondary Education Act, the Vocational Education Act, the School Lunch Act, the Individuals with Disabilities Education Act, and the Higher Education Act. As the chief expert on education for the U.S. House of Representatives, Jennings spoke at hundreds of meetings in the United States and has traveled to China, the former U.S.S.R., Italy, and several other countries representing the United States. His activities have included editing several books, writing a national legislative newsletter, and publishing numerous articles. His book, *Why National Standards and Tests*, was published by Sage Publications in 1998.

**Eugene G. Johnson** is the chief psychometrician of the American Institutes for Research. Johnson's research interests include the design and analysis of complex sample surveys and applications of item response theory. He is technical director for the National Assessment of Adult Literacy and for the Foreign Language NAEP. He is senior technical advisor for all of AIR's assessment projects and the sampling director for state, national, and international surveys. Johnson is a member of technical advisory boards for state, national, and international large-scale assessments. He has been involved with NAEP since 1976, was the research coordinating director for NAEP from 1991 to 1995, and was senior technical advisor for NAEP until leaving ETS in 1999. He is still a technical consultant for NAEP. He is a member of the National Research Council/National Academy of Sciences Committee on Educational Excellence and Testing Equity. He holds a Ph.D. in statistics from Princeton University. Johnson is co-recipient of the 1988 National Council on Measurement in Education triennial award for technical contributions to educational measurement.

**Lyle V. Jones** is Research Professor of Psychology at the University of North Carolina at Chapel Hill, where he also served as Alumni Distinguished Professor, director of the L.L. Thurstone Psychometric Laboratory, and vice chancellor and dean of the Graduate School (1969-79). Earlier he was a National Research Council postdoctoral fellow and then a faculty member at the University of Chicago. As a member of the Technical Advisory Committee from 1965 to 1969, he helped to design NAEP and helped to monitor its progress while serving on the Analysis Advisory Committee from 1969 to 1982. He also was a member of the Alexander-James panel that recommended a trial state NAEP and of the National Institute of Education panel that evaluated the trial state assessment. Jones attended Reed College, became a communications officer in the Army Air Corps, and then received B.S. and M.S. degrees from the University of Washington and a Ph.D. degree in psychology and statistics from Stanford University. He is an elected member of the Institute of Medicine and a Fellow of the American Academy of Arts and Sciences, the

American Psychological Association, the American Psychological Society, and the American Statistical Association. Since 1991, as a member of the Report Review Committee of the National Academies, he has monitored the pre-publication reviews of many National Academy reports, some of which pertain to NAEP or to related issues of education assessment.

**Archie Lapointe** has extensive experience in measurement and in assessment methodology. In 1981-82 he and Willard Wirtz conducted an assessment of NAEP to examine its strengths and weaknesses (*Measuring the Quality of Education*). Many of their recommendations became part of ETS' winning proposal of 1983, of which he was a co-author, and are accepted characteristics of NAEP today. As executive director of NAEP from 1983 to 1997, Lapointe implemented the new design, initiated the SREB project, and encouraged the use of NAEP technologies by several states. He also planned and implemented the International Assessment of Educational Progress (IAEP), using NAEP items and methods to conduct an international comparative study, and was the principal author of its report, *A World of Differences*. Lapointe's understanding of cognitive test development and its relationship to instruction was developed while he served as general manager of the California Test Bureau. While vice president for development at Science Research Associates (SRA), he managed the test scoring and reporting operation, as well as the development activities for the SRA Achievement Test, the Iowa Tests of Educational Development, the National Merit Scholarship Tests, and the American College Testing program tests. As director of the Center for Assessment at American Institutes for Research, he directed projects for the USDOE, the *Voluntary National Tests*; for the City of Philadelphia, *Standards Based Tests K-12*; and for California, the *California High School Exit Exam*. He currently is serving on Italy's seven-member Comitato Scientifico, Tecnico (Scientific and Technical Committee), which advises the national ministry on issues of curriculum reform, standards, and technology in the schools.

**Stephen Lazer** has been the executive director for the National Assessment of Educational Progress at Educational Testing Service since 1997. He received a bachelor's degree in English and political science from McGill University in 1980, a master's degree in political science from Princeton University in 1982, and completed coursework and qualifying examinations that were part of the doctoral program there in 1984. His academic areas of interest include modern history, comparative politics, American government, and political theory. Between 1984 and 1985, he was an editorial and research associate of the World Policy Institute. Between 1984 and 1992 he served as a part-time lecturer in political science at Princeton University. In 1985 Lazer joined ETS, where he served as an assessment developer in the Advanced Placement program. In 1991 he joined the NAEP staff, where he served as director of social studies programs and director of development before taking on the responsibilities of executive director. Lazer's expertise and experience at ETS include the development and design of assessments and the management of complex programs. He also has expertise in computerized test development, item banking, and computer-delivered testing. He has published widely on matters related to large-scale assessment, with particular emphasis on NAEP.

**Irvin J. Lehmann** is professor of measurement at Michigan State University, where he has been since receiving his Ph.D. in measurement, evaluation, and statistics from the University of Wisconsin-Madison in 1957. He received three bachelor's degrees and his master's from the University of Manitoba. At Michigan State University, he taught courses in measurement and evaluation, research methods, and survey research. He was on leave of absence to the National Assessment of Educational Progress from 1968 to 1971 in Ann Arbor, where he was assistant staff director for research. He is the author or co-author of 11 texts in education research and measurement and evaluation. He has served as executive officer and president of the National Council on Measurement in Education. Lehmann was co-founder, with Frank Womer, of the Large-Scale Conference on Assessment that was sponsored by the Education Commission of the States. He has been a visiting professor at the Technion in Israel and Perth University in Australia. He has been a consultant to local, state, national, and international organizations and has been a member of the New Jersey Department of Education Technical Advisory Committee for State Assessment since its inauguration.

**Robert L. Linn** is Distinguished Professor of Education at the University of Colorado at Boulder and co-director of the National Center for Research on Evaluation, Standards, and Student Testing. He received his Ph.D. from the University of Illinois at Urbana-Champaign with a specialization in psychometrics in 1965. He worked as a senior research psychologist and director of developmental research at Educational Testing Service and as a professor of education and of psychology at the University of Illinois at Urbana-Champaign before moving to Colorado in 1987. He is a member of the National Academy of Education and is a past president (2002-2003) of the American Educational Research Association. He served as co-chairperson of the NAE panel on the evaluation of the Trial State Assessment for the National Assessment of Educational Progress and as chairperson of the National Research Council's Board on Testing and Assessment.

**Wayne Martin** (1945-2003) completed his undergraduate work at the University of Michigan and his graduate work at the University of Connecticut. At the time of his death, he was director of the State Education Assessment Center at the Council of Chief State School Officers (CCSSO), where he oversaw the council's efforts to design and develop standards and assessments for students, beginning teachers, and beginning school administrators. He also oversaw the work of CCSSO in the areas of data definition, development, and reporting. Before joining CCSSO, he worked for 12 years at the Colorado Department of Education, where he was actively involved in the state's education reform efforts. He served as the state assessment director, staff director for the State Standards and Assessments Council appointed by Governor Roy Romer, and as principal investigator and associate director for CONNECT, the state's systemic reform initiative for mathematics and science education funded by the National Science Foundation. He was a member of the staff at NAEP for 11 years prior to joining the Colorado Department of Education.

**Lloyd Morrisett** graduated from Oberlin College, did graduate work in psychology at U.C.L.A., and earned his Ph.D. in experimental psychology from Yale University in 1956. After teaching at the University of California at Berkeley for two years and being on the staff of the Social Science Research Council for one year, he joined the staff of Carnegie Corporation of New York in 1959, where he remained until 1969. At Carnegie he held various positions, including that of vice president. During the formation of the Exploratory Committee and subsequently of NAEP, Morrisett, working with John Gardner, was the primary staff member at Carnegie responsible for those developments. After leaving Carnegie, Morrisett was president of the John and Mary R. Markle Foundation for 28 years. He also co-founded the Children's Television Workshop (now Sesame Workshop), producers of "Sesame Street" and other educational programs for children; and he was chairman of its board for 30 years.

**Frederic A. Mosher** is a senior advisor to the Spencer Foundation, which specializes in the support of education research. In 2000 and 2001 he also was a consultant to a RAND Corporation project supported by the U.S. Department of Education's Office of Education Research and Improvement to explore ways of improving the government's support and management of education research, and a consultant to Achieve Inc. In 1998, after 36 years as a program specialist and policy analyst, he retired from Carnegie Corporation of New York, a general purpose philanthropic foundation supporting "the advancement and diffusion of knowledge and understanding." Over those years he worked in the full range of the corporation's programs, including international affairs, U.S. governmental reform, education at all levels, and the role of African universities in the development of their countries' education systems. In the 1980s and early 1990s he chaired the corporation's program on Avoiding Nuclear War (later Cooperative Security), which dealt extensively with U.S.-Soviet relations. In recent years he returned to focus on the policy issues involved in transforming the U.S. public education system into one that would enable substantially all students to reach or exceed significant standards of achievement. He is a cognitive/social psychologist by training, with a Ph.D. from Harvard University.

**Ina V.S. Mullis** is co-director of the International Study Center at Boston College and co-director of the TIMSS (Trends in International Mathematics and Science Study) and PIRLS (Progress in Reading Literacy Study). Mullis also is a professor at Boston College in the Lynch School of Education's Department of Educational Research, Measurement, and Evaluation. Prior to joining the TIMSS International Study Center, she was project director for NAEP. Mullis received a Ph.D. in education research from the University of Colorado, where she was the 1983 recipient of the Distinguished Alumni Award from the School of Education. She joined NAEP in 1972 and played a major role for more than two decades in designing the assessments, directing project activities, and reporting results. She is the author or co-author of more than 25 NAEP reports. From her work on NAEP and TIMSS, she has considerable management experience and technical expertise in a wide range of large-scale national and international assessment methods and issues. Mullis also serves on several advisory panels, including the NAEP Validation Studies Panel.

**Daryl Nichols** (1927-2000) assisted developing nations in Africa and Asia to create effective, low-cost, primary education programs over a period of three decades. During the earlier years he also helped some of these nations develop testing programs. His M.S. in psychology was from Iowa State University. He joined the American Institutes for Research (AIR) in 1955 and directed the Social and Educational Research Program there during the first cycle of national assessment. He and Vincent Campbell co-directed AIR's citizenship assessment for NAEP, leading the team in exercise development, administration, and reporting results for the first national assessment in citizenship. Other areas of national assessment in which he played a leading role during its early years were reading, social studies, music, and career and occupational development. At AIR, he also initiated a program of research on diffusion of innovations sponsored by the National Institutes of Health.

**Ingram Olkin** is professor of statistics and education at Stanford University. Previously he was on the faculty of Michigan State University and the University of Minnesota. He was a Fellow at the National Center for Education Statistics and is currently chair of the Design and Analysis Committee, which is the technical advisory committee to the National Assessment of Educational Progress. He has served on various national panels of the National Research Council and was the founding chair of the NRC Committee on Applied and Theoretical Statistics. Olkin attended the College of the City of New York, was a meteorologist in the Army Air Corps, and received a master's degree from Columbia University and a doctorate from the University of North Carolina. He co-edited the book, *Education in a Research University*; co-authored and edited more than 15 books; and is an author of more than 150 articles. His co-authored book on combining information from independent studies has served as a basis for research synthesis in medical and educational research.

**Gary W. Phillips** was designated the acting commissioner of the National Center for Education Statistics (NCES) effective 22 June 1999. Earlier at NCES, he was the deputy commissioner. Previous responsibilities at NCES included overseeing NAEP, the National Adult Literacy Study (NALS), and the Third International Mathematics and Science Study (TIMSS). He also was the architect, and served as the executive director, of President Clinton's Voluntary National Test (VNT). Phillips has a Ph.D. from the University of Kentucky with an emphasis in statistics and psychometrics. He has published or presented more than 200 papers, taught more than 30 graduate-level courses, and presented more than 50 workshops on advanced statistical topics. He is nationally and internationally known for his expertise in large-scale assessments and complex surveys. During his tenure at NCES, Phillips' main emphasis has been on the translation of statistical data into information that is understandable, useful, and timely for policy makers. He has authored several reports that have been instrumental in informing the debate about our national education policy agenda: *The Lake Wobegone Effect: A Skeleton in the Testing Closet* (1988); *A World of Differences: The First International Assessment of Educational Progress* (1990); *The State of Mathematics Achievement: The First NAEP State-by-State Assessment* (1991); *Toward World Class Standards: The First Linking Study Between NAEP and International Assessments* (1993); and *Technical Issues in Large Scale Performance Assessments* (1995). The main purpose of each of these reports was to provide new and innovative information to help education researchers, policy makers, and the public better understand the condition of education in America.

**Keith Rust** is vice president and associate director in the Statistical Group at Westat, a research corporation with headquarters in Rockville, Maryland. He is also research associate professor in the Joint Program in Survey Methodology at the University of Maryland at College Park. He holds a Ph.D. in biostatistics from the University of Michigan. Rust is a Fellow of the American Statistical Association; a former member of the Committee on National Statistics, an activity of the National Research Council; and is currently chair of the Social Statistics Section of the American Statistical Association. Rust has been heavily involved in statistical activities associated with sampling for NAEP since 1987 and has directed Westat's activities in this area since 1990. He also participated in a number of international studies of education achievement and has taught courses in survey sampling methods and inference from complex surveys.

**Ramsay Selden** is vice president and director of the assessment program at the American Institutes for Research (AIR). He leads and coordinates AIR's efforts to develop assessment programs and to conduct research and other activities on assessment at the local, state, national, and international levels. Earlier at AIR, Selden was director of the Education Statistics Services Institute (ESSI). The ESSI was created by the National Center for Education Statistics (NCES) to support its efforts. ESSI develops new data collections in areas that are not addressed well in current education statistics, helps analyze and disseminate NCES findings, and supports NCES programs in planning, evaluation, project management, and training. Before joining AIR, Selden directed the assessment programs of the Council of Chief State School Officers, leading CCSSO programs on assessment, standards for students and educators, accountability in the education system, standards-based education reform, and education indicators and statistical improvement. Before joining CCSSO, Selden worked for the U.S. Department of Education, Office of Educational Research and Improvement/National Institute of Education, where he served on the staff of the National Commission on Excellence in Education and managed programs at NIE on reading, literacy, and language education. Selden came to Washington, D.C., in 1977 on the Education Policy Fellowship Program of the Institute for Educational Leadership; and he served as an adjunct professor at American University. He has published on reading and literacy, textbooks in education, education assessment, accountability, and standards-based reform. He has served on many panels and written papers on education assessment, reform, and statistical improvement. He did his undergraduate work in English at Duke University and his graduate work in English and education at the University of Virginia.